OUR STORY IN MANY VOICES

THE ALASKA STATE MUSEUM CATALOG AND GUIDE

Charles Wohlforth

Design by Sarah Asper-Smith

University of Alaska Press

FAIRBANKS

PAGE II

Detail of Sanightaaq Rain parka

Seal skin, seal fur, bird feathers and beaks, St. Lawrence Island, Siberian Yupik

ASM-II-A4458

Published by University of Alaska Press
An imprint of University Press of Colorado
1580 North Logan Street, Suite 660
PMB 39883
Denver, Colorado 80203-1942

Printed in the United States of America

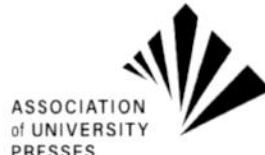

The University Press of Colorado is a proud member of Association of University Presses.

The University Press of Colorado is a cooperative publishing enterprise supported, in part, by Adams State University, Colorado School of Mines, Colorado State University, Fort Lewis College, Metropolitan State University of Denver, University of Alaska Fairbanks, University of Colorado, University of Denver, University of Northern Colorado, University of Wyoming, Utah State University, and Western Colorado University.

∞ This paper meets the requirements of the ANSI/NISO Z39.48-1992 (Permanence of Paper).

ISBN: 978-1-64642-651-5 (paperback)
ISBN: 978-1-64642-652-2 (ebook)
https://doi.org/10.5876/9781646426522

Library of Congress Cataloging-in-Publication Data

Names: Wohlforth, Charles, 1963– author. | Asper-Smith, Sarah.
Title: Our story in many voices : the Alaska State Museum catalog and guide / text by Charles Wohlforth ; design by Sarah Asper-Smith.
Other titles: Alaska State Museum catalog and guide
Description: Fairbanks : University of Alaska Press, [2024] | Includes bibliographical references and index.
Identifiers: LCCN 2024008339 (print) | LCCN 2024008340 (ebook) | ISBN 9781646426515 (paperback) | ISBN 9781646426522 (ebook)
Subjects: LCSH: Alaska State Museum—Guidebooks. | Alaska State Museum—Catalogs.
Classification: LCC F901.5 .W64 2025 (print) | LCC F901.5 (ebook) | DDC 979.80747986—dc23/eng/20240228
LC record available at https://lccn.loc.gov/2024008339
LC ebook record available at https://lccn.loc.gov/2024008340

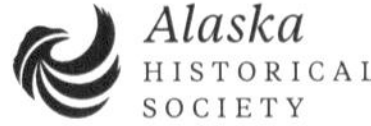

The Alaska Historical Society, sponsor of this project, disclaims all responsibility for statements of fact or opinion made herein. Financial support provided by Rasmuson Foundation, Block Foundation, Atwood Foundation, and Friends of the Alaska State Library, Archives, and Museum.

All photos of pieces in the collection taken by Brian Wallace, Lou Logan, David Gelotte, and Sara Boesser

OUR STORY IN MANY VOICES

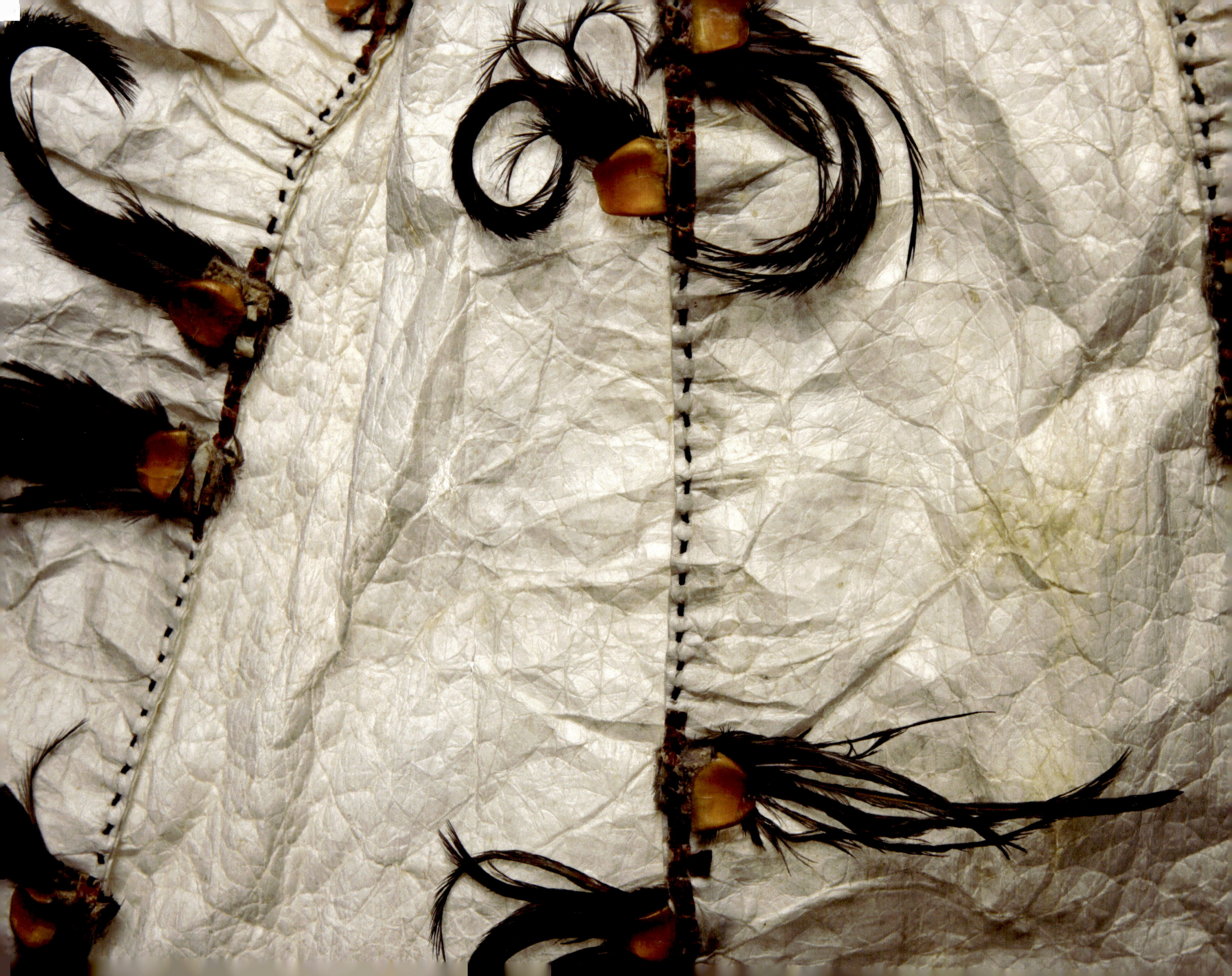

To all Alaskans, past, present, and future, to whom this museum belongs, and for whom it will perpetually preserve, reflect, and expand the Alaska story.

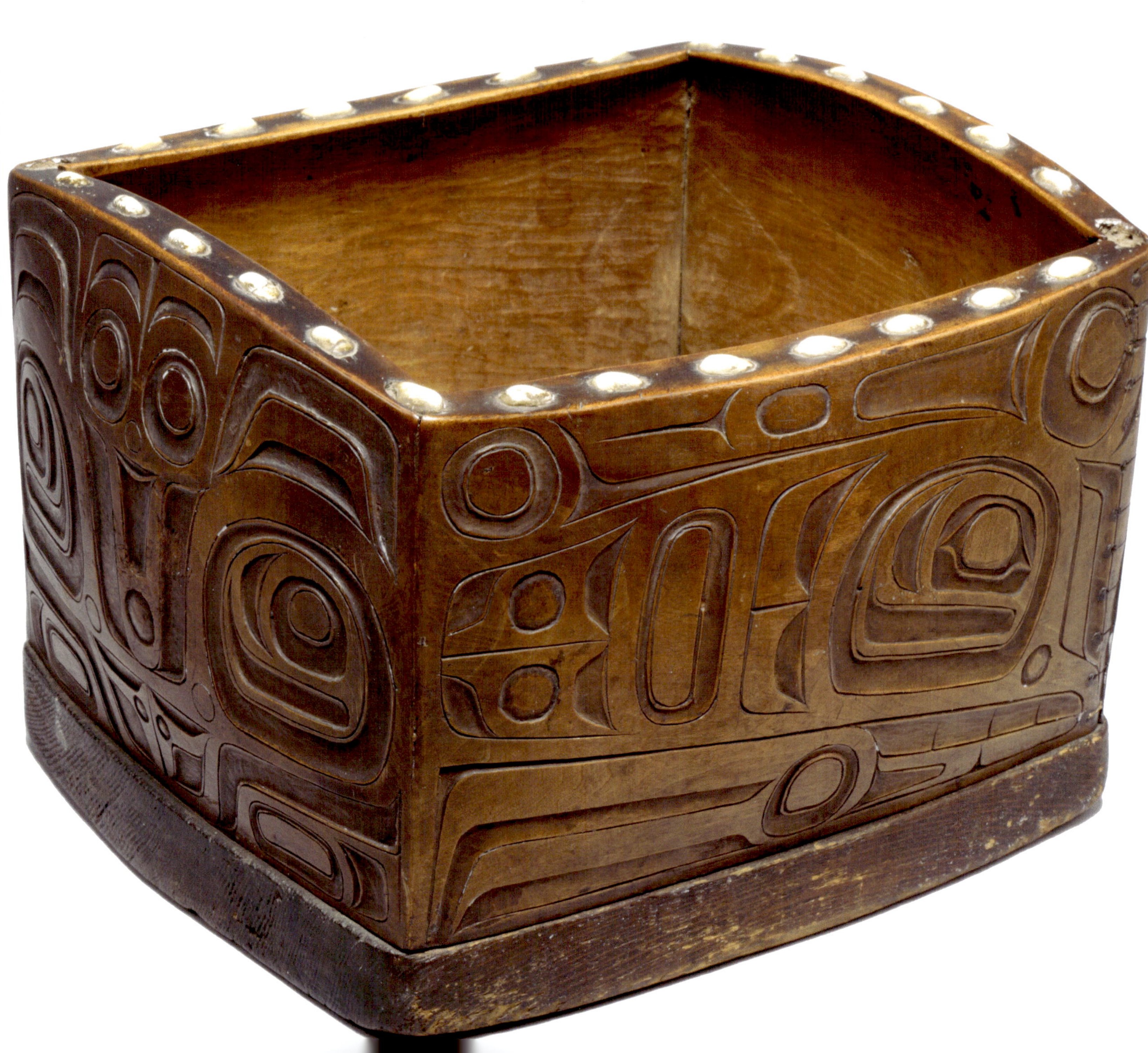

Laakt s'íx'I
Bentwood bowl

Decorated with clan crest design in formline style.

Tlingit or Haida, late 19th c.

ASM-96-54-1

CONTENTS

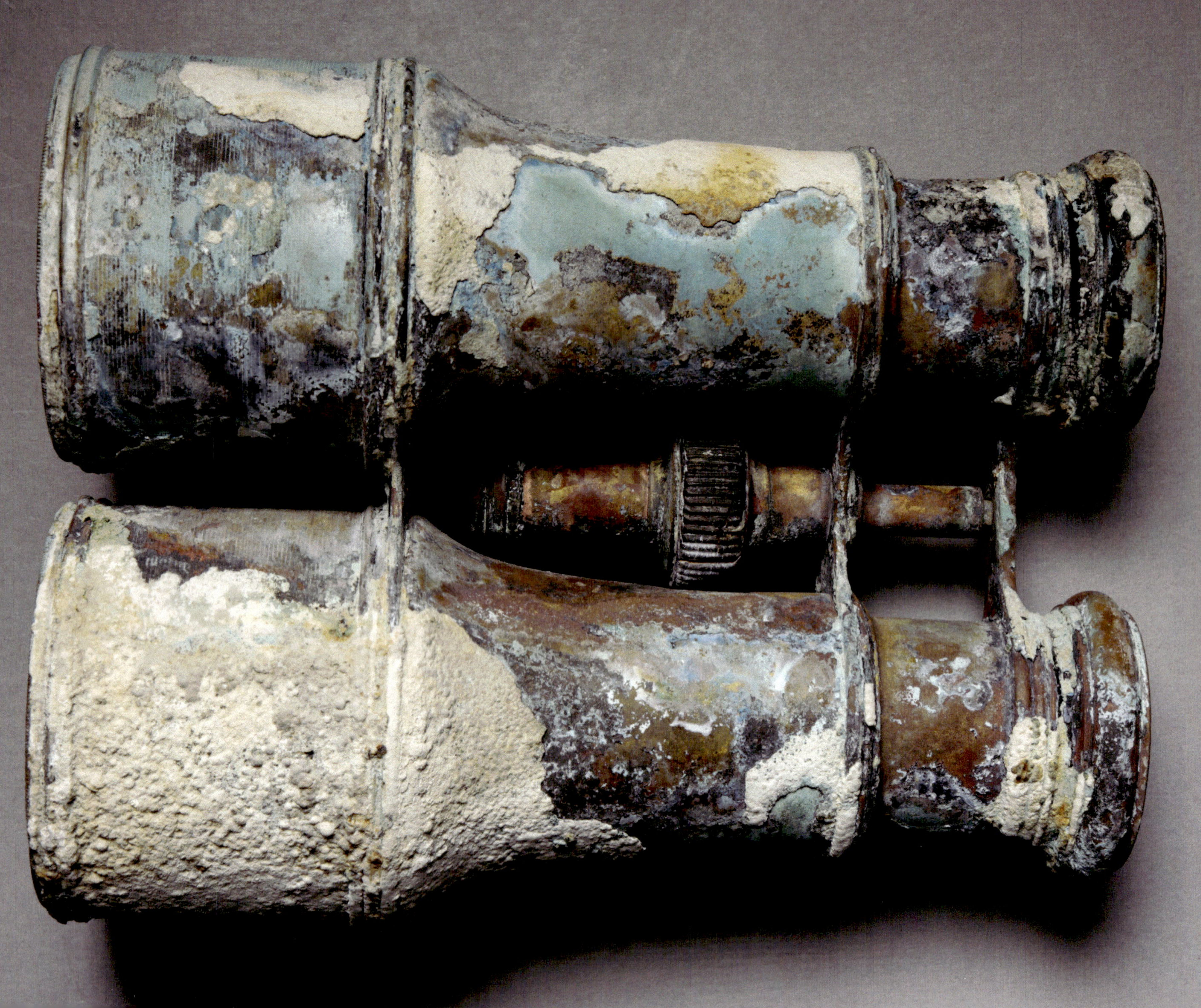

FOREWORD

LEFT
Binoculars from the *S.S. Aleutian*
ASM-2008-11-8

As the curator of collections for over thirty years, I have many favorite objects in the Alaska State Museum that I especially enjoy presenting to visitors—extraordinary objects that represent important moments and ideas in our Alaska story. One example is a bronze crest representing the Russian double-headed eagle that was presented to Alaska Natives in 1804 as both a peace offering and as a visual sign to colonial competitors that Alaska was claimed by Russia. Since the fifteenth century, European powers had recognized a "Doctrine of Discovery" that dictated they could seize new lands if the people they found there were not Christian. This concept, although recently repudiated by the pope himself, is still reflected by the lines drawn on our modern maps. The crest helps us to think about who really owned Alaska, how the concept of ownership has changed through time, and what it means today.

Author Charles Wohlforth and designer Sarah Asper-Smith, who created this book, present their own unique perspective and favorite objects, adding a valuable perspective. They made the book independently of the museum or the State of Alaska, raising money for the project from grants, and it received academic peer review rather than museum review. Asper-Smith played an integral role in creation of the exhibit, which opened in 2016, as a contractor with her firm ExhibitAK. She engaged Wohlforth to edit the exhibit labels, as his final essay here explains. Their exceptional work in Alaska over many years has prepared them to present their interpretation of Alaska's people and history.

Many objects chosen for the exhibition tell multiple and sometimes contradictory stories. Each museum visitor is encouraged to think deeply about the many meanings represented. As we discovered from our many conversations with Alaskans about the exhibit design, the meaning and significance of many key episodes of the history are still unsettled. Fittingly, the exhibit often reflects the conflicts and contradictions, encouraging visitors to be flexible, consider the evidence, and draw their own conclusions. We embrace different perspectives as a way of understanding and pondering Alaska's unique human history.

The Alaska State Museum welcomes all visitors. We believe all who come will learn something here, no matter the level of knowledge you bring, and regardless of how much time you are able to devote. All will appreciate the beauty and power of the objects. And we welcome this book, as well, as a fitting guide and interpretation, which will orient you to Alaska, carry you through the exhibits, and help you understand, in your own way, the complex history and changing meaning of this place.

Steve Henrikson
Curator of Collections

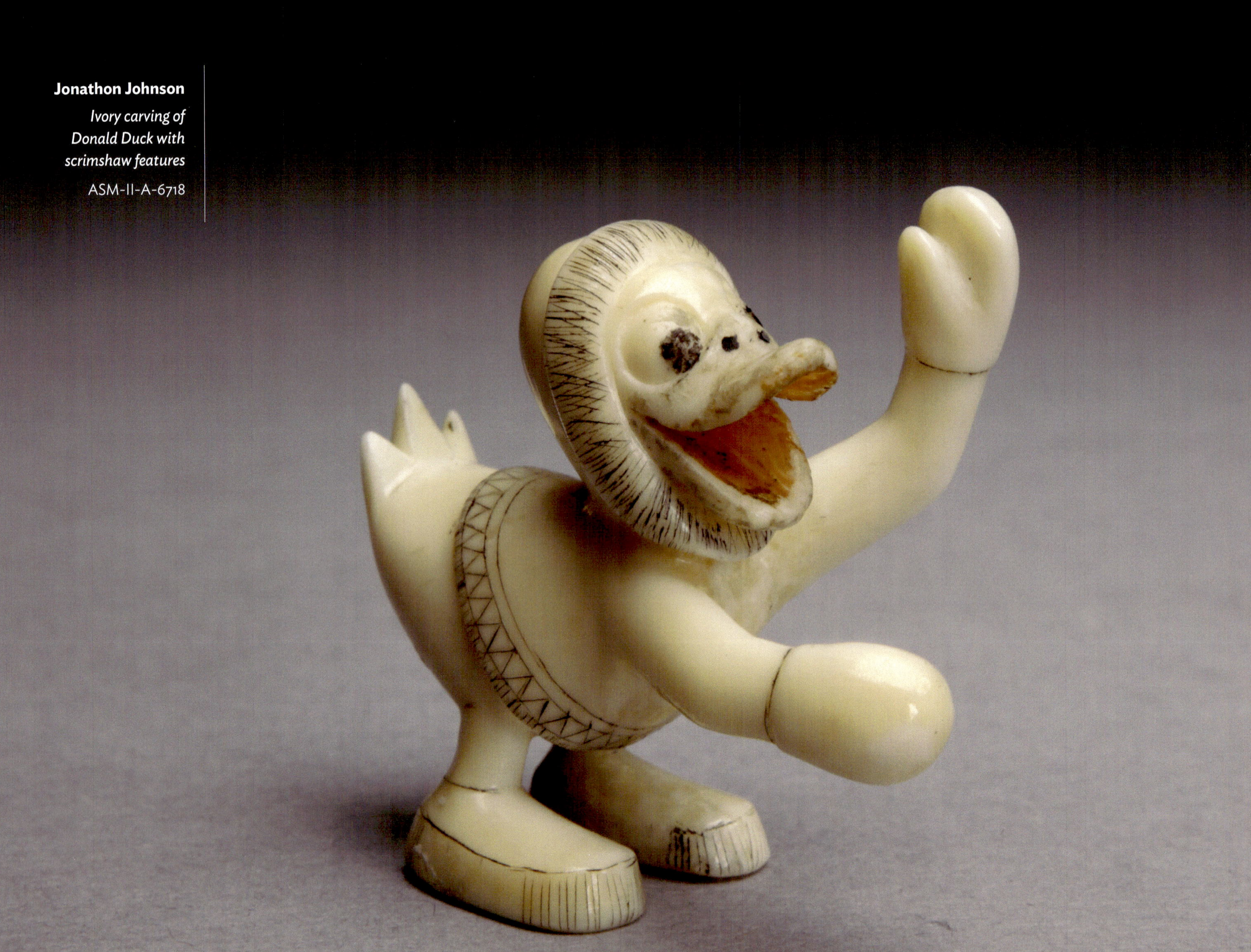

Jonathon Johnson
Ivory carving of Donald Duck with scrimshaw features
ASM-II-A-6718

OUR STORY IN MANY VOICES

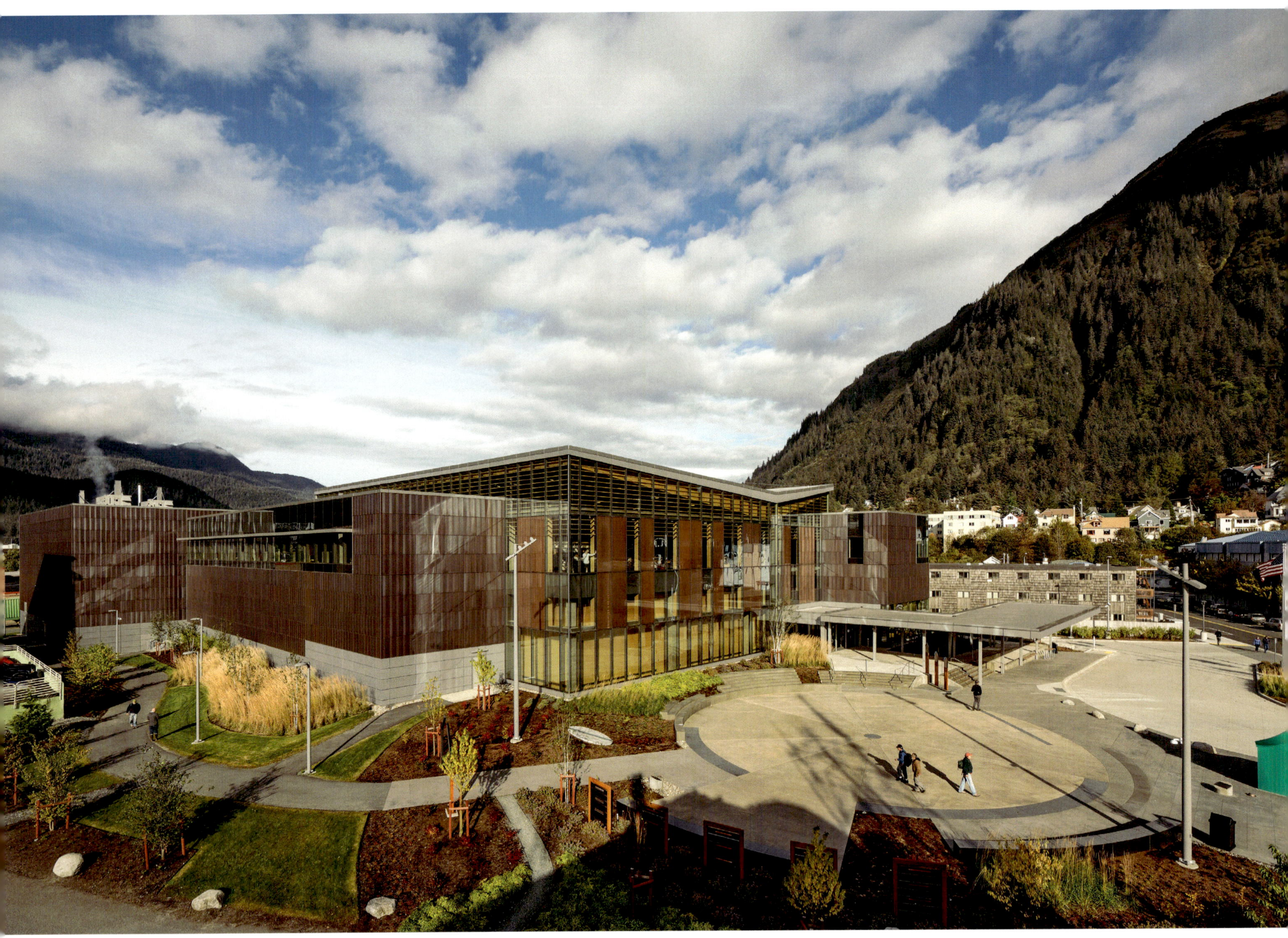

INTRODUCTION

LEFT
The newly opened Andrew P. Kashevaroff Building in 2016.

No building could encompass Alaska, but the Alaska State Museum attempts to do so like no other. This book seeks to assist in that impossible task by placing the museum's exhibits in their context—in time and place, and in the cultural landscape. For newcomers, we hope to help with mental mapping, so you can arrange the objects into a story that makes sense for your own exploration of our state. For vintage Alaskans, we would guide you into a deepening Alaska story in this current moment of change, as familiar characters and incidents reorient themselves in new dimensions.

None of this is easy. Indeed, the exhibits' designers believed it should be hard. That challenge was essential, because the curators refused to dictate how visitors should understand the past and each other's cultures. Instead, they created a rich, complex, nonlinear space without a defined pathway to follow. Each visitor chooses where to look and in what order. Sometimes perspectives conflict. As you see each object, you can choose to perceive it for its beauty, its use, or for what it can say about the people who made it and their relationship to this place.

As the museum was built, we worked alongside the gifted curators who created these permanent exhibits. Asper-Smith helped conceive and manage the exhibit project and led the graphic design. She recruited Wohlforth to edit the museum labels, melding the language of the many diverse co-curators who brought to the project their own cultures and areas of historical expertise. When this work was done, in 2016, we stepped back with pride.

Several years later, however, Asper-Smith noted the absence of a museum catalog, and again recruited Wohlforth to help. This time, our roles would be fundamentally different. Instead of being collaborators with the museum, we became observers and even, at times, critics. Generous donors who are mentioned in the acknowledgments made this possible, without any cost to the museum or the State of Alaska. This independent funding allowed us to interpret the museum without the institution's oversight (although staff members were extremely helpful in the process). We determined the design and content of the book, with the quality control of anonymous academic peer review. Thus this book does not promote the museum but describes it, taking our own informed but particular point of view.

Of course, ours is only one perspective. The Father Andrew P. Kashevaroff Building, housing the Alaska State Library, Archives, and Museum, contains thousands of unique records and objects representing a state that is larger than all but sixteen nations, is home to more than twenty indigenous languages, and has speakers of one hundred more. Alaska's story is rapidly being made and remade. We are honored to offer this catalog and guide to interpret the exhibits, as a companion to those ready to enter this extraordinary tale, so you may draw your own conclusions.

Charles Wohlforth
Sarah Asper-Smith

MAPS A BRIEF ATLAS OF ALASKA'S CULTURAL AND HISTORIC LANDSCAPE AND THE MUSEUM ITSELF

SELECTED OBJECTS FROM THE MUSEUM

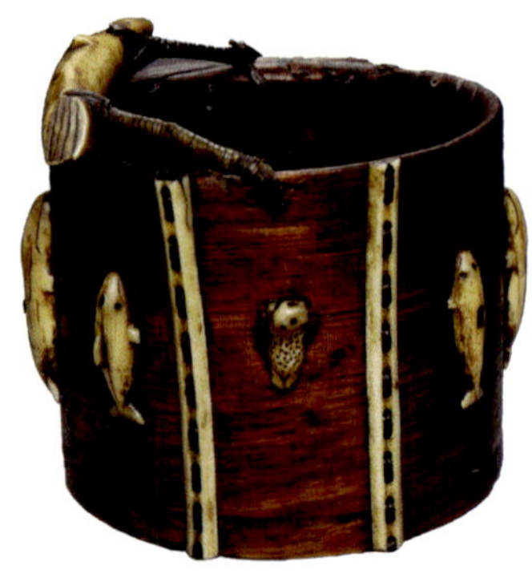

1. Iñupiaq ceremonial bucket from Pt. Barrow. Iñupiaq hunters sometimes show respect to harvested animals by offering them water.

ASM-II-A-6853

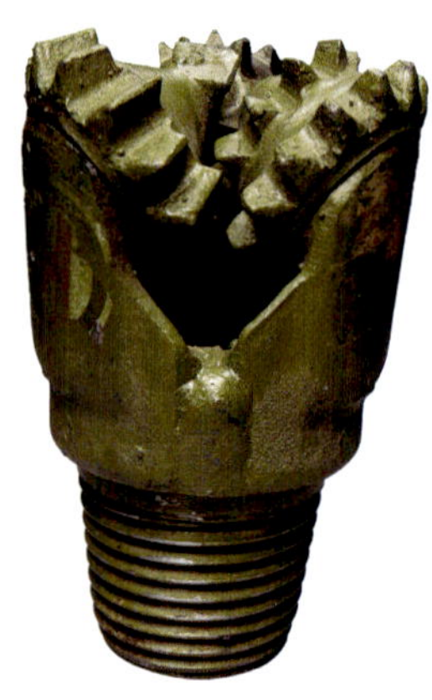

2. In 1968, Atlantic Richfield found the largest oil field in North America near Prudhoe Bay. This bit is for taking samples for analysis.

2015-12-3

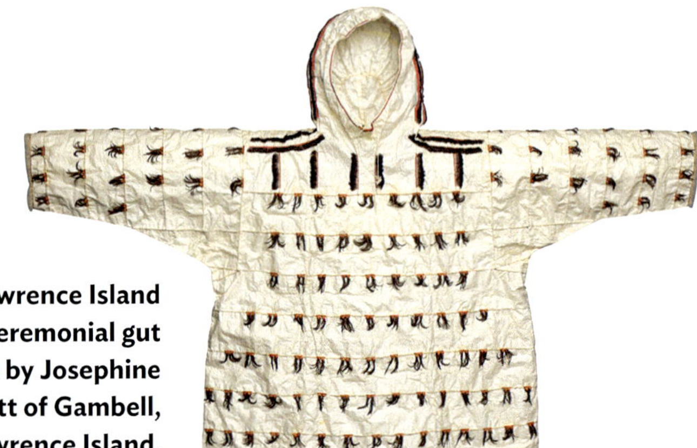

3. St. Lawrence Island Yupik ceremonial gut parka made by Josephine Ungott of Gambell, St. Lawrence Island.

ASM-II-A-5806

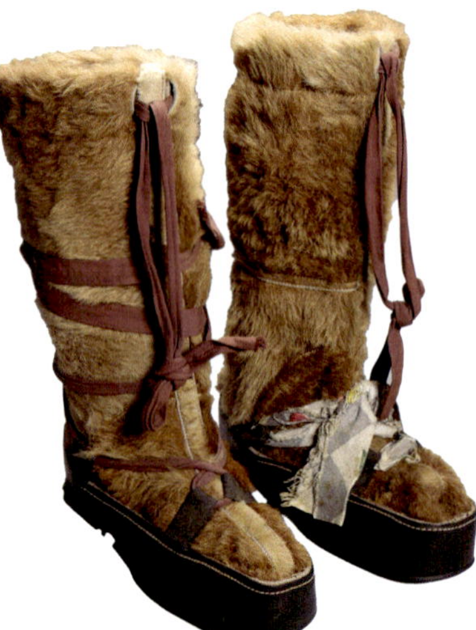

4. Experimental mukluks. An Army laboratory at Ladd Field, near Fairbanks, evaluated Army equipment in the extreme cold.

99-11-1

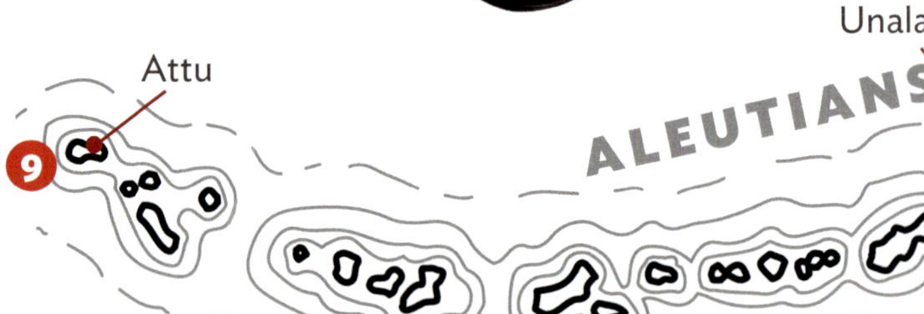

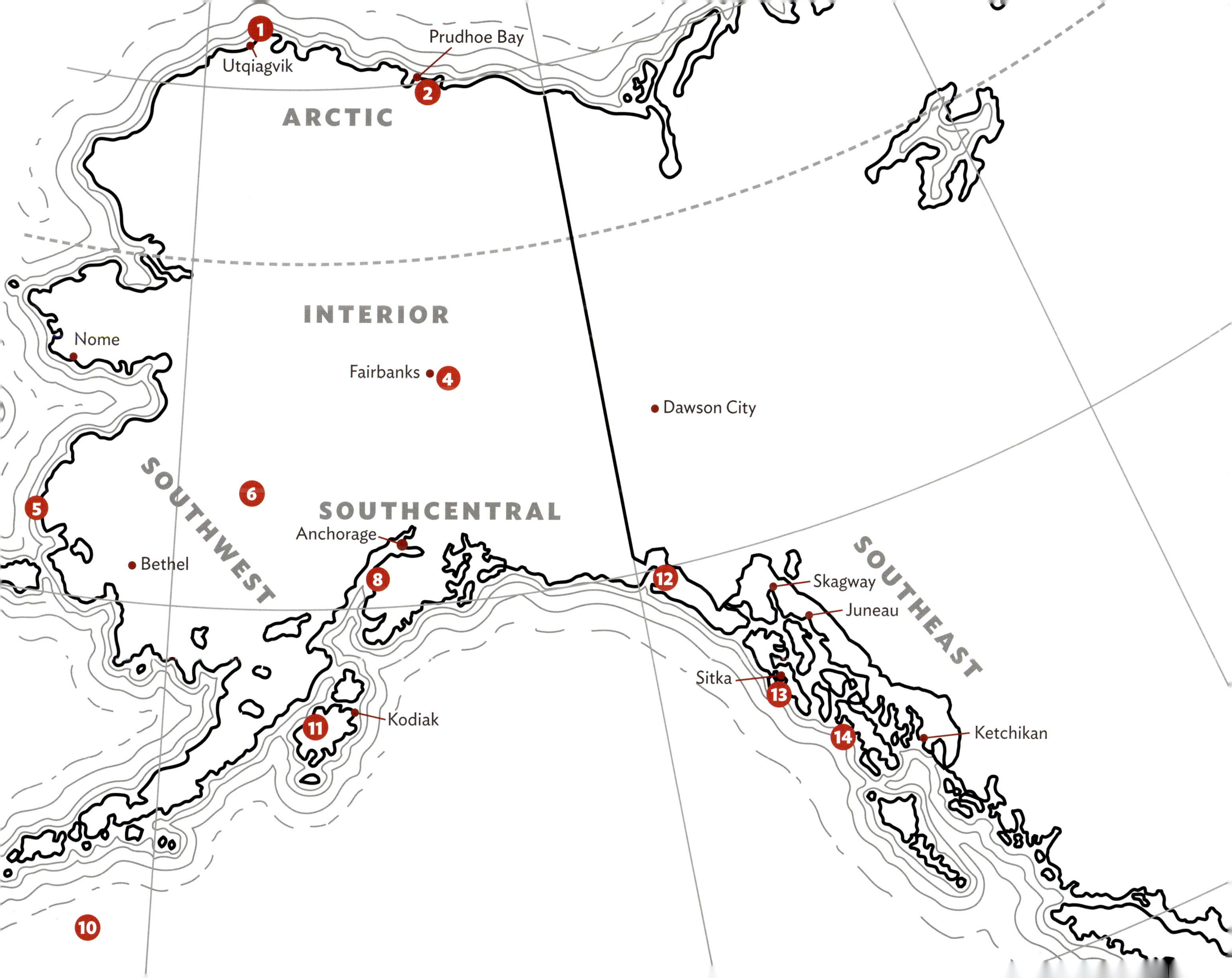

1
Utqiagvik
Prudhoe Bay
2
ARCTIC
INTERIOR
Nome
Fairbanks
4
Dawson City
SOUTHWEST
6
5
SOUTHCENTRAL
Anchorage
8
Bethel
12
Skagway
Juneau
SOUTHEAST
Sitka
13
11
Kodiak
14
Ketchikan
10

5. Sam Hunter, a Yup'ik carver in Hooper Bay, made this seagull mask at the request of Walt Disney documentary film makers in 1945–1946.

ASM-II-A-5398

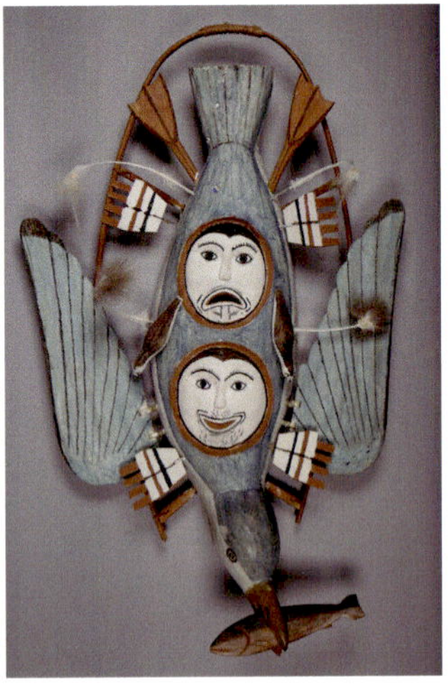

6. Upper Kuskokwim Athabascan people of Nikolai used a peg calendar to track Russian Orthodox holidays.

II-C-166

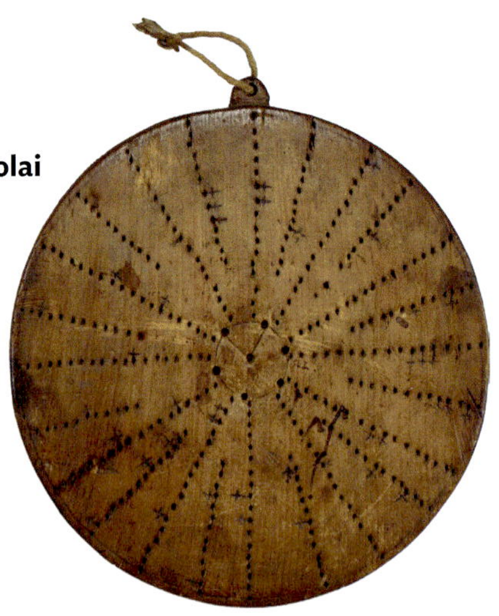

7. *The Reef Rookery, St. Paul's Island, Prybilov Group, Bering Sea, Alaska* By Henry W. Elliott, 1872. The artist could foresee that the seemingly endless seal population, of sufficient vastness that clouds of their collective exhalation condensed over the herd, could not survive an unlimited harvest.

2005-41-1

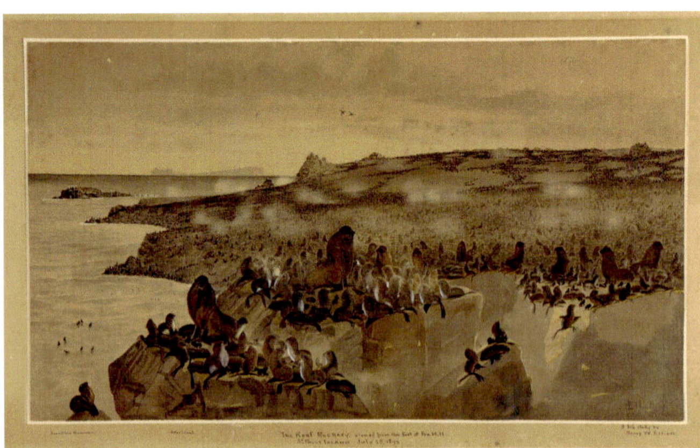

8. Dena'ina Athabascans of the Kenai Peninsula used this counting cord as an aid to remembering historical stories, which they passed orally down with startling accuracy.

II-C-316

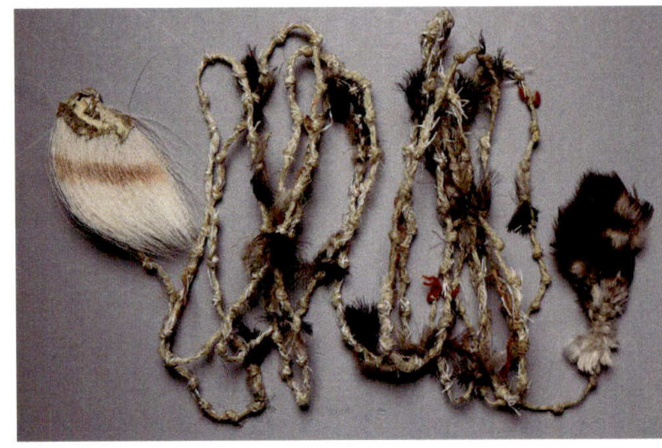

9. More than 2,300 Japanese soldiers lost their lives in the battle of Attu in May, 1943. This is a Japanese officer's pistol—a Nambu Type 14, 8mm caliber, with custom jade grips.

2003-24-2

10. Model of the Cutter *Bear* made by a Yup'ik or Iñupiaq carver from walrus ivory.

II-A-5134

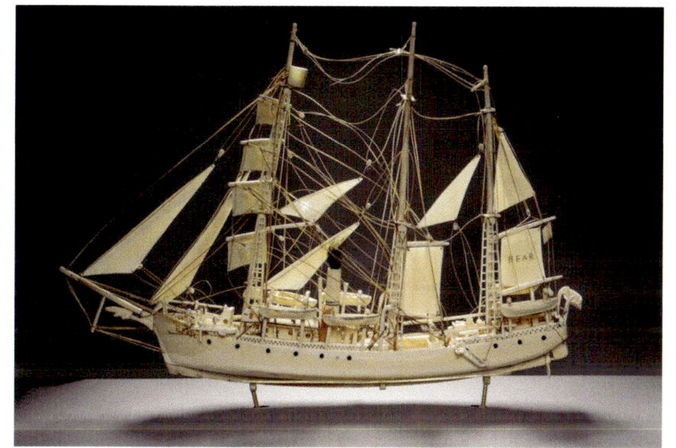

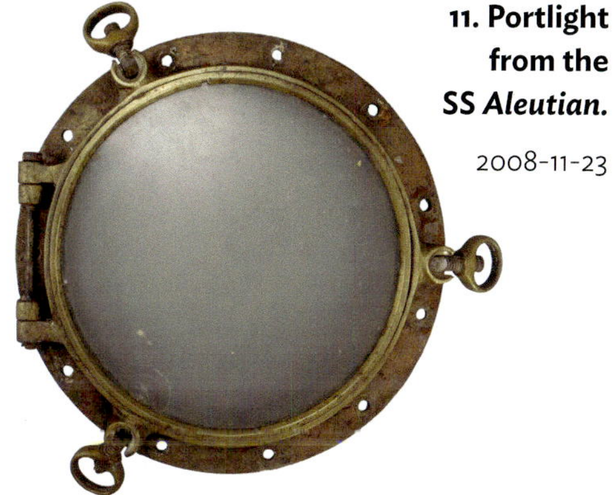

11. Portlight from the SS *Aleutian*.

2008-11-23

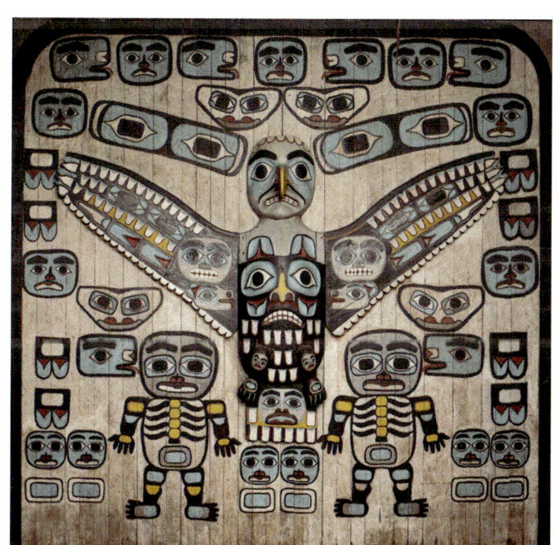

12. The Xeitl X'een *Thunderbird Screen* from the Thunderbird House (Xeitl Hít), Shangookeidí clan, Yakutat Tlingit, tells the ancient origin story of the house.

II-B-845

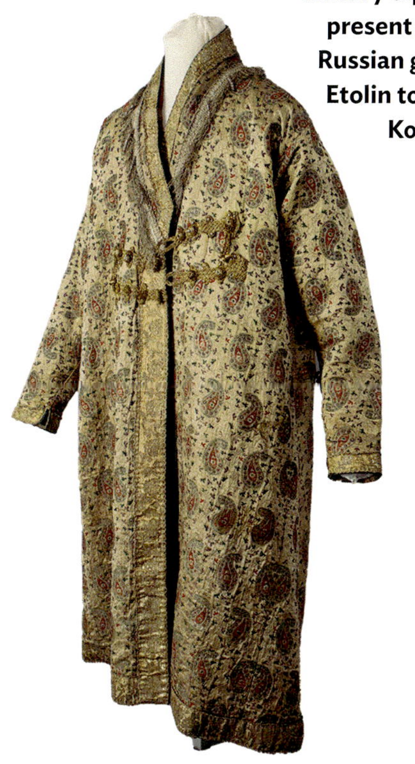

13. Kaftan, a 19th century diplomatic present given by Russian governor Etolin to Mikhail Kooxx'aan.

94-39-1

14. Cutting old growth trees supported the timber industry in Southeast Alaska during in the twentieth century. This Sitka spruce was cut in 1929 at approximately 556 years of age.

2004-1-1

INDIGENOUS PEOPLES AND LANGUAGES OF ALASKA

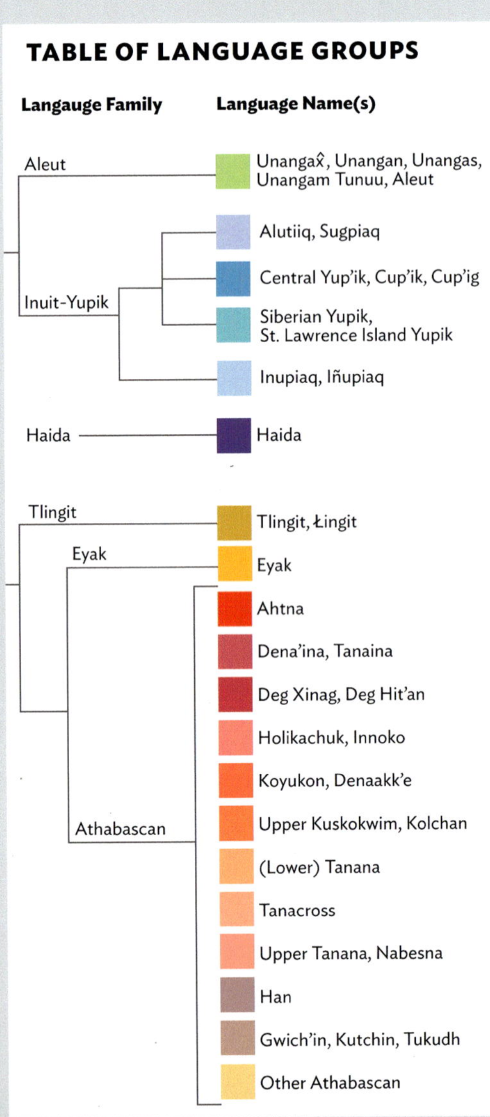

TABLE OF LANGUAGE GROUPS

Langauge Family	Language Name(s)
Aleut	Unangax̂, Unangan, Unangas, Unangam Tunuu, Aleut
Inuit-Yupik	Alutiiq, Sugpiaq
	Central Yup'ik, Cup'ik, Cup'ig
	Siberian Yupik, St. Lawrence Island Yupik
	Inupiaq, Iñupiaq
Haida	Haida
Tlingit	Tlingit, Łingit
Eyak	Eyak
Athabascan	Ahtna
	Dena'ina, Tanaina
	Deg Xinag, Deg Hit'an
	Holikachuk, Innoko
	Koyukon, Denaakk'e
	Upper Kuskokwim, Kolchan
	(Lower) Tanana
	Tanacross
	Upper Tanana, Nabesna
	Han
	Gwich'in, Kutchin, Tukudh
	Other Athabascan

This classic map is a handy guide to learn about Alaska Native cultures. The language groupings correspond generally to the cultural groupings covered in the museum.

Alaska Native people speak many distinct traditional languages. Although almost everyone also speaks English, Native languages are used at home in some parts of the state, and many school programs seek to pass them on to new generations. The languages incorporate worldviews and knowledge unique to tribes and their lands and keeping the languages vital is a key to cultural health.

Grouping Alaska's languages yields a simplified cultural map. The related Iñupiaq, Yup'ik, and Alutiiq/Sugpiaq languages of the Inuit-Yupik language group are spoken by peoples with related cultures spanning the mainland coast from the Arctic to Prince William Sound. The Athabascan languages and cultures of the Interior are more closely related to American Indian languages and cultures in interior Canada and all the way to the American Southwest. The Tlingit, Haida, and Tsimshian cultures of coastal Southeast Alaska have much in common with other Pacific Northwest tribes.

Credit: based on Krauss, Michael, Gary Holton, Jim Kerr, and Colin T. West. 2011. Indigenous Peoples and Languages of Alaska. Fairbanks and Anchorage: Alaska Native Language Center and UAA Institute of Social and Economic Research (https://www.uaf.edu/anla/collections/map/).

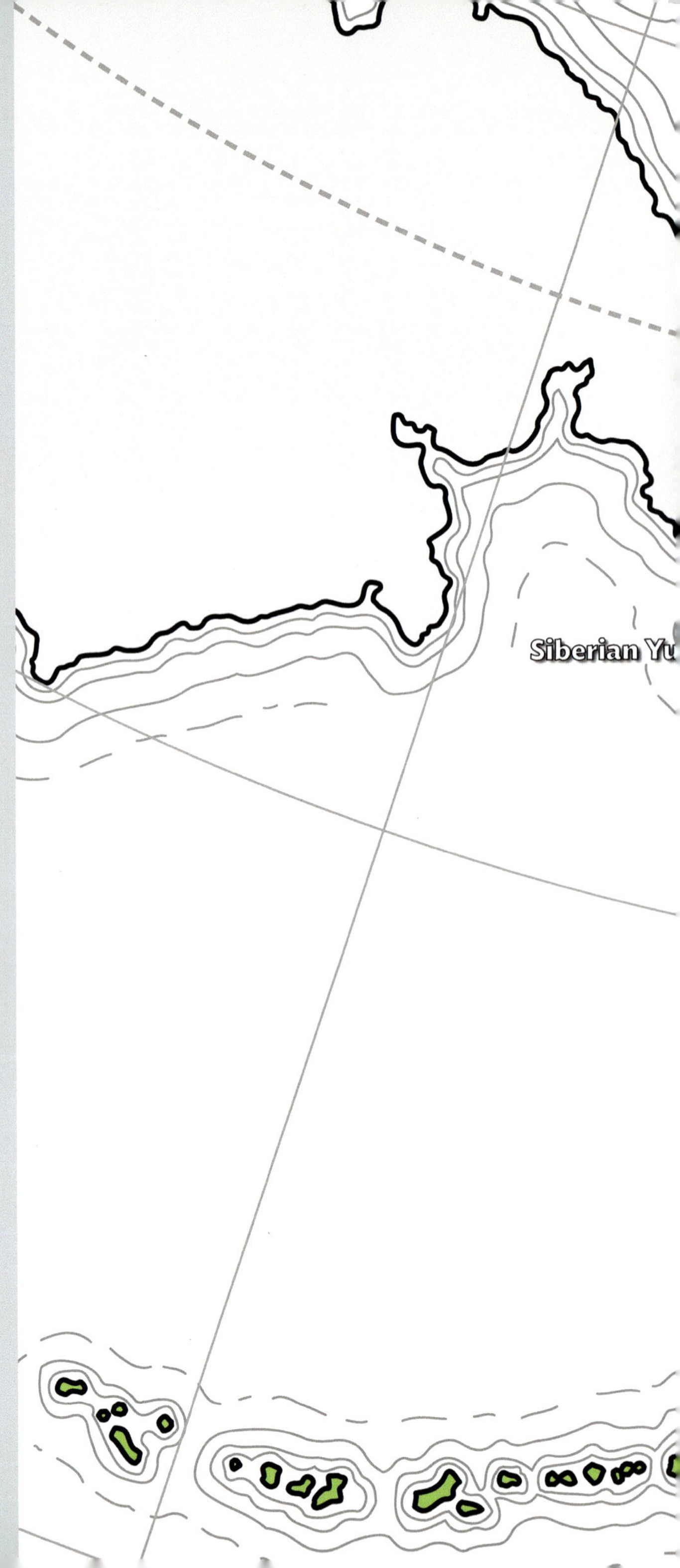

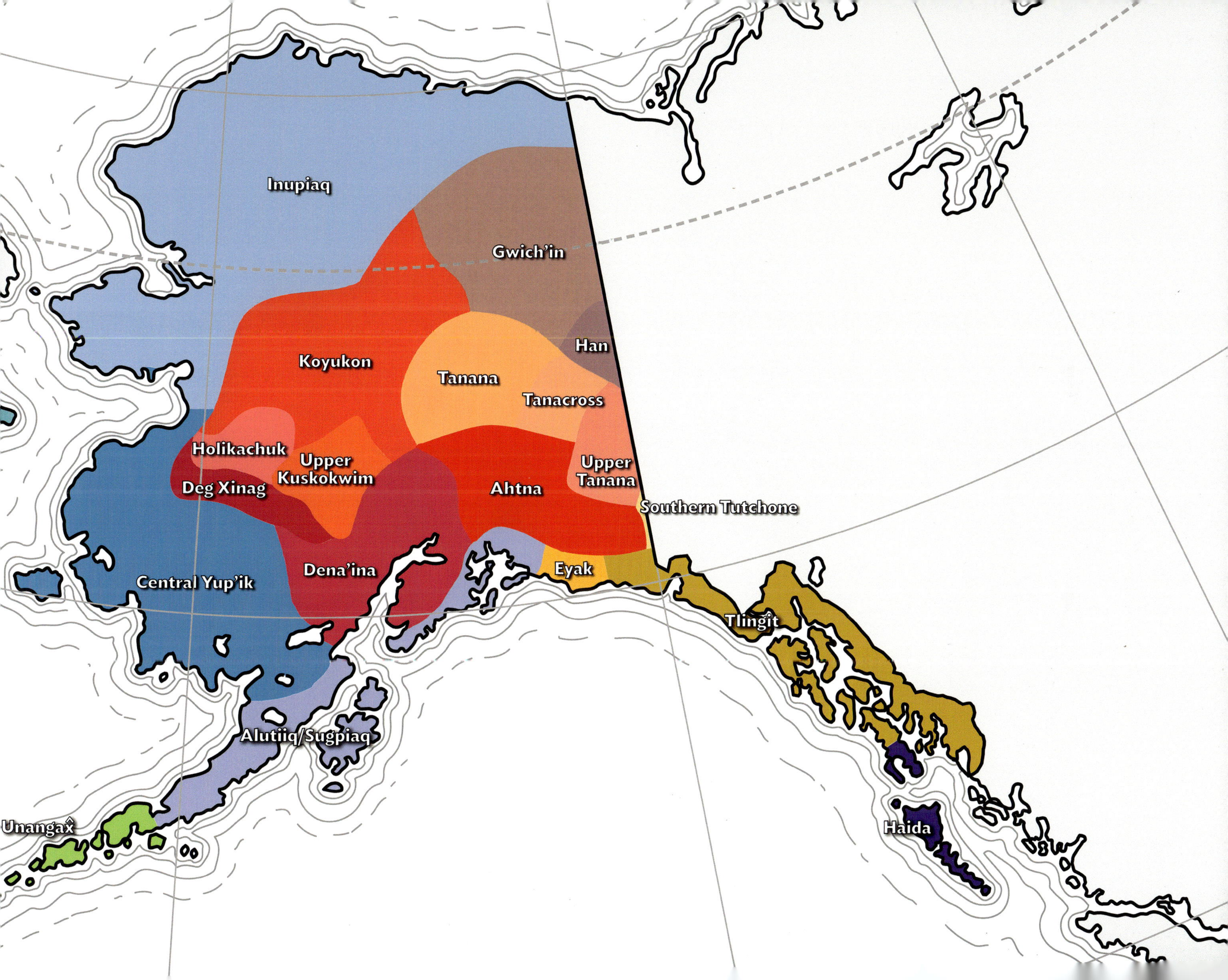

Inupiaq
Gwich'in
Han
Koyukon
Tanana
Tanacross
Holikachuk
Upper
Kuskokwim
Deg Xinag
Upper
Tanana
Ahtna
Southern Tutchone
Dena'ina
Eyak
Central Yup'ik
Tlingit
Alutiiq/Sugpiaq
Unangax̂
Haida

ALASKA STATE MUSEUM GALLERY MAP

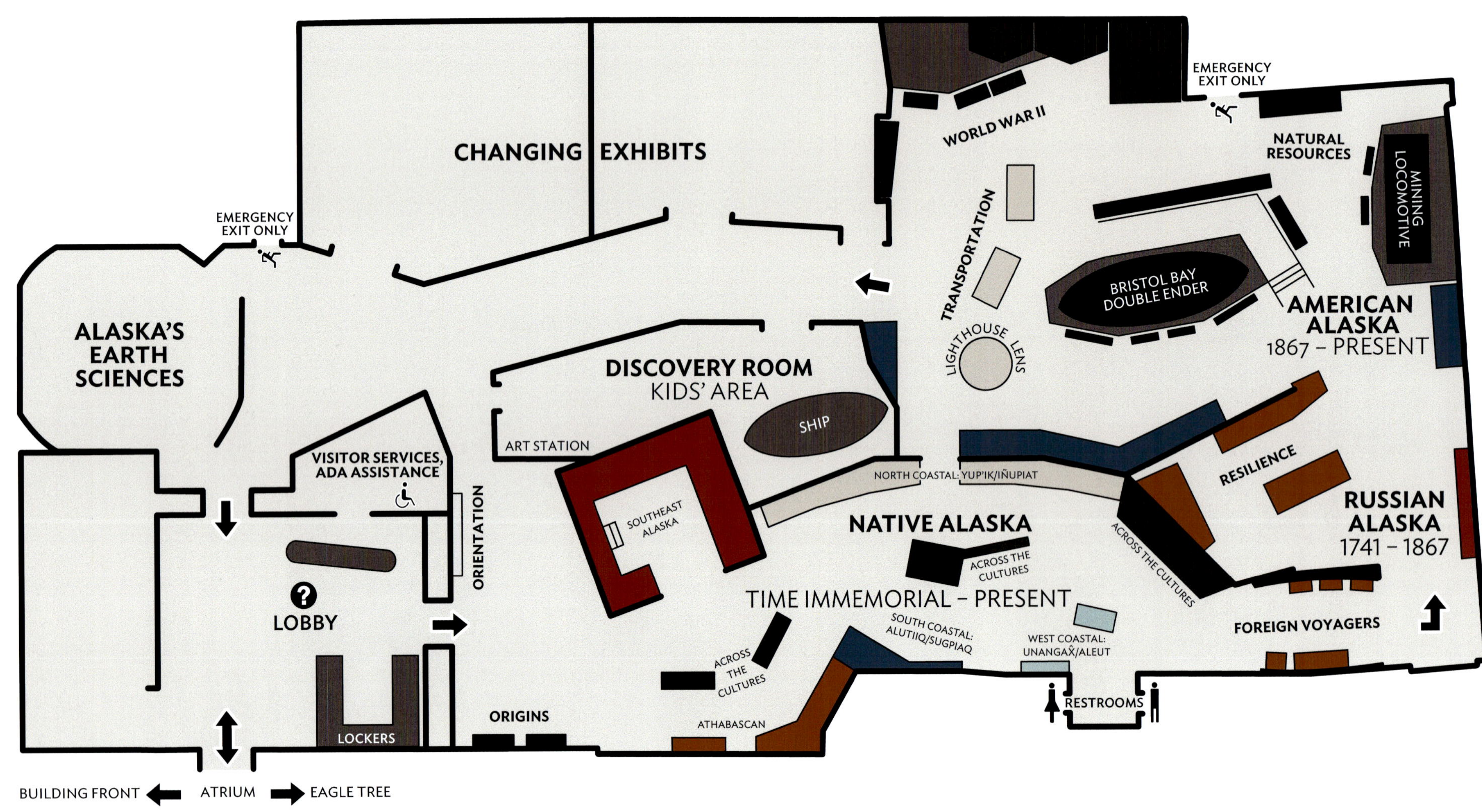

OUR STORY IN MANY VOICES

Wonder Wall
A visual overview of a wide range of creatures, geology and paleontology representing the museum's natural history collections.

Orientation
In this space you will encounter faces of Alaska and a digital map that orients you to the vastness of this place that the museum seeks to explore.

Origins
Leading theories (both scholarly and traditional) of the peopling of the New World are supplemented with precontact tools and ivory carvings, archaeological baskets, a petroglyph from Southeast Alaska, and a Tlingit screen illustrating an ancient story.

NATIVE ALASKA

Southeast Alaska: Tlingit, Haida, Tsimshian, Eyak
Objects are housed within a representation of a traditional Tlingit plank house. Visitors may enter through an open side of the house, or by going through a traditional doorway in the front of the house.

Interior: Athabascan
This section features a birch bark canoe and beaded Dena'ina clothing of caribou hide, as well as hunting and fishing implements, basketry and beadwork.

North Coastal: Yup'ik and Iñupiat
Look up to see a large skin boat (umiak) above casework featuring the museum's large collection of Arctic artifacts.

West Coastal: Unangax̂ / Aleut
Look for a high-density exhibit on twined basketry, a gut parka, and contemporary art from the region.

South Coastal: Alutiiq / Sugpiaq
Katmai masks, stone lamps, and contemporary art are featured.

Across the Cultures
Island cases in the Alaska Native gallery feature cross-cultural comparisons to illustrate the interconnectedness of tribal groups living on the crossroads of continents. Look for trade, masks, baskets, art, clothings and regalia, and kayaks.

Foreign Voyagers
The walls of this ship-like gallery display maps and charts from 18th and early 19th century European and American expeditions to Alaska.

Resilience
This section explores the response of Alaska Natives to the encroachment of Russians and Americans upon their lands, and their subsequent efforts to colonize Alaska and destroy and assimilate Native cultures.

RUSSIAN ALASKA

This section interprets the Russian colonization of Alaska during the late 18th and early 19th centuries. Cases represent daily life in the colony, the complexity of trade in the colonial capital, and the Russian Orthodox Church.

AMERICAN ALASKA

Starting with the Alaska Purchase of 1867, visitors can trace the development of American culture in Alaska.

Maritime Industries
A Bristol Bay double ender anchors this section. Surrounding exhibits interpret the rise of commercial whaling and fishing, the development of support infrastructure, and related social issues.

Mining
Displays of mining equipment and personal artifacts representing miners and their families surround an 18-ton electric mining locomotive. Both the Klondike and Nome Gold rushes are covered.

Oil & Timber
A huge spruce cross section highlights the harvest of timber. The development of Alaska's rich oil fields forever changed life here, and this display examines the growth of the industry.

Tourism
The development of Alaska as a tourist destination is outlined in this section.

Transportation
This section traces Alaska's growing transportation connections to the rest of the world, and how Alaska has coped with finding itself no longer at the ends of the earth, but at the crossroads of continents.

World War II
Alaska played a strategic role during the war, which brought many changes.

Discovery Room
A climbable version of the HMS *Discovery*, the 18th century vessel used by the expedition of Capt. George Vancouver to the north Pacific, is the focal point of this kids' learning and playing area, as well as Olivia the Octopus.

Earth Sciences
Specimens interpret Alaskan earth sciences in changing exhibits.

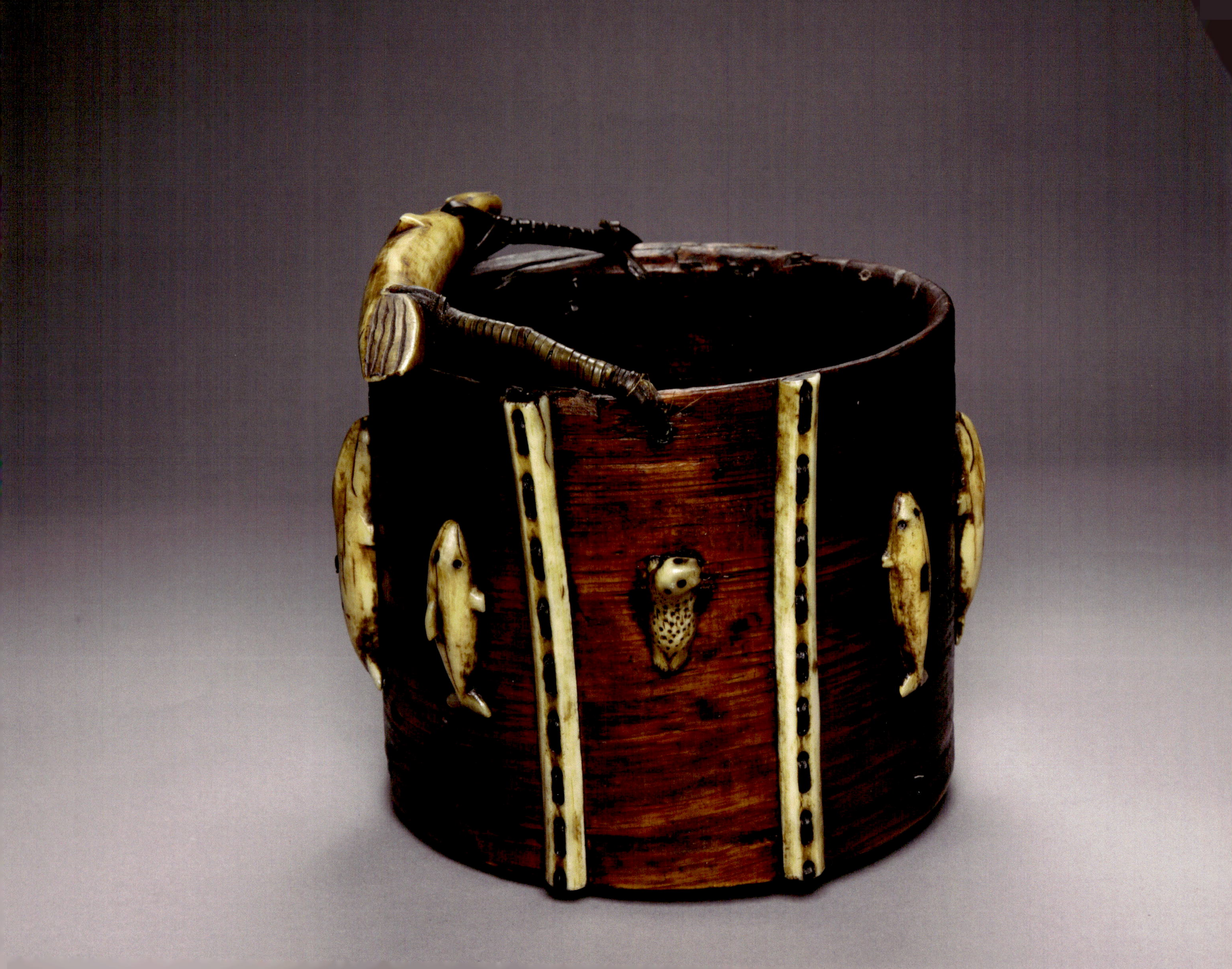

THE SETTING

ALASKA'S GEOGRAPHY, NATURAL HISTORY, AND HUMAN ECOLOGY, AND THE KASHEVAROFF BUILDING

LEFT
Ceremonial bucket
Pt. Barrow, Nuvugmiut, Iñupiaq.
ASM-II-A-6853

1.

Almost anyone can find Alaska on a map, but most maps are of little use to appreciate Alaska's size and geographic diversity. Many maps of the United States depict Alaska as a disconnected afterthought, at a reduced scale, shrunken so it won't dominate the representation of the other states. Many world maps squeeze the Arctic regions. Maps are made for people, as are political boundaries, but the North is barely inhabited, with only one-twentieth of 1 percent of the world's population spread across its vastness. Nearly the entire Arctic is encompassed in only four nations, all among the world's largest: Russia, Canada, Greenland, and a part of the United States, Alaska.

Where people are so scarce and space so plentiful, places can best be described by their nature rather than by their names. Alaska does have regions, peoples with unique cultures, towns and cities with their own economic lives—most of the Alaska State Museum is about that. But when you fly over the expanse of Alaska, the human story is not evident. You see wilderness, intact and unconstrained by roads, fences, wires, or much of anything else that humans have made. Everything built is lost in this immensity. At night the darkness stretches as far as you can see, except for rare scattered specks, the outposts where people live, even the largest of which—Anchorage—is infinitesimal and alone in this space. To consider the setting, it's best to start with the natural history of the land, not the human history.

Processes of nature write the land differently in each part of Alaska. The southern tip is temperate and damp, with huge rainforest trees on steep rocky shores, while the northern tip is desert-dry and usually frozen, with tundra heather and no trees at all—and for most of the year, its flat, white land blends into the flat, icebound sea. These differences manifest natural forces in systems that support unique communities of life. To understand Alaska, you learn to read these systems and how life responds.

We'll start from the south. Along the arc of the Gulf of Alaska and southeast to the strip of coast called the Panhandle, a rim of mountains—still building—intercepts the storms of the North Pacific, wringing from them prodigious rain and snowfall that powers the growth of huge spruce, hemlock, and cedar trees and builds ice fields that spill down the valleys as great glaciers. The glaciers scrape mineral-rich sediment from the mountains, which washes down the rivers in spring, fertilizing ocean plankton blooms at the foundation of some of the world's most productive fisheries. The salmon fed by that ecosystem climb up the rivers to spawn and die, feeding the bears, who in turn fertilize the trees. This mossy, temperate rainforest—a dim, drowsy, eternal place—ranges from well south of Alaska all the way north and west to Kodiak Island and near Anchorage, but it grows only on the front of these mountain peaks. On the back side, in the rain shadow of the mountains, an entirely different biome prevails.

When you climb over the coastal mountains, the light changes. Now the trees, mostly small spruce as well as birch and aspen, leave the sky open, and the forest floor is brush, grass, or mossy ground cover. Besides the drier weather, it's colder and the tree line on the mountains is lower, leaving more room for alpine tundra. Moving farther north, beyond the towering Alaska Range, this boreal forest grows as thin as a teenager's beard, as the robust white spruce give way to spindly, gnarled black spruce, trees whose trunks add only a few inches of thickness in a century. Here in the Interior, distant from the coasts and the moderating influence of the ocean, temperatures in winter are very cold and the summer is hot and dry. Permafrost lies under much of the landscape, soil that never thaws, preventing surface water from draining, even in summer. It's a hard place for vegetation to grow and the land is poor, but shrubs and heathery plants have adapted, like the black spruce, to survive and reemerge during the short summers.

Great rivers drain this central part of the state from east to west, the largest of them, the Yukon River, flowing almost two thousand miles from British Columbia to a vast delta with the Kuskokwim River, on the southwest shore of Alaska. The Yukon-Kuskokwim Delta's wetlands shimmer with gigantic flocks of migratory birds. The rivers open a pathway for fish to cross Alaska, especially salmon. They spawn in the world's most abundant runs on Bristol Bay, just to the south of the delta. Storm tracks from the frigid Bering Sea cool and dampen this land, where trees are scarce. Those damp conditions become ever more dramatic, continuing southwest along the coast to the Alaska Peninsula and the Aleutian Islands. The Aleutians protrude from the waves like the backs of beasts, their black volcanic cliffs blanketed by heather and shrouded in mist, as the incessant wind and fog sweep across them from the vast North Pacific.

The Interior's boreal forest, already described, covers the great center of Alaska, bounded on the north by another east-west mountain range, the old and craggy Brooks Range, which is certainly cold enough but is too dry to accumulate much glacier ice. To its north, a truly Arctic climate keeps the land frozen. Snowstorms are not uncommon in mid-summer, and in winter the sky stays dark—at the northern tip of Alaska, the sun doesn't rise from mid-November to mid-January. Although precipitation is sparse—Tucson, Arizona, gets more than three times as much annually as Utqiagvik, the main community here—the summer thaw exposes wet, spongy ground with innumerable shallow lakes. This water stays in place, on flat land, held to the surface in summer by deep and continuous permafrost, and in winter frozen into a white and featureless tableland. During the brief summer, insects and migratory birds thrive, and herds of hundreds of thousands of caribou migrate north, birthing calves on the tundra and digging through thin snow for lichen.

All this happens naturally through the processes of nature, without people. But people are changing Alaska. The warming climate has dramatically altered the timing of the seasons and ice coverage, average and extreme temperatures, storms, water temperatures in the ocean and rivers, erosion, permafrost depth and extent, wildfire frequency and severity, and many other parts of the system. Brush has grown where formerly there was only tundra, tree lines have risen higher on the mountains, forests over thawing permafrost have slumped in landslides, lakes have drained, and newly destructive insects have killed millions of acres of trees. Salmon runs have failed, ocean fish species have moved north or declined, plankton blooms have sputtered, and enormous die-offs of seabirds have left piles of their dead on beaches. Biological changes due to climate change became evident in Alaska around 2000. At this writing, in 2023, this natural world has remarkably, unavoidably, irreversibly changed, and it is still changing, rapidly.

So we cannot leave people out of the story after all.

Oil lamp

Late Kachemak tradition (900–2700 years ago), ancestors of the Sugpiaq/Alutiiq people.

ASM-II-A-1776

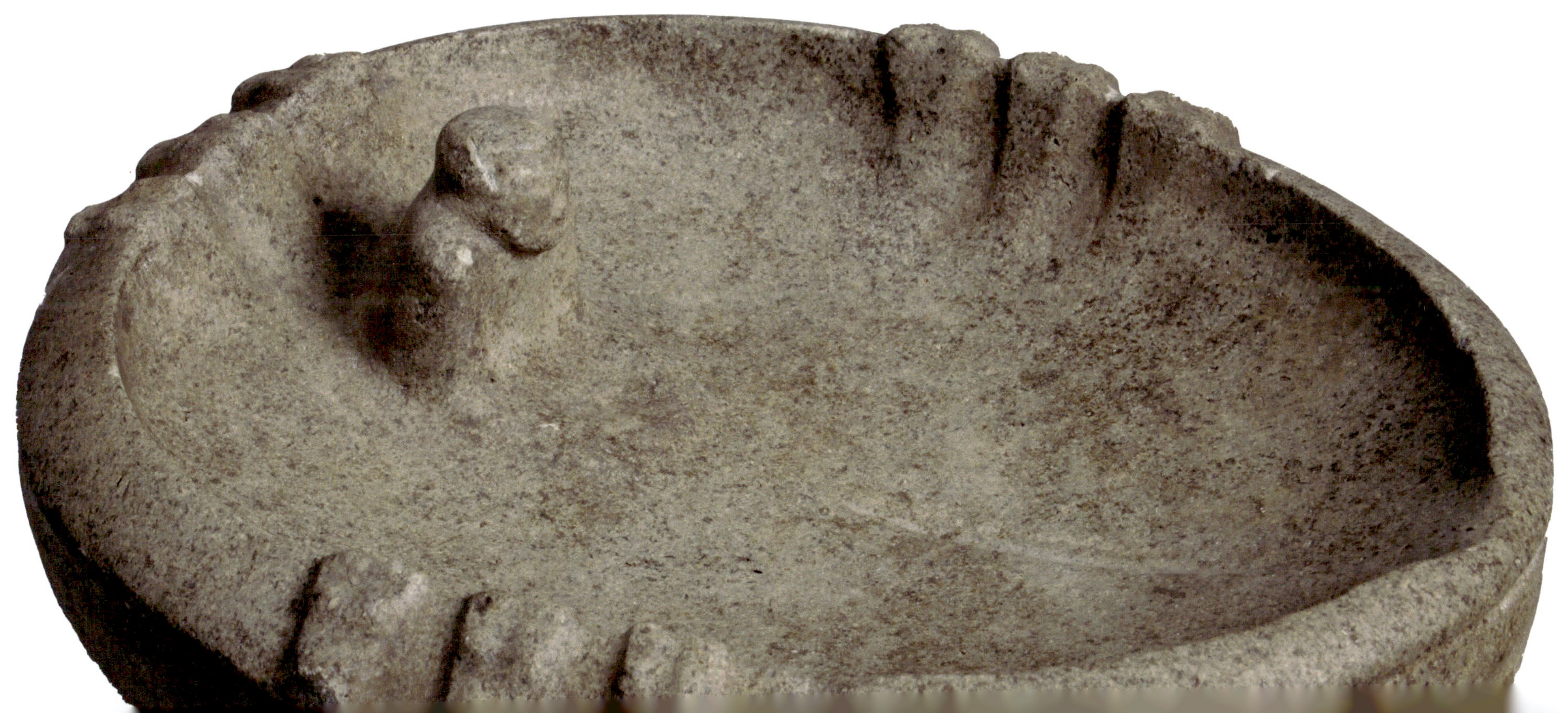

Sam Hunter (Yup'ik), 1945-6

Seagull mask Hooper Bay, Naparyaarmiut.

ASM-II-A-5398

2.

Why are people here? All animals rely on their habitat, including homo sapiens, but in Alaska this question of human ecology is a complex riddle whose solution is not entirely resolved.

In most places in the world, where patterns of development were established centuries earlier, human populations grew around the resources that support life. We humans cannot escape our environment—the land and weather determine where we can harvest food and get water. Alaska's first peoples lived where they could eat, but their populations were small, within the carrying capacity for hunting, fishing, and gathering on northern lands and waters, beyond which capacity survival would not be assured. But today's population is much larger, and it is almost entirely dependent on food and goods that arrive from elsewhere, mostly on ships, with most of those supplies coming across a single dock in Anchorage. Large-scale agriculture has been unsuccessful in Alaska, and the state grows only a tiny proportion of its own food. Most stores contain almost nothing made here. Alaska is an outpost at the end of the supply chain, its sustenance largely unconnected from its environment.

The contemporary private economy depends on natural resource exports of oil, minerals, and fish, as well as tourism and global air freight—all industries whose health varies with unpredictable

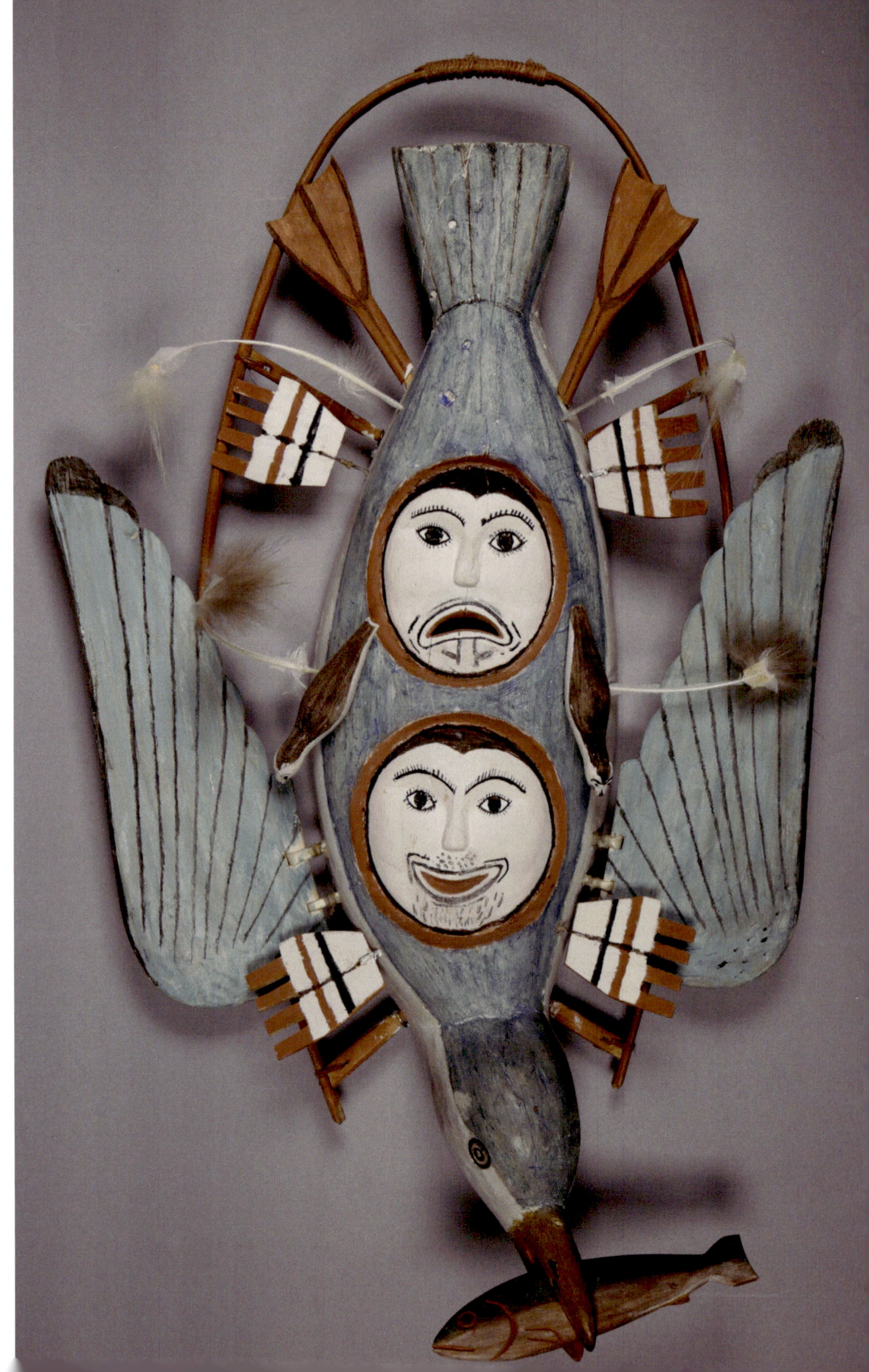

world markets and distant investment decisions. Government expenditures instead make up the greater part of the Alaska economy. The U.S. military maintains large bases in Alaska, and the federal government is generous with services, investments, and direct payments, far in excess of Alaskans' tax payments to the national treasury. The state government's own enormous Alaska Permanent Fund investment account—built on past oil revenues—generates enough earnings to help power the economy through expenditures and direct payments called dividends that are given to every resident. The state also collects and spends revenues from oil production, although that flow of wealth has long been in an unsteady decline.

The Iñupiat of the Arctic continue to subsist on marine mammals, including bowhead whales, walrus, and seals, but the core of their region's private economic activity comes from the oil fields and a zinc mine. Small Iñupiaq communities are connected only by air. A single, mostly unpaved road, five hundred miles long, links the oil fields at Prudhoe Bay with the outside world.

The economy of western Alaska, the Aleutians, and the Gulf of Alaska coast depend mostly on fish, with a frenzy of salmon coming in the summer and crab and bottom fish throughout the year, although much of that takes place offshore without much local involvement. Communities here are small and transportation is by air or water. The tiny population of the western mainland is mainly Yup'ik, mostly in river villages, where people preserve among the most traditional lifeways in Alaska.

The Aleutian Islands are even more sparsely populated, with the industrial Dutch Harbor fishing port in Unalaska and a few tiny Unangax̂ villages. The first people of Kodiak Island and around Prince William Sound and the lower tip of the Kenai Peninsula are the Sugpiaq/Alutiiq. In these regions, village life continues, but most people live in ethnically diverse hub communities where fishing, tourism, and government drive the economy.

The south central region—including the Kenai Peninsula, the Matanuska and Susitna Valleys (known as Mat-Su) and, especially, Anchorage—is the commercial and health-care center of Alaska, holding the majority of the state's population, its only city of over 100,000 people, and a racially and ethnically diverse urban core. The main airport's geographic position makes it a global cargo hub. A large military base north of Anchorage also creates many jobs.

Farther north, Fairbanks is the only city amid the vast Interior region. Large military installations, the University of Alaska, tourism, and gold mining generate the area's economic activity. The Alaska Railroad and a skein of two-lane highways connect Anchorage, Fairbanks, and Seward, south of Anchorage.

The indigenous people of the Interior and from the Anchorage area north and east are Athabascans. They traditionally subsisted by hunting caribou and other game and taking fish from the rivers, but the ecosystem here is far less generous than on the coasts. Their villages are broadly scattered along the rivers.

The traditional indigenous people of Southeast Alaska developed larger communities and greater wealth than those in the north thanks to the relative richness of their coastal rainforest home, with huge salmon runs in the rivers, plentiful food from the sea, and animals and materials from the forests. The Tlingit at the north and central part the Southeast Alaska Panhandle and the Haida and Tsimshian to the south were traditional travelers, traders, and warriors. Today, some of

Tthiggide'on Adze

Used for general woodworking. Deg Hit'an Athabascan (attributed).

ASM-96-51-12

their ancient villages remain as tribal enclaves, but other communities have grown into towns where Alaska Native people are in the minority.

Together with the Athabascans, these Southeast Alaska cultures have more commonalities with American Indians of the western United States than they do with the indigenous people of the Arctic and western Alaska. Southeast Alaska is an extension of the Pacific Northwest. Likewise, Athabascan peoples also live in interior western Canada, and their languages bear similarity to Navajo in the American Southwest.

On the other hand, the lifeways and art of the Iñupiat of the north, the Yup'ik of the west, and the Sugpiaq/Alutiiq of the south central coast are more closely related to the circumpolar Inuit of Arctic Canada (formerly known as but today rarely called the Eskimos). In the Aleutians, the Unangax̂ (formerly called Aleut) are a distinct ethnic group of their own with elements in common with each of their neighbors.

In Southeast Alaska, the cities of Sitka, Ketchikan, and Wrangell grew during the twentieth century on big timber harvests and wood-processing plants. That ended in the 1990s when the federal government protected the old-growth rainforest, and the area's economies transitioned to tourism. Commercial fishing and mining employ people in the region, too. But development is limited by geography. The coastal mountains block highway construction. With transportation only by air or boat, and little flat ground, the primary commercial product is beautiful vistas. Well over a million cruise ship passengers come each summer.

If Alaska were a country, these regions would be its provinces, as different and as unconnected as American states. Because of Alaska's size and the weak transportation network, most people rarely travel beyond their own region, and they tend to be oblivious about what is happening elsewhere in the state. Links in the fishing or tourism industries are as likely to tie Alaskans to other parts of the world as to companies elsewhere in Alaska.

Instead, the cultural connections of Alaskans—like their most important economic lifelines—run through government. The federal government controls most of the land, makes most of the development decisions, and provides the most jobs through the military, health care, land agencies, and many other expenditures. The Alaska state government also pays for health, education, transportation, and the one thing every Alaskan has in common—man, woman, and child—the cash payment of the annual Alaska Permanent Fund dividend.

Chance placed Juneau along the narrow, windy Gastineau Channel, in a corner of the state where a huge gold mine was dug beginning in the 1880s. It lies far from the center of the population and can be reached only by air or water—there is no road. Indeed, there's not much reason for Juneau to be here but for the timing of that gold find, which made it the largest Alaska city when Congress designated it as the territorial capital in 1900 (the capital actually located here in 1906). And, in a state so dependent on government, the capital is exceptionally important. Much of the economy flows through its buildings. And, with that distinction, Juneau is, in some practical ways, at the center of Alaska.

3.

Juneau pulses with its own rhythm. In January, with cooler weather and snow in the mountains, the legislature arrives for its annual session, which is legally designated to last ninety days but almost never does, instead continuing until late spring, and sometimes reconvening to go through most of the year. In May, with a few more sunny skies and the dark conifers shedding their cloaks of snow, the summer visitors arrive, mostly from white ships that tower above the docks and the gifts shops along the downtown waterfront. High energy continues until the fall, when, muffled by the cover of an overstuffed gray sky, with heavy rains and empty streets, Juneau pauses in the dimness, waiting for the holidays and the return of the legislature.

The Father Andrew P. Kashevaroff building, home to the Alaska State Library, Archives and Museum, remains awake through this annual cycle. In summer, light streams in; in winter, the building glows outward. It is a cultural center of this central city, a fifteen-minute walk from the Marine Park where most visitors arrive. Public parking is open below the building and on the street in front of the circular entrance plaza, where public artworks stand and an extensive covered area provides shelter from the rain.

The center of the building is a high, narrow atrium. At the far end from the door, a sculptured tree stands as tall as the ceiling, three stories high, with a staircase that wraps around its branches. This is the museum's largest natural history exhibit: the Sitka spruce, Alaska's state tree. It towers as the king of the temperate rainforest, precious for lumber with its straight grain and light weight—it once was a strategic war material for its use in airplanes—and precious for the vertical habitat it scaffolds in the mossy, dusky forest. This model of a tree symbolizes the region. Mounted bald eagles perch in its branches and in a huge nest near the top, where you can see a juvenile eagle, with brown plumage but without a white head—these birds take five years to fully mature. Here is a chance to see eagles where they live, close up.

At the top of the stairs, the state library and archives face south, toward the water. Take a look at the airy, calming research center, which serves both the Alaska State Archives and the Alaska State Library Historical Collections. Changing exhibits are usually on view, often with historical photos and video, as well as contemporary topics of interest. Visitors can also browse a collection of selected Alaska periodicals and books. The ocean and mountain view is on one side, and on the other is an extraordinary masterpiece of stained glass by one of Alaska's most recognizable and characteristic artists, Evon Zerbetz of Ketchikan. Zerbetz interprets the people, animals, and cathedral forests of her home with bright, thickly decorated woodcut imagery, at once endearing but also mysterious with its iconlike flatness. The window expands this vision to an overwhelming dreamscape. The entire window is sixty-five feet long, with designs that extend from the glass onto etched alder-wood panels. Titled *We Are Written in the Layers of the Earth*, the piece explodes with sea life, birds, and land animals, all entwined with strands representing human stories—it reminds me of the sacred grandeur of a great church window, but evokes instead the spirituality of Alaska's swirling ecosystems. Zerbetz's woodcut style suggests the black lead borders of historic stained glass. In fact, Zerbetz created the piece first as a twelve-foot linoleum print, traveling to Germany to fabricate the glass with the aid of experts.

More of the museum's essentially artistic treatment of natural history continues downstairs, in the "Wonder Wall" to the left

A glass mural by Evon Zerbetz separates the library and the research area: *We are written on the layers of the earth.*

© Lara Swimmer Photography

of the entrance desk. Here curators exhibit a rich and diverse collection of animal mounts in a single set of huge cases, with clear glass on the front and back, forming a wall through which visitors can pass on the way out of the main exhibits. The display freezes the wildlife in their beauty, but out of their context, as a kind of three-dimensional mural of once-living beings—something like the profusion of life depicted in Zerbetz's glass wall upstairs.

Finally, a room near the southeast corner of the building, in the museum area, contains a theater and sometimes exhibits relating to earth science.

The Alaska State Museum lacks any single natural history narrative, nor does it really make much attempt to explain the natural systems that define Alaska. But the pieces that are here—the eagle tree, the Zerbetz window, and the Wonder Wall—do say something powerful about how Alaskans feel about the overwhelming natural world in which we live.

And then there is the map. In the atrium, carved into the terrazzo floor, a metal outline of Alaska's coast reaches from wall to wall. The map is to scale and oriented to the north, so that standing upon it you can feel like you are somehow scientifically located at the center of the representation of Alaska that the museum represents. But, as I noted at the beginning of this essay, maps don't capture Alaska well. This map is huge, but its true location is off in a corner of Alaska—notice the spot that picks out Juneau, on the extreme lower right. And notice also how small and far apart all the towns really are. They're nothing more than dots. The coast itself is just a line, an abstraction, at this scale.

The museum seems to point to this vastness and to acknowledge that even here, Alaska is too large to be modeled or enclosed. But within the humility of that acknowledgment, there is much to learn in the details and specificity of the human experience within this immensity. And that is primarily what the museum is about, in the galleries devoted to things people made—as we shall learn in the following sections.

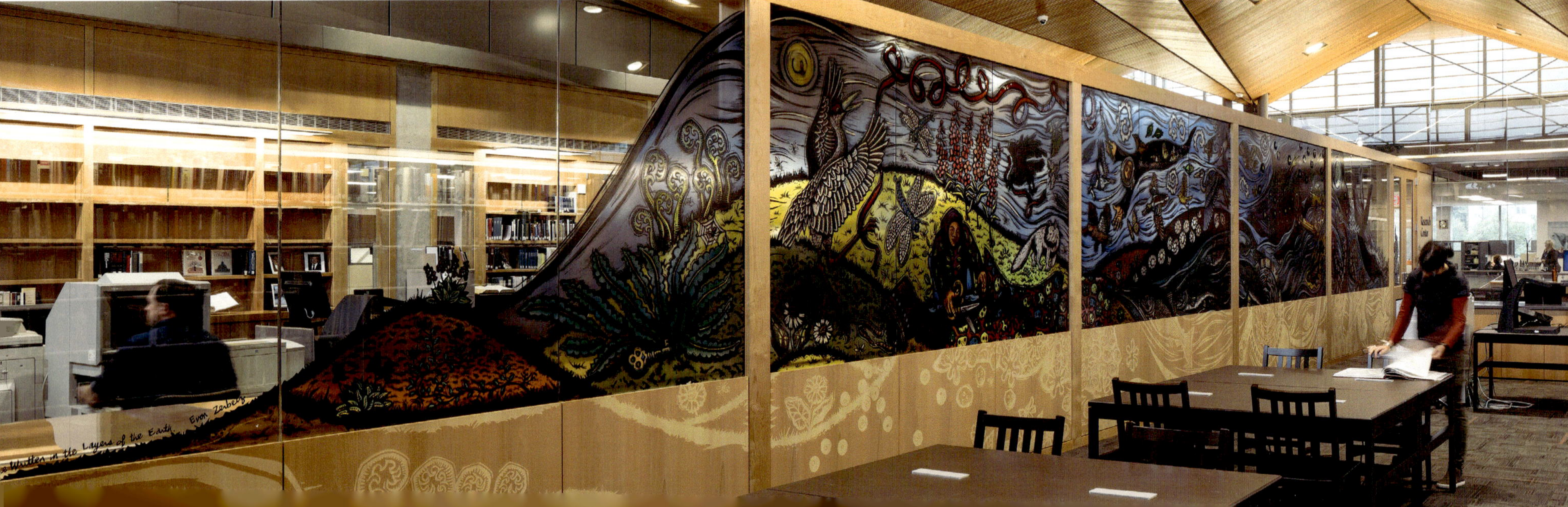

THE STORY IN THE EXHIBITS

1. Native Alaska

INDIGENOUS ALASKA CULTURES BEFORE CONTACT AND TODAY

The first gallery of the Alaska State Museum tells of Native cultures as if they existed outside the dimension of time. A sign declares that the exhibit covers "Time Immemorial–Present Day," or, to put it simply, all known time. Alaska's first people are still Alaska's people—about 20 percent of the population—and their cultures do not belong only to the past. The exhibit makes that point by showing ancient art and artifacts side by side with contemporary Native art and newly made traditional Native art, creating a sense of an evolving but unbroken continuum. But all Alaska Native cultures underwent deep changes after contact with outsiders, often traumatically, and in some cases so disastrously that memory and tradition were broken. That is not much represented here—the next set of rooms tells that story. Instead, this first big, roughly oval gallery—this harmonious, richly occupied, dignified place—presents an ideal form of these indigenous cultures, with their pride, their artistry, and their continuity, largely as if none of those bad things had ever happened. It's a magical space.

In keeping with the lack of a timeline, you will find few straight lines through the exhibit. Wandering steps set the viewing sequence. But there is logical organization. For the most part, cases and objects along the walls represent distinct cultures and their geographies, allowing visitors to absorb their characteristic styles and understand their settings. The most dramatic of these sections will draw your attention immediately: the clan house to the left at the entrance of the gallery, with its oval entrance portal, containing the Southeast Alaska collection, with belongings from the Tlingit, Haida, and Tsimshian peoples. In the middle of the gallery thematic cases labeled "Across the Cultures" bring together objects from various indigenous peoples, with displays of art, masks, baskets, bent wood, and other shared themes, and at the opposite end of the gallery and overhead is a remarkable and arresting collection of watercraft from different cultures.

Starting to the right after you enter, a part of the exhibit called "Origins" contains archaeological objects that seem to predate the indigenous traditions familiarly passed down to the present. Replicas of stone microblades and lanceolate points offer early evidence of human habitation. These may date from 14,500 years ago, when the world was thawing at the end of the last glacial period. Archaeologists and some indigenous cultural leaders debate when people from Asia first came to North America—it may have been much earlier—but most agree they traveled through Alaska or along its coast before peopling the rest of the New World, during a period when the oceans were as much as four hundred feet lower than they are today because

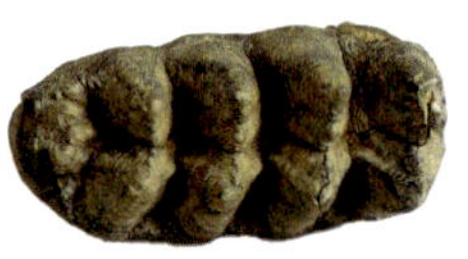

Mastodon tooth fragment

IV-C-59

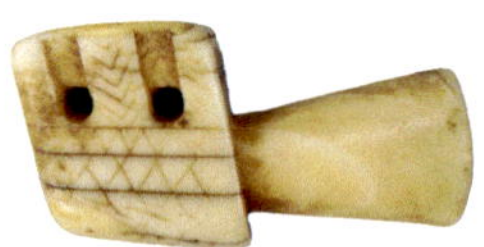

Inflation valve for float

II-A-1316

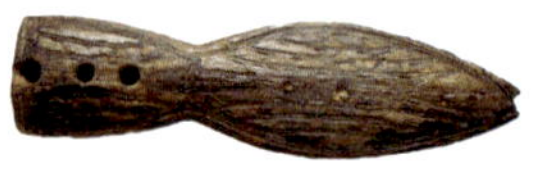

Unknown object

Punuk culture, St. Lawrence Island.

ASM-II-A-2629

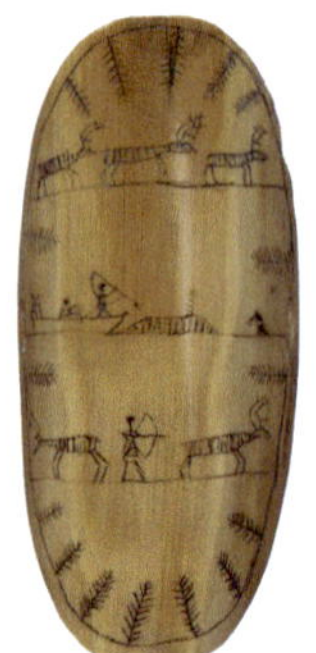

Wrist guard

Made of excavated mammoth ivory, to protect wrist from bowstring, Cape Prince of Wales.

II-A-909

glacier ice had removed that much water from the sea. It's unlikely archaeologists have found the earliest of their camps and settlements.

These cultures may have hunted species that never made it out of the Pleistocene epoch (see the mastodon teeth) and may have been succeeded on the same ground by several other cultures that came and went. As is true everywhere in the museum, deciphering how their technology solved problems is a key to understanding these people's lives. For example, see the ancient harpoon head from Cape Prince of Wales, the westernmost point of the Americas, and the nearby ivory inflation valve—hunters would harpoon marine mammals such as walrus, attaching them to inflated floats made of skins. The animals tired as they pulled the floats, and when they died, their carcasses would be held near the surface. Related, here is a tool for twisting sinew into rope, a socket for holding a harpoon head, a harpoon counterweight, and a carving with markings that apparently record the number of walrus taken. And these same cases also contain objects whose functions are unknown, because the technology from hundreds of generations ago is now lost to us.

Much of what follows in the exhibit shares a theme with these ancient objects, as the weapons, tools, shelters, boats, and clothes manifest the human ingenuity needed to subsist on these northern lands. Tools for hunting marine mammals recur and improve, with adaptations that reflect the conditions of different parts of Alaska. And cultural continuity is evident, too. The Thorne River basket, 5,450 years old, was found preserved in wet mud on Prince of Wales Island, near mussel shells that it probably once held. A contemporary Haida weaver, Dolores Churchill, made a reconstruction following a form known for gathering shellfish in the early 1800s. Likewise, see the remarkable stone lamp carved with the figure of a man, made by a culture we now call the late Kachemak Tradition—a people whose exact identity is lost, but whose work suggests that of the Sugpiaq/Alutiiq culture that followed it and still persists on the south-central Alaska coast.

Exhibits in each part of the gallery teach about cultures. Learn about Iñupiaq and Yup'ik whalers at the far end of the gallery, about the Haida in Southeast Alaska in the clan house across the gallery, about the Sugpiaq/Alutiiq a bit farther down to the right, and about baskets all over the room, including through a comparison of the basketry of many cultures in the first set of "Across the Cultures" cases in the center.

A good way to avoid being overwhelmed is to pick a theme that interests you and explore the exhibit through that frame of reference. For example, looking at art is a way to understand ecosystems. Work from Southeast Alaska and from the Interior reflects the characteristics of these vastly different natural homes in ways both obvious and subtle. In the clan house on the left, which holds treasures of Southeast Alaska's indigenous people, especially the Tlingit, the weight and warmth of the rainforest comes through in the colors of wood and the red and black dyes. The detail of the decoration reflects the wealth and social complexity of these societies that enabled carvers and other artists to dedicate themselves to creation. The Tlingit built big boats and houses, wore armor, fought battles, and held slaves, and they traded far inland through mountain passes they controlled, gathering exotic materials and amassing great wealth. Note the delicately engraved bracelet, commonly made of silver fashioned out of coins obtained in trade. Another remarkable beaten-coin silver Tlingit piece hangs in the "Across the Cultures" case on trade, a blanket clasp in the shape of a ceremonial shield. The clan house contains carved hats and woven regalia that would have taken artists many months or years to create, all for ceremonial uses. A spectacular Tsimshian bentwood box by David and Zach Boxley exemplifies the intricacy of the form-line design that developed in these cultures.

Across the way, the color palette differs—the light blue of the open sky gleams around the caribou above the Athabascan exhibit and in the lighter colors and airy design of the objects people made. These tribes occupied the vast expanse of central Alaska and western Canada, mostly away from the coasts, with big sky, on tundra, and in poorly growing forests with open canopies, enduring severe weather and harvesting lean animals that themselves fought to survive in the spare and unforgiving ecosystem. Their villages were small and mobile, traveling through an annual round in pursuit of fish, game, and plants, in their seasons, often living in tents made of skins. The art tends to be lightweight and functional. The beadwork is especially beautiful and weightless, done in early days with dyed porcupine quills and later with tiny seed beads, adorning clothing, boots, and bags—see the beaded Dena'ina clothing made of caribou skin or the Gwich'in beaded moose-hide bag for holding hunting tools. People also made functional baskets of birch bark, a light, waterproof, portable material widely available on the uplands of the boreal forest. (To pick up more on this theme of how environment influences art, see the case in between the Southeast and Interior exhibits, which explores the commonalities and differences among Alaska Native peoples'

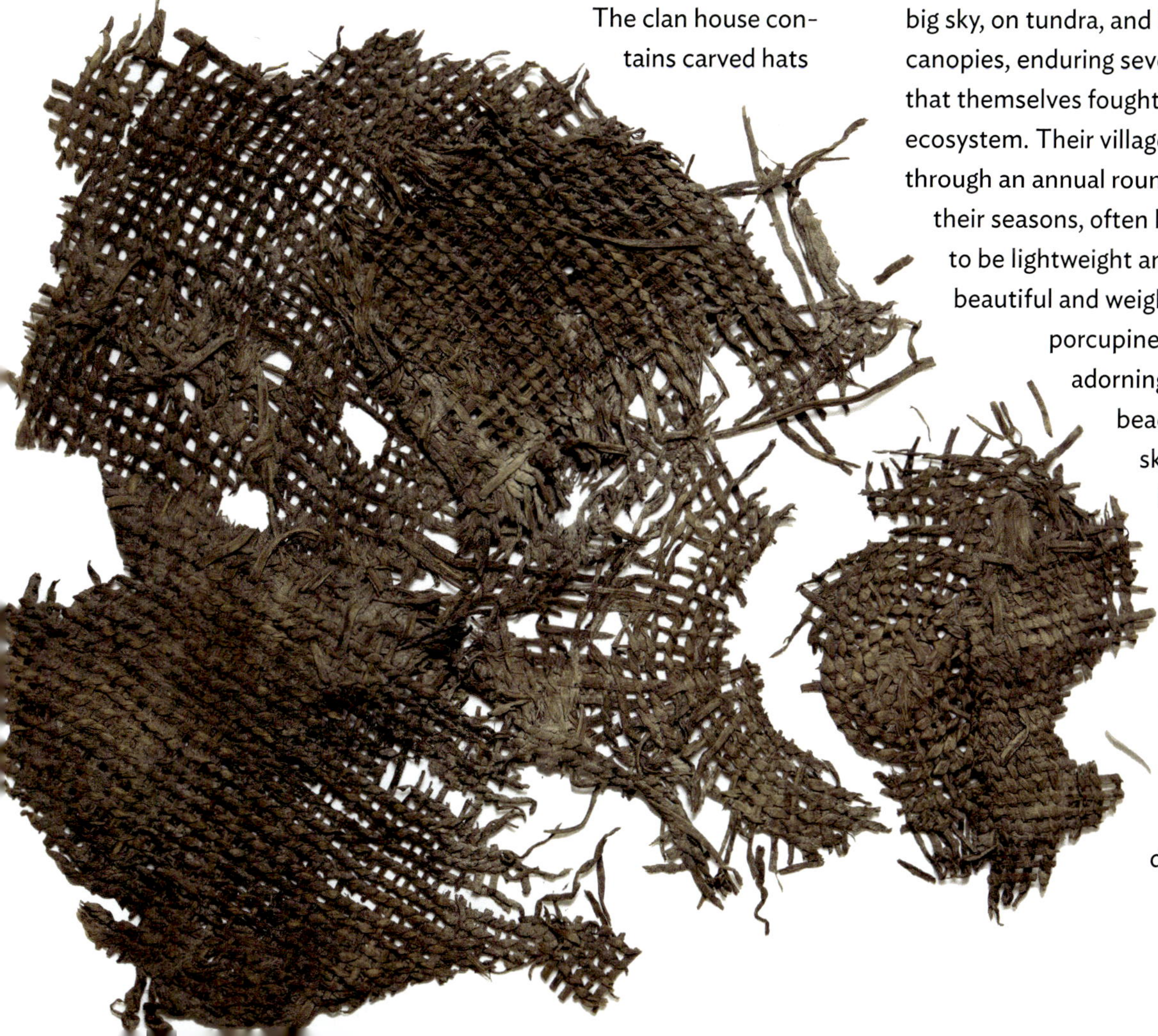

Thorne River Basket

Twined of spruce roots, it is radiocarbon dated to approximately 5,450 years old. Found buried in wet mud with mussel shells nearby, thought to be its original contents. Prince of Wales Island.

ASM-94-31-1

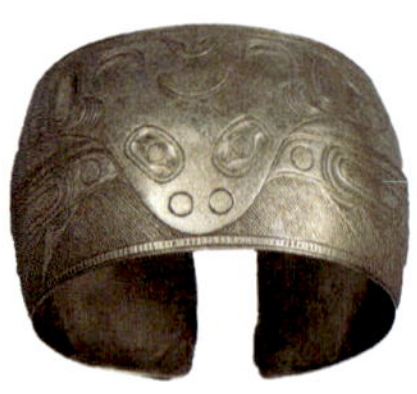

Dáanaa kées Silver bracelet

Mud shark or dogfish design. Tlingit.

II-B-1789

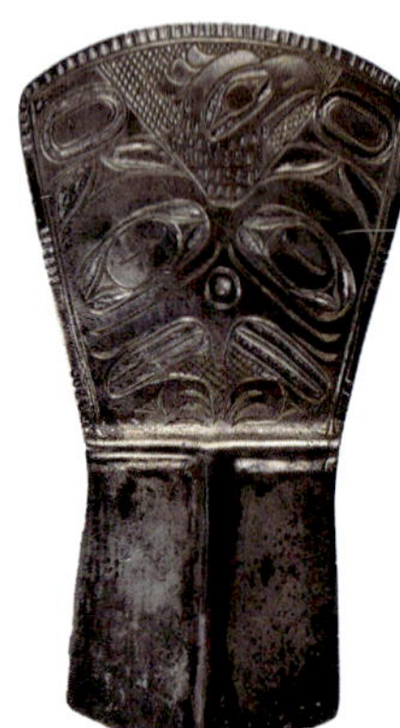

Blanket clasp

Yakutat, Tlingit.

II-B-836

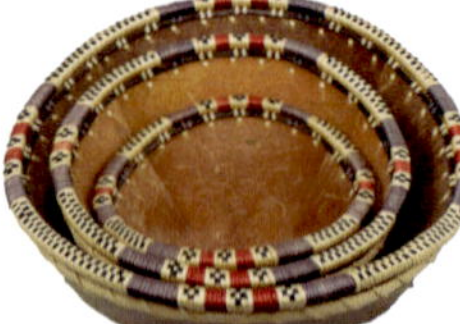

Tetth'og Nesting birchbark baskets

By Belle Deacon [1905–95] (Deg Xinag Athabascan)

II-C-165

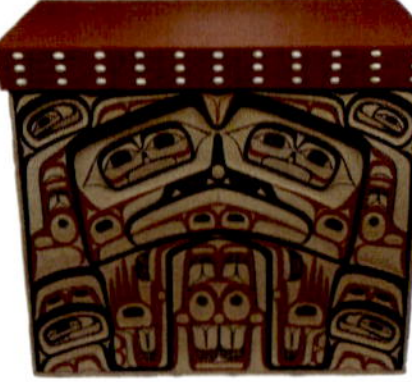

Large box

By David and Zach Boxley (Tsimshian), 2014.

LC.430-1

art and decorative motifs, in masks and everyday objects. Some styles quickly become recognizable.)

The mobile, river-dwelling Athabascans built functional, lightweight watercraft they could carry, paddle with small groups in moving water, and easily repair with nearby materials—the birch bark canoe. It is as graceful as an object of art but is unadorned. Hanging above you, a dugout canoe from Southeast Alaska has opposite characteristics. A heavy, seaworthy craft for the ocean, with high gunwales, it required many paddlers. Carvers made these boats from huge, single logs as long as fifty feet and decorated them with artistic forms prescribed by the clan.

Watercraft appear all through the museum. In these boats, strands of meaning unite, connecting technological and cultural adaptation to the differing conditions of life around Alaska. Beyond Southeast Alaska and the Interior, the other Alaska Native groups represented in the exhibit all lived on the ocean and all made kayaks and other boats covered with skins. But the boats and tools they made reflect interesting differences, based on their function and traditions. On the left of the gallery, explore things made by the Iñupiat of the north and the Yup'ik of the west, and on the right the Sugpiaq/Alutiiq of the Gulf of Alaska and the Unangax̂ of the Aleutian Islands. At the far end, a comparative exhibit of kayaks, with models of other boats, illustrates how indigenous people solved the problem of navigation and hunting on Alaska's rough, ice-clogged waters.

You'll pass under an overturned umiak, the boat used by the Iñupiat to hunt whales from the sea ice, which is also used for transportation and hunting by the Yup'ik and Siberian Yupik. To build an umiak, a driftwood frame is covered by the skin of walrus or bearded seal. The form may be 30,000 years old, but these boats still ply the Arctic Ocean and Bering Sea from Alaska villages—because the design has never been improved upon. Indeed, in 1888, Yankee whalers hunting from shore in Utqiagvik quit using their own wooden boats because they were ineffective and instead adopted the watercraft and methods of the far more successful Iñupiat, who likewise implemented some Yankee technology in their own hunts.

The umiak is probably the technological predecessor of the kayak. Both have the advantage in Arctic waters of being strong and light. Iñupiaq whalers build trails across the shore-fast sea ice to reach open water where they can launch their boats, pulling umiaks on sleds behind snowmachines (as snowmobiles are called in Alaska). Several of the traditional kayaks exhibited here also were designed to

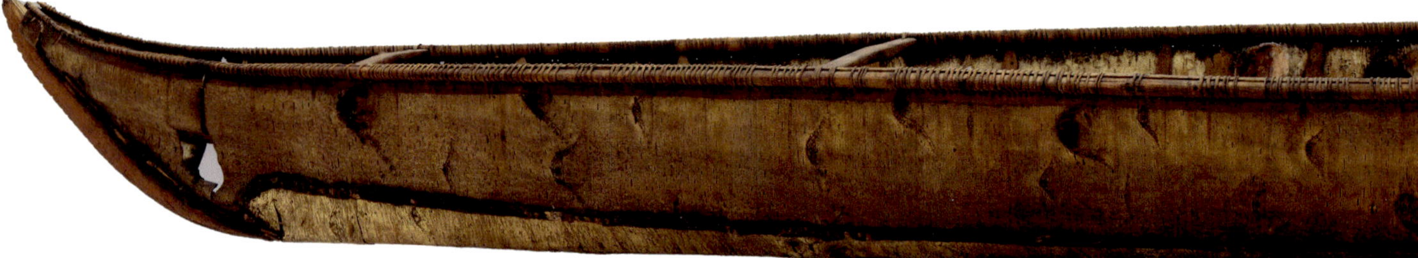

carry sleds on their back decks so that the hunters paddling them could emerge onto the ice and pull the boat along. (Except for some recent cultural revival, however, practical indigenous use of kayaks died out in Alaska generations ago.)

Two obvious innovations in the development from the umiak to the kayak are the smaller size and the enclosed deck. One paddler can handle a kayak, although some kayaks had two holes, and traditionally family members might ride below decks on trips. (A third hole was added by Russian colonial overseers, who enslaved Unangax̂ and Sugpiaq/Alutiiq paddlers for hunting and warfare.) The Unangax̂ covered theirs with sea lion skins, using them to hunt seal, sea lions, waterfowl, and other fast-moving animals. In the north, Yup'ik and Iñupiaq hunters also killed swimming caribou from kayaks. Besides being maneuverable for pursuing game, kayaks were light enough to drag or carry. The closed deck allowed the boat to navigate rough water, as waves could wash over it without the paddler getting wet or the hull swamping and losing buoyancy. When a kayak overturned, these seafarers knew how to roll it back upright with a jerk of the paddle.

Many coastal people hunted whales. The Iñupiat in the Arctic continue to whale in large crews with their open umiak boats, using harpoons with floats, as in ancient times, but today with projectile harpoon tips of brass instead of ivory and with floats of rubber rather than sealskin. They kill the whale at sea and tow it to the ice for butchering by the entire community, following traditions of sharing and respect that are intended to honor the gift that the whale's spirit has made of its body to the people, including giving the dead whale water from a bucket. The Unangax̂ and Sugpiaq/Alutiiq no longer hunt whales, but in the past they killed them from kayaks, using darts or harpoon tips of bear bone or slate that were treated with poison from the root of the monkshood plant—a dangerous occupation only for specially gifted and trained shamans who hunted alone. A good shot would paralyze a whale's tail so the animal would drown, to be recovered when it drifted ashore. A single kill could feed a village for months and provided needed bone, sinew, and baleen. The Yup'ik people of Norton Sound built the longer, sleeker Unaligmiut kayak for their form of whale hunting. They pursued the speedy beluga whale, with many boats corralling the animals into shallow water where they could be stranded by the falling tide. The Unaligmiut kayak on exhibit here is also interesting because it shows teeth marks: the builder used his bite to shape the wood into the vessel's frame.

Human beings needed boats to people the north. Another key technology was waterproof clothing. Even today, water is the most dangerous killer in Alaska's outdoors, either through drowning or getting wet and losing body heat. People solved this problem in a land with scant fiber sources by making parkas of waterproof animal or fish skins, sometimes constructing light and functional garments of startling beauty. An Unangan or Sugpiaq/Alutiiq maker created an extraordinary parka made from the skins of tufted puffins—birds of the alcid family that

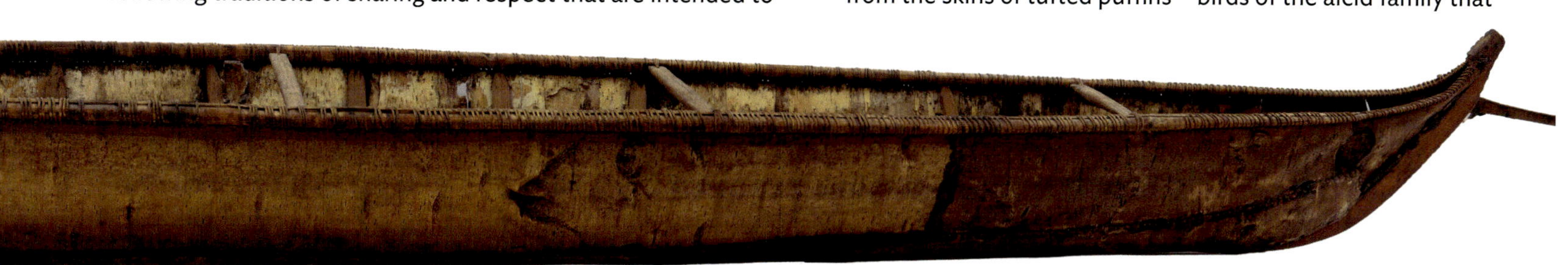

Vanq'ashli
Birchbark canoe

Originally from the vicinity of Lake Iliamna. Dena'ina

II-C-197

Three-cockpit kayaks were apparently developed after the arrival of Russian fur traders, who sometimes traveled by kayak with two Native paddlers. The figures in this model wear special headgear used by sea mammal hunters. The hunter up front holds a bow at the ready. Alutiiq/Sugpiaq (attributed).

II-F-165

live perpetually at sea—which was collected by an early American military expedition. Besides the remarkable detail of the piece, one is also struck by the skill required to catch enough of these small diving birds to make a parka. (Do not miss, in this same case, the extraordinary "Walrus Man" carving, a weird and unsettling ivory figurine of a half man, half walrus, about which little is known.)

A Sanightaaq parka (page ii) made of seal gut struck me as one of the most beautiful objects in the collection. It hangs in the first Yup'ik exhibit case, on the left side of the room. The parka comes from the Siberian Yupik of St. Lawrence Island, which lies in the windy Bering Sea, closer to Asia than America, with the villages of Savoonga and Gambell, which are among the most traditional subsistence communities in Alaska. The parka, probably made in winter and used for ceremonial purposes, is shimmering white. It was sewn with sinew and decorated with crested auklet feathers and the hard rictal plates that come from the side of the beak of the tufted puffin. Unfortunately, as is the case with many objects, nothing is known of its maker or how the parka was collected.

The same case contains other traditional aids against the weather—snowshoes, whose use is obvious, and, less obvious, eleven pairs of snow goggles, each slightly differently made. In the Arctic, on bright snow under bright sun, eye protection is essential to avoid snow blindness, or photokeratitis, which is temporary damage to the cornea due to excessive exposure to ultraviolet light. The thin slits in the wooden goggles protect the eyes by reducing the total light from the overwhelming Arctic glare. Here, each pair takes a slightly different approach to the problem, using visors, round or slit-shaped openings, or even colored glass, like modern sunglasses. One pair looks a bit like the eyepiece on a welding helmet—not a coincidence, since they perform the same function—while the shape of another pair suggests an animal's sharp nose ridge, with a brow that acts as a visor.

Most Alaska Native tribes made masks, and still do, with functions ranging from the practical, such as the snow goggles, to the spiritual, as seen in the Yup'ik mask representing Tuunraq, a deity who controls the availability of game, in the "Across the Cultures" mask case. That mask's distorted face suggests to me the passage between two worlds—which is the purpose of many of the masks.

Here, once again, is the link between nature, culture, and art. In many northern cultures, traditional spirituality attributed a spirit life to all animals, and even to objects such as glaciers, trees, and rocks. Sentient animals could choose to give themselves to people, who were their equals. Even from a materialist, Western worldview, we can imagine how Native people thrived through these beliefs. Lives relied intimately on nature, with survival dependent on mastery of animal behavior, weather patterns, and environmental change. Even today, that intuitive knowledge, and its predictive skill, can seem magical to an outsider, as capabilities we don't understand often do. Traditional indigenous spirituality also addressed the terrible risks inherent in subsistence lifeways, when a failure to harvest animals or other resources could bring famine to a village. Early visitors to the Iñupiat, for example, describe hunters' complex rituals before going out, as they sought the favor of many supernatural beings in nature and requested the spirits of animals to give their bodies for the village's sustenance. Even today, some hunters—although now mostly Christian—give water to animals they kill and pray for the safe return of their spirits so they can live and come again.

In many cultures, shamans aided people with their particular gifts of seeing the future, passing between the spirit and tangible worlds, helping with the success of hunts, and spiritual healing. Colonial religious authorities early on suppressed shaman skills, sometimes with the help of indigenous Christians who came to believe that shamanism was satanic, and today shaman masks and tools are rare. In addition, some Native cultures traditionally destroyed masks after a single ceremonial use. For the Sugpiaq/Alutiiq people, whose culture Russian invaders disrupted more than two centuries ago, old masks are rare. Those that survived, such as three on exhibit here, bring a powerful presence from the past. But masks are becoming more common, as mask makers continue their work, inspired by objects like these, and as tribes continue to use them in traditional ways. You'll see many examples in the "Across the Cultures" part of the exhibit, including a Tlingit shaman's spirit helper mask made by artist Richard Beasley in 1989.

Masks in the exhibit span time and worlds with their expressive faces and enigmatic meanings. Unlike the other objects we see—the tools, clothing, boats—the masks look back at us. A collection of Yup'ik masks from Hooper Bay bridges unexpected links, coming to us by an odd fluke. A married pair of documentary filmmakers, sent to Alaska by Walt Disney in 1946 to make a movie titled *The Alaskan Eskimo*, asked the Yup'ik people of this Southwest Alaska village to appear in the film, and the villagers worked with an elderly former shaman to make a collection of masks for a filmed dance. Afterward, they prepared to burn the masks in the traditional fashion, but the filmmakers bought some of the works to preserve them, which we see now in the museum. These few are masterpieces, such as the graceful and complex seagull mask by Sam Hunter. Note as well the walrus ivory Donald Duck, (page x), which Yup'ik carver Jonathon Johnson made as a souvenir for the visitors.

Donald Duck was not originally part of Yup'ik culture, so why is the piece here? Outsiders commonly make the mistake of encountering Alaska Native cultures with an expectation of purity, comparing them to a mythic past from before White contact. It's true that modern technology has irrevocably loosened connections to nature, separating people from the days when each village existed in its own world, in touch with the spirits of animals whose harvest determined its families' survival. But almost all the world's peoples have similarly changed. All kinds of people now are connected with one another, most living at a remove

Yuktuktaak Snow goggles

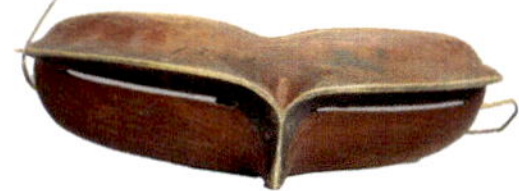

II-A-318

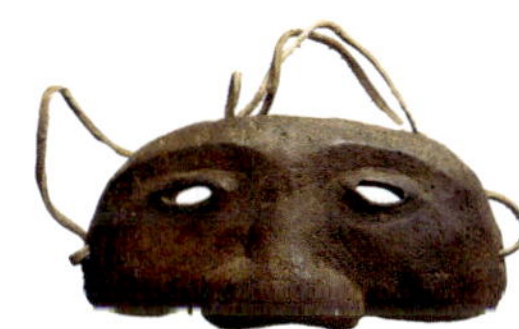

Point Hope, Iñupiaq, Taġiuqmiut.

II-A-328

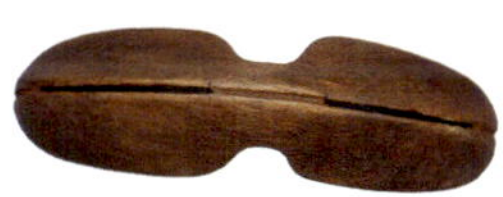

II-A-5150b

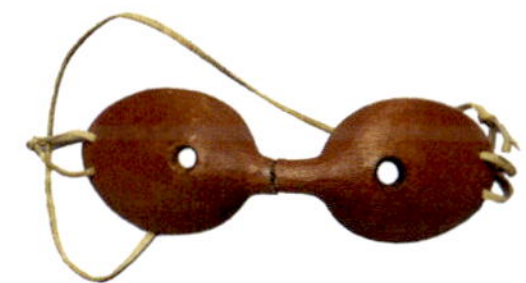

Kivalina, Kivalliñiġmiut, Iñupiaq.

II-A-326

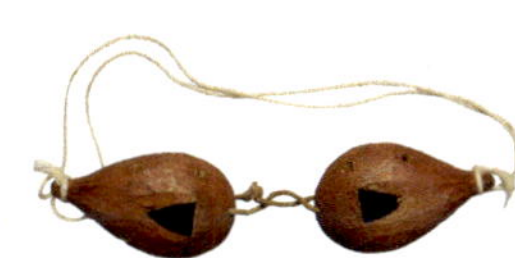

Blue glass in eye holes, Bethel, Kusquqvagmiut, Yup'ik.

II-A-5013

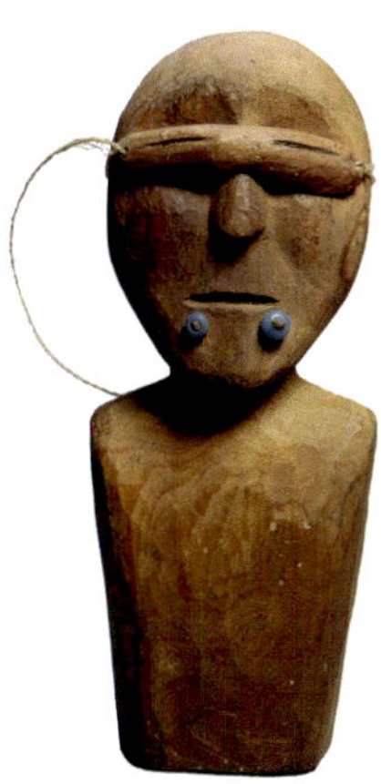

Figure wearing removable snow goggles, tied with sinew.

II-A-5237

from the production of their food, and often in less parochial societies than in ancient times—but that doesn't mean our cultures are dead or contaminated. Every culture flows and grows through time with myriad influences. The walrus ivory Donald Duck need not symbolize colonial corruption of Yup'ik culture—it can be seen as a Yup'ik carver's affirmative reinterpretation of material that reached him in Hooper Bay, just as his Hooper Bay colleague Jim Lake interpreted a killer whale on a mask with crayon colors and a smiling yellow face on its back.

The technology in the exhibit makes a similar point about how living cultures innovate and adapt. Some outsiders believe Native subsistence ways of life are less valid if hunters use modern technology, suggesting that spiritual meaning can only be achieved with spears and arrows, not guns, or they question the validity of hunting at all when food can be bought in stores and restaurants. In 2017, an internet mob attacked a sixteen-year-old Siberian Yupik boy who had successfully harpooned a fifty-foot whale from a small boat in the Bering Sea after he had been hailed online as a hero by his own people for providing for their village. These hunts observe age-old customs of sharing and prayer, and the harvest is closely regulated and sustainable. The harpooner used an aluminum boat and a black-powder-charged harpoon point called a darting gun, but northern people have always adopted the best available technology that allows them to live in this harsh place—the constant is continuing innovation, not the particular tools.

The oldest objects in the exhibit—the chipped blades—come from a time, more than fourteen millennia ago, when the now-dominant Western culture was at about the same technological level, in the Stone Age. The Thorne River basket, from nine thousand years later, may reflect a similar rate of tool development in the two cultures. The ingenious tools that follow in the exhibit parallel progress with change elsewhere in the world. The toggling harpoon head was invented here, as we can see from ancient examples, and adopted later by Yankee whalers. When Captain James Cook arrived in Southeast Alaska in 1778, the indigenous people he met were living a healthier, wealthier lifestyle than he had known growing up back in England, where he had been raised in small thatch hut, and where three of his five siblings had died as children. Cook's English technology had far more in common with the Alutiiq's than either does with ours today.

Now technology is global, and cultures evolve together within that context. But they haven't all become the same. We can observe what is essential to a culture by learning what practices its people conserve during times of change. All around the exhibit, contemporary works of traditional Alaska Native art conserve the forms and imagery of the past, although the artists use modern tools and materials to make them. One of the most dramatic masks in the exhibit, carved of wood, with ivory and leather, was made in the 1970s by a King Island Iñupiaq, Sylvester Ayek, after his village had departed their steep, rocky homeland in the Bering Sea and moved to Nome—where the village remains, to this day, a distinct King Island cultural group among the larger community. A shiny sculpture conserves meaning in a different way. Larry Beck's *Ooger-uk Inua #3, Walrus Spirit* conveys its traditional subject using metal hubcaps, rubber from car tires, and oil can spouts.

Nothing is truly timeless, but these works step outside of time and play with it, like the sometimes mischievous spirits of many Alaska Native stories. Which brings us to an item that is deeply part of Athabascan culture yet is not Alaska Native at all. A fiddle and bow played by Bergman Silas, a Tanana Athabascan elder from Minto, represents his people's extraordinary musical traditions, which have included American oldtime and Scottish fiddling since around 1850, but with words and music fully incorporating the indigenous culture. Masters including Silas sing in Tanana (one of eleven Athabascan languages), playing for festive dances, performing hymns and gospel music, and composing special songs for memorial potlatches—in their tradition, a newly written song is performed to express mourning and to praise the deceased person's life and good qualities with detailed lyrics. Mysterious medicine or shaman's songs are intended to heal or have other purposes, but outside researchers say they generally have not been allowed to record or study them.

Minto elders teach young people to play and to sing in Athabascan languages even today, despite the challenges of keeping their indigenous tongue alive in the sea of English flowing from media, schools, and everyday life, even in rural Alaska. In that sense, Native cultures continue to change in negative ways, with loss, pressured by colonists who began arriving centuries ago. That story is told in the next group of exhibits.

But here, in the Native Alaska exhibit, which was made and co-curated by Alaska Native people themselves, time has stopped. We can see what is essential, conserved, and lasting from these ancient cultures. This has great worth.

Deneldogee Fiddle

Used by Bergman Silas of Minto, Alaska. Tanana Athabascan. Non-Native manufacture.

2000-36-1

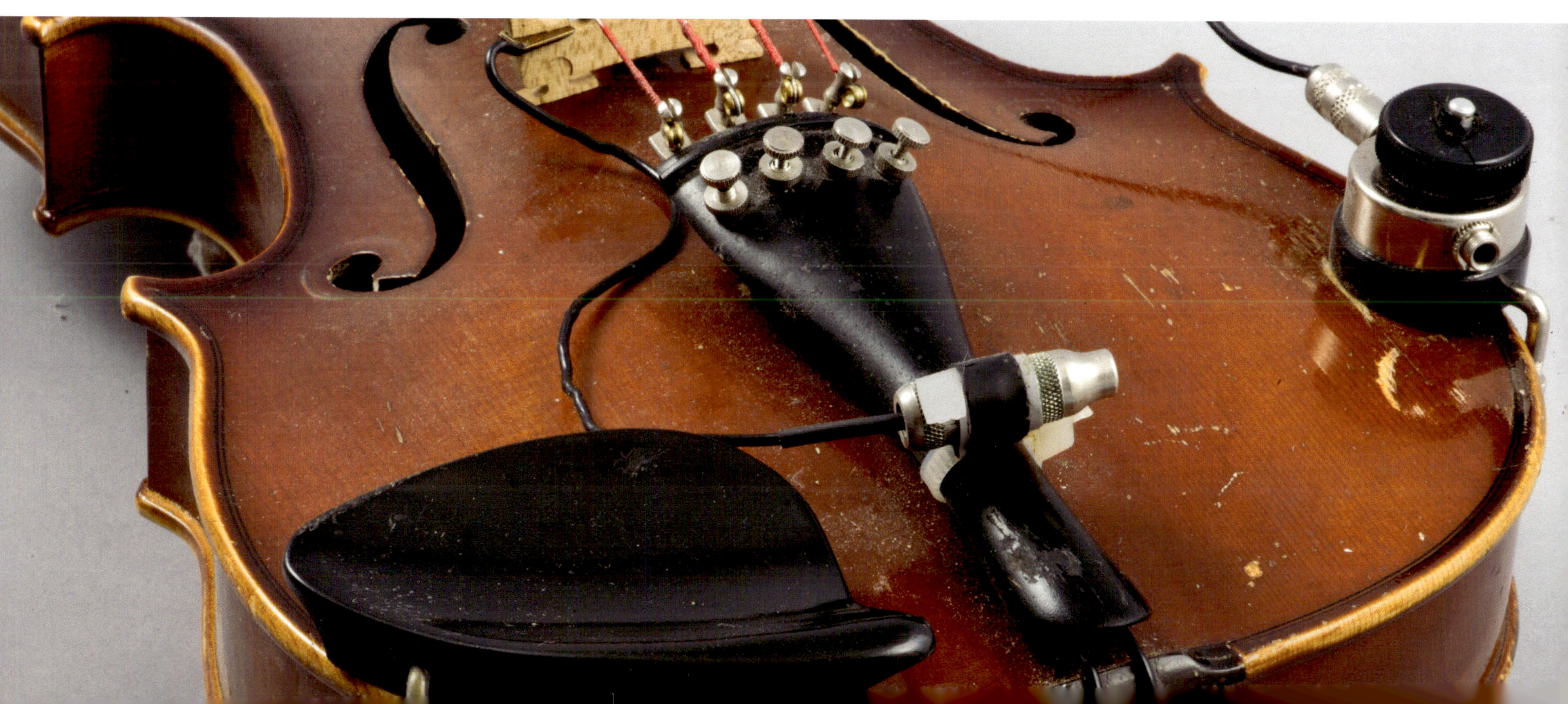

Early Russian map, 1773. Depicts the known and unknown coasts of Siberia and Alaska.

97-24-1

2. Conquest and Resistance

RUSSIAN AMERICA, U.S. EXPANSION, AND TRIBAL POWER

At the end of the Alaska Native section, the museum gallery narrows to a corridor with wooden walls and a floor like those of a square-rigged ship, representing the seafarers from Europe and Asia who arrived in the eighteenth century to expand their nations' empires and to map the world. Taking a hard left after this Foreign Voyagers section leads to the Russian American exhibit and, through a passage farther left, to the Resilience section, which addresses the response of Alaska Natives to conquest by the Russians and later the Americans. Just beyond you can see historical items from the U.S. purchase of Russia's claim to Alaska in 1867.

Even the shape of the walkway has meaning here, as the path of history narrows and branches through events that remain contested more than two centuries later. Who owns Alaska, legally and morally? The vast majority of Alaska was never conquered by Russia or the United States, nor did indigenous people sign treaties ceding their lands. Instead, cultures collided with different conceptions of what ownership meant—of what and who could be owned, and how—and that conflict continues, certainly in the moral and cultural realm, and to some extent politically, too, as tribes reassert their sovereignty.

The incompleteness of Alaska colonization reflects its odd place in world history, situated on the far side of the globe from the European monarchs who dispatched their explorers. Russia got here first, surging eastward and claiming a huge swath of North America, butting up against the British and Spanish. But after a century, Russia couldn't hold Alaska and the United States raised its flag, finishing its westward spread, and largely completing the shape of the country we know today. You can see alternate realities here, with settlers coming eastward or westward, with those from each direction bringing completely different customs and traditions, and with both in conflict with the cultures that were already here.

Vitus Bering was traditionally credited as the discoverer of Alaska (back when historians discounted the perspective of people already living in the places Europeans "found"). Russia dispatched Bering on two incredibly arduous expeditions eastward, by land across the entire breadth of Asia to build ships on the Pacific, and to sail further east, seeking the western extent of the Americas. In 1741, after seventeen years of effort, Bering managed only a single brief landfall in Alaska before heading for home and being shipwrecked and stranded on an uninhabited island, where he died. As it happened, the survivors on that island killed and ate many sea otters, and when they eventually got back to Asia, they discovered they were rich men. The thick otter pelts were extremely valuable in China. Soon, hardy fur traders from eastern Russia set out to find more otters, and the resource colonization of Alaska had begun.

Voyagers from Spain, France, and Britain competed with Russia in the late eighteenth century to explore Alaska and claim lands. Captain Cook came on his last voyage in 1778, and his officers landed near present-day Anchorage, on what is now Cook Inlet, where they buried a parchment in a bottle as a claim of ownership. English and American traders later sailed these shores buying furs, and the British set up trading posts inland, beyond areas the Russians penetrated. But Russia prevailed, over decades, in taking control of the coast, and buried more

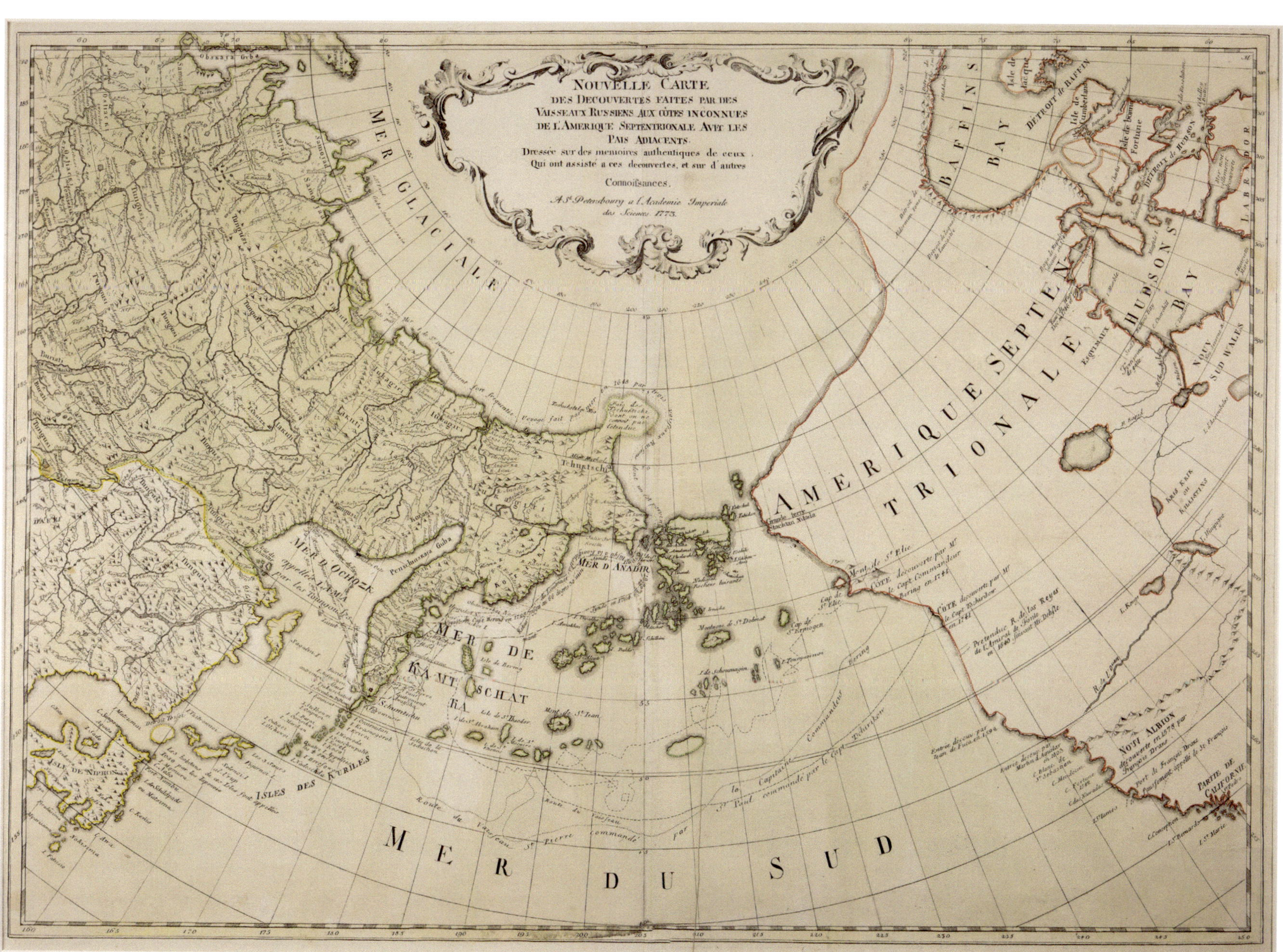

Nouvelle Carte
des Decouvertes faites par des
Vaisseaux Russiens aux côtes inconnues
de l'Amerique Septentrionale avec les
Pais Adiacents.
Dressée sur des memoires authentiques de ceux
Qui ont assisté a ces decouvertes, et sur d'autres
Connoissances.
A St. Petersbourg a l'Academie Imperiale
des Sciences 1773.
MER GLACIALE
BAFFINS BAY
HUDSONS BAY
LABRADOR
NOUV SUD WALES
AMERIQUE SEPTENTRIONALE
MER D'ANADIR
MER D'OCHOZK
MER DE KAMTSCHATKA
ISLES DES KURILES
MER DU SUD

than twenty iron markers, called "possession plates" as evidence. Only one was ever found, in 1935, and a replica of it is behind glass under the floor at the entrance to the Foreign Voyagers exhibit.

This concept of ownership can be hard for us to understand—the notion that burying an object in the ground would transfer vast lands from the people who had always lived there to someone who had just arrived. But the indigenous people's concept of ownership also would be unfamiliar to us. It differed among Alaska's first peoples. The Chugach Sugpiaq/Alutiiq whom Cook met in Prince William Sound owned their tribal lands collectively as villages, and any divisible animal a hunter harvested—the meat of a seal, for example—similarly remained community property. Other rules governed the ownership of indivisible objects, such as tools or clothing. For example, only women could own houses or large boats, and Cook noticed women in command. When Chugach paddlers met Cook, they took one of his boats and various objects from his ship's deck, which under their code belonged to the tribe, but happily gave it all back when the Englishmen objected. Neither side understood what the other had in mind.

Once the newcomers wanted things of real value, however, violence would settle the matter.

Many of the early Russian fur traders were peasants escaping poverty and a repressive class system in Siberia, traveling at extreme risk. They used their guns and extraordinary brutality to force the Unangax̂ people of the Aleutian Islands to hunt for them, destroying the homes, food, and survival supplies of those who resisted, and torturing men's families to gain compliance. Only the Native people could effectively take the wily sea otter, using their silent kayaks and thrown weapons—guns scared the animals away, damaged the pelts, and caused the carcasses to sink.

Later, competing fur-trading companies enslaved Unangax̂ and Sugpiaq/Alutiiq people somewhat like serfs in Russia. In 1784, forces led by fur trader Grigorii Shelikov mounted an unprovoked attack on Kodiak Island Natives, killing hundreds of Sugpiaq/Alutiiq people on Refuge Rock, torturing and massacring prisoners, and holding hostages to assure obedience (in Alutiiq the place is called Aw'auq, which means "to become numb"). They also pressed the Unangax̂ and Sugpiaq/Alutiiq into service as a kayak navy for further battles to capture other villages and to fight competing fur companies.

Besides greed, the Russians' tactics were driven by necessity. Unlike the British and American traders with their square-rigged ships, the Russians got supplies from home overland across Asia, too far to carry many valuable trade goods, iron, or other materials. In the eighteenth century, they usually lived off the land in much the same fashion as the Alaska Natives, using indigenous technology such as skin boats and obtaining furs through force. Many lower-ranking Russian men married into Alaska Native communities and settled with them culturally. The matrilineal kinship system of the Tlingit made the children of Russian men and Tlingit women full members of their clans and houses. For those of low status in Russia, life in Alaska indigenous villages was probably better than life back home. Tribal and Russian culture merged in some ways, such as in the banya steam bath, a core part of Sugpiaq/Alutiiq and Russian life. In some villages, the social and leadership system transformed, as indigenous church lay readers became de facto chiefs.

In 1799, Russian aristocrats formed the Russian-American Company as a monopoly to control the fur trade and to govern the country's American possessions. Alexander Baranov, who had been hired by Shelikov in 1790, became the governor and top manager of the monopoly, and violently expanded the company's area of control to new hunting grounds. The Tlingit resisted, in 1802 destroying a Russian fort and killing its occupants. The decisive battle came in 1804, when Baranov sent a swarm of kayaks and a square-rigged warship, the *Neva*, against Tlingit warriors in Sitka. Facing Russian cannons, the Tlingit were forced to retreat and Baranov built his capital there.

On the same voyage, the *Neva* innovated a new route for supplying the colony by sailing from St. Petersburg, Russia, westward around South America, stopping in Alaska, and then continuing west around the rest of the world back to St. Petersburg. Sitka became a fortified and up-to-date city, the

Embroidered Russian kaftan presented to young Kiks.ádi leader in 1843.

ASM-94-39-1

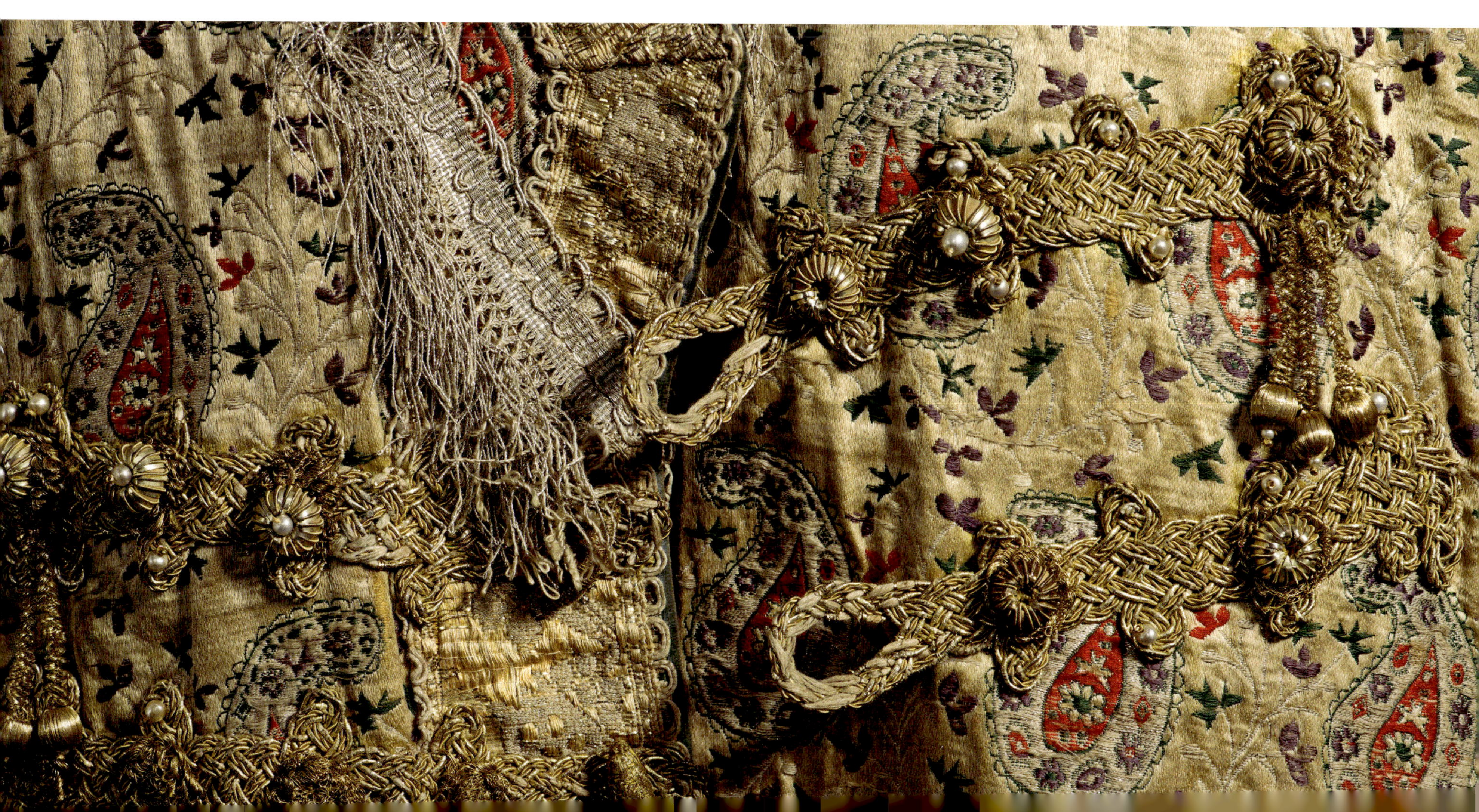

Seward Brand canned salmon Alaska Packer's Association, mid 20th century.

96-60-1

largest on the Pacific coast of North America, and the region's most important international port as well. Eventually Sitka had a residence for the governor called Baranov's Castle (although it was built after his death), a cathedral, and a grand house for the Russian Orthodox bishop, as well as a library, museum, and other public buildings. Officers and clerics, dressed in all the splendor of their rank, held religious services with glittering icons and attended grand balls. Some of their buildings still stand in Sitka, and pieces from others are in the exhibit.

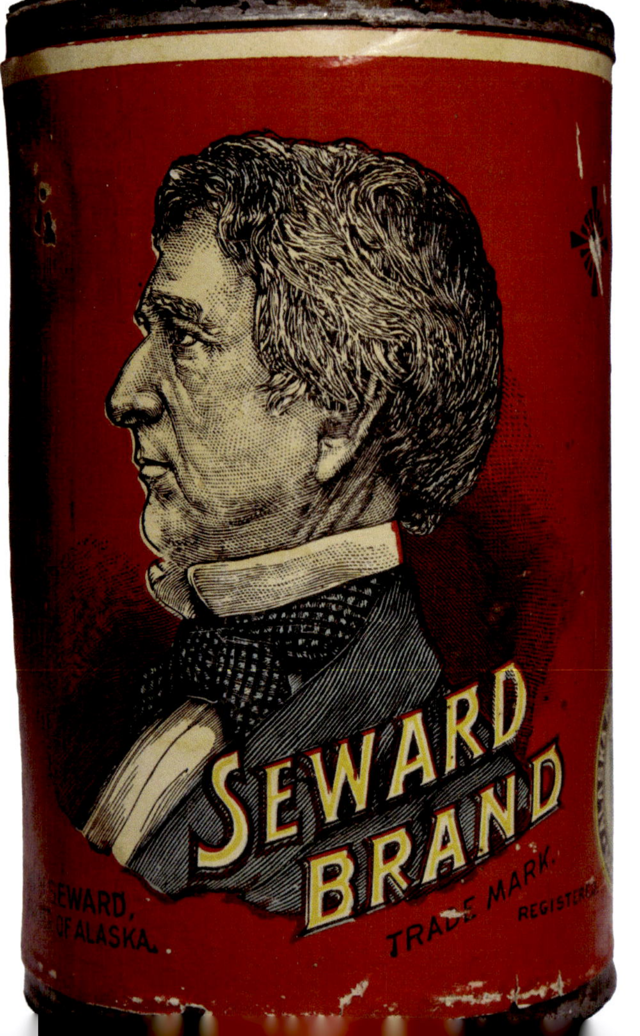

Baranov pushed onward, building a fort in California, where he sent Alaska Native hunters for furs, and on the Hawaiian Island of Kauai. The Russian fur operation had to keep spreading because it rapidly killed off all the furbearing animals in each new area it entered. Sea otters were driven nearly to extinction and, after being protected in 1911, remained rare into the 1970s, although they have largely recovered today.

The Unangax̂ and Sugpiaq/Alutiiq peoples were systematically devastated. Russian fur traders destroyed entire villages, moved and mixed others, and decimated the population through warfare, disease, and starvation. Amid the carnage, many traditions were lost. The Tlingit of Southeast Alaska fared somewhat better. They lost the battle of Sitka, but went on to destroy a Russian outpost at Yakutat, and Russian officers always considered them a threat. Sitka depended on Tlingit trade for food, and the clans could have starved the city or overwhelmed its defenses. The Russians tried to co-opt clan leaders with gifts and symbols of power, including bestowing one weak, young leader with a title and an embroidered kaftan, sword, and tri-cornered hat.

The Russian Orthodox Church also mitigated the violence in the later years of the Russian colony. Priests interceded after seeing the abuses of the early fur traders. For the most part, the priests did not try to eliminate Alaska Native cultures or languages. Many indigenous people were forced to convert to Christianity, but were not required to discard their traditional beliefs. Russian priests translated services and parts of the Bible into Native languages (which also required them to create written versions of those tongues). Despite the brutality of the early Russian invaders, many coastal Alaska Natives today bear Russian names, attend Orthodox churches, and appreciate their Russian heritage as an important part of their identities.

But Russia's hold on Alaska weakened. In 1818, after Baranov retired (he died on his way home to Russia), naval officers took charge of the colony and the fur trade. The Russian-American Company lost profitability due to the overhunting of animals and these military leaders' lack of business acumen. Internationally, Russia's military lagged behind that of other powers, and its ability to hold on to this far-off colony came into doubt. British trading posts were operating widely and American whalers were hunting in the Alaska Arctic. Unable to police most of Alaska and fearful the British could take it by force, the Russians were receptive to America's interest in buying their claim there.

Secretary of State William Seward negotiated the deal in Washington, DC, for $7.2 million. An oil painting captures the scene of the negotiations, and you can also see a cloak Seward is known to have worn—he wasn't a large man. A ceremony to take down the Russian flag in Sitka and raise the American flag took place on October 18, 1867. The flag exhibited here was long thought to be that one, but recent scholarship suggests it is a flag carried by William Healey Dall on an Alaska expedition two years earlier. Dall's findings influenced debate in Congress to appropriate the payment for Alaska—public opinion mocked the purchase and newspapers called it Seward's folly—and the money wasn't approved until a year after the Russians had left.

No more than 823 Russians had ever lived in Alaska, and their economic and cultural impact had been limited to the southern coasts and islands. Russian dominion over Alaska was recognized under international law, but in no real sense did Russia possess most of Alaska. At first, the Americans seemed intent on little more. The army sent a small garrison of soldiers to Sitka and a few other small outposts to protect Americans moving there, but few came, and so the outposts quickly closed. In Sitka, the bored soldiers developed a reputation for drinking and sexual assault, and their commanders dealt with minor conflicts with the Tlingit by lashing out militarily against entire villages.

After ten years, the army withdrew its garrison as a useless expense, since so few American residents were coming to Alaska. With the soldiers gone, a Tlingit clan planned to attack and destroy Sitka. Another clan interceded. Panicked residents called for help, and the U.S. Navy arrived with force. In 1882, three warships converged on the village of Angoon after a dispute about a whaling accident. They shelled the Native civilians, burned their homes, storehouses, and boats, and destroyed or stole precious clan objects—an operation carried out, as an officer wrote, "as a punishment and as a guarantee for future good behavior."

For the most part, however, the American takeover of Alaska occurred without overt violence. The newcomers—fish cannery owners, market hunters, and gold prospectors—simply took resources that the indigenous people had always relied upon, such as fish and marine mammals, while introducing disease, alcohol, and social disruption that tore apart their communities. Alaska had no civil government at all until 1884, and many more years passed before U.S. authorities established anything we would recognize as law and order. Moreover, even when laws were enforced, they gave Alaska Natives little protection since indigenous people could neither hold American citizenship nor legally own land. Newcomers did as they liked, self-organized to settle disputes, and often treated the indigenous people as less than human. Legendary Nome sled dog musher A. A. "Scotty" Allan, whose trophy stands in the next part of the exhibit, wrote in his autobiography of seeing gold prospectors feed their dogs on the bodies of Iñupiaq people who lay on the ground dead of epidemic disease.

Protestant missionaries such as Episcopalian Hudson Stuck and Presbyterian Sheldon Jackson documented abuses against Alaska Natives with outrage in books and lectures for eastern U.S. audiences. Jackson, the most important of the missionaries, held the belief, considered progressive at the time, that Alaska Natives could attain equality with Whites, and avoid extermination, if they became more like typical American small-town residents. He advocated a

Dahlgren type artillery shell found in 1938 at Angoon, likely from the 1882 bombardment.

98-1-1

School bell from Yup'ik mission school at Eek, Alaska.
III-R-171

crash program for Natives to disavow their own cultures and languages and assimilate to the religion, values, and behavior of the American middle class, speaking English, working in the cash economy, wearing Western clothes, living in nuclear families in homes built of lumber, attending church, and sending their children to school.

In 1880, Jackson met with leaders of other Protestant denominations at a New York hotel to divide up Alaska's territories for this project. Each denomination would take responsibility for civilizing the indigenous people of its assigned zone. Jackson excluded Roman Catholics from the meeting, as well as the Russian Orthodox, who had co-existed with Native cultures and allowed use of Native languages. In 1885, Jackson's close friend Benjamin Harrison, then a U.S. senator and later the president, helped him gain appointment as Alaska's general agent of education, putting the resources and authority of the federal government behind his effort to eliminate Native cultures in order to save Native people. Missionaries fanned out to all parts of the Alaska territory, settling nomadic people into new permanent villages around schools, churches, and clinics, and taking for themselves quasi-governmental authority.

The assimilation policy lasted a long time. In 1915, the Alaska Territorial Legislature passed a law allowing indigenous people to become territorial citizens only with the signed certification of five Whites assuring that applicants had "abandoned all tribal customs and relationships." Prospective citizens were also required to take an oath renouncing their tribes "for all time." In 1924, Congress granted U.S. citizenship to all American Indians and Alaska Natives, and during President Franklin Roosevelt's New Deal, federal assistance supported cultural projects, creating totem poles and clan houses. But discrimination and assimilation continued. A notorious boarding school that took Native children from their families and villages, the Wrangell Institute, operated until 1976. I was privileged in 2016 to interview Molly Hootch, the Yup'ik woman who gave her name to the 1970s lawsuit that forced the construction of schools in students' home villages. She explained that her last name, Hootch, which means alcohol, had been assigned to her family by a missionary before her grandparents' generation because one of their relations drank too much. Consequently, Molly knew nothing about her family before her grandparents.

Children of the mid-twentieth century were punished in school for speaking their parents' languages, and they sometimes grew up internalizing resistance to their own cultures and avoiding knowledge of their traditions. The Resilience section of the exhibit presents evidence of these painful policies, including powerful contemporary art that expresses their continuing legacy. Nicholas Galanin's 2006 sculpture *What Have We Become?* depicts a person's head as a book of pages, showing how Alaska Natives of the current generation have been forced to turn to books written by anthropologists a century ago to learn about their own cultures and restore their traditions.

But some rare elders survived to bridge this period and pass traditions on directly. Lela Kiana Oman, born in 1915 in Norvik in Northwest Alaska, lived 102 years, long enough that she was able to publish the Iñupiaq stories her father had taught her. He passed on stories and dance to his children secretly, at night, attempting to hide the lessons from the Baptist missionary family that controlled their newly created village. He himself had been born in a snow cave from a family of shamans and umialiks (respected leaders). As Oman said to me in 1997, "He would tell us, 'If we tell you the stories tonight, don't spread them around, don't tell people about them, because then you will be known as children of sin.' And some of those strong Christian people did think we were evil."

As with race relations elsewhere in the United States, racism against indigenous people has never entirely ended in Alaska, but milestone events in the last eighty years removed its official sanction and opened the way for equality and eventually for Alaska Native power. Alaska Natives suffered segregation and exclusion in the early part of the twentieth century. Some towns—including Anchorage—forbade indigenous residents, and they had to live in separate villages outside city limits. Unangax̂ people in the Pribilof Islands, forcibly relocated and made to harvest fur seals for the Russians, were kept at that

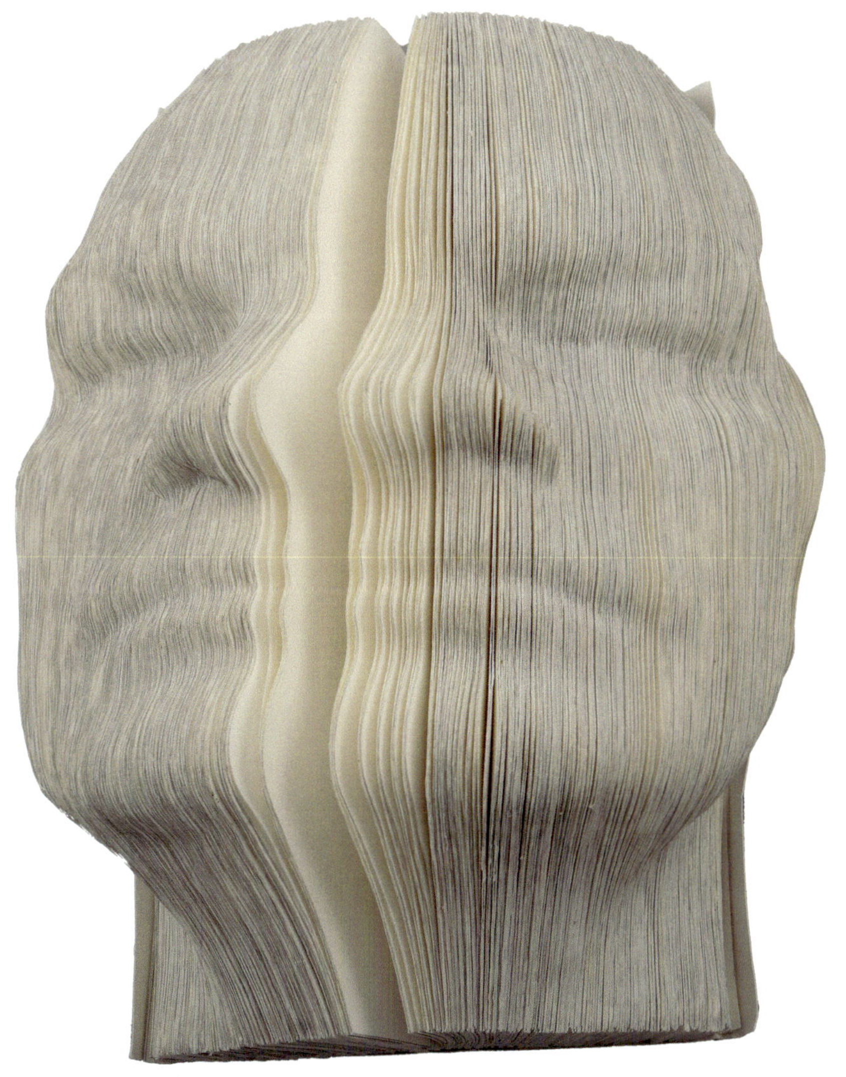

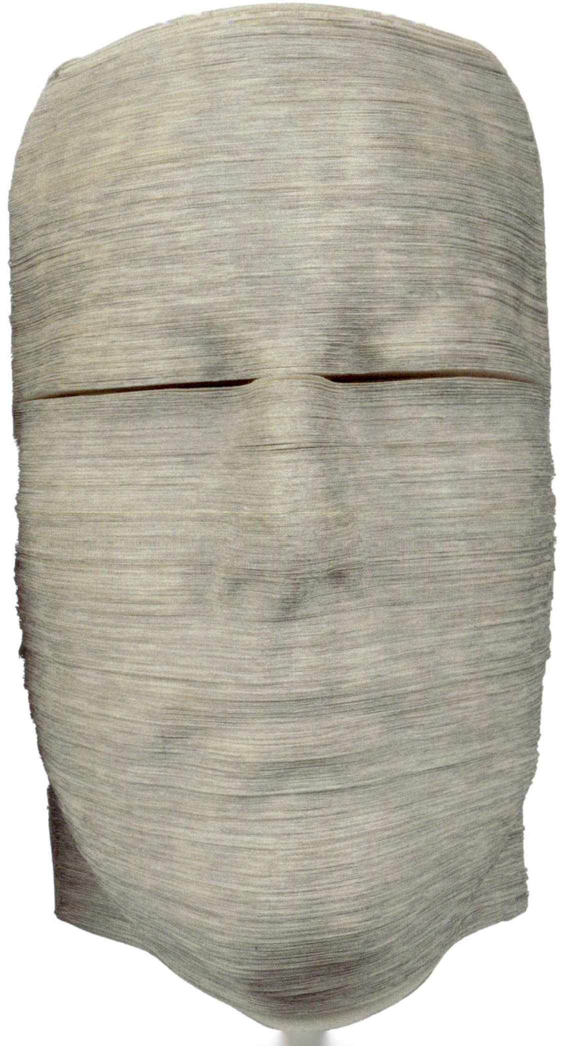

What Have We Become?

By Nicholas Galanin (Tlingit/Unangax̂), 2006.

2006-4-1a, b

ANB/ANS sashes

2012-3-2, 2002-18-1

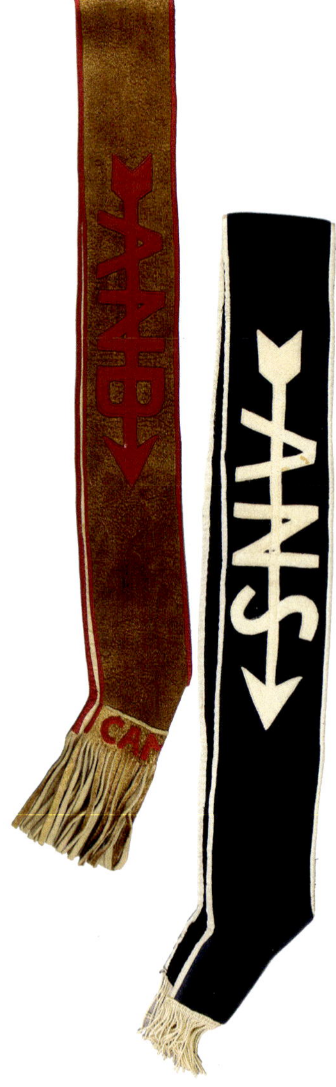

work in conditions akin to slavery until 1946, in an arrangement managed by the U.S. government.

World War II brought increased segregation and then progress for equality. Signs saying "No Natives Allowed" went up on some businesses after the army general in charge of Alaska, Simon Bolivar Buckner—the son of a Confederate general of the same name—forbade soldiers to enter businesses where Alaska Natives were served—even as Alaska Native soldiers, national guardsmen, and intelligence scouts courageously fought for the United States. Major M. "Muktuk" Marston, who organized indigenous men into guard units, protested the racist treatment, joined by Ernest Gruening, a liberal intellectual who had been appointed governor by his friend President Roosevelt. In the exhibit, a letter to Gruening from civil rights icons Elizabeth and Roy Peratrovich denounces segregation on behalf of the Alaska Native Brotherhood and the Alaska Native Sisterhood (formed in 1915, these were the first indigenous civil rights organizations in the nation). With Gruening, their combined efforts led to passage of Alaska's landmark anti-discrimination law in the territorial legislature in 1945. Although the law proved flawed and was little enforced, its powerful symbolism helped change behavior.

In the latter half of the twentieth century, the federal government became the ally of Alaska Native rights—against adversaries in the state government. When Congress made Alaska a state in 1959, it granted its new government the right to select 103 million acres for its own, since virtually the entire land mass then remained federal property. Alaska Natives correctly saw state land selection as a threat to the places they hunted, fished, and lived, and they filed claims with the U.S. Department of the Interior that ultimately covered the entire state. In 1966, Interior Secretary Stewart Udall acknowledged those claims by freezing all Alaska land transfers until the issue could be resolved. White leaders of the State of Alaska screamed in protest. Most opposed any land for the Natives beyond small allotments. But they changed their minds with the discovery of oil at Prudhoe Bay. To build a pipeline to move the oil, land rights would have to be resolved. In 1971, with state and Native support, Congress passed the Alaska Native Claims Settlement Act (ANCSA), which conveyed 44 million acres to new corporations owned by Native shareholders and endowed them with $1 billion.

ANCSA was hailed as an innovative solution. It transferred an unprecedented amount of land while avoiding creation of more Indian reservations, which at the time were seen as failures. But the law's flaws soon became apparent. At its heart, it continued the assimilationist program, imposing the Western hierarchy of moneymaking corporations on villages and regions—by design, as White leaders within Alaska saw the profit motive as a good way to advance resource and industrial development on lands that had been used for traditional subsistence and wilderness. But many Alaska Natives still lived off the land and spoke Native languages, and inadequate state and federal schools left them unprepared to run large companies. Many of the new corporations did poorly and some went bankrupt before Congress stepped in, two decades later, with measures that shored them up. Meanwhile, a tribal sovereignty movement rose in rural Alaska, with indigenous people demanding recognition for their own traditional forms of self-government, rather than the corporate boards or town councils imposed by outsiders.

In 1993, the federal government recognized Alaska tribes—out of 574 recognized tribes in America today, 229 are in Alaska, mostly encompassing single villages—and agencies began contracting directly with them to provide services on a government-to-government basis. But the State of Alaska fought the concept of tribes and resisted Alaska Natives' preferential rights to fish and game on their traditional waters and grounds. In 1999, Alaska Natives proved in court that the State of Alaska racially discriminated against them by providing inferior schools.

In the years since, the balance has shifted, although the outlines of these conflicts remain. Alaska Native corporations became the state's largest and most powerful businesses. Voters elected an Alaska Native lieutenant governor, speaker of the State House, and member of Congress. In 2022, Native corporations sponsored a voter initiative to force the state to recognize tribes, and the legislature belatedly agreed—but with only a symbolic law.

The Resilience section, the museum's most controversial and important contemporary statement, was something new for Alaska. On the floorplan, the section branches from the main path that visitors follow, taking a turn from the progress from Foreign Voyagers through Russian America and the American purchase of 1867, suggesting that this history has now frayed into divergent strands. They represent unfinished business started by men such as Vitus Bering, James Cook, Alexander Baranov, William Seward, and Sheldon Jackson. Today, as courts and politicians continue to contest the status of tribes, Native corporations, and the state government, the question of who owns Alaska remains unanswered.

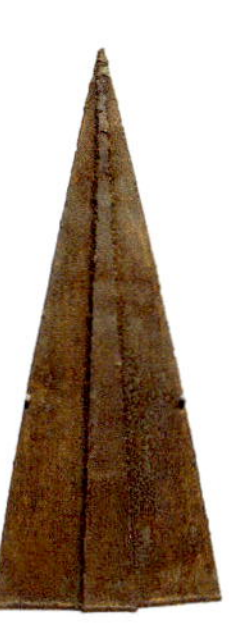

Double-Headed Language Dagger #2 (Gunalchéesh)

By Da-ka-xeen Mehner (Tlingit/N'ishga), 2012

2016-9-1

3. American Colony

RESOURCE BOOMS AND THE BIRTH OF MODERN ALASKA

Alaska grew in the twentieth century though three major spurts of frantic development: the gold rush that began in 1898; World War II and the following Cold War military buildup; and the era of big oil, which peaked in the early 1980s. After each boom came a bust, the extended economic and social hangover that follows any party of get-rich-quick exuberance. That pattern left behind a history of disconnected episodes and places, with a changing cast of characters from a transient population. Boom times brought young Americans surging north and busts sent them back again. Even today, Alaska's non-Native population comes and goes at a rate higher than in any other state, and the percentage of residents who were born here or die here remains among the lowest of all the states.

The museum's American Alaska Gallery reflects this truth. Rather than focusing on chronological storytelling, the exhibit primarily presents objects in discrete sections about industries and individual events. A mining locomotive. A lighthouse lens. A Quonset hut barracks. Each stands for its own story. Work happened in Alaska. Ships navigated. War was waged. Progress wasn't always permanent, and it usually reached only a limited

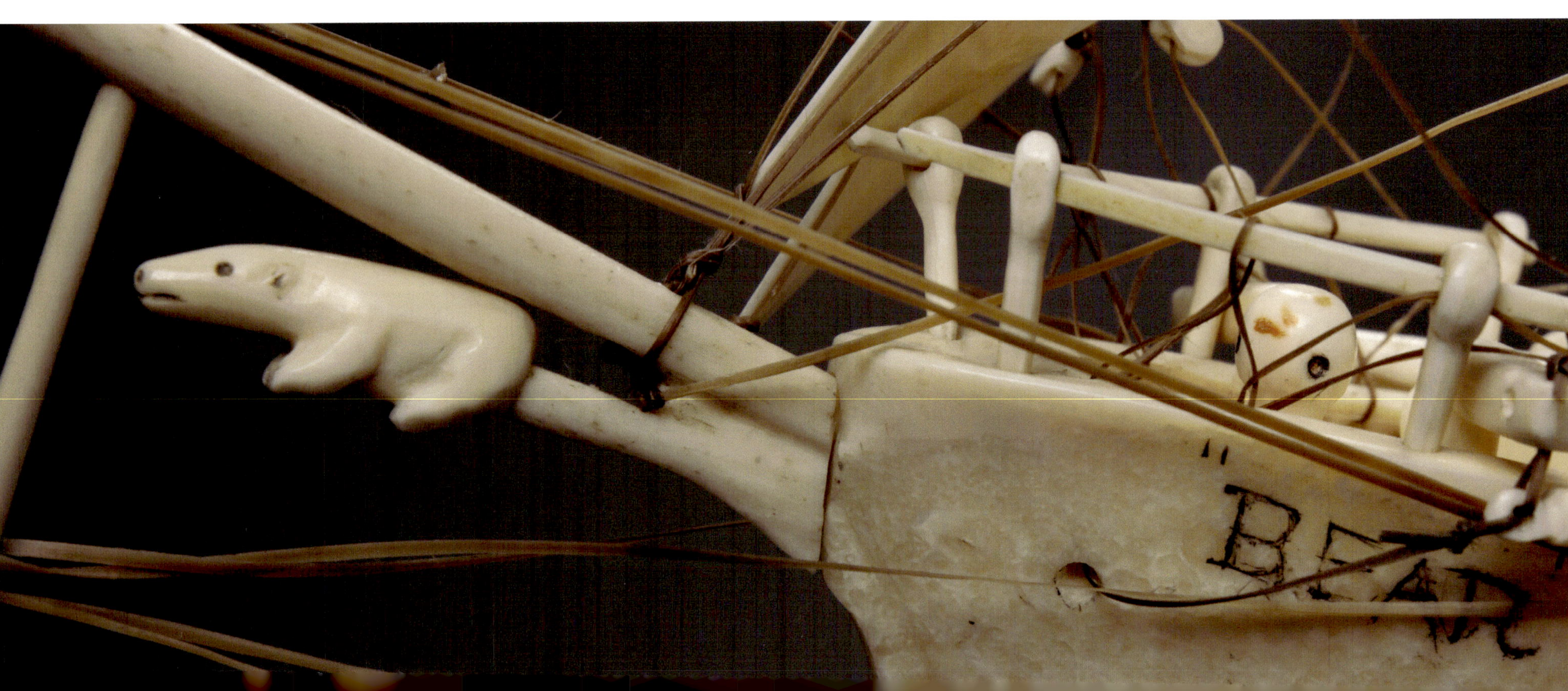

part of the immense land mass. But Alaskans had some things in common, even if only briefly, and we still do: the cold, the wildness of the place, and the excitement and fear of living at the edge of humanity's web of machines and rules. They endured, perhaps profited, or otherwise proved themselves where success required strength, ingenuity, and respect for forces far larger than we are. As in the Alaska Native gallery, the objects here speak of those struggles and the Alaskans who faced them.

That's most of the gallery. Along its left side, however, a timeline and series of labels tell the story more conventionally, in the order that events happened. Besides providing a primer of modern Alaska history, the crowded cases here contain rare and fascinating objects characteristic of the periods covered, including both things of historic import and charming curios, such as the souvenir spoons that tourists began bringing back as early as the 1890s.

As these displays show, the American period began with expeditions before the 1867 transfer of control from Russia to the United States. Soon after, fishing companies and whalers exploited rivers and coastal waters from ships and seasonal camps, and gold finds in Southeast Alaska brought local development, particularly in the founding of Juneau with its hard-rock mines. But the vast expanse of Alaska remained the domain of Alaska Native people living in their traditional ways, and they remained the majority of the population.

Modern Alaska started like a cinematic jump cut. In 1897, news flashed around the world of a group of prospectors getting off a steamer in Seattle with trunks and gunnysacks containing two tons of gold they had found on the Klondike River, which joins the Yukon River just east of the Alaska border in Canada's Yukon Territory. At the time, gold backed the U.S. dollar, and a global shortage of gold had produced deflation and an economic crisis that put legions of men out of work. In 1898, some 100,000 stampeders from around the world set out to find their own Alaska gold, plunging into a wilderness journey for which few were prepared, across a land that was not prepared for them. A gold rush in Nome soon followed, on the far side of Alaska, and more at points in between. The discoveries produced prodigious gold—enough to help increase the world money supply and change the direction of presidential politics. And enough, in just a few years, to populate Alaska with greed-driven adventurers. Alaska Natives would never again hold the majority.

For Americans coming north, Alaska beckoned as a last extension of the Wild West, with land free for the taking, since most did not respect the land ownership of the indigenous people. U.S. policy designated the vast majority of Alaska as open for mineral claims or homesteading, processes that allowed U.S. citizens—not Alaska Natives—to obtain ownership of public land or resources by locating it and following rules for registering, occupying, or using their new property. That system of an open frontier lasted for most of the twentieth century, and became deeply embedded in Alaskans' self-image as tough, self-reliant folk taming the wilderness. Indeed, there was

LEFT

Model of the Cutter Bear made by a Yup'ik or Iñupiaq carver from walrus ivory, early 20th c.

II-A-5134

BELOW

Gold and poke.

III-O-839

Governor Gruening signs the anti-discrimination act of 1945. Witnessing are O. D. Cochran, Elizabeth Peratrovich, Edward Anderson, Norman Walker, and Roy Peratrovich. Image by Amy Lou Blood [Barney].

ASL P274-1-2

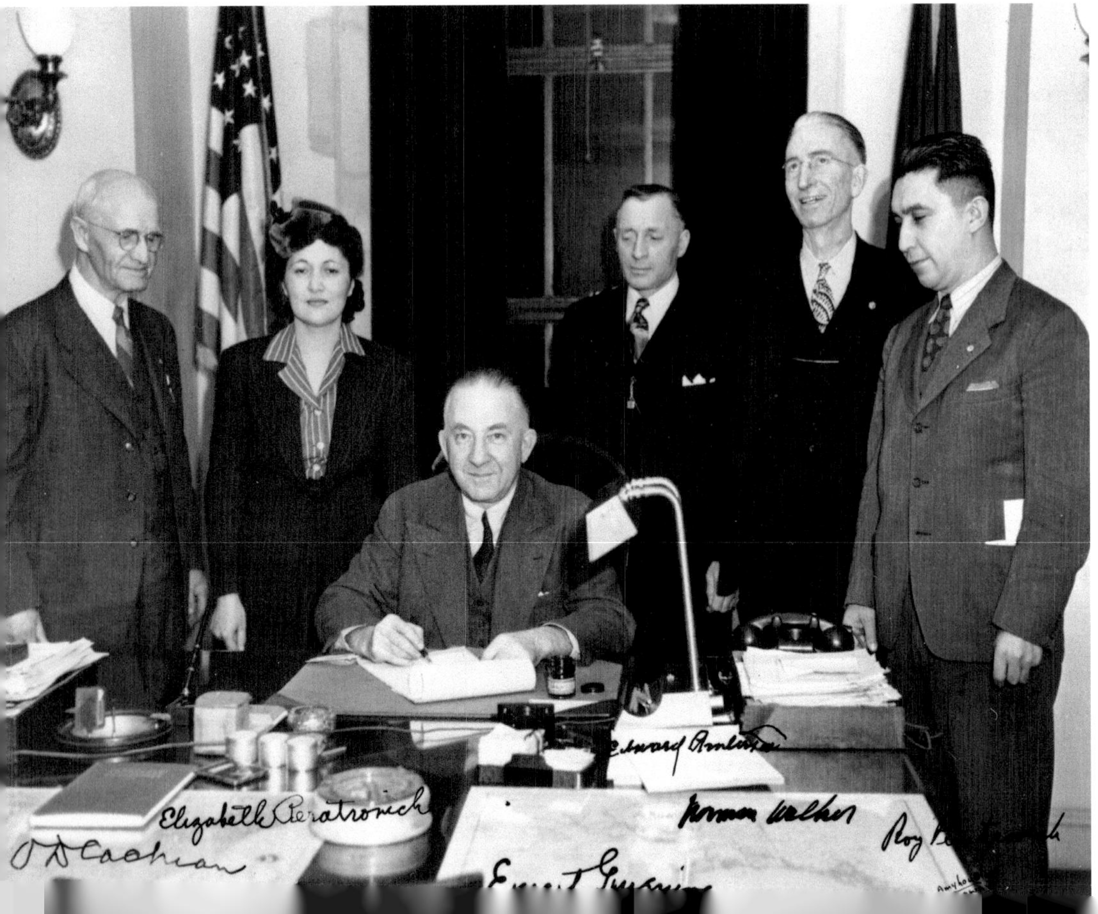

nothing fake about the hardships these pioneers overcame—surviving extreme cold and extraordinary isolation—even if their backwoods challenges were romanticized by Jack London's stories (he stayed on the Klondike through but one terrible winter) and more recently by largely phony reality TV shows.

The gold rush period slowly lost energy and came to a halt in 1917, when America entered World War I, as young wealth seekers left to fight or to pursue better opportunities elsewhere. The non-Native population dropped by almost one-fourth. But even as Alaska stagnated economically, it retained the Americanization that had come with the gold rush influx of people, including the new towns of Anchorage and Fairbanks and the federally funded Alaska Railroad connecting them to tidewater at Seward, as well as improvements to navigation, a growing tourism industry, and laws passed by Congress that elevated Alaska's political status from district to territory. That change had allowed Alaskans to elect a legislature with some limited powers to make laws and impose taxes, and to choose a non-voting delegate in the U.S. House of Representatives. They picked James Wickersham, a fascinating character: mountain climber and adventurer, judge, hustler and dealmaker, and a powerful orator. He and his successors also fought for more self-determination, but after the gold rush Alaska remained a remote, undeveloped resource colony, frozen in time, with transportation, communication, and industry as if from the previous century.

Then came another of history's jump cuts, when the Japanese attacked Pearl Harbor and, in 1942, captured the Aleutian Islands of Kiska and Attu—with Guam, the first U.S. territory to be occupied by foreign forces since the War of 1812. The enormous defensive response mounted by the U.S. military jerked Alaska into the twentieth century and transformed it, rejuvenating the population with a new flood of young people. The military headquarters in Anchorage caused that small town to explode into Alaska's largest city. For the first time, a highway through Canada connected Alaska to the outside world. After the war, former GIs and other newcomers used that road to come north to make their fortunes. The booming economy didn't disappoint them, with the military's Cold War military buildup of the 1950s, which made Alaska a high-tech fortress to fend off feared nuclear attack from the Soviet Union.

This vigorous new generation pushed for Alaska to become a state, outraged by their lack of a vote in national elections and eager for the wealth they believed a new state could unlock from Alaska's resources. Momentum came from a successful constitutional convention in the winter of 1955–56, and the discovery of oil on the Kenai Peninsula, south of Anchorage, in 1957. Alaska became the forty-ninth state in 1959, electing its first members of Congress (all Democrats, as conservative statehood opponents had feared), and made Bill Egan the first governor. Egan was a small-town grocer with a legendary memory and extraordinary personal skills, which he had used as chair of the constitutional convention and as a statehood leader. As governor, Egan selected promising oil lands for the new state from the endowment granted by the federal government. In 1968, those lands fulfilled the statehood boosters' wildest dreams, when a drill rig hit the largest oil field in North America, near Prudhoe Bay on the Arctic Ocean, and made Alaska fabulously rich.

Prudhoe Bay disrupted Alaska history with a third and final jump cut (at least so far). First came construction of the nine-hundred-mile pipeline to bring the oil from the Arctic to Port Valdez on Prince William Sound, then came the money from selling that oil. The black gold rush dwarfed all the other booms, and the political and social changes it brought were among the deepest. The frontier closed, ending Alaska's open-for-all tradition of land development, as Congress passed three landmark laws in a decade: settling land claims for Alaska Natives, authorizing construction of the pipeline, and designating more than 100 million acres of parks, wilderness, and other conservation lands—an area the size of California. Homesteading passed into history, replaced by big company projects that delivered collective government wealth. The state government canceled all taxes on individuals and began giving away money to every citizen through the Alaska Permanent Fund Dividend. And the culture changed, too. The distance to the rest of America suddenly shrank, as communities fully integrated into the mainstream of national corporate businesses and instant communications, creating urban lifestyles just like those in any western U.S. city, except for the weather, wildlife, and nearby wild lands.

The museum's timeline ends in 1989, the year the tanker *Exxon Valdez* hit a rock in Prince William Sound, causing the most environmentally damaging oil spill in America to that date.

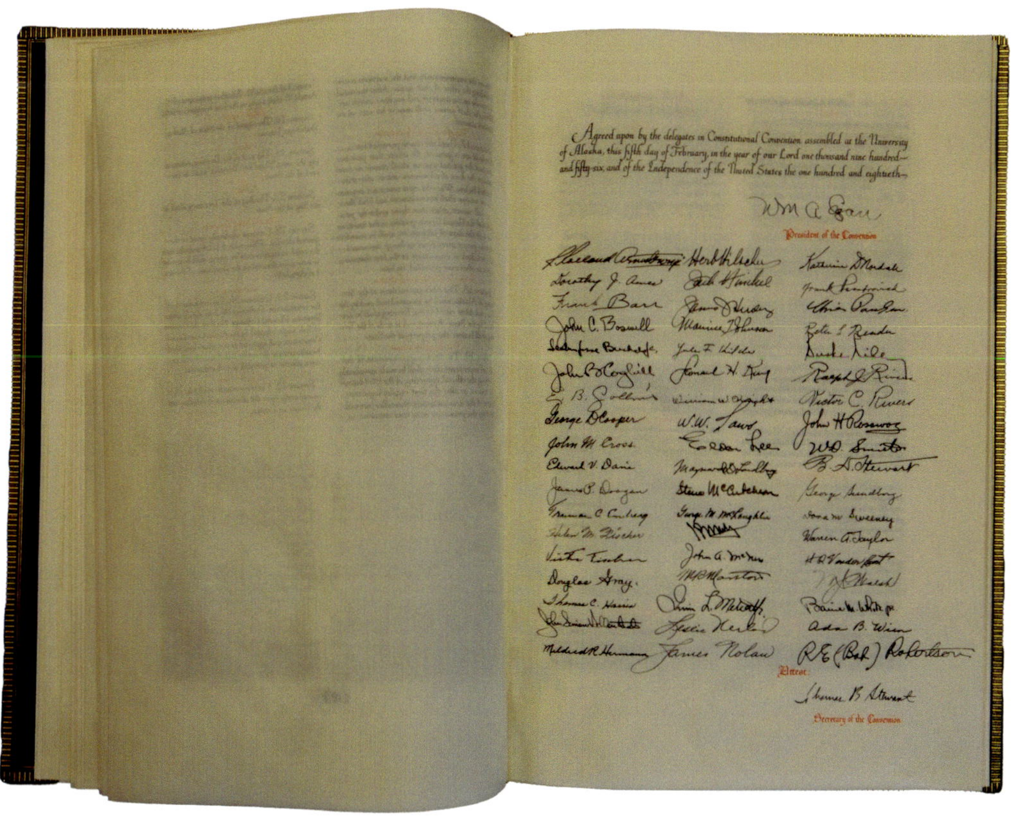

Alaska State Constitution, hand lettered on parchment by Walter W. Ferris, retired chief calligrapher of the U.S. Government Printing Office, 1956.

III-O-311

Spruce round cut on Heceta Island, Tongass National Forest, in 1929. Estimated number of years at cut: 556

2004-1-1

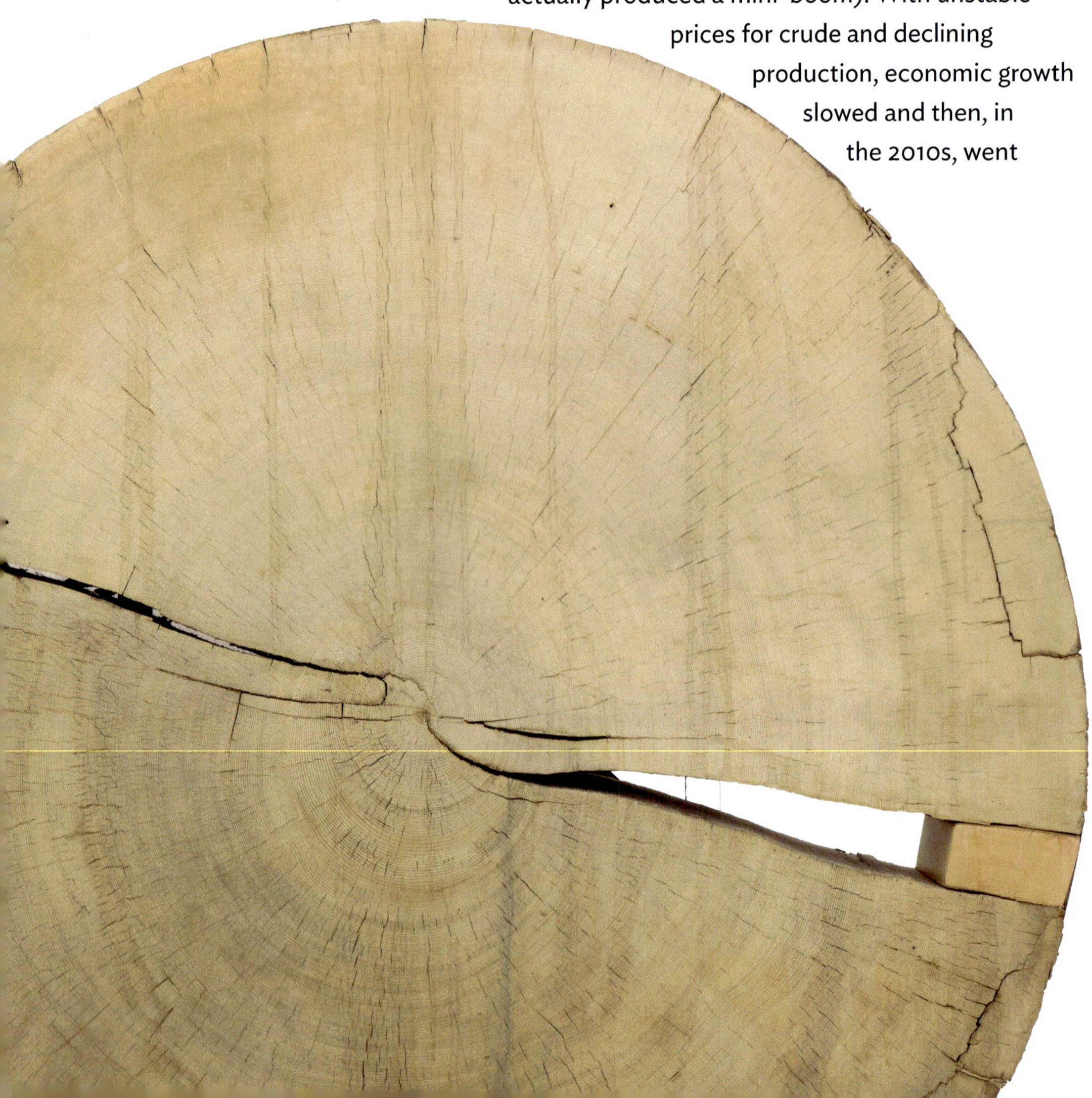

The oil spread to more than one thousand miles of beaches and killed thousands of marine mammals and a quarter million birds—their carcasses rolled up in oily berms on some shores. Even some of the oil industry's most ardent Alaskan admirers were disillusioned. In the exhibit, the spill stands metaphorically for the bust following oil's Alaska peak (although spill spending actually produced a mini-boom). With unstable prices for crude and declining production, economic growth slowed and then, in the 2010s, went in reverse. An economy that still depended on government spending and oil money contracted for a decade, a long, slow bust that, at this writing, had not ended.

The timeline gives visitors an outline of when things happened. In the rest of the gallery, exhibits stand alone like individual chapters.

On the far side of the gallery, mute giants represent the extractive resource industries that moved Alaska. A mining locomotive that operated a century ago in the tunnels under Juneau stands on a short section of track. A section of the forty-eight-inch-diameter Alaska Pipeline looms above on its support structure. In between those behemoths, the huge round of a felled old-growth tree is next to a giant chain saw and a photo mural of a clear-cut. In Alaska, large-scale timber was an extractive industry, too, not a renewable one.

Small sawmill operations produced lumber for building, and still do, but the giant pulp mills in Ketchikan and Sitka fed on huge first-growth trees that would take too long to replace for the cutting to become sustainable—although the forest is lush, it grows slowly this far north. In the 1990s, to save the remaining rainforest, President Bill Clinton canceled long-term contracts that fed the mills. The industry never recovered, and today large tracts of the Tongass National Forest remain in their primeval state. Alaska Native corporations that once cut and sold their timber began selling their standing trees for carbon credits, agreeing for compensation to keep the forest alive and sequestering carbon dioxide from the air. All that happened on the southern coasts of the state, near the Pacific. Alaska's inland forest never faced much large-scale harvest, as those dry, cold areas generally grow trees too small or low in quality for commercial use.

The eighteen-ton Baldwin locomotive from the Alaska Gastineau Mining Company pulled cars through a two-mile tunnel—the longest in the Western Hemisphere at the time—bringing rock dug from inside Mount Harris to Thane, just south of Juneau on the Gastineau Channel, where it could be crushed to release its gold. This huge mining operation, with its own hydroelectric energy project, operated from 1915 to 1921, when it closed because of unprofitability. But other large-scale, hard-rock mining around Juneau lasted until World War II.

Mount Harris and Mount Juneau, the city's backdrop, were named for the prospectors who brought mining to Juneau. They were guided here from Sitka in 1880 by Chief Cowee of the Auk Tlingits, who had already located the gold. At first, miners could find gold near the surface, in the Silverbow Basin in the mountains above Juneau, but soon needed major investment to blast shafts into the mountains. A modern city grew on those corporate riches. Scheduled steamers unloaded passengers onto streets that glowed with early electric lights.

A similar pinprick of development in the wilderness surrounded the world's richest copper deposit, in the remote Kennicott Glacier valley, reached by way of the 196-mile Copper River and Northwestern Railroad from the town of Cordova on Prince William Sound. The railroad and Kennicott mine operated from 1911 to 1938 and then were abandoned back to the wilderness. Today the buildings are part of Wrangell St. Elias National Park, and the adjoining ghost town has been resurrected for tourists.

But these hard-rock mines were exceptions in Alaska, and did not drive huge gold rush migrations of people. Placer mining was more common, in the Yukon, near Fairbanks and Nome, and many other places. Placer miners dug gravel containing gold—it had already been extracted from the mountains by erosion—and used water to separate the metal from the rock. Placer gold inspired middle-class dreams because theoretically anyone could find it. A single prospector could sift pay dirt with a shovel and a pan, or just a few miners could operate a small sluice—a simple ramp for washing gold from sand. Still, most of the gold came from major operations, such as the multistory mechanical dredges that crept across the landscape. In any case, placer mining was hard work and damaging to the environment, as the waterworks hurt fish-bearing streams and the gravel tailings remained sterile of vegetation for many decades.

Today, Alaska miners continue to dig for gold and other metals from some of the most productive mines in the world in Southeast Alaska, the Interior, and the Arctic. Prospectors and small-time operators continue to seek wealth from the gravel, too. Alaska's vast land mass contains an extraordinary variety of minerals, but only particularly rich deposits can overcome the challenges of distance and remoteness and, today, the hurdles of environmental concerns and permitting. Mining supports relatively few jobs in the state economy.

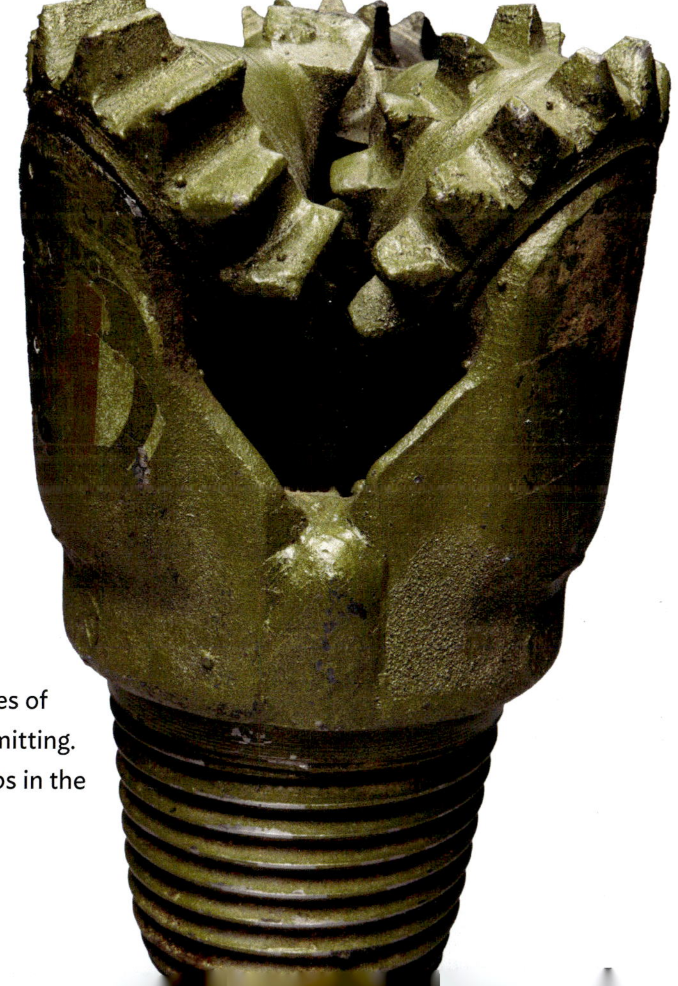

Drill bits for obtaining samples for analysis for the oil industry. Dispersing ports allow lubricating "drilling mud" to flow as bit cuts.

2015-12-3

Wood Lures from Sitka from a commercial salmon troller.

98-40-1

Alaska's oil industry has produced the vast majority of the state's private economic activity since the Alaska Pipeline began flowing in 1977. Oil discovery in Alaska began with relatively small finds on the Gulf of Alaska, beginning at the now-disappeared town of Katalla in 1902, and continuing later on the Kenai Peninsula and offshore in Cook Inlet in the 1950s and 1960s. The Prudhoe Bay discovery, orders of magnitude larger, changed Alaska's population, first with the influx of workers and wealth seekers who came to build the pipeline—said to be the largest private construction project in history to that time—and then as the state government set off an economic and building boom by spending the money it received from its oil. Migrants from southern oil-producing states also changed the social and political profile of Alaska, as it switched in less than a decade from a solidly Democratic state to a Republican one.

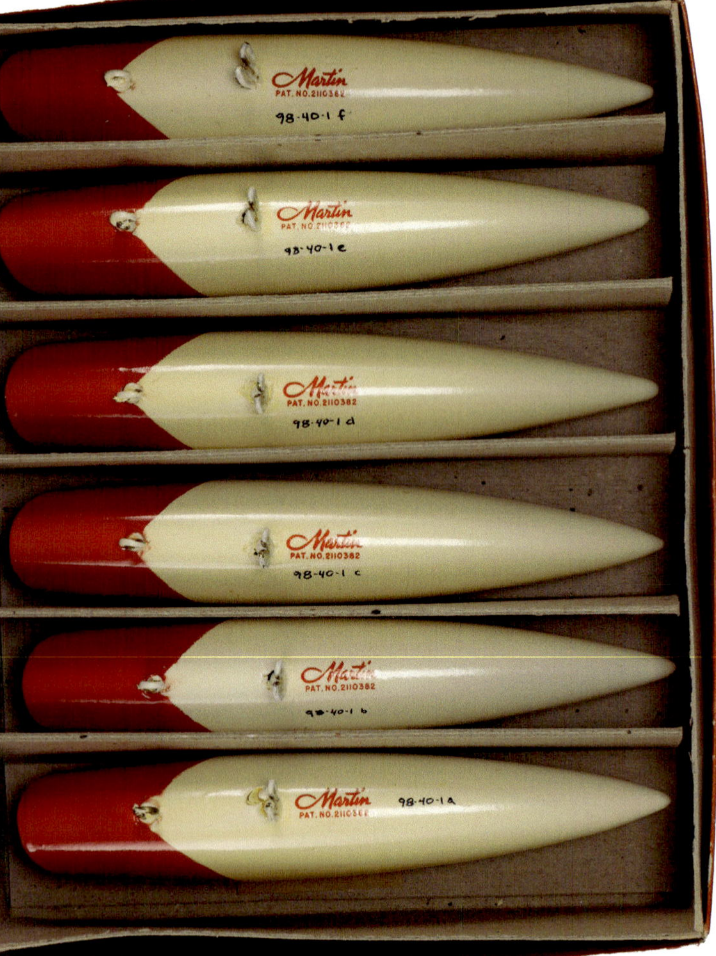

Alaska's outpost economy drives these population changes. Economists explain that states with high population turnover tend to be ones that rely on resource extraction, such as oil and mining, and are hosts to large military installations—two of Alaska's key attributes. Big resource projects attract workers with high wages, but those jobs may not last long amid fluctuating commodity prices and construction schedules. Military personnel constantly cycle through, although some settle down on retirement, and Alaska has the highest proportion of veterans of any state (11 percent of the adult population). Consistently, over a tenth of Alaska's population changes every year, as residents come and go, especially in the larger cities of Anchorage and Fairbanks. That has enabled Anchorage to rapidly gain ethnic and racial diversity, mostly since the 1990s, as immigrants from all over the world moved to Alaska from other states and made the city's schools among the most integrated in the United States. In the tolerant and egalitarian Alaska ethos—Alaska is also the state with the least income inequality—that change happened with little overt conflict and a fair share of civic pride.

The exhibit feels lighter and more positive when it moves to the main renewable resource industries, fishing and tourism. They represent stability amid the boom and bust, and the towns these industries support tend to be older and prettier.

Fishing takes up the center of the gallery, around the double-ended sailboat from the Bristol Bay salmon fishery. It's a beautiful, functional vessel, full of romance for those who love the sea and can imagine bringing in nets full of sockeye salmon while under sail—but this strange fishery, without motors until 1951, represents the problems with fishery management that helped drive the statehood movement. Alaskans believed, probably correctly, that large fish companies outside Alaska used influence in Washington, DC, for preferential access to the territory's catch. The federal requirement for the use of sail in Bristol Bay, which lasted thirty years after fisheries elsewhere converted to motorized vessels, benefited cannery owners by holding down their costs and allowing them to control fishermen. Weak federal management also failed to conserve fisheries, and salmon catches repeatedly crashed.

At the Alaska Constitutional Convention, the biggest controversy surrounded how the new state would select its fish managers. When the document came up for public approval, its supporters lured voters to the polls by also including a referendum on fish traps—the hated barriers, mostly owned by companies outside the state, capable of blocking salmon rivers—and that ban passed by an even larger margin than the constitution itself. After statehood, however, salmon stocks failed to recover. The new constitution called for sustainable harvests, but also equal access for all—both imperatives intended to correct the problems of the federal era. But the two requirements proved to be in conflict, because equal access allowed too many fishermen to chase too few fish. In 1972, Alaska voters amended the Alaska Constitution to allow for a limited entry program, which keeps the fishing fleet from growing and gives fishermen a property interest in conservation. That change ushered in fifty years of sustainable management that is still held up as an example worldwide.

A similar pattern followed in other fisheries, as responsible managers gained control of fisheries and then limited them by creating permits or quotas as private property. In 1976, Congress excluded foreign fishing vessels from within two hundred miles of U.S. shores. Later, fishermen received legal allotments of offshore fish they could catch themselves or sell for other fishermen to catch. The results improved fisheries management, but also gradually rearranged society in coastal communities, making them something like farming towns, with rooted owners and migrant workers. Harbor towns prosper through the booms and busts in the rest of the state, anchored by those who own permits, quotas, and boats, who are assured a share of a sustainable resource. Families staying for generations have built the state's loveliest communities in places such as Petersburg, Cordova, and Kodiak. But entering the industry as a fisherman is difficult and expensive. Most workers in the fishing industry—which is the largest private employer in Alaska—arrive for brief fishing seasons to work long hours in processing plants or on factory ships, and then depart the state for other seasonal work.

The Alaska tourism industry is as old as commercial fishing. Steamships began bringing visitors not long after Alaska became part of the United States, for the same reasons visitors come today: first, to see the scenery and wildlife; after that, Alaska Native culture; and then, perhaps, some gold rush history or a museum. The attraction of seeing this wild, grand place hardly needs to be explained to those who have visited—naturalist John Muir was among the first to tell of this beauty in his popular writings after making the first of many trips in 1879, when he paddled to Glacier Bay in a Tlingit canoe. Sightseers traveled the

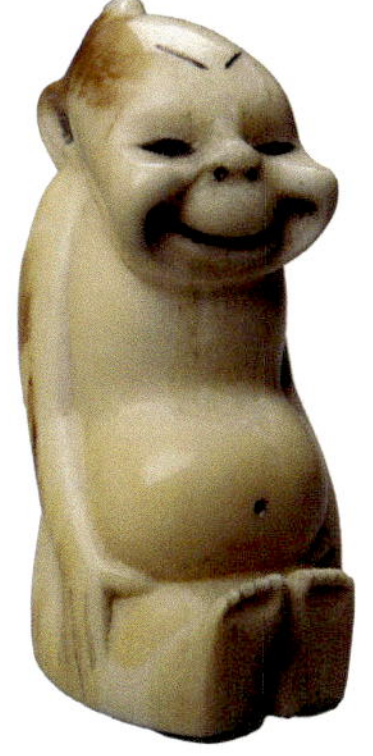

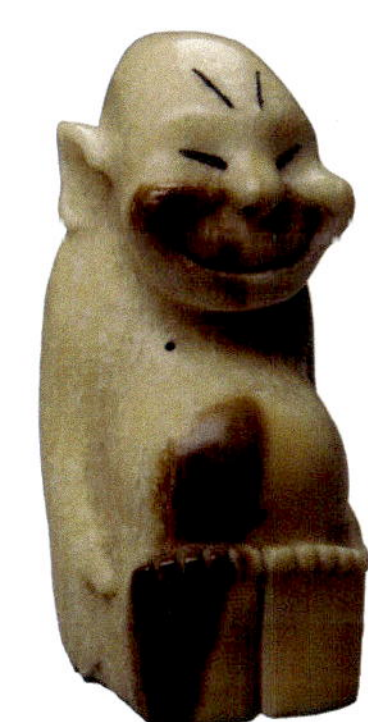

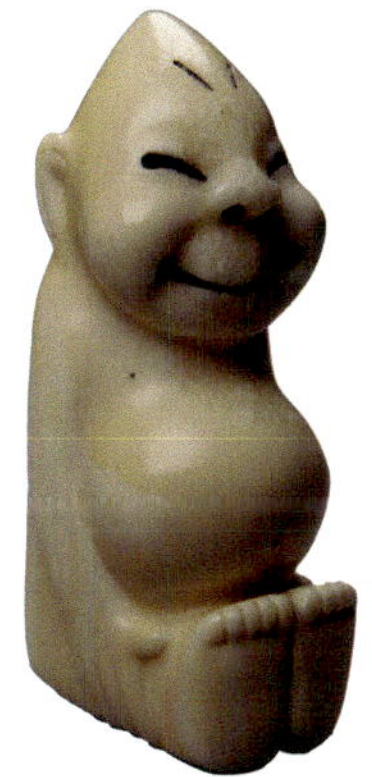

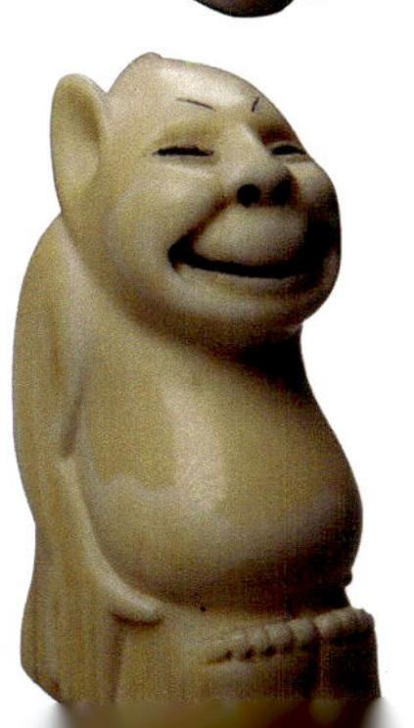

The original billiken—God of Things as They Ought to Be—was a good luck charm popular at the turn of the century. A traveler brought one to Nome and soon after it was copied by carvers, including Happy Jack (Angokwazhuk), who carved the top billiken.

98-7-60, 98-7-57, 98-7-59, 98-7-61

Life ring from the *Princess Sophia*.
III-O-254

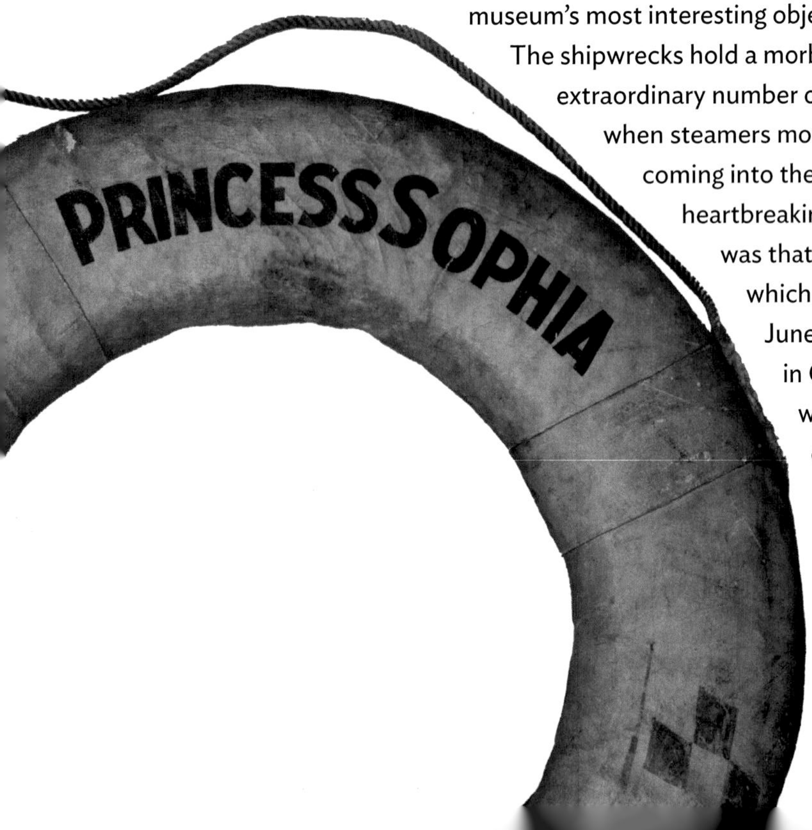

inside passage on steamers before the gold rush. They stopped in indigenous villages to see totem poles and bought Alaska Native art, mostly made specifically for this trade, with new styles and influences intended to appeal to the visitors. When the gold rush stampede came through Skagway in 1898, that event soon became an attraction, too. The first sixty tourists arrived that same year, and more after 1908, when local businessmen rearranged the buildings to improve the look of the main street, Broadway, and create a more dramatic Wild West setting. Skagway's heyday only lasted a year or two, but the visitors keep coming—well over a million arrive on cruise ships annually, more than forty times the town's peak population during the gold rush (today the year-round population is about 1,100 people).

Tourism leads into Transportation, where some of the museum's most interesting objects are on exhibit. The shipwrecks hold a morbid fascination. An extraordinary number occurred during the years when steamers moved almost everyone coming into the territory. The most heartbreaking of these wrecks was that of the *Princess Sophia*, which went aground north of Juneau with 343 on board in October 1918. No one was hurt in the crash and other vessels came to the ship's aid, ready to rescue the passengers, but the captain refused them, hoping to refloat his ship at high tide. Instead, a storm came up overnight and the ship slid off the rock and sank in the darkness and spray, taking the lives of all on board, except for a single dog, an English setter. Investigation showed that some passengers had escaped into the water wearing life vests but suffocated on oil spilled from the ship. Items from the wreck are on on exhibit here, as well as the *Princess Sophia*'s chilling final radio messages, which were sent as water rushed in.

Alaska's greatest treasure ship sank in 1901. It carried successful gold miners from the Klondike returning with their new fortunes. Steaming near Juneau, the luxurious *Islander* hit something—no one knows what—and sank rapidly, taking forty-two lives and untold wealth in gold. Some passengers jumped overboard with their pokes of gold and went to the bottom. Treasure seekers have searched for more than a century and found the objects exhibited here, including a tuxedo and a poke of gold nuggets, both recovered 114 years after the wreck. But much more may still be under the water.

Among other transportation adventures represented in the exhibit, some charming, others hair-raising, the story of the airship *Norge* may be my favorite. In 1926, polar explorers Roald Amundson and Lincoln Ellsworth became the first to fly over the North Pole, leaving Norway in a 348-foot-long dirigible with Italian aeronautical designer Umberto Nobile, his little dog Titina, and a crew of thirteen. When they reached Alaska, a storm caught the huge, slow-moving airship and carried it west, over the Bering Strait, and the adventurers finally were forced to land their damaged craft wherever they could, without knowing their location. The spot happened to be near the tiny Arctic community of Teller, north of Nome. Pieces of the *Norge* were given away to the surprised residents, including some we can see on exhibit, and one of the locals carved an ivory model of the *Norge*.

Such prewar adventures seem frivolous compared to the desperate journeys and slaughter of World War II in Alaska. The museum's extensive exhibit on those events is vivid and full of detail, but most people are unaware of the battles fought here or their permanent impact.

As the Japanese took on the United States, they planned to seize a defensive perimeter of islands across the broad expanse of the Pacific. After bombing Pearl Harbor in Hawaii on December 7, 1941, and Dutch Harbor in Alaska's Aleutians on June 3, 1942, the Japanese planned a simultaneous attack on the island of Midway, west of Hawaii, and on the outer Aleutian Islands of Kiska and Attu. But the Americans broke the enemy's codes and foiled their plans by concentrating their defenses at Midway, where the United States won a decisive battle, while the Japanese were allowed to take the Alaskan islands without resistance.

As the war progressed, Kiska and Attu lost strategic significance, but the Japanese left forces dug in there because of the enormous effort that would be required to remove them—an effort the United States was bound to expend due to the symbolic importance of having land occupied by a foreign invader. The closest air base, Dutch Harbor, was more than 600 miles distant from Kiska and 850 miles from Attu. Attempts to bomb the Japanese off Kiska failed, despite heroic efforts, foiled by the storms and fog of the North Pacific and the difficulty of pilots finding their targets. The U.S. military would have to build its way closer, extending its forces out along the undeveloped chain of islands. Rapidly constructed bases at Adak and Amchitka brought the enemy within 250 and 50 miles of Kiska, respectively. With that foothold and an enormous military buildup, the United States finally mounted an amphibious assault on Attu in May 1943. It was America's first encounter with fanatical Japanese bravery and suicide tactics. In the long battle for that forlorn, treeless island, more than 2,300 Japanese soldiers fought to the death or took their own lives to avoid capture. Only 23 survived. On the American side, 549 died, 1,148 were wounded, and 2,100 were injured by the harsh weather and terrain. The Japanese then evacuated Kiska, slipping away unseen in the fog on eleven war ships. A large U.S. and Canadian force attacked the island but found it abandoned.

The sheer size and astonishing speed of American war work in Alaska is mind boggling, as was the impact. Americans really feared further Japanese invasion. They built forts with guns in the mountains above Resurrection Bay to protect Seward's port and constructed a navy base on Kodiak Island. Big new airfields,

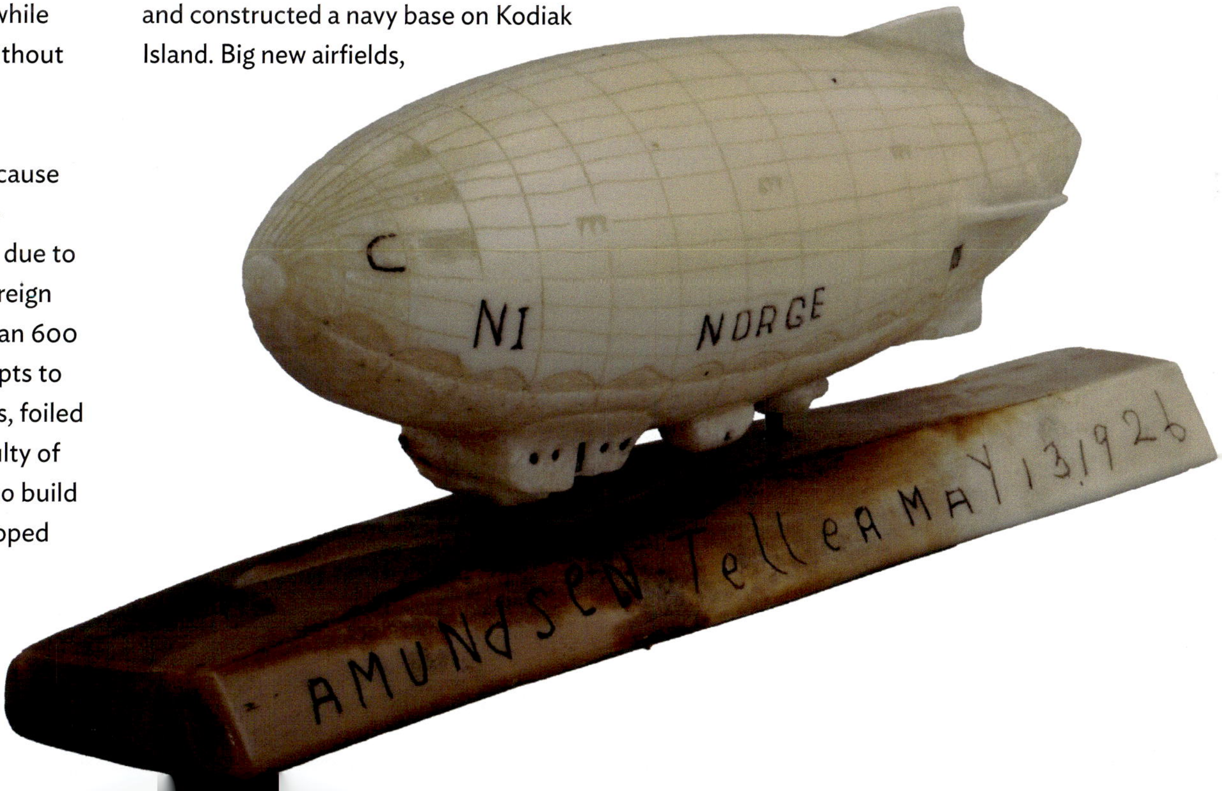

Ivory carving of the Norge.

A souvenir carved by a Yup'ik or Iñupiaq artist.

II-A-3318

A Japanese Army officer's pistol—a Nambu Type 14, 8mm caliber, with custom grips of jade, manufactured 1935.

2003-24-2

some built in a matter of days, turned the page of transportation history to aviation, and became the nucleus for new communities. Construction changed the economic future for towns, and new roads made it possible to drive to Alaska for the first time. The military even built sewer, water, and electrical systems that would serve Alaskans for generations.

Changes came among the people, too. The army's top general took control, ordering dependents to leave, and requested civilian families to depart. He invoked censorship of communications and the media. And he imposed new racial segregation rules—which helped inspire Alaska's civil rights movement. Cities established civil defense groups to patrol streets and enforce blackouts, and in rural Alaska, indigenous villagers organized into National Guard and scout units to defend the shores and gather intelligence on the enemy. The invading Japanese had imprisoned about fifty mostly Unangan residents of Kiska and Attu, half of whom died in camps during the war, and the Americans also evacuated the indigenous population from the rest of the Aleutians, interning 881 people and destroying their ten villages to deny the Japanese those modest assets should they advance. These American internees also fared poorly in degrading camp conditions, with many deaths.

With the end of fighting in Alaska in 1943—after just one year—most of the new military facilities were left with skeleton crews or abandoned. Kiska and Attu became uninhabited outdoor museums of the brutal battles there, where thousands had died for land that would be left to the seagulls when the fighting was over. The war ended and the world moved on.

History never stops, but the Alaska Gallery essentially ends here, with something of a question mark. What does all this tell us about ourselves and our future? Unlike the Alaska Native section, with its continuity to the present, this American section depicts people firmly in the past, represented by things that we no longer use, objects whose meaning is assigned by those bygone people's lives and not our own. The discontinuities are more notable than the commonalities. As historian Terrence Cole noted, "The history of Alaska is punctuated by one shocking surprise after another, and there is no reason to think this pattern is going to change in the future. Historical patterns cannot predict the future of Alaska's economy."

Next in the museum comes the Discovery Room for kids, with its fun square-rigged ship to climb on and the giant colorful octopus up above, made of plastic cups and other found objects. That's about the future. The galleries for temporary exhibits also define today's Alaska.

But I think there is a bigger lesson here as well. The entire museum is a statement about Alaska's identity as we see it today. The exhibits were not created by any single mind but by a collaboration over many years, encompassing many voices that sometimes spoke in harmony, sometimes in conflict. These conversations happened during a time of deep cultural change in Alaska, at the sunset of the oil era and during the rise of Alaska Native organizations' power and assertiveness. On the surface, the museum exhibits say what they say: visitors learn important information about, for example, World War II or the fishing industry or many other topics. But the way these things are said also carries a message, and perhaps a deeper one, as Alaskans assess the meaning of our past and gaze into a hazy future.

That story of how we tell our story is next.

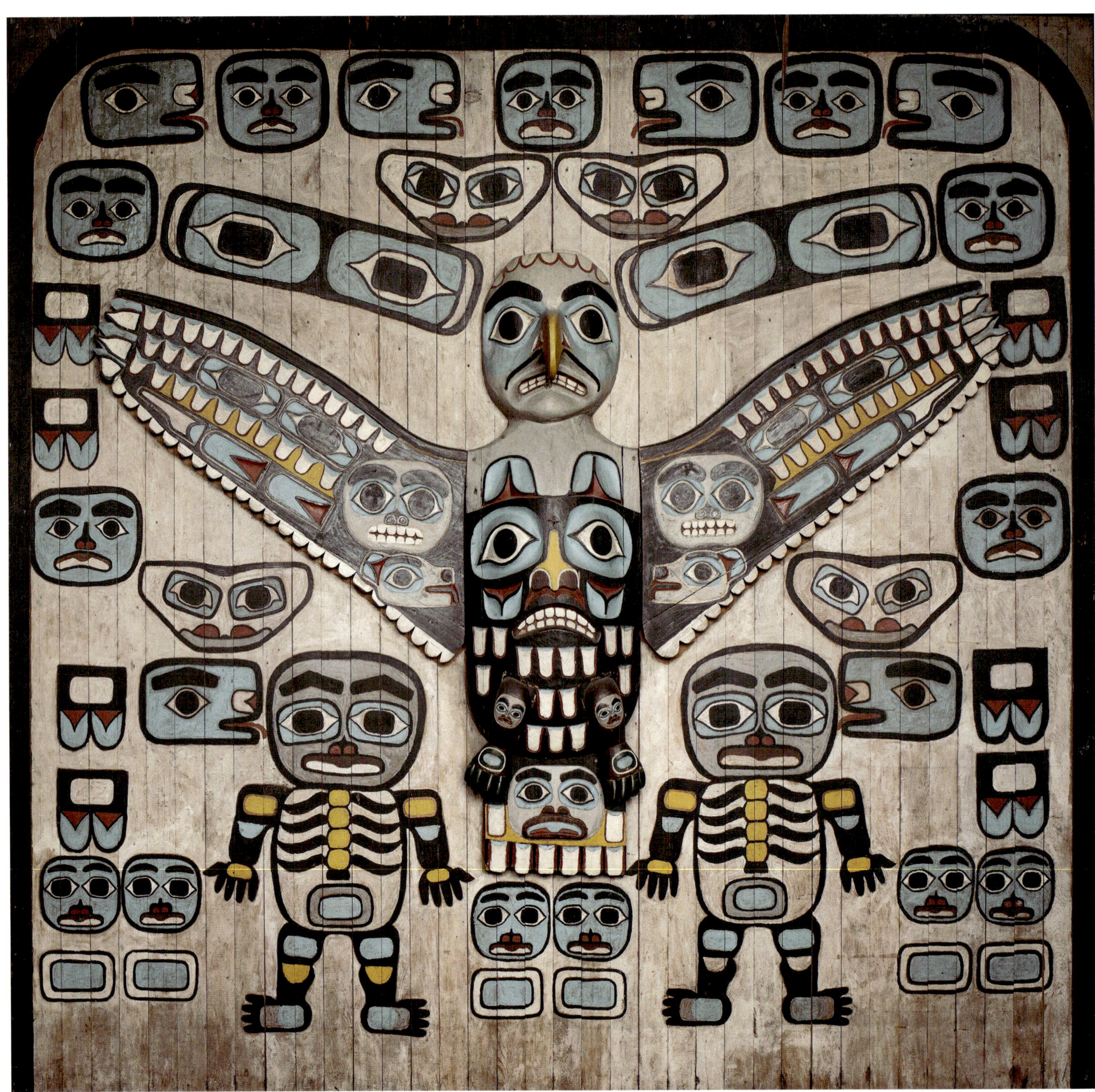

Xeitl X'een
***Thunderbird Screen* from the Thunderbird House (Xeitl Hít), Shangookeidí clan, Yakutat Tlingit.**

II-B-845

VOICING ALASKA'S STORY

THE CREATION OF THE MUSEUM AND ALASKANS' CHANGING IMAGE OF OURSELVES

1.

At the beginning of the Alaska State Museum's permanent exhibit, text by a respected scholar described the arrival of the first people in North America in the way it is currently understood by science, as a migration from easternmost Asia to westernmost Alaska during the last glacial period, at least 14,500 years ago, when much of the ocean was locked in ice. But Ernestine Saanklalaxt' Hayes disagreed. The museum resides in the lap of her Aak'w Kwaán clan Tlingit village, where docks and industrial yards stood when she was a girl, and where, before that—before gold miners' rock waste filled the area—a lagoon of fish fed the people who lived there. The tide still remembers those days, and comes in twice a day among the sediments under the building. That was the place, below however many layers of history that hide the essential past, from which Hayes said her people came.

"I do believe that people were always here, even during glaciation," said Hayes, an author and past Alaska State Writer Laureate. "My essential belief is that the language and the culture emerged from this place and could not have happened anywhere else but here, where we are, in what is now Southeast Alaska. I think it is rooted, rooted very deeply in this place."

Steve Henrikson, the curator of collections, didn't necessarily disagree. He is an honorary member of Angoon's Dakl'aweidí clan and participates in its ceremonies, having been adopted before marrying his wife Janice Criswell, a weaver (something we learned of from a media clipping, as he is too humble to brag of his membership). But neither did Henrikson dispute the physical evidence for the timing of the first human arrivals in Alaska offered by Joshua Reuther, an archaeologist at the University of Alaska–Fairbanks. In the end, he let stand both truths. Reuther's statement, on a gallery label titled "first arrival of the first people," explains the origin in terms of Western science, while a carved Tlingit house screen tells the ancient origin story of the Xeitl Hít (Thunderbird House) of the Shangookeidí clan of Yakutat in pictures. And, as if to connect the two, a quote from Hayes insists on equality between the knowledge systems of indigenous people and academic science, rejecting the very concept of "prehistory" used by archaeologists.

These statements aren't exactly contradictory, but they call visitors into distinctly different worlds, places where the essential nature of what we see in the museum is fundamentally different. Do we see objects or belongings? Do we see evidence of past lives that are gone, or are these things alive in themselves, with spirits that still yearn for use and meaning? Indigenous

Shirt with beaded eagle design. Made by a Tlingit patient for Dr. Bertrand K. Wilbur's son, Bert, adopted by the Kaagwaantaan clan of Sitka.

Loan courtesy Wilbur Family. LC. 438-1

Alaskans have told me that everything has a spirit, as we do, with a moment of creation and a moment of death, arising from nature, like us, and then subsumed back into it. Traditionally, the Tlingit carved totem poles from rainforest trees to tell of clan heroes and histories, but then they let the poles rot back into the forest floor, allowing them to die as all living things die. In the museum, we can see a collection, a hoard of culture, which is permanent as only inanimate things are permanent. Or we can see a process that continues, still alive, of which even our presence and our gaze are part.

Museums are not permanent. Even if they persist physically, what they mean changes with each generation. The Father Andrew P. Kashevaroff Building, which houses the Alaska State Library, Archives and Museum, opened in 2016, replacing a museum on the same site that had been built in 1967 to honor the centennial of the treaty that made Alaska part of the United States. In 1967, Alaska had been a state of the union for only eight years, and pioneer optimism powered the construction of a series of public facilities to celebrate the centennial of the Alaska Purchase, as the exchange with Russia was then called. But even then, some Alaska Natives had other views, saying Russia could never have sold Alaska because Russia had never owned it—the indigenous people did. In 1971, Congress recognized Native land rights by conveying 44 million acres and almost $1 billion to newly formed Native corporations—the largest such settlement in world history to that day. In the half century since, those corporations have become the richest and most powerful companies based in Alaska.

Fifty years also brought another anniversary to celebrate the treaty with Russia, in 2017. In part as a commemoration, this new, very different museum had just been finished—while many Alaska Natives said the treaty was no cause for celebration at all. A Tlingit from Yakutat, the late Byron Mallott, held official responsibility for the sesquicentennial in his role as lieutenant governor, but, although as a patriot he praised the United States, he told me that Alaska Natives were ambivalent and increasingly sensitive about the anniversary. Some refused to participate in commemorative events. Some considered the arrival of the United States a tragedy, and a few, as curator Henrikson related at the time, even said that Alaska Natives who had served in the military should not have fought on the side of an oppressive government. Sentiments and sensitivities were high.

A section of the Alaska exhibit called Resilience reflects the anger, channeled through Henrikson from ten years of meetings with Native elders and his own family. It begins with a series of contemporary works by Tlingit artists on themes of displacement, identity, and loss, including a pair of child-size handcuffs by Nicholas Galanin that speak to the mid-twentieth-century removal of Native children from their families to attend assimilationist boarding schools. A label with the heading "Genocide" quotes the United Nations definition of that crime against humanity, noting that "many people" feel the Russian and U.S. governments committed genocide against Alaska Native people. After the exhibit went up, Alaska's most respected academic historians challenged that statement in newspaper columns, arguing that genocide in any literal sense never occurred here. Henrikson pushed back. "I do strongly feel that the evidence of genocide is on display," he said. "The part the government played, the part the missionaries played, and the part American capitalism played—that's what it amounts to." But he also admitted receiving complaints about the handcuffs, since no such child's handcuffs ever were used—indeed, handcuffs are a one-size-fits-all device—and so this artistic conception misrepresented at least one form of truth.

Several kinds of truth are present even within the Resilience section. Various voices have their say. We learn about the government-backed work of Protestant missionaries, led by Presbyterian leader Sheldon Jackson, to erase Native cultures by ending ceremonies and prohibiting children from speaking their indigenous languages or learning stories and dances from their elders. But we also read a formal apology from the Presbyterians, and an explanation of the missionary's benign intent to protect Native people by including them in the dominant society—an odd kind of protection, since it demanded a traumatic a loss of identity, but also a poor fit for the word *genocide*, since that term assumes a malicious intent to destroy. Alaska Natives had an active hand in these events, too. Henrikson, who wrote the "Genocide" label, also included in this section his wife's grandfather, Rudolph Walton, who was among Jackson's first pupils in 1878 and became a Presbyterian deacon, but also kept his Tlingit traditions alive as leader of the Kiks.ádi clan. He carved the extraordinary house posts that are here, bearing the year 1904 inscribed in the wood, which he made for the famous "last potlatch" of that year. Walton used his knowledge of White ways as an early leader in the Alaska Native Brotherhood, which fought in court for Native rights, but itself also advocated assimilation.

"They said, 'Well, we're going to send some of our kids to their school and learn their ways. And then we're going to use those ways to fight for our rights.' And that's exactly what happened," Henrikson said. "Everybody always emphasizes the victimization. And they were. But they also did a lot to prevent it from being worse. And they had collaborators in that, like Dr. Wilbur." Dr. Bertrand K. Wilbur worked at Jackson's school in

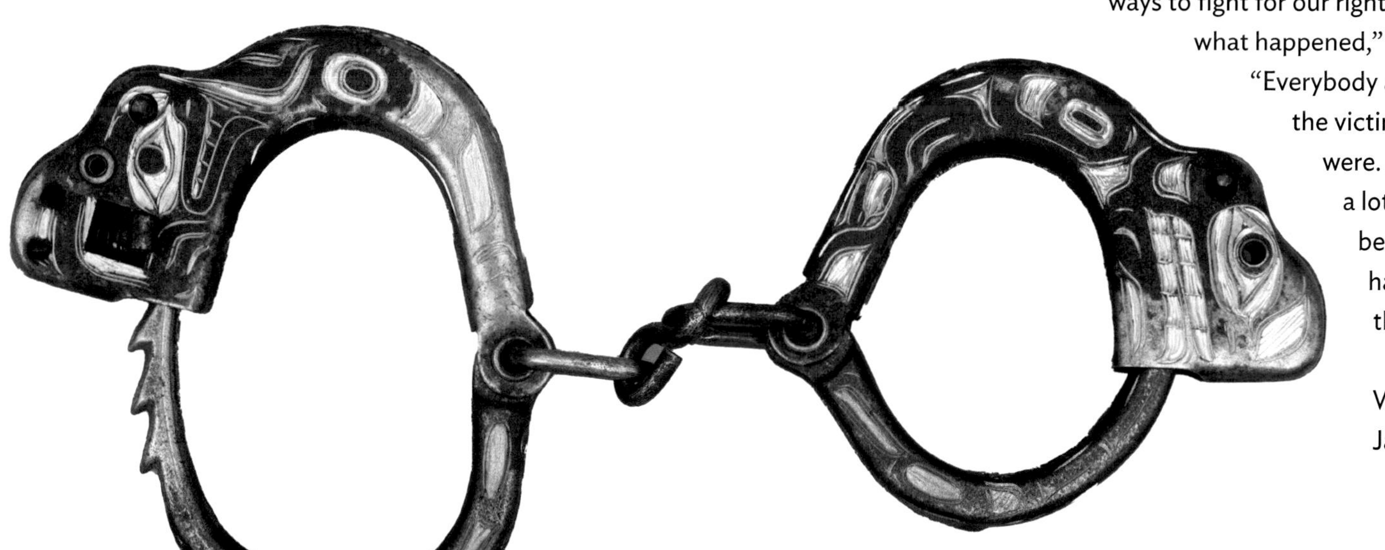

Indian Childrens' Bracelet by Nicholas Galanin (Tlingit/Unangax̂), 2014. The piece speaks to the practice of removing Native American children from their families to attend boarding school.

2014-17-1

Interior house post. Carved by Rudolph Walton, a Kiks.adi carver in Sitka, on commission by the leaders of the Kaagwaantaan Wolf House, for their potlatch in Sitka, 1904.

II-B-1110-1

Sitka, but refused to exclude non-Christian people from his care and saved the lives of children in the village and the chief himself. In the Resilience area, Henrikson showed me a child's shirt, beaded with an eagle design, that was given to Wilbur's son by the grateful mother of one of his patients. Father and son were adopted into Tlingit clans and a potlatch at Wilbur's house celebrated his retirement and departure from Sitka in 1901. In 1990, Henrikson met Wilbur's son in San Diego, when he was one hundred years old, and the old man brought out the beaded eagle shirt he had worn as a toddler to be shown here in the museum.

Henrikson said some visitors have complained about this part of this exhibit, too, saying it is too positive toward the missionaries. "It really struck me as a perfect story to bring in here, to kind of add balance," he said. "They weren't evil. They were trying to do their best. And there were probably some that were pedophiles and criminals, but a lot of them were, you know, good people."

This story and another helped me understand the museum and accept

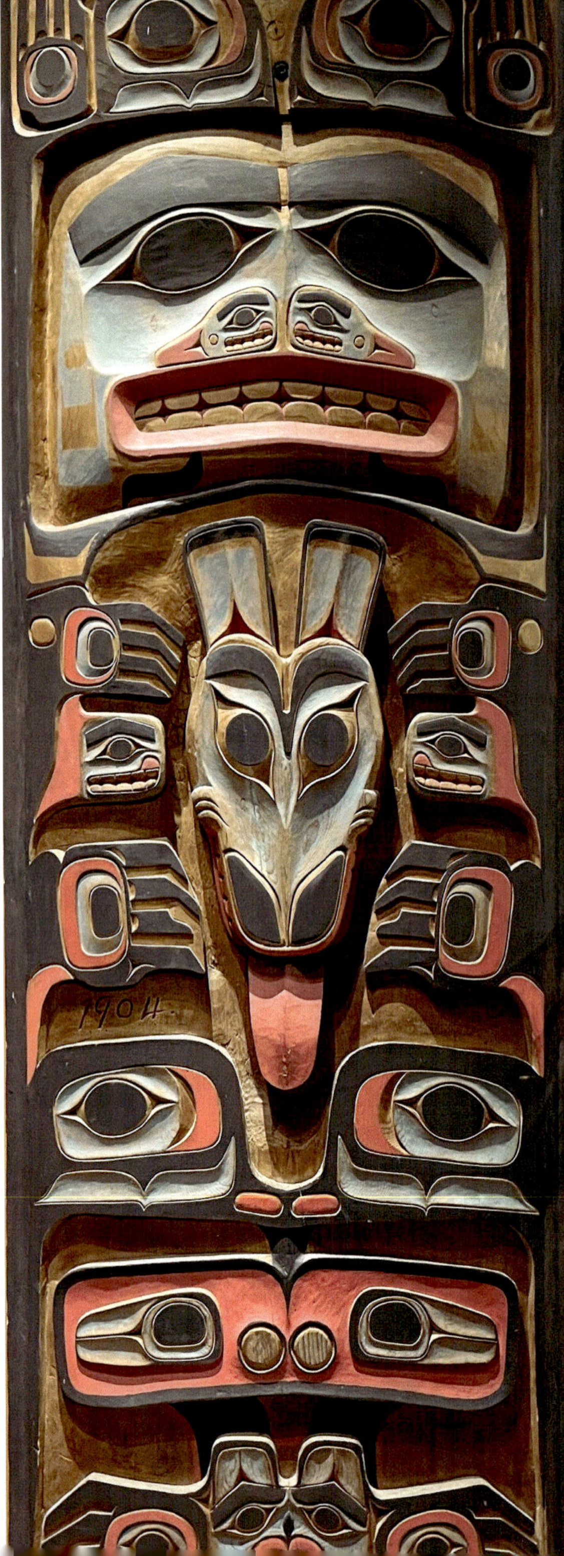

its contradictions. The truth here emanates from each of the things we see, which connect to individual Alaskans who lived complex lives with many meanings—not villains and victims, just people. The refusal of the exhibit to impose broader messages from above forces the engaged viewer to do the work of completing the story, as we do in life, by assembling what we see and others' points of view into our own perspective and ideas.

One day when I visited, the man who was working at the front desk, Brian Wallace, told me another such story. Henrikson had earlier pointed out perhaps the most important historic piece in the collection, the bronze double-headed eagle crest that was given as a peace offering and payment for land by Russian conquistador Alexander Baranov to a Kiks.ádi clan chief after the battle of Sitka in 1804, ending the largest and most decisive armed conflict of Russia's invasion. It may be the only such Russian American peace offering that survives. Wallace told me his grandfather, a Kiks.ádi chief, had owned the bronze crest, which came down through the family for more than a century, its meaning eventually forgotten, until it resided in his mother Dorothy Wallace's toy box in Juneau when she was a girl. Dorothy said the eagle lost its wing tip when she was wrestling with her brother over it. In 1940, the director of the museum, Andrew Kashevaroff, visiting the Wallaces' home, recognized the crest and acquired it for the collection. And here it lives, representing war, peace, and the ownership of a continent, but also a piece of household clutter underfoot when a little girl left out her toys. It can be both.

This is why the Alaska Exhibit represents Alaska in a way that is found nowhere else. Alaskans built this exhibit by accretion, designed and assembled it by discussion, and reached an unspoken consensus that they would agree to disagree, allowing the many voices of the belongings and objects here to continue speaking—in harmony and in cacophony. The experience can be incomplete and overwhelming at the same time. As is Alaska.

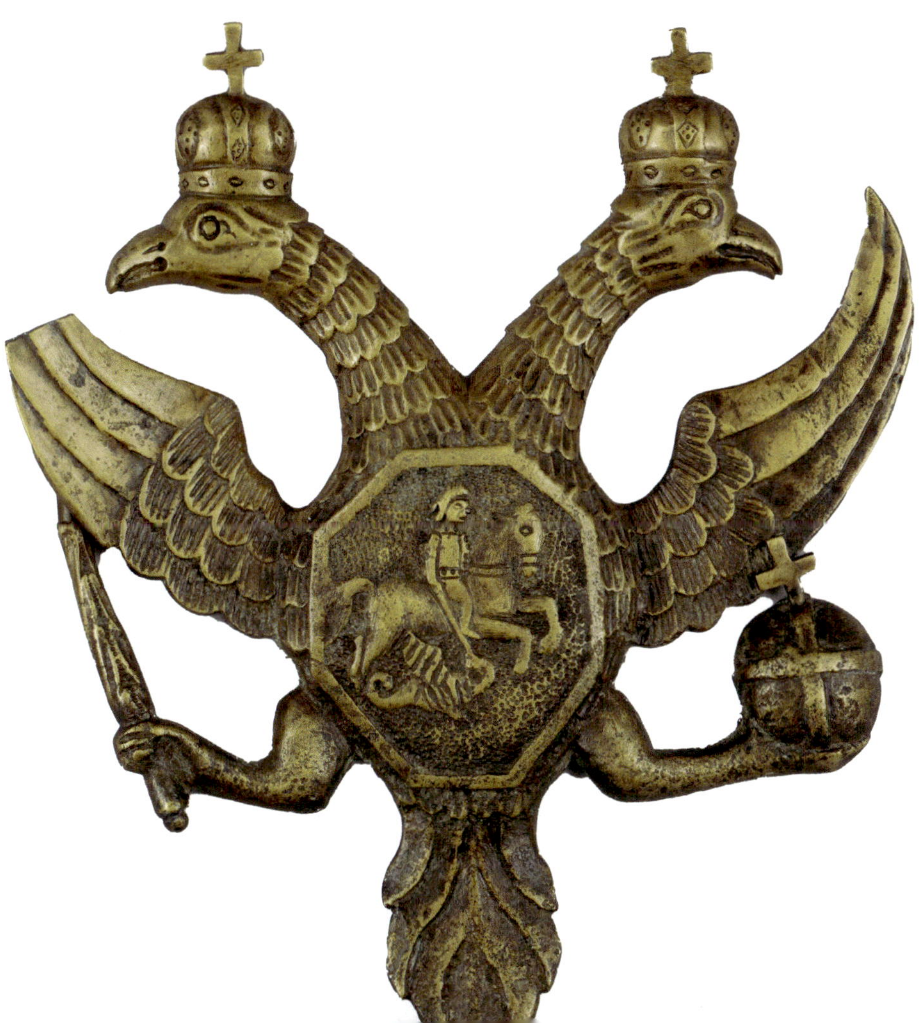

The double-headed eagle was the crest of Imperial Russia. Beginning in the late 1700s, Russian traders presented bronze crests as gifts to Alaska Natives. The presence of the crests also signaled to rival colonial nations that the land was claimed by the Tsar. According to clan history, this crest was presented to a leader of the Kiks.ádi clan of Sitka as a peace offering following the Battle of Sitka in 1804.

III-R-150

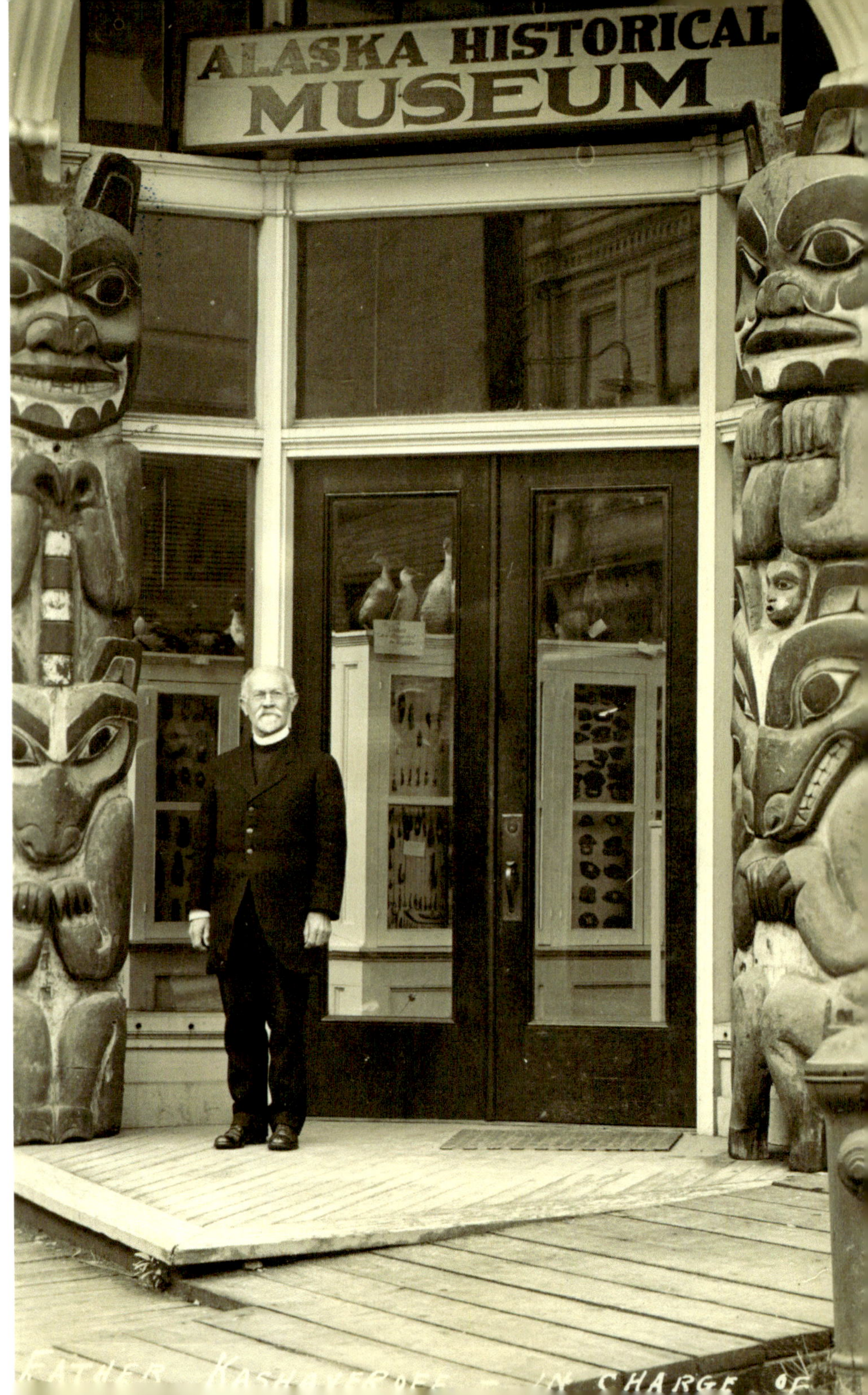

RIGHT
Father Kashevaroff (1863-1940) at the entrance to the Alaska Historical Library and Museum, circa 1930.
ASL-P44-03-003

FACING PAGE
Photos of the Alaska (Territorial) Museum
ASL-P243-3-003, ASL-P243-001

2.

Congress created the museum in 1900, before Alaska was a state or even a territory, and for twenty years it had no exhibits or permanent home; it was only a collection stored in various places that grew as the federally appointed governors of the District of Alaska gathered items. Although the early U.S. rulers of Alaska sought to extinguish Alaska Native cultures, they coveted artifacts those cultures had created. Sheldon Jackson arrived as a Presbyterian missionary in 1877 and became the government's general agent for education in 1885, and John Brady, a missionary with Jackson who opened a school in Sitka in 1878 and later a trading post, was appointed governor in 1897. Brady requested the establishment of the museum, which was headquartered in his official residence as governor, and he was a collector himself, although his widow sold that collection to the Smithsonian Institution. Jackson also voraciously gathered Native art, eventually sending his private collection to Princeton, New Jersey, where he had attended seminary, and the material is still there in the Princeton University Art Museum. Many other items collected by Jackson's colleagues reside in a museum that still bears his name in Sitka, now part of the Alaska State Museum.

Brady and Jackson may easily be despised for their cynicism, collecting art while suppressing the culture that created it, but their stories and legacies are more complex. While Jackson expressed disgust at tribal social organization, especially polygamy, slavery, and a role for women he regarded as degrading, both reverends wrote admiringly of the indigenous people they knew in their first years in Alaska. In the pre-dawn of the gold rush, White miners and prospectors were infiltrating indigenous country, seeking wealth and sex, and using alcohol as a tool of conquest while spreading chaos, disease, prostitution, and child sexual abuse. Brady, traveling by canoe in 1878, wrote to Jackson of meeting clan members who were "far away from the whites, and are, therefore, virtuous . . . If we could only anticipate the miners by three years, untold misery and vice would be prevented."

The protection the missionaries offered, however, came with a profound cost: their charges were required to become Christians and renounce a culture that had succeeded richly for millennia and that gave meaning and order to life, instead conforming to American nuclear families and abandoning ceremonies such as the potlatch, a gift-giving celebration that linked the living and dead, connected clans and communities, resolved debts and grievances, and cemented class relationships in a complex social system. The potlatch was capitalism in reverse, with the rich gaining status by giving rather than hoarding wealth. In 1902, as governor, Brady made an agreement with a group of Tlingit leaders who had prospered as Christians to hold one last potlatch, and obtained federal funding to support that grand event in 1904. The posts created for the potlatch by Rudolph Walton eventually became part of the museum collection. (The Tlingit leaders did not stop holding

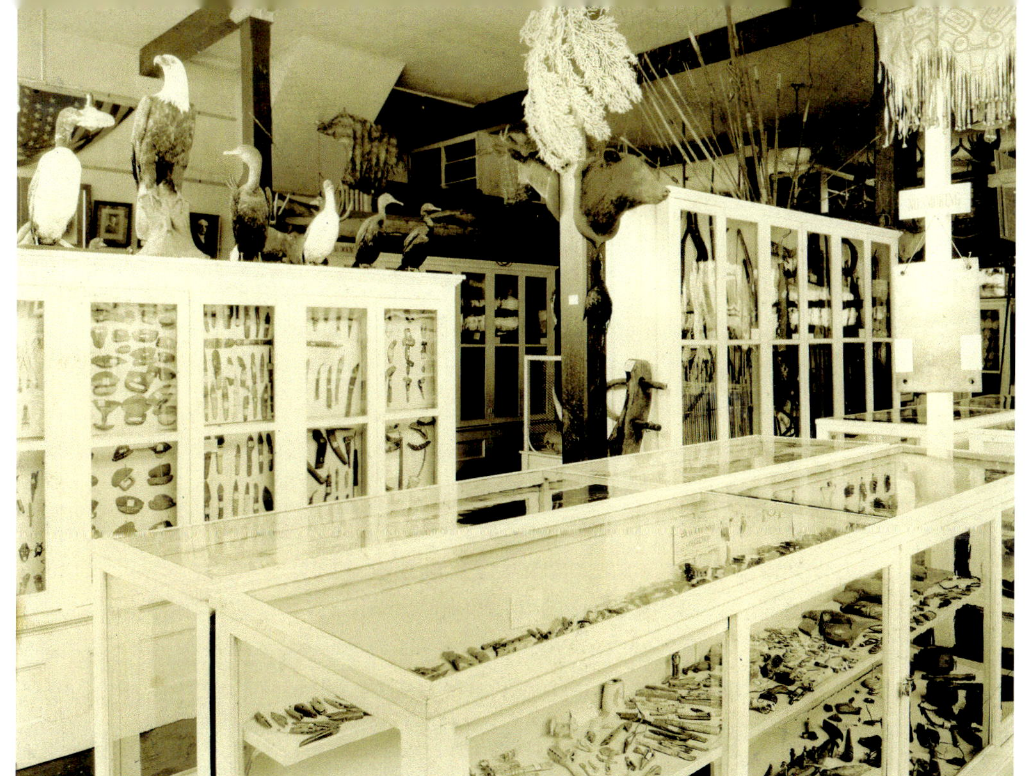

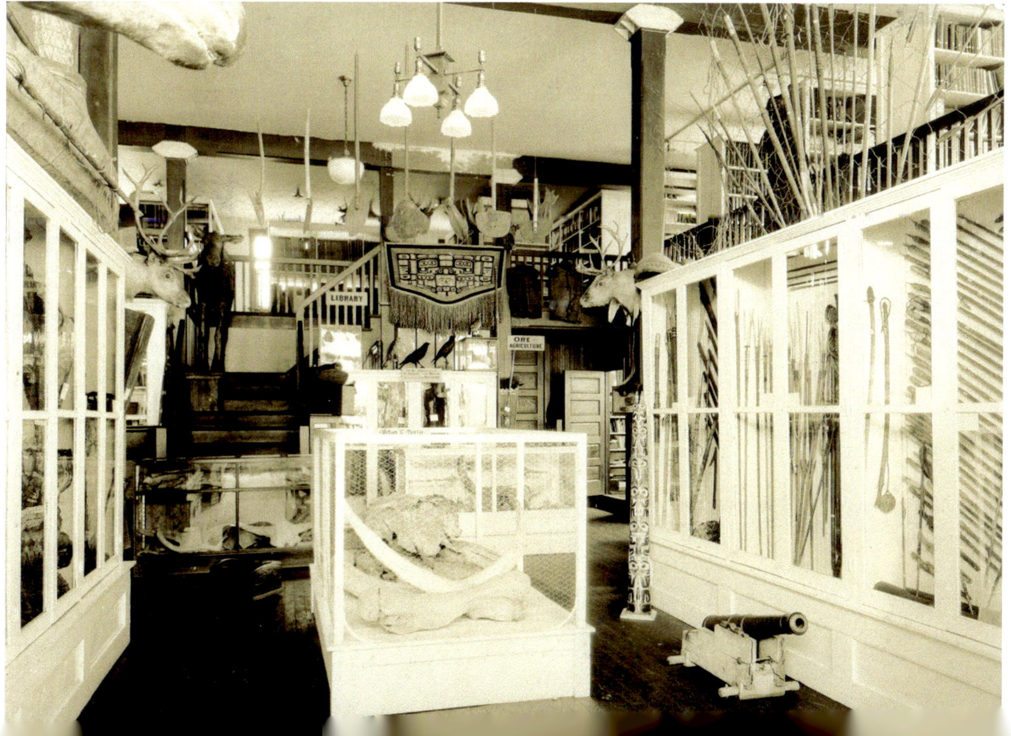

S'igeidí S'íx' Beaver Bowl

On loan from the Deisheetaan clan of Angoon LC.99-1

potlatches, however; they merely moved them underground for the next sixty years.)

Brady also preserved totem poles and ordered carvings for an exhibit, the Louisiana Purchase Centennial Exposition at the 1904 World's Fair in St. Louis. Boosters designed that huge national event to publicize the resources and cities of the West, and Brady wanted to promote Alaska opportunities that could bring development. Exposition organizers premised the anthropology exhibits on the pseudoscientific ideas of the eugenics movement, endorsed at that time by the nation's most prestigious academics, which later inspired Germany's Nazis. In St. Louis, they taught that indigenous people were racially inferior through exhibits that showed "living peoples in their accustomed avocations," displayed like animals in a zoo. They measured and examined these indigenous people as scientific specimens, and, when some died, dissected them. After the exposition, the house posts and some important art returned to Alaska and became foundational holdings of the museum. They stand today at the entrance of the Alaska Gallery, where they were placed with the consultation of Tlingit clans that own the symbols—whose people participate now not as human specimens but as co-curators.

Brady felt the need to commission these works of Southeast Alaska tribal art—as the museum continues to do—because the best work had been stripped from the region by collectors who were funded largely by major universities and big-city museums. The attraction was obvious: the tribes of coastal Alaska and the Canadian northwest created objects of unique beauty and grace and, from the perspective of museum visitors in New York or Berlin, seeing them out of context, impressive objects that emanated mystery and romance. A rush to grab as much as possible kicked off around the time Jackson and Brady arrived, and continued for almost fifty years. Museums leaders called for haste—as did Jackson and Brady—because they expected the cultures that produced the art to soon be eliminated. But competition among the museums drove the real frenzy. George

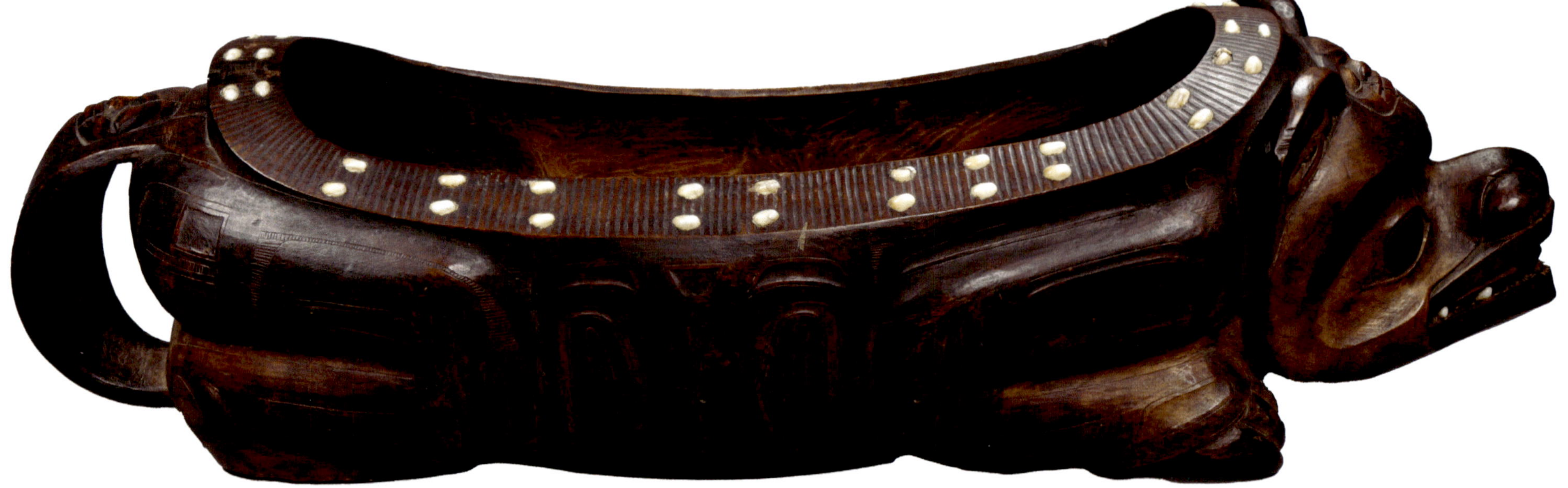

Dorsey of the Field Museum in Chicago kept a count of how many totem poles his museum had acquired compared to the American Museum of Natural History in New York, and called for increased effort when his side wasn't winning. Both museums acquired more art than was left in Alaska, as did museums in Washington, DC, Seattle, Berlin, and elsewhere.

Unfortunately, some of the hurried collectors cared mostly about their trophies and failed to document what the objects meant or who they had belonged to, squandering the cultural and scholarly value of the things they gathered. For example, in Kachemak Bay (outside Southeast Alaska), a village that had been depopulated by Russian fur traders was erased from existence in 1883 by a collector from the Berlin Museum, who took everything that had been left behind without even recording its location, which is permanently lost. In 1930, after this collecting era was complete, a visiting anthropologist observed Native people in British Columbia pretending, during a ceremony, that they were using certain serving pieces in the shapes of animals, imagining they had bowls that now resided in storage cabinets in New York or Paris. Collectors had made sacred objects into commodities, but the spiritual meaning stayed behind with the people through their relationships, practices, and beliefs—and in that sense the tribes retained their patrimony.

Although museums stole some artifacts, they mostly bought pieces from communities that needed money. The lost art is a surface manifestation of a deeper and more important economic story. The rich culture of the Tlingit and Haida of Southeast Alaska had developed amid the great wealth of their salmon streams and trading relationships, but late in the nineteenth century these peoples were under siege from American miners and fishing companies. The first salmon cannery appeared in 1878, and soon companies from the U.S. West Coast had blocked streams across the region, attempting to catch every fish, which left too few to feed Native communities or for spawning that would allow runs to return in future years. Overfishing inflicted hunger on villages that relied on salmon across much of Alaska. Killer epidemics and social disruption also weakened communities and their ability to support themselves. When museum collectors showed up with large sums of money to buy traditional objects, accepting the deal may have been an act of survival, and hardly a fair exchange.

This history is reflected in the strengths and gaps of the Alaska State Museum's collection, which in turn tells the story of difficult times for Native peoples. The 32,000 pieces, of which 3,281 are on display, include relatively little from the Unangax̂ and Sugpiaq/Alutiiq peoples of the Aleutian Islands, Kodiak, and the central Gulf of Alaska coast. Russian fur traders brutally conquered and enslaved those groups beginning in the mid-eighteenth century, and few of their belongings survived outside of Russian museums. But the Russians never penetrated the Interior or Arctic Alaska to a significant degree, and those areas also escaped the extreme competitive collecting that swept through Southeast Alaska. The Iñupiat of the north and the Yup'ik of the west did face hunger from resource loss—Yankee whalers in the late nineteenth century slaughtered whales and other marine mammals they relied on, and miners arrived with diseases and social pressures—but they lost fewer of their cultural treasures. The Alaska State Museum contains much more from those cultures because more art and artifacts remained in the early twentieth century when it began its own collections. Perhaps big-city museum collectors also didn't

Father Andrew P. Kashevaroff in church robes.

ASL-P01-1949

RIGHT

Original flag design by Benny Benson.

Writing below, in Benson's hand, states "The blue field is for the Alaska sky and the Forget-Me-Not, an Alaskan flower. The North Star is for the future state of Alaska, the most northerly in the union. The Dipper is for the Great Bear, symbolising strenth [sic]."

III-O-410

like that art as much as they did the rainforest art of the Tlingit and Haida. Their carvings from big trees bear a resemblance to the highly ornamented style of Beaux Arts decoration that was popular at the time, while the indigenous art of the Arctic is generally sparer and more linear, appealing to modernist sensibilities. Of course, none of the work was originally intended to be décor, but the act of removing it from its context diminished it, in the way that the dominant culture often takes expressive ideas to create products and stereotypes.

What lives did these absent works of art live in distant cities? Nadia Jackinsky-Sethi recalls taking students to the Louvre when she was teaching high school English in Paris. As a member of the Ninilchik tribe of Lower Cook Inlet, she traces her ancestry to the Sugpiaq/Alutiiq people of Kodiak, but Jackinsky-Sethi had earned a degree in art history without ever studying Alaska Native work. In the Louvre, she and her students discovered a spectacular trove of it, mixed with indigenous art from other parts of the world. "That kind of inspired me to think," she recalled. "Why wasn't that part of my own art history education to this point? Why didn't I know that we have all these beautiful things from this region that are no longer there?" Jackinsky-Sethi eventually earned a PhD in art history studying Alaska Native art and has dedicated her career to reviving these ancient artistic traditions. She has also visited works of Alaska Native art in museums around the world.

"For many indigenous peoples, the idea of collections is that they are relatives and they are not just objects, but they have a living soul that is meant to be used and meant to be part of our communities and our everyday life," she said. "I want to be given privacy with the materials that I'm working with. And I feel like that really makes a difference when you can pick something

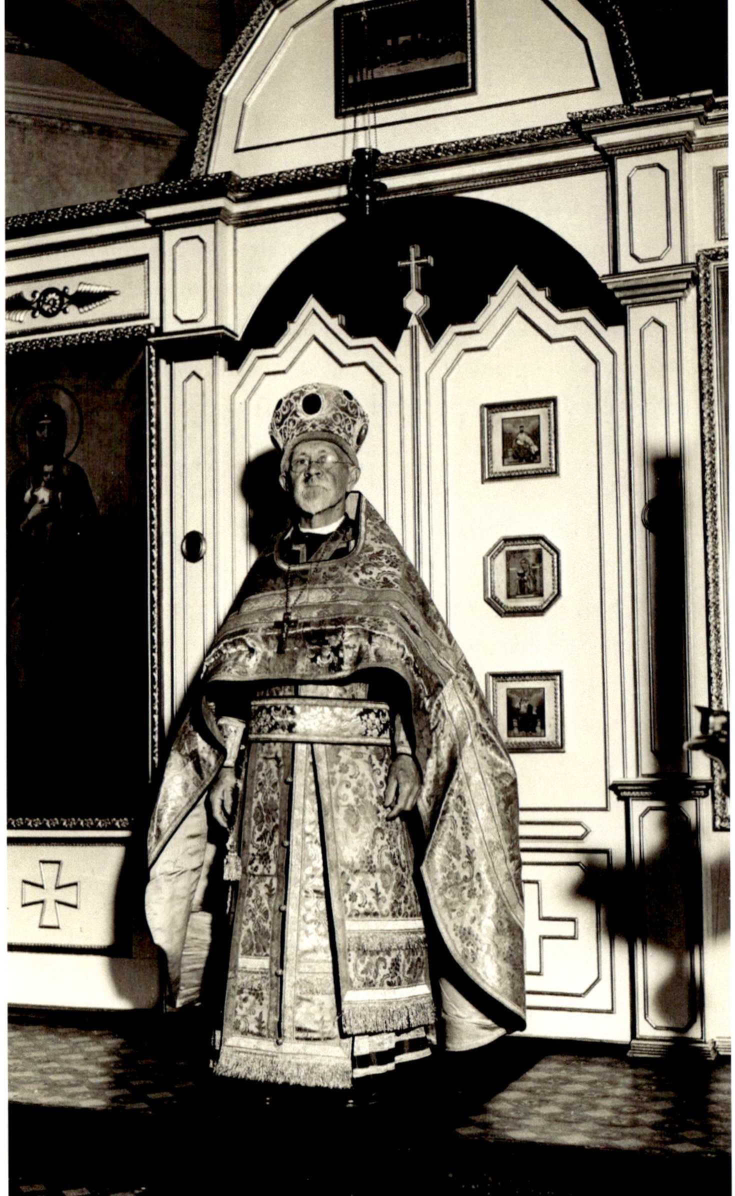

The blue field is for the Alaskan sky and the for-get-me-not, an Alaskan flower.

The north star is for the future state of Alask the most northerly of the Union. The dipper is for the Great Bear or Symbolizing, strength.

up and when you can hold it and you get that sense of feeling and touching something that someone you were related to might have made. I think that's really powerful. And when you see something on display, that same emotion, does that really happen? And sometimes it's really sad and painful. You see things that are on display being unused or being ignored."

A man of Alaska Native ancestry first made Alaska's museum something more than a storehouse. In November 1919, Father Kashevaroff needed a job. Two months earlier, the Russian Revolution had halted his salary as the priest at the St. Nicholas Russian Orthodox Church on Fifth Street in Juneau, although he never stopped performing his duties there, even when he became the full-time museum director. Kashevaroff had been born in 1863 on Kodiak Island, the descendent of an eighteenth-century Russian colonist and an indigenous woman he had married. As a teacher and priest, Kashevaroff served indigenous people across the coast of the Gulf of Alaska, sometimes traveling by kayak or dogsled, at churches in Kodiak, at Nuchek (a village in Prince William Sound that was later abandoned), and, in Southeast Alaska, at Angoon and Juneau, as well as at Sitka, where, in 1893, he married Martha Bolshanin. She was a member of the Kiks.ádi clan of the Tlingit, and Kashevaroff

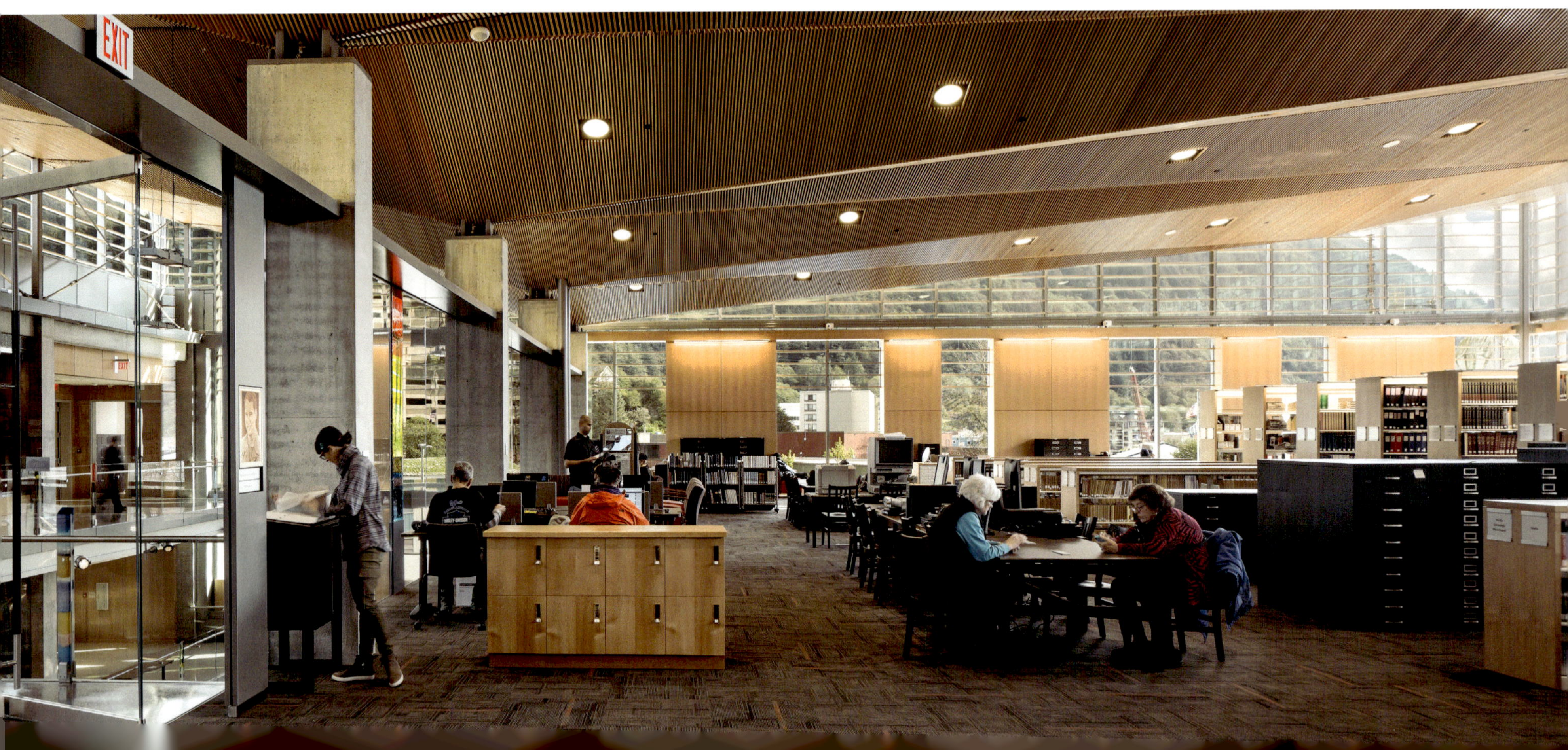

The Alaska State Library on the second floor of the Andrew P. Kashevaroff Building.

© Lara Swimmer Photography

was adopted into an Eagle moiety clan upon their marriage (the Tlingit are divided into two moieties, and custom strictly forbade marriage to a member of one's own moiety). The couple had eleven children. By the time Kashevaroff became the director of the museum, he was widely liked and trusted for his warmth and his unequaled knowledge of Alaska history and cultures, as curator Henrikson wrote in a brief biography. As a beloved teacher, musician, and scholar, with skill in languages and many friends, Kashevaroff coaxed out new objects for the museum from villages that the well-heeled collectors of big-city museums had declared already stripped clean, enabling him to add thousands of items to the museum.

A writer from Milwaukee recalled a 1930 Juneau meeting with Kashaveroff: "Our favorite refuge from the rains was the Territorial Museum, whose most interesting 'exhibit' was its curator, Father A. P. Kashevaroff. There was an old-world charm about him that seemed incongruous in that lusty mining town. His dark, clerical garb accentuated his snow-white Van Dyke. He was small and retiring, but to talk with him for a minute was to feel the force of an extraordinary personality."

Kashevaroff guided the museum for twenty years, until his death in 1940, a period between the two world wars when time slowed down in Alaska. The chaotic population boom of the gold rush had ended and many of the boomtowns had disappeared, leaving the north country a forgotten frontier with technology and lifestyles left over from the previous century. It was during this time that Kashevaroff visited the Wallace family and acquired the 1804 Russian double-headed eagle crest from their toy box. He also recovered an unexploded shell from Angoon, where the U.S. Navy had bombarded the Xutsnoowú Tlingit clan in 1882 without meaningful provocation, killing six children and destroying homes, canoes, and winter food supplies. And, in 1927, when the territorial governor announced a contest to design a new flag, which boosters hoped would someday become the flag for a new state of Alaska, Kashevaroff saved all the entries, including the winning Big Dipper design by Benny Benson, an Unangan boy living in a Seward home for displaced children. Benson's flag flew over the Territorial Capitol, built in 1931, where the museum itself resided for thirty years.

The museum depicts that prewar period, but the objects often look much older than they are. Henrikson said the material culture on display from early twentieth-century Alaska, if found in a museum representing another region of the United States, would be typical of the 1870s or even earlier. But change came rapidly. "After World War II, we had all this new modern infrastructure that the government and industry built upon to create a much more modern place," he said.

Benny Benson's life spanned that change. When he entered the Jesse Lee Home orphanage as a toddler in 1916, Alaskans traveled by boat and dogsled and communication was slow and uncertain—and that pioneer life persisted, even in the cities, until the U.S. military arrived to fight the Japanese, with bloody battles in the Aleutian Islands and fortifications all over the territory. Development leapt forward sixty years in less than a decade after the war, as a new flood of Americans arrived, many of them veterans looking for new country. They demanded that Alaska be allowed to become a state so they could vote and participate as full citizens. The discovery of oil on the Kenai Peninsula in 1957 and Alaska's increasing political sophistication persuaded Congress to admit it and put the forty-ninth star on the American flag in 1959. The Territorial Capitol became the State Capitol, with Benson's flag still flying there. In 1969, when

Apollo 11 carried the Alaska flag to the moon, Alaskans were able to watch the landing live on television. In the museum, you can see the flag that went to the moon, with its golden Big Dipper and North Star on a field of blue. Benson was fifty-six years old when that happened. He told a TV interviewer, "I think that was quite a deal."

At that time, in the late 1960s, Alaska stood on the threshold of a burst of change that would dwarf all those that came before. The discovery of oil on the North Slope would bring extraordinary wealth. Congress would settle Alaska Natives' land claims, which led to their new economic and political power. And the map of Alaska would be resolved, with the final closing of the westward expansion of American settlement in the public domain. In that moment of optimism, Alaska finally established a proper state museum, with its own building, the predecessor of the current Kashevaroff building. As the state came into its own identity, that building rose in Juneau as an intentional act of self-definition.

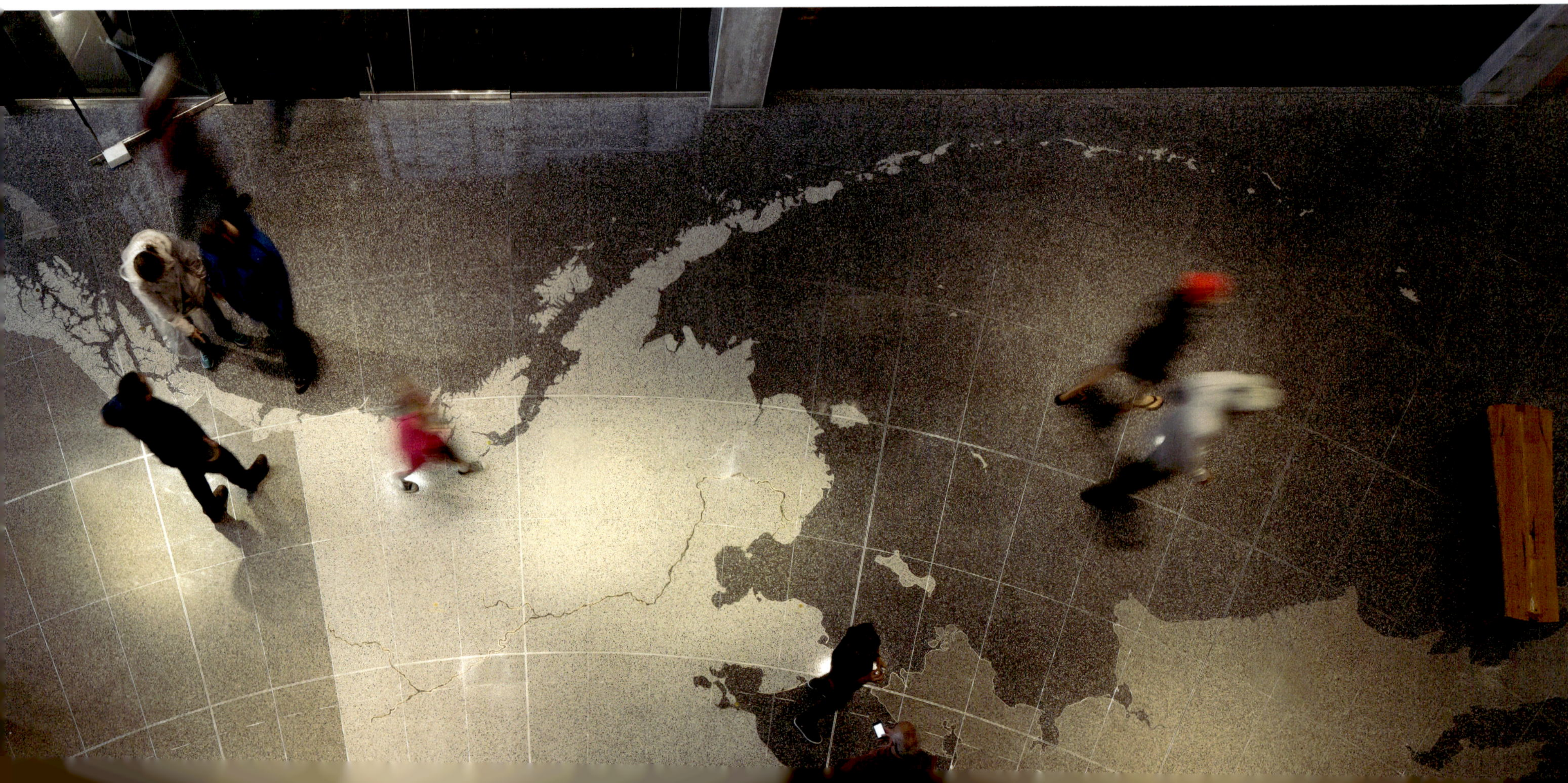

A map of Alaska in the terrazzo floor of the atrium.

© Lara Swimmer Photography

3.

Bob Banghart, who came to work at the museum in 1974, received the assignment to install a spruce tree within the spiral ramp inside its rotunda, upon whose limbs would perch a group of taxidermied bald eagles. For decades, that tree stood as a beloved touchstone of the museum and of Juneau itself, for children, including young versions of me and of Sarah Asper-Smith, my partner in creating this book, and also for adults, as all were enchanted by the circular walk up into the branches, with the occasional sound of the eagle's cry, and the changing perspectives on the vertical diorama of the rainforest gradually unfolding from every angle.

Forty years after construction of the 1967 museum, Banghart found himself again involved, now responsible for dismantling the tree as the building came down to make room for the new Kashevaroff building. During the old museum's life, he'd had a successful career as a facility developer—and as a musician—and now he returned as deputy director of the division overseeing the museum, library, and archives, and was tasked with rebuilding it. He'd hitchhiked to Alaska as a young man, studied art at the University of Alaska–Fairbanks, and taught himself cowboy fiddle playing. When we talked for this essay, after his lifetime in Alaska, he still had the drawl and mustache of a cowboy, and the frankness of one, too. Back when he had originally erected the tree, he had been so new an Alaskan that he couldn't tell a Sitka spruce branch from a pine or hemlock. Now he knew a lot about Alaska, but the job would be harder in other ways. The world had changed. The tree he had preserved in the 1970s with formaldehyde and assembled with a compound containing asbestos, and which so many treasured for so many years, now had to be designated a hazardous material site, to be encapsulated and disposed of by specialists in protective suits before the building could be demolished.

The cultural changes since 1967 were even more complicated. Even the meaning of Alaska had changed. In 1967, Alaska was a proud, brand-new state celebrating the centennial of the Alaska Purchase. Alaska Natives were fighting for their land and rights, but participated enthusiastically in the celebration—Don Wright, a key leader in that fight, at the same time worked as director of one of the centennial celebration facilities in Anchorage, and indigenous communities around the state mounted their own centennial projects. As the next anniversary approached, fifty years later, Republican governor Sean Parnell and lieutenant governor Mead Treadwell supported another vigorous celebration, including replacing the museum, and worked with Banghart to commission a bronze statue of William Seward, the secretary of state who negotiated the Treaty of Cession with Russia in 1867 (Seward was also an important abolitionist and President Abraham Lincoln's right hand during the Civil War). Alaska has a Seward Day holiday and many places are named after him. But attitudes had changed. After 2014, when Bill Walker and Byron Mallott, running as independents, replaced Parnell and Treadwell, some indigenous people opposed the statue. Mallott tried to mitigate concerns by redesigning the state seal to include indigenous references, but gave up on the effort, Banghart said. When the Seward statue went up in 2017, some Native leaders supported it, but the preeminent cultural leader of the Tlingit, Rosita Worl of the Sealaska Institute, reminded Walker and Mallott that her people had opposed the treaty back in 1867. She linked Seward to imperialism and White supremacism.

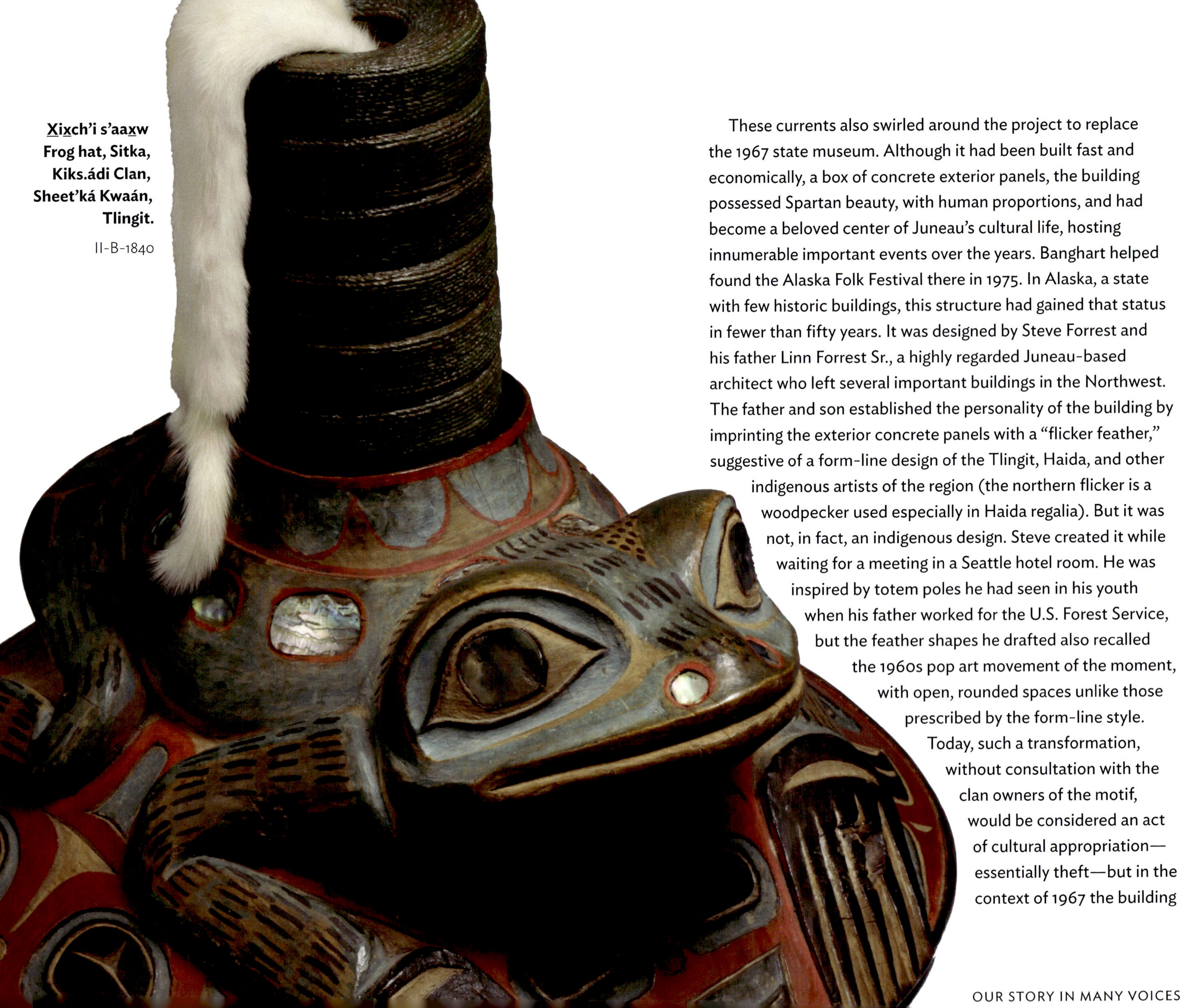

Xixch'i s'aaxw Frog hat, Sitka, Kiks.ádi Clan, Sheet'ká Kwaán, Tlingit.
II-B-1840

These currents also swirled around the project to replace the 1967 state museum. Although it had been built fast and economically, a box of concrete exterior panels, the building possessed Spartan beauty, with human proportions, and had become a beloved center of Juneau's cultural life, hosting innumerable important events over the years. Banghart helped found the Alaska Folk Festival there in 1975. In Alaska, a state with few historic buildings, this structure had gained that status in fewer than fifty years. It was designed by Steve Forrest and his father Linn Forrest Sr., a highly regarded Juneau-based architect who left several important buildings in the Northwest. The father and son established the personality of the building by imprinting the exterior concrete panels with a "flicker feather," suggestive of a form-line design of the Tlingit, Haida, and other indigenous artists of the region (the northern flicker is a woodpecker used especially in Haida regalia). But it was not, in fact, an indigenous design. Steve created it while waiting for a meeting in a Seattle hotel room. He was inspired by totem poles he had seen in his youth when his father worked for the U.S. Forest Service, but the feather shapes he drafted also recalled the 1960s pop art movement of the moment, with open, rounded spaces unlike those prescribed by the form-line style. Today, such a transformation, without consultation with the clan owners of the motif, would be considered an act of cultural appropriation—essentially theft—but in the context of 1967 the building quickly became an admired and beloved landmark for its beauty and the unique combination of modernist brutalism and this regional theme.

In 2010, when discussion of the replacement project went public, community meetings flowed with affection and nostalgia for the old museum, the eagle tree—and the flicker feathers. At the same time, the state's Office of History and Archaeology declared the building eligible to be a historic landmark, citing its one-of-a-kind design. The Juneau Planning Commission called for at least one of the concrete panels to be preserved, and the state historic preservation officer made that one of three conditions of tearing down the landmark. Banghart didn't like the idea. He wanted to start clean and sympathized with Native people who found the flicker feathers inauthentic and objectionable. Architect Brian Meissner recalled how that issue hung over the project as contractors tried to remove the panels, which were attached to the building's steel frame by rusted connections, and were coated with dangerous friable asbestos. He said, "Ultimately the panels ended up getting destroyed as the building was taken down just because of the way they were attached, and with that asbestos, you had to take them apart, and they all broke. Which is probably in the end fortuitous because they were so loaded with this cultural pain." But he said the feather concept did survive. A renowned Native artist executed a new flicker feather design using the correct form-line style, which the museum has occasionally used as a motif.

Meissner's firm, ECI, also commissioned a book about the 1967 centennial celebration to mitigate the demolition of the old museum (ECI, based in Anchorage, partnered in the overall project with Portland's Tom Hacker, who was lead designer of the new museum). Meissner contracted with Tricia Brown, a respected Alaska book editor, and she engaged six of Alaska's best writers and six of its best photographers to fan out across the state, documenting the history and fate of the forty-two projects funded by the Alaska Purchase Centennial Commission in the 1960s. The book, *The View from the Future—2017: Fifty Years After the Alaska Purchase Centennial*, is a fascinating read. It brings back a time that was remarkably different, in good ways as well as bad. The State of Alaska was brand new in 1962, when Governor Bill Egan began planning for the centennial. Still wobbling on training wheels, the government was chronically short of money and lacked public facilities far more basic than a central museum. Alaska in those days lacked, in fact, a sense of permanence, and lacked even a firm agreement, among its youthful and highly transient non-Native population, that Alaska would ever be a place to stay and raise a family, rather than just a place to make a buck and leave. The centennial focused on the future: on building community institutions of connection and stability, on building a home. Every town nominated a project, offering to match federal funding. Those that were selected doubled the number of Alaska's museums, added many community centers and libraries, preserved totem poles, and created centers for indigenous and contemporary art. A good many of the facilities did become permanent.

Juneau was engaged at that time in a many-year battle to retain its status as the state capital against *Anchorage Times* publisher Bob Atwood, who believed the capital should be nearer the state's population center, and who had the power to repeatedly force the issue. The Alaska Centennial State Museum was intended to help cement Juneau's position, and to show the city's resolve. City leaders donated property the military had created during World War II, when engineers dumped mining waste onto the intertidal lands in front of the Native village, and voters overwhelmingly approved a sales tax to pay for much of the cost of construction. The building went up in a rush, Juneau transferred it to the state, and Governor Wally Hickel received the keys just after the centennial year ended. It was nicknamed the Million-Dollar Museum—locals considered that a high price for a museum—with the federal government contributing two-thirds of the cash and the sales tax one-third (adding the value of the donated land made the contributions even). Many Alaska Natives joined in the community's pride in the museum, as several elders have told me. The centennial, whatever its underlying meaning, had succeeded in uniting Alaskans, honoring their cultures, and lending a new sense of purpose and permanence to their shared state.

But even this good story, beautifully told in Brown's book, could not escape the crosswinds of December 2014. Banghart's boss, the director of the Division of Libraries, Archives and Museums, which was officially the book's publisher, essentially disavowed it, writing in a preface on page 10 that its narrowness was forced by the dictates of the historical preservation authority, and denouncing America's "imperialist" takeover of Alaska Native lands as unworthy of celebration. In my opinion, the preface was wrong, imposing today's frame of reference on the events of 1967, and attributing a view to the Alaska Natives of that time that the evidence shows many did not share. The book itself disappeared, with distribution only by a single shop in Juneau. Its carefully prepared digital version was not released by the state library.

Banghart does not believe his state agency intentionally suppressed the book (at this writing, he no longer works for the state). The more important point, he said, is that the old museum evolved culturally as Alaska's people did, because it kept a close relationship with those it represented. There were flaws in the exhibits in the old museum that even its lovers admit. The Alaska Native section treated indigenous cultures as largely a thing of the past, rather than communicating their vibrant contemporary life. The history section started with the arrival of pioneers and told their triumphal story without enough context about their impact on the land or the first people, or about the setbacks and busts that have made Alaska's economic progress far from linear. But, all in all, the old museum told the story of its

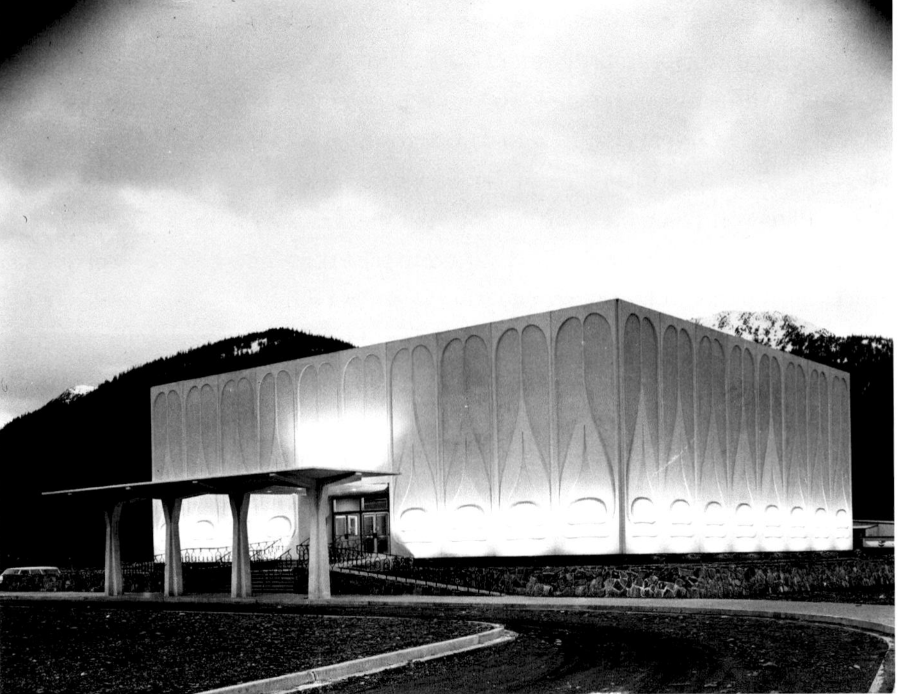

The newly constructed Alaska State Museum in 1968.

AHS-P283-2-468

objects honestly and was not afraid to change. Even at the end, it did not feel dated or irrelevant.

The museum changed, in part, by recognizing that the meaning of some of its holdings would not remain static. It began sharing its objects with tribes almost a decade before Congress passed the 1990 Native American Graves Protection and Repatriation Act, which governs the return of sacred items and human remains. A key example is the Xixch'i s'aaxw, or frog hat (see page 64), from the Kiks.ádi Tlingit that sits in the clan house exhibit, but has frequently been taken out for use. The hat, which is at least ten generations old, was made for the clan's most respected leaders to wear during important ceremonies. The six rings on top represent the six slaves who were ceremonially killed in honor of the formal naming of the hat in the early nineteenth century. It belonged to the entire clan, but in the 1970s the hat disappeared into a private collection after a member sold it without permission. In 1981, it came up for auction in New York, and the only way to recover the hat was for the clan to buy it back—which the clan could not afford to do. So the museum teamed with the Native-owned Sealaska Foundation and the Central Council of the Tlingit and Haida Indians of Alaska to purchase the hat, with a joint ownership agreement that allows the clan to use it whenever it desires. The hat was taken out and worn eighty or ninety times in the next forty years.

Around that time, various other museum objects also began to be used as they were originally intended. On a visit, you will often see empty spots in the cases where clan belongings are absent because they are in use. Tribal members walk out the door with these treasures—something that would normally drive a museum professional mad with anxiety, but here they are accustomed to it—and the items leave in the trunk of a car or down the ferry ramp, off to mark a funeral or another rite of passage, to be returned in due time. "That came with a set of rigid applications at one point, which I kind of just dispensed with when I was running the show," said Banghart, who became curator of exhibitions in 2007 and chief curator in 2009. "I just said, 'You want it, come get it. No insurance, no nothing. I don't want to see a special bag built for this or anything. Bring it back when you're done with it.'" He believed something else was more valuable than the objects in the collection. "The only thing of value in an institution like this is trust," he said. And nothing bad has happened yet. (A curator said the museum currently does provide appropriate containers and insurance.)

Banghart said these cultures are alive and their belongings are part of that life—until a museum or collector kills the connection by putting their things in storage or locking them behind glass. Even elevating the artifacts' scientific value can be fatal, he said, akin to viewing them as financial assets, as in the antiquities market. Cultural meaning is not static, to be gleaned from examination of a thing, but can only be understood fully through the ongoing connection to living humans. But once down the road to commodification, Banghart said, human greed, of various kinds, makes it difficult to bring back an object to its true context, and most indigenous art from this part of Alaska left a long time ago.

Banghart told me of his frustration when he traveled to Berlin for a weeklong museum symposium with academics holding a vast collection of Alaska indigenous art, who wanted to reinterpret it for a new exhibit in the Humboldt Forum. Their intent was right, he said, to dispel the romanticism that had clung for a century to the interpretation of these objects. But the

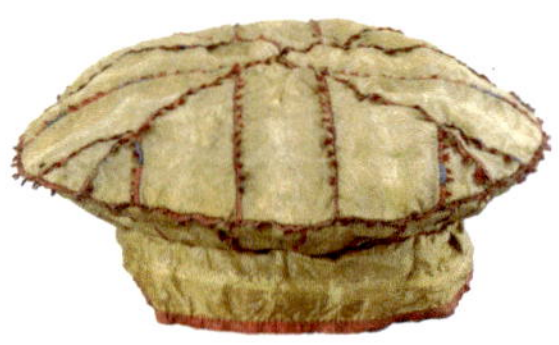

Sailor-style hat

Made with sea mammal gut.

Unangax̂ or Sugpiaq/Alutiiq, circa 1888.

2008-10-1

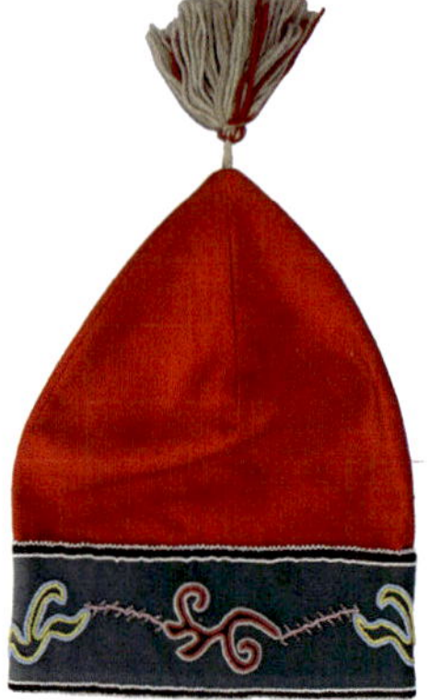

Touque-style hat, likely styled after hats worn by French-Canadian fur traders.

Tlingit, early 20th century.

II-B-1601

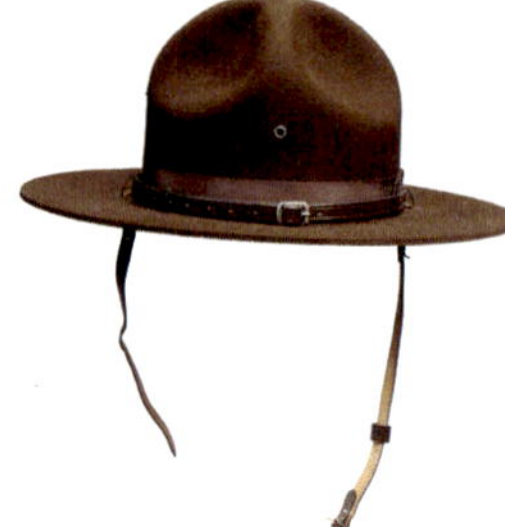

Brown felt Alaska State Trooper hat with chin strap.

2008-28-8

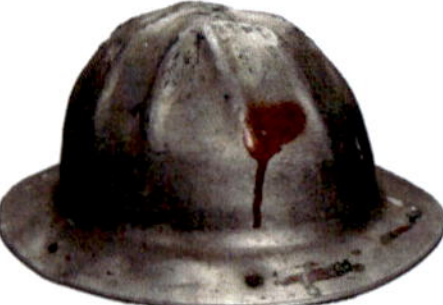

Sawmill hardhat.

2015-15-6

professors still talked about the belongings as content, not as part of a cultural process—they still didn't get it. "It was remarkable how uneducated those educated people were when it came to understanding that an indigenous culture is a dynamic that only needs to be examined through the eyes of another human being to gain insights. It's people. You don't want to put all of these edifices of academics around and try to identify it by pulling it out of context. You have to get in the middle of it. You have to be part of it. You have to laugh, cry, die with the community."

In 2004, Henrikson brought a truckload of objects from the museum to Sitka for a potlatch the Kaagwaantaan clan held to commemorate the centennial of its "last" potlatch. The University of Pennsylvania brought four hats it had held since the 1920s, buying an airplane ticket for each hat and four more tickets for a staff member to ride next to each hat. Henrikson brought the huge house posts and screen from the museum, the pieces that had been carved for the event Governor Brady ordered in 1904, as well as other tribal items grand enough to transform a gymnasium at Sheldon Jackson College into a clan house. He recalled, "I'll never forget driving that large, rusty old UPS-type van with a history of brake problems, loaded with millions of dollars' worth of priceless artifacts, down the ramp onto the ferry—with an open door and open water immediately ahead. I had plans, if the brakes failed, to sideswipe an RV on the way down and try to wedge the van against the hull to keep it from hitting the water. Luckily, we made it over and back to Sitka without any trouble. It sure was about the greatest ceremony I've been to."

With the museum's new openness, it participated in a great cultural change in Alaska over a half century. In the 1990s, as Alaska Native corporations rose in economic power, media carried reports of anti-Native racism and politicians pushed against indigenous rights. A ballot initiative proclaimed English the official language, shunting aside languages spoken here thousands of years earlier. Legislators neglected dilapidated rural Alaska schools while spending generously on city schools, until a court ruled their policy was racist and unconstitutional. The legislature refused to acknowledge Native subsistence hunting and fishing rights, even when federal law required a rural priority. Alaska Native groups held large protest rallies in the streets of Anchorage. A new, more militant generation rose, reclaiming disused cultural symbols and practices—although with meanings that were in some cases reconstructed rather than having been passed on through generations. Today, practices not seen in a century have returned, such as facial tattooing, and many young Alaska Natives have begun using names from their indigenous languages. Power shifted. In 2014, the State of Alaska added to its official languages, in addition to English, Iñupiaq, Siberian Yupik, Central Alaskan Yup'ik, Alutiiq, Unangax̂, Dena'ina, Deg Xinag, Holikachuk, Koyukon, Upper Kuskokwim, Gwich'in, Tanana, Upper Tanana, Tanacross, Han, Ahtna, Eyak, Tlingit, Haida, and Tsimshian.

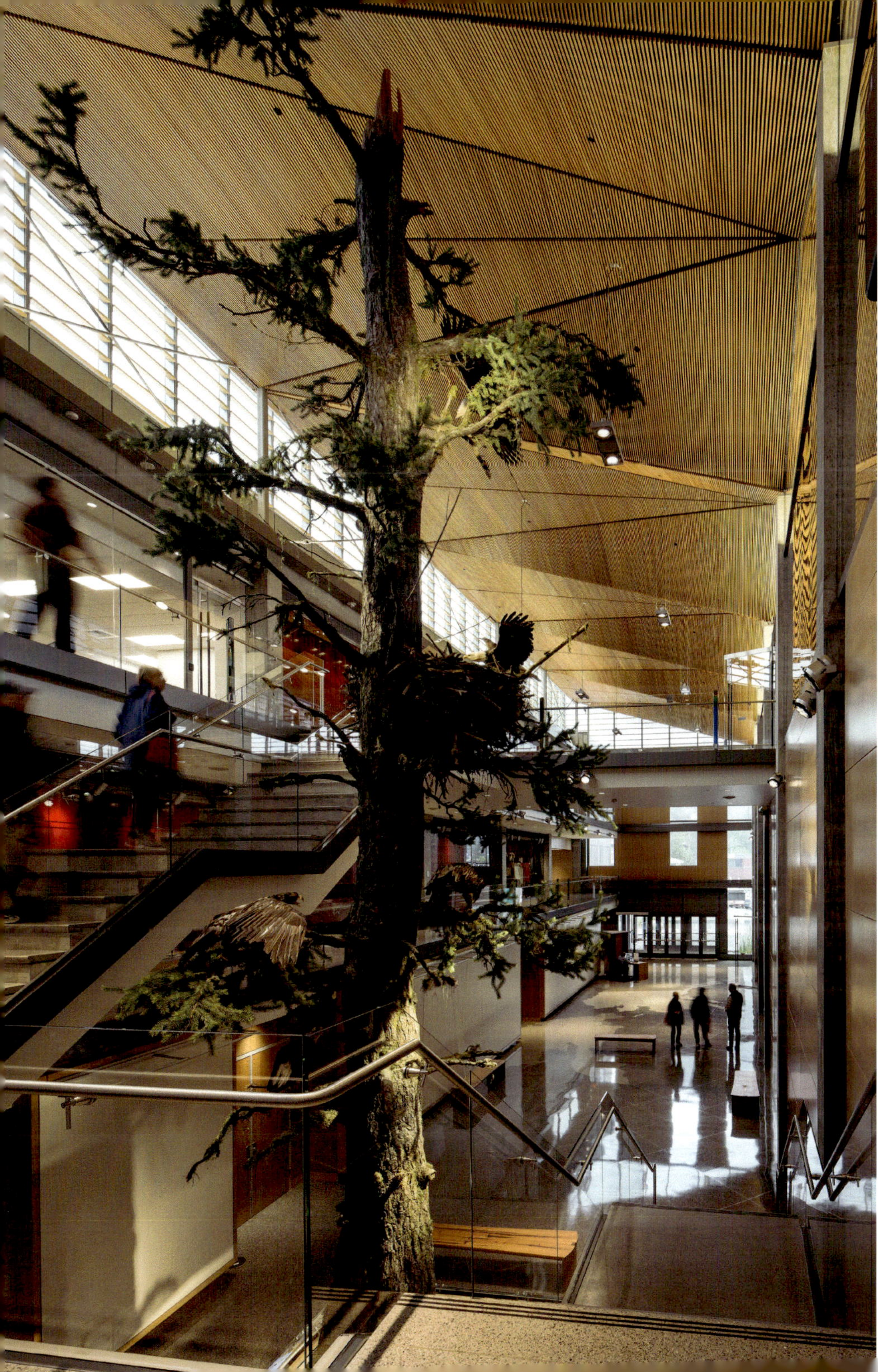

Eagle tree.

© Lara Swimmer Photography

Bob Sam participated in this movement, and is an example, with his life, of how culture evolves. As an elder of Juneau's L'eeneidí clan who lives in Sitka, he takes care of cemeteries, a responsibility to the ancestors that comes from his Tlingit heritage by virtue of his name, Shaagunnastkaa, which came from his shaman great-grandfather—but he also lives part of the year in Hokkaido, Japan, and is a Shinto priest. Sam told me he became involved in repatriating tribal belongings from museums when he saw what he believes were the remains of his great-grandfather on display in New York. He never succeeded in recovering those remains, but he became expert at using the 1990 Native American Graves Protection and Repatriation Act early on, challenging museums holding tribal artifacts, and he has brought back a great trove of his clan's belongings from the American Museum of Natural History and the Smithsonian Institution, including the many shamanistic tools of his great-grandfather. Now those items reside in the storage facilities of the Alaska State Museum, which he trusts and believes is a safer place than his own home in Sitka (at the request of the tribe, funerary and shaman objects are not displayed). "It can be said that shamanism is dead. I could take those objects and burn them, like some Christian people want me to, but I chose to keep them in the museum under my care, and we've never brought them out," Sam said. When he walks into the museum today, he feels pride and belonging. "I just don't have the words for how beautiful the artwork is," he said. "There's a term called feng shui. That's what that represents to me. . . . When I walk into the museum and see that artwork, it is 'everyone is welcome.' And you immediately feel that welcome. And when you look at the artwork, it's pure traditional Tlingit art. Pure."

Like everyone, he likes the eagle tree, which in the new building occupies a corner of the high, light atrium, with a staircase that wraps around. The 1975 tree was a real tree, assembled by a recently graduated art student who would have attached pine branches to its spruce trunk if not for the timely intervention of an older woman at the museum who gently corrected him—the young Bob Banghart. This time around, Banghart just watched. A museum exhibit company in Minnesota called Split Rock brought on an artist to create the tree out of completely synthetic materials, bigger than the old tree because the space is bigger, but with an appearance of startling verisimilitude. Architect Meissner said builders left the roof off the atrium so the tree could be lowered carefully into place by crane, and that is how it was planted, gliding slowly down from the sky.

4.

On a Monday during his lunch hour in July 2013, Aaron Elmore, a junior member of the Alaska State Museum's small staff, wrote an email to his colleagues outlining a set of reasons for supporting a provocative plan: to fire the company designing the new museum's exhibits and have in-house employees do it themselves. He copied Banghart and Henrikson; Asper-Smith, a home-grown exhibit consultant who had recently received a museum studies master's degree; Paul Gardinier, the curator of collections as well as a gregarious and well-loved sculptor and musical instrument maker; and Elmore's fellow exhibit specialist Jackie Manning, whose abstract paintings had been shown in the museum. All had either many years of experience at the museum or deep roots in Juneau. Elmore wrote, "I think we are uniquely qualified for the job."

Meissner's architectural firm had partnered with an exhibit design company from Vancouver, British Columbia. That's a conventional approach in museum construction, as the exhibits can represent a substantial portion of the total cost. Here the building cost $100 million and the contents another $39 million. Elmore wrote in his email about the impossibility that the Canadian contractors, simply by visiting Juneau, could learn what the museum's collection truly meant to members of Alaska's cultures—they would inevitably make errors. Asper-Smith said, "A lot of the time you hire a firm from Outside and you spend half the time explaining what Alaska is all about." Her master's thesis advocated for Alaskans to tell their own stories. Banghart worried that outsourcing the project to a hired firm risked damaging the trust the museum had built with the people it represented. When initial designs arrived, Banghart's fears were realized. "It was Anyplace, U.S.A. Put your name here," he said. The Vancouver firm's design reflected a style recognizable from National Park Service visitor centers, with little use of artifacts, many technological and constructed artificial features, and an easy-to-grasp instructional approach open to a single interpretation.

For Meissner, the museum staff's complaints were unwelcome news and a professional challenge. A long process ensued as contracts with the first and then a second outside exhibit design company were set aside, and as the clock ticked down for opening the building on schedule in 2016. But in hindsight, he said, the decision to have the Alaska staff build the exhibits was right—and indeed was the only decision that would have worked. The Alaska State Museum should not be like a visitor center. "There's a lack of authenticity, whether it's the constructed animal or the simulated landscape or the simulated whatever," he said. "A Sesame Street reality. And what the Alaska State Museum wanted to try and do was: We have objects, and they're real, and they can help us tell a story or engage in a difficult conversation. That hopefully can lead to some cultural healing and understanding. So, let's use the real things. Let's be authentic."

Besides, he said, the museum had a strong team, with artistically talented designers equal to anyone from an outside firm, and a depth of knowledge about the collection that would take a lifetime to replicate. Gardinier drew floorplans of the exhibits with contours and sightlines that matched the flow of Alaska's story: a big, connected space where you can see continuities among Alaska Native cultures and times; a narrow chokepoint at the historical break and cultural disruption when Europeans first arrived; and then branching paths in the complex

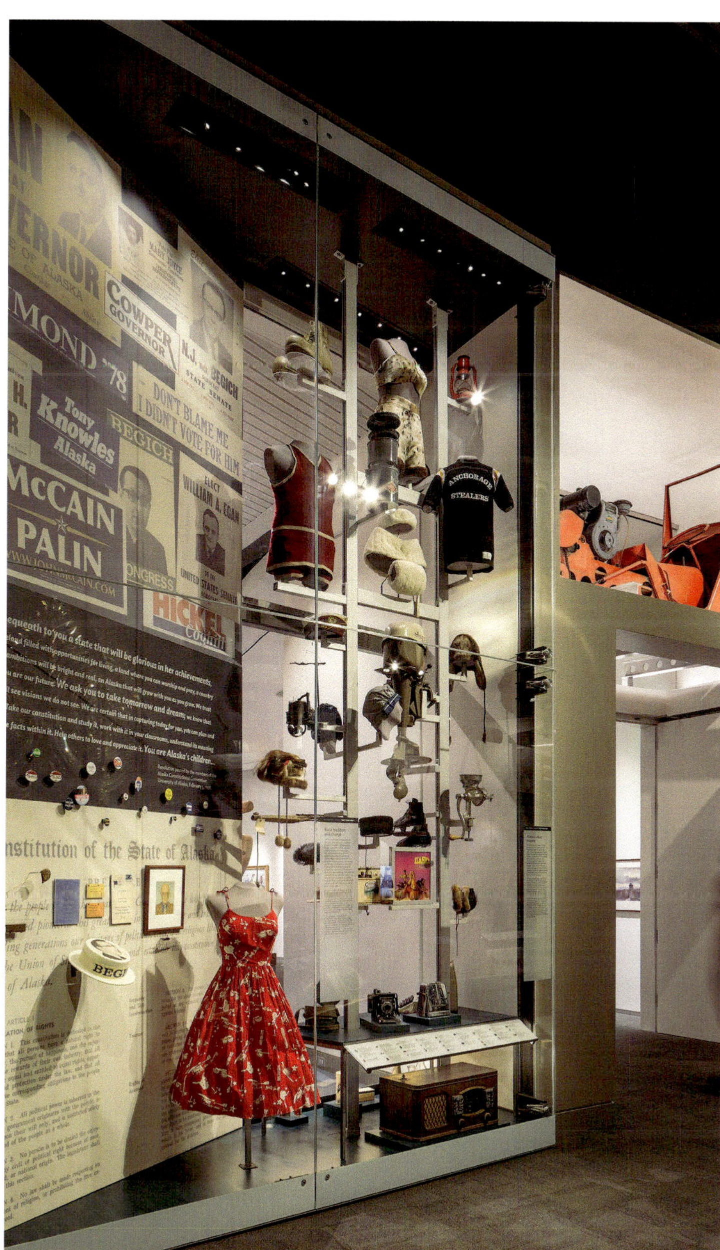

Contemporary Alaska exhibit.

© Lara Swimmer Photography

and unsettled twentieth-century period. Manning experimented with layouts of the display cases on butcher paper, creating artistically pleasing compositions of shapes and colors, while Henrikson, at her side, countered with his views on the objects' meaning and relationships, and advocated always to add more. The designs sometimes placed contemporary art next to ancient artifacts or mixed cultures and geographies, making surprising and subtle connections.

"The artifacts were their medium," Henrikson said of the artists. "They loved having conversations between two or three objects in the same area." In this vision, the galleries would become three-dimensional art installations through which visitors could walk, with learning that would feel more like an artistic experience than an instructional one. Henrikson said, "We really wanted it to reflect reality and we didn't want to make it easy for people. We knew that some people were not going to get it, and some people would be threatened by it. But other people would start to make some of these connections between different people and cultures and time periods, too."

How many visitors would deeply understand those ideas? Most would be coming briefly from docked cruise ships, often bringing only superficial knowledge of Alaska. But Banghart wasn't concerned. "I don't care about that," he said. "What I was more concerned about was establishing and reinforcing the relationship we had with the communities that produced that material." He hoped the museum could contribute as a participant to future generations of Alaska cultural development. "If people come in and they're confused and they are internally challenged by what they see, because they're not sure how that all plays out, then that's fine. I don't have a problem with that," he said. "I'm at odds with a lot of my museum cohorts in that respect, because there's this idea you've got to run everything down into an educational format of comprehension for a ten-year-old. I'm like, 'Oh, fuck that.' I don't really like having a conversation with someone that teaches me as if I'm ten years old."

It's surprising that a conservative state with a conservative Republican governor—Parnell—entrusted this group of employees with the money and the mission to tell the state's story in this way—actually, it's amazing. Several fortunate circumstances combined to make it possible, besides Parnell's personal support and his relationship with Banghart: a period of high oil prices filled Alaska's oil-dependent treasury, a gradual rise of community momentum grew behind the project, and a deadline approached with the anniversary of the treaty with Russia that made Alaska part of the United States. Museum supporters had begun working on the idea, trying to acquire land, in 1995. Their efforts over two decades shaped relationships with state leaders of both parties in the Capitol, who live much of the year in Juneau's small-town culture. A pair of Democratic state senators who became close friends made the building their cause—Dennis Egan of Juneau and Johnny Ellis of Anchorage, and Ellis got money for the land in 2002 and more to begin design five years later. Henrikson began meeting with community and cultural groups around that time to discuss what they wanted from the exhibits. When Parnell became governor in 2010, he let the project go ahead, even though it was not fully funded—not even the design was fully funded—and Meissner's firm came on board with the goal of opening in six years, in time for the sesquicentennial.

Although he partnered with Hacker from Portland, Meissner wanted to create an Alaskan building that would fit its place and community. Frequently, architects from outside Alaska arrive to make grand statements about the landscape, an impulse evident in the major museum in Anchorage, with its façade like an icy block of glass, and in Fairbanks at the University of Alaska, whose museum features a swooping shape as white as an iceberg. Alaska-made architecture, to the extent that there is a local style, instead says more about living in this landscape than copying it. As a northern design exponent has observed, we have enough ice already. The best Alaska building exteriors use warm colors and welcoming, protective shapes, with interiors that take advantage of their spectacular settings by looking outward on them—as the Kashevaroff building's design ultimately did, after many community meetings and iterations, with an approach that Meissner described as letting go of exciting architectural ideas to do what people wanted and needed.

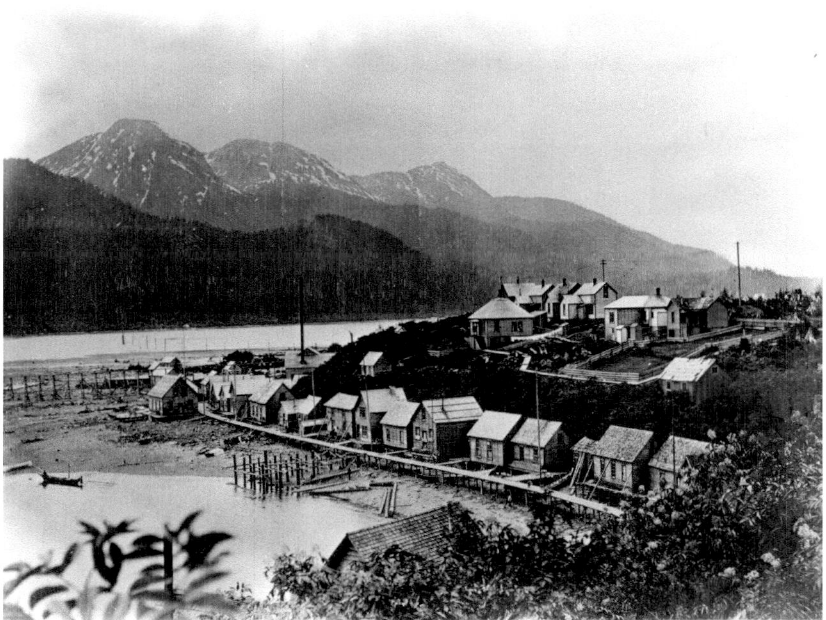

Aak'w Kwaán village in the early 1900s, now the site of the Alaska State Museum.

ASL-P155-1-01

The place—the site—had wounds. A 1940 aerial photograph shows the area as a bay among long piers and boardwalks in front of the Aak'w Kwaán village and fishing waters. During World War II, military engineers filled those tidelands to create port property, using waste rock generated by the Alaska-Juneau Gold Mine, which for thirty years had tunneled into the mountain behind the city (and which shut down because of the war). The fill buried a creek crossing the shore, which thenceforth flowed inside a pipe. A tank farm operated on filled land nearby, behind the spot where the centennial museum went up in 1967. By the time the tanks were removed, fuel spills had dripped for years into the rocky ground of mine tailings, which also continued to leach their own toxins, and which were, besides, unstable and poorly suited for supporting buildings. And below those layers, not forgotten, fish and people had once lived here. Ernestine Saanklalaxt' Hayes helped dredge those memories. She recalled the area from her childhood in her sadly vivid memoir, *Blonde Indian*, published in 2006. Meissner assigned his team to read the book as they grappled with the ghosts of this dirty ground.

"Through today's eyes, it's really ugly and traumatic what they did to this place," he said. "And this is the place that we were building on. And it had these memories, through the contaminated soil below, both through the tank farm and the toxins, this weird little outfall creek on the back, and this thing that was built in 1967, which is so loved, that now we're going to have to take down. So, it went through an extensive public process. We spent so much time in public meetings. They were really well attended, and they were very fun. We workshopped the heck out of this thing and the people of Juneau were great to work with."

Advocates of Juneau arts and history wanted to save the old museum building to be reused as a cultural facility, or even to house the Juneau City Museum, and pointed to an alternate waterfront site for the new state museum that was available, recalled Gary Gillette, president of the Gastineau Channel Historical Society. But by the time those discussions began, the state had committed to its plan and didn't want to change course. Besides, Banghart said, the 1967 building had worn out. Its leaks and rot were too difficult to fix because of the asbestos in the walls. Down in the basement, sump pumps were keeping the collection storage vault dry twice a day, when high tide infiltrated through the crushed rock below. Various retrofits had attempted to address the lack of space, with offices added to the back and, after a boiler explosion filled the building with soot, a separate mechanical structure outside. The state library and archives, housed elsewhere, also needed new space, and would be more efficient under the same roof with the museum. The Kashevaroff building would be five times larger but would operate at the same cost, with room for all three entities, and would be built to last a century, with the collection stored at an elevation safe from the future flood waters of climate change.

In January 2013, contractors broke ground behind the old museum, constructing a storage vault that would ultimately become part of the new building. Later that year, the project team made the final decision that the Alaska staff would mount the new exhibits rather than outside contractors. But the work needed to begin immediately, and the museum lacked the skilled workforce of museum professionals that would normally tackle such a large project. They resorted to having a barn raising. Scott Carrlee, the curator of museum services, recruited twenty-seven museum workers from a dozen tribal and small-town museums all around Alaska, some of whom had no formal training at all. In return for their travel costs, these workers would come to Juneau in repeated waves, learning how to build cardboard mounts and containers to safely transport each item in the collection—and they would get the whole job done. Scott's wife, Ellen Carrlee, the state museum's conservator, taught the visitors how to do it, as did some other skilled helpers. The idea saved money and spread professional museum skills around Alaska (and some of those workers came back again later, learning to build permanent mounts of brass and plexiglass and making manikins for the new exhibits).

Early in 2014, the museum closed for the next thirty months. Contractors excavated around the old museum's foundation, opening a door directly into its basement storage vault and connecting that to a temporary corridor made of steel shipping containers, which led across the property to the newly built vault. Objects glided on carts through that tunnel to their new home. Then the old museum came down and the new museum went up around the new vault, with the collection already inside.

Time now was short for the design of the exhibits and for the gathering of ideas and opinions from cultural groups and experts to guide what the museum would actually say. Banghart believed the museum's relationships and Alaska-rooted staff would make that easy, and in some ways, it was. Among the Tlingit of Southeast Alaska, where Henrikson had been so long embedded in the culture, meetings to discuss the exhibit had been going on for some time. Henrikson already had decided on the major changes: the exhibit would present Alaska Natives as people of the present, not only of the past, with mixed contemporary and historic objects, and would not shy away from the hard topics of colonization and oppression. Meetings elicited

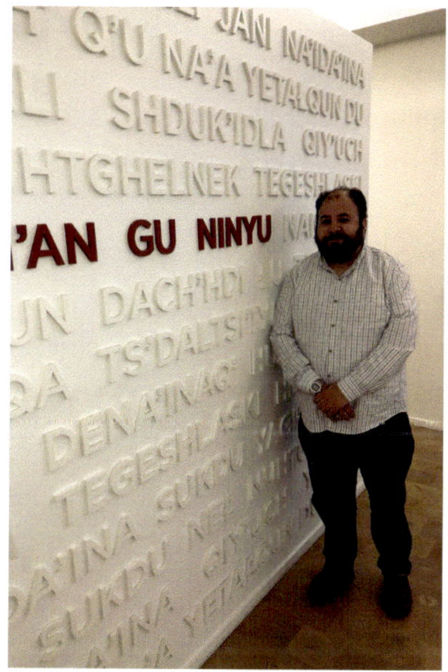

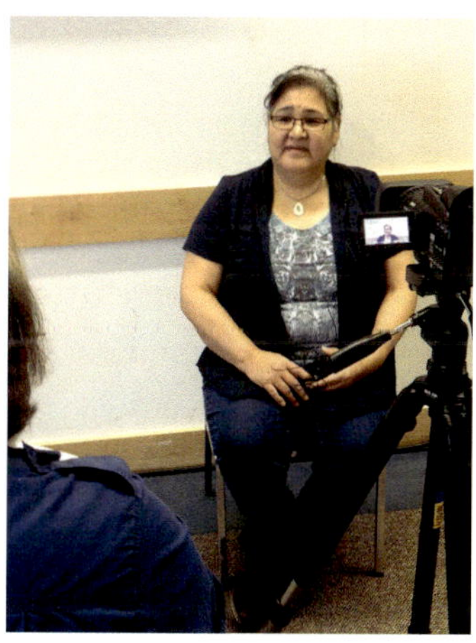

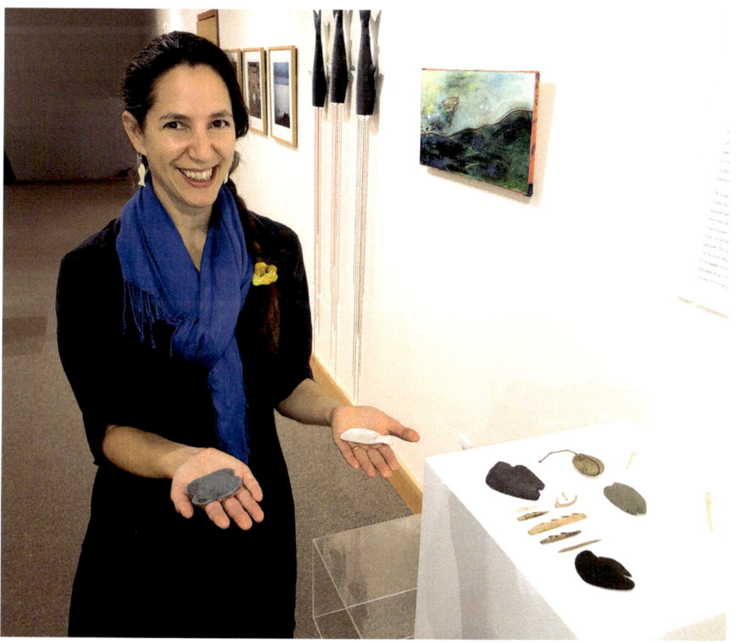

permission for telling the region's deepest stories. At one session, Ben Didrickson, a Tlingit elder, declared, "Elders said, 'Don't talk about it.' They didn't have the tools. The time is right for something to happen . . . We were taught for many years not to talk about these things. Now it's time to talk about these things."

Everyone wanted a clan house exhibit, as in the old museum. But whose clan house? The social organization and art of the Tlingit people are complex. Tribes are subdivided by clans and clans by houses. Each has its own crest, stories, and songs that it uniquely owns, and each clan is a member of one of the two moieties, or lineages (as is every Tlingit person), the Raven on one side and the Eagle or Wolf on the other. The carving of traditional art observes these formalities, with imagery appropriate to each clan and moiety, reflecting the social structure and depicting the heroes and villains of the clan's stories. To create a generic house that mixed these designs would be untrue to the culture and potentially disrespectful of the place where the museum stands, in the lap of the village site, directly upon the fishing grounds that had once fed its people. But that meant the art in the house must come from a single clan owner. Henrikson turned to Aak'w Kwaán tribal elders to determine which clan's house would be represented in the museum's permanent gallery.

Bob Sam participated in those discussions as the elders agreed upon representation of his Gaatáa Hít (Trap House) of the L'eeneidí (Dog Salmon) clan of the Raven moiety, with its dog salmon crest, and with a house screen that would tell the people's migration story. "I'm being very careful with my words out of respect of other clan houses in Juneau," Sam said. "We decided to use that story to welcome all the clans of Juneau. . . . And all of this was approved by the elders of Juneau. It was

CLOCKWISE **Co-curators Aaron Leggett, Diana Martin, and Nadia Jackinsky.**

Photos by Charles Wohlforth and Sarah Asper-Smith

Souvenir hat.

2009-3-4

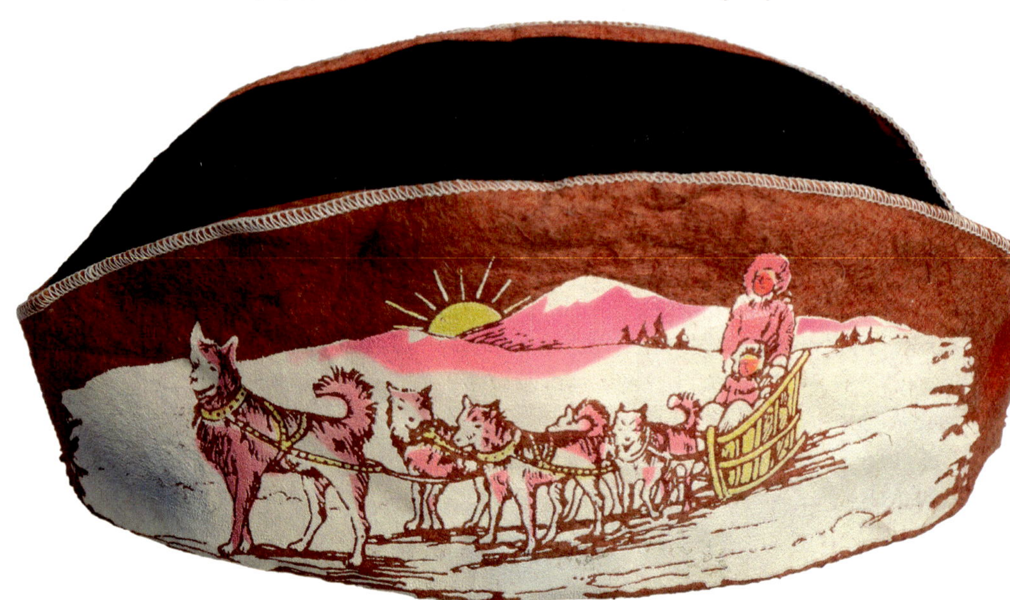

a struggle at first, but we couldn't have done it without their approval." The museum project paid for the artwork, but Sam acted on behalf of his clan to commission the carvings. For the house screen telling the clan's story he selected Nathan Jackson, the beloved and venerable carver who appeared on a U.S. postage stamp in 1996, and for the house posts, he selected master carver Steve Brown. Workers in Wrangell shaped the boards for the walls using traditional tools. The projects took many years to complete.

The museum collaborated with other tribal groups, but less thoroughly. Perhaps it is inevitable, and appropriate, that the indigenous exhibit emphasizes the people of Southeast Alaska, especially the Tlingit, within whose homeland it resides. Visually, their objects dominate. The grand carvings that impressed the curators of big-city museums a century ago impress still. The museum's local community connections naturally opened deeper access to the content and influenced the tone of the exhibit. But Alaska Native peoples are diverse and different. They fought wars and their leaders sometimes face off today in legal and political battles. The militancy and indignation that come through in the exhibit is largely a Tlingit voice, in my opinion. Some other Native peoples suffered far less directly from the arrival of White settlers and from assimilationist government policies, because, in this vast land, the two sides didn't encounter one another until much later. In 1997, in the Interior village of Minto, I interviewed Peter John, traditional chief of the Athabascans, born in 1900, who lived his first decade without ever seeing a White face. John's life had been more like that of his precontact ancestors than like ours. His stories about change were much different than the Tlingit's story of the last potlatch—they were stories of hardship and loss, but not of anger.

Asper-Smith attended Juneau meetings with Henrikson, and other meetings around Alaska, and brought in more than twenty co-curators, experts who would interpret their own cultures, or, in the case of those addressing historical topics of the twentieth century, the events or industries they had studied. These points of view might conflict, and the museum did not avoid those conflicts. Although the exhibit designers had adopted an overall theme, the co-curators who wrote material about their areas of expertise did not communicate with one another and turned in vastly different products. Some wrote dense, learned prose in the style of an academic paper, some expressed their ideas in casual language, and some wrote long, funny tales that could never come close to fitting in a museum exhibit. Asper-Smith hired me to edit these documents into labels with strict word-count limits, in a unified tone, and language that would be digestible by visitors on their feet reading from the wall—all while retaining the original author's ideas, perspective, and voice.

I didn't try to impose the theme, and I don't know how I could have, because the words given to me to edit were diverse and idiosyncratic. The themes could only emerge organically from the expressions of these very different people—or not. To me, that was the theme.

Some co-curators outside Southeast Alaska were disappointed by the accelerated process. Without the opportunity to visit the objects—already selected by museum staff—or the time for in-depth consultations with community or tribal members, the undertaking felt incomplete to them. Aaron Leggett, president of the Native Village of Eklutna, co-curated the Athabascan section, covering the peoples in Interior Alaska and western Canada to Cook Inlet, where his Dena'ina people live. Leggett was confident of his ability to do the task, as the senior curator of history and indigenous cultures at the Anchorage Museum, and as a participant in many similar past efforts for various institutions. But he said the process didn't compare favorably with the well-funded, decade-long consultations that went into the Smithsonian Institution's Arctic Studies Center in Anchorage, which brought an extraordinary trove of indigenous objects from a century of storage back to Alaska. The center had opened a regional office in Alaska in 1993 but didn't complete its permanent exhibit until 2010. The Alaska State Museum's deadlines would be counted in months rather than years. "It was certainly a challenge," Leggett said. "I just do feel like it was a little bit of a missed opportunity."

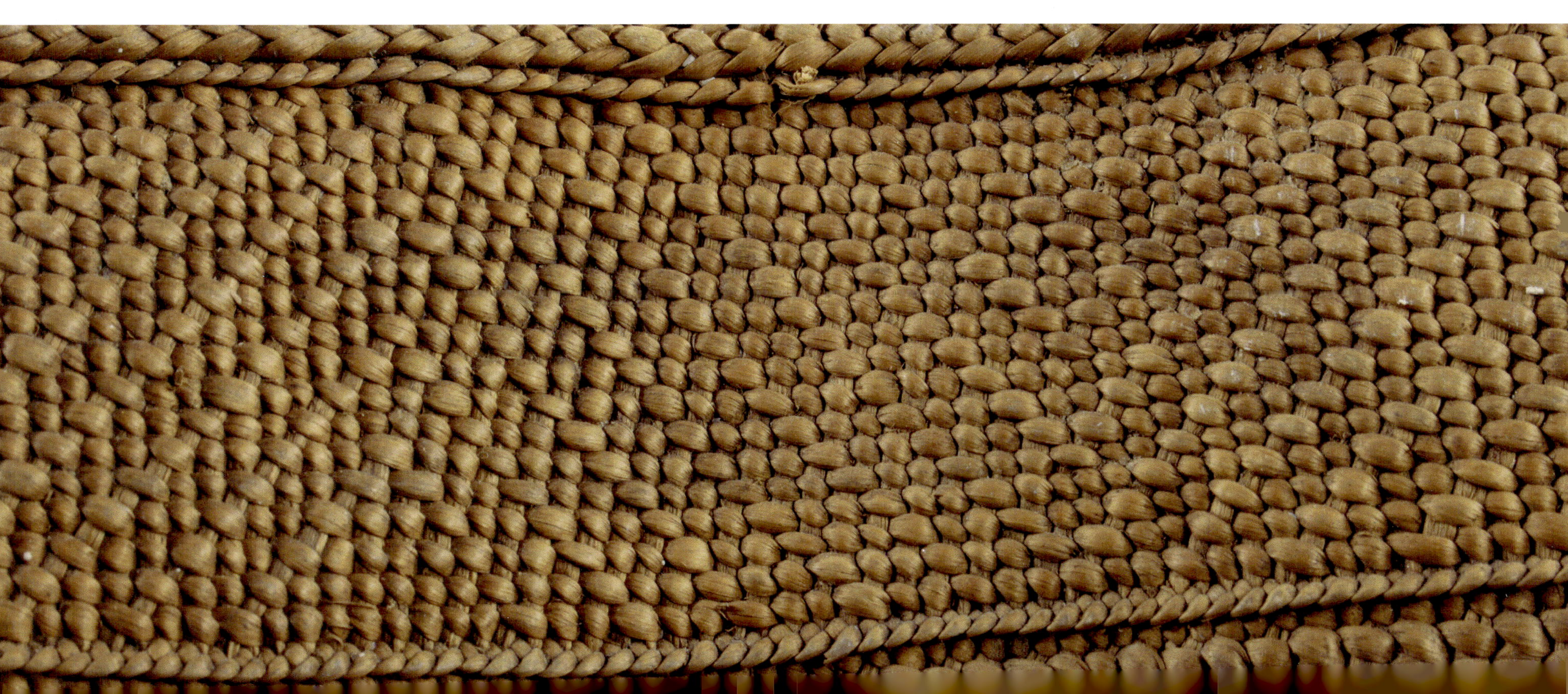

Twisted split spruce root basket, Tlingit.

II-B-636

Niłnuqeyishi
Counting cord
A memory aid recording history and stories.
Kenai, Dena'ina Athabascan.
II-C-316

I apologized for my part in this, years later, to Ron Inouye, whose work I severely compressed for labels on the World War II internment of Japanese Americans and the similar, less-known wartime internment of the indigenous people of the Aleutian Islands. Inouye began investigating these injustices in 1970, as a teacher in Ketchikan, when he went into the woods to explore a rotting Civilian Conservation Corps camp from the 1930s and learned from locals that it had been used to hold Unangan people taken from their homes as far as two thousand miles away in the Aleutians when the war arrived there in 1942. For decades, Inouye gathered evidence and testimony about the deaths and abuses that occurred, and in 1995 he mounted a powerful exhibit documenting those events at the University of Alaska Museum of the North in Fairbanks. The state museum invited him to co-curate here as well, but with few artifacts to show, the complex story ended up much shortened—hardly more than a picture and

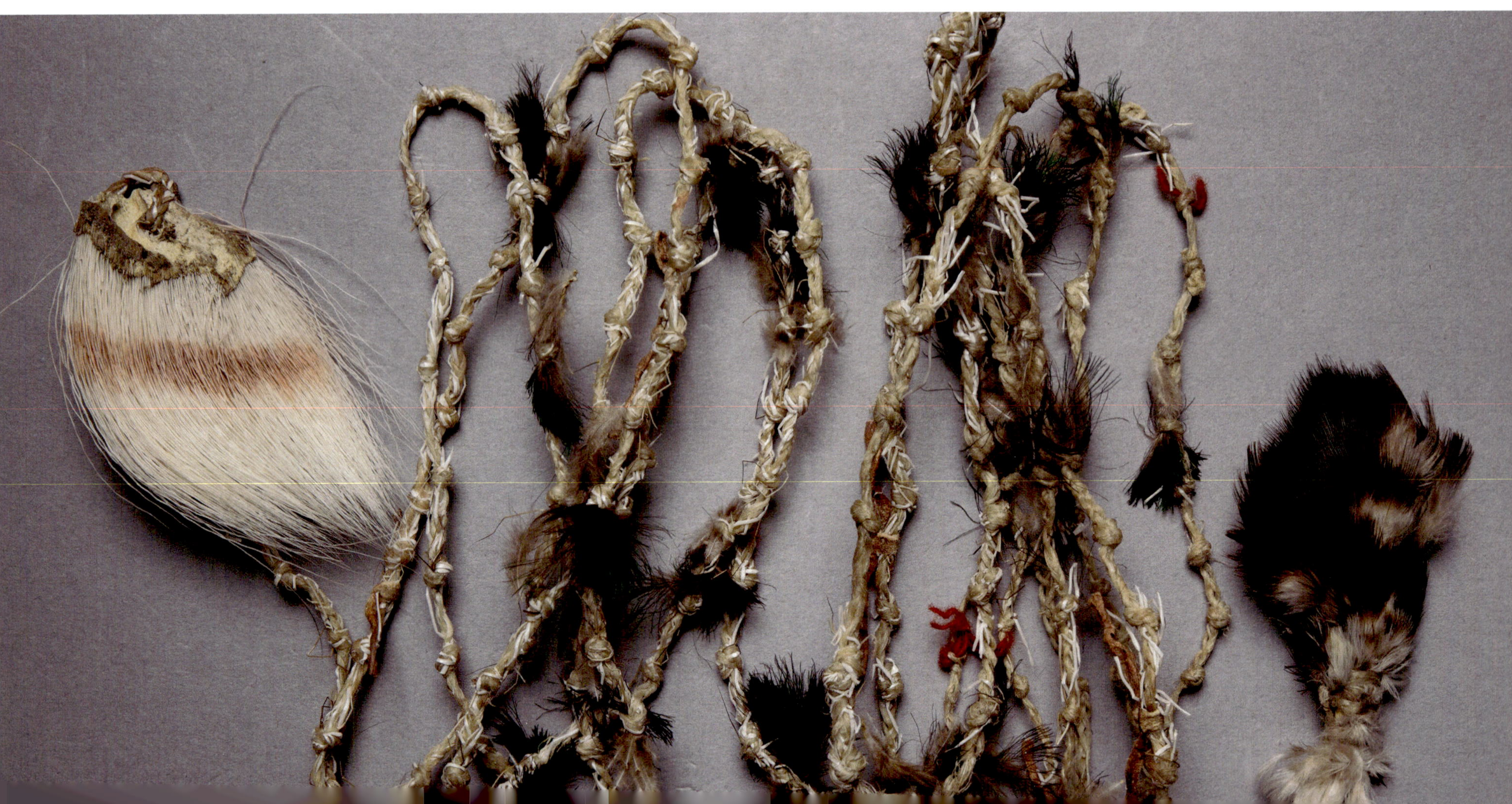

a mention. The museum's artifact-based approach depended on showing artifacts, but society saves few souvenirs of its most shameful mistakes.

Inouye graciously accepted my apology. Alaska is so huge, and so many things have happened, he said, that just being part of the museum at all was important. He had dedicated many years to saving from obscurity the truth of how the United States abused its Japanese and Unangan citizens during the war. In 1988, President Ronald Reagan had apologized on behalf of the nation. Inclusion in the state museum validated and preserved that knowledge by leaving a strand of the story evident for those who might later wish to pull it out of the past and learn more. "Once you're there, people realize that there was something that happened," he said. "Until it's there, they have no clue. And I think that's the real value, having the kind of public presence of things that people previously had some inkling of but never really knew."

All these different goals, concerns, and memories came together from around Alaska as if from a big, swirling vortex. At least the exhibit would be thoroughly Alaskan. The process creating it had been casual, vigorous, opinionated, and somewhat chaotic, like any Alaskan public process. And the people involved felt a lot of pride about the results—even those who wished they'd had more time or more space or deeper involvement. This is what Banghart wanted. "We were putting [curators] in people's living rooms right off the bat and making it personal," he said. "And that is, from my perspective, probably the singular element that gave us those stories to those depths, with that kind of acceptance, because it's your neighbor."

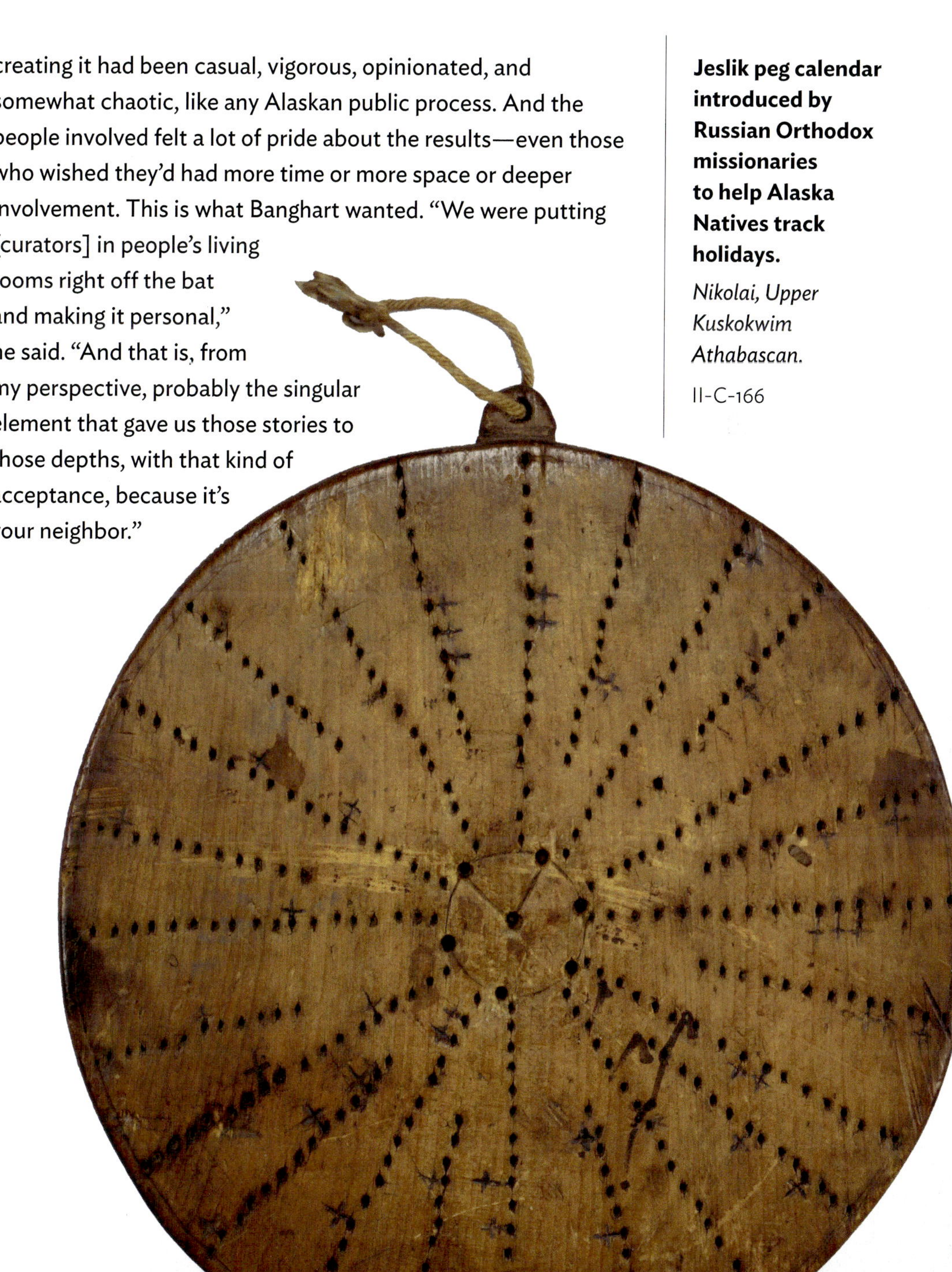

Jeslik peg calendar introduced by Russian Orthodox missionaries to help Alaska Natives track holidays.

Nikolai, Upper Kuskokwim Athabascan.

II-C-166

Tl'otth'eghee
Steel dagger
by Old Man Esau, Toklat River. Tanana Athabascan, 1904.
II-C-39

5.

The museum could barely hold the huge, heavy objects representing the natural resource economy of Alaska. Construction workers built railroad tracks to roll a mining locomotive into place, reinforcing the floor so it could sustain the weight, then removed the tracks except for directly underneath the boxy, black machine. The museum collection lacked objects representing the oil industry and requested donation of a piece of the trans-Alaska pipeline for the exhibit, which the Alyeska Pipeline Service Company unearthed from an equipment yard, rusted and worn. It stands high on its two steel legs like a battle-scarred giant, less obviously a conduit to move oil than a harsh monument representing that industry's dominance and decay. Again, the builders had to reinforce the floor. For logging, the message is even clearer. A chain saw with an extremely long bar lies near the round of a tree that a logger felled when it was 556 years old, near a wall-sized photo mural of a mountain devastated by a clear-cut. Over more than a century, these industries developed in spasms, building cities around them, and then sputtered and subsided, leaving behind ugly marks. When the museum was completed, that boom-and-bust cycle had just entered a lasting bust, as oil prices and production declined, deflating the economy and shrinking the population. The building itself is an artifact of that last boom.

Telling Alaska's resource development story would have been relatively simple as recently at 2009, when Alaska celebrated fifty years of statehood with great hoopla and self-congratulation, but it's not so simple anymore. The triumph of statehood seemed to crystallize Alaska's pioneer spirit at its optimistic best. At the time of the celebration, some of the statehood movement's revered leaders were still living. In that simpler historic narrative, pioneers tamed Alaska. They arrived as the self-reliant gold seekers of 1898, going north to create a new society, and fought for recognition and fairness against colonial oppressors down south—the moneyed interests and the federal government—to gain access to trees for logging and oil for drilling and to control their own destiny as the forty-ninth state. In that story, recurrent economic booms and busts were merely steps on an upward climb. Alaska had been a colony like the original thirteen, but under the thumb of Washington rather than London, and statehood had brought freedom in the same way the American Revolution had—freedom with wealth, as the resources of this great land came under the control of those who lived here.

As the twenty-first century progressed, however, that pioneer tale became threadbare through retelling, and

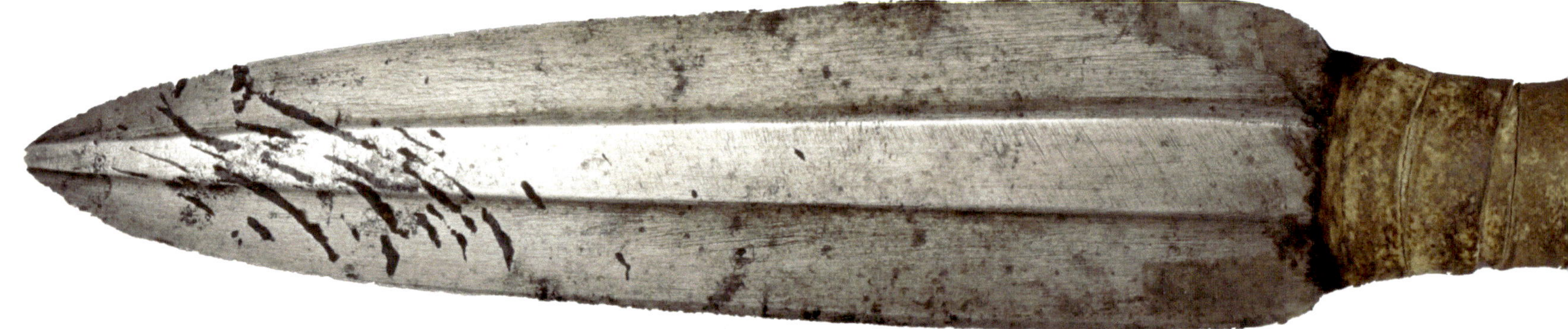

appeared incomplete and even upside down as characters who had been left out of the story began to assert themselves. The museum's photo mural depicting the admission of Alaska as a state now seems to belong to a distant epoch, showing men (none still living) in 1950s suit jackets and narrow ties, joyfully holding aloft the forty-nine-star flag, which was in use only until Hawaii became the fiftieth state later in 1959. The famous *Anchorage Times* headline read simply, "WE'RE IN." But who was in? From the Alaska Native point of view, Alaska statehood posed a threat, not an opportunity, and it motivated the final, more aggressive stage of their fight for recognition of their land claims, ultimately leading to the rise of indigenous-owned corporations. In hindsight, the pioneers who had accused their federal sponsors of colonialism looked like more like colonists themselves—or at least members of the same team.

In 1970, when historian Steve Haycox arrived in Alaska, scholars had already rethought the pioneer myth of the American West, showing that the frontier had not been empty before the pioneers' arrival, and that their ability to conquer it relied not just on hardiness and pluck, but also on extensive federal support, both monetary and military. It took much longer for that revision to take place in Alaska. Haycox worked at it over a long, distinguished career as a professor at the University of Alaska–Anchorage. The reassessment lagged, among other reasons, because, in 1970, the frontier essentially remained open in Alaska. Alaskans could still enact Manifest Destiny by seizing unsettled land as their own. Although Alaska Natives had filed land claims over most of the state, the vast majority of the land remained public domain, essentially free for the taking by any pioneer tough enough to stake it out—although such homesteaders now would arrive in float planes rather than covered wagons.

The final and largest resource boom was rolling in as well with the era of big oil, a black gold rush that rapidly washed over Alaska with a new population and waves of irreversible modernization. And another, contrary current crashed into oil—and into the Natives and the pioneers—as the nation's environmental movement, then at its apex of popular strength, turned its attention to protecting this last wild land. With the resolution of these conflicting forces, the 1970s became the conclusive and most consequential decade in Alaska's history. The oil companies got their pipeline, the Alaska Natives got their lands, and the conservationists got their parks. The pioneers, as many sturdy Alaskans still saw themselves, rallied behind politicians and economic boosters pushing for development—for oil—but in the process, they wrote the final page of their own story. When the decade was over, three huge acts of Congress—for oil, for Native lands, and for conservation—had closed the frontier, leaving the pioneer with no more room to run. In this new, relatively domesticated Alaska, abandoned mines and leveled old-growth forests no longer looked so much like steps on the way to great new heights. They slowly transformed into regrettable scars left behind by people trying to make a buck on finite resources. Those who made them had been colonists indeed.

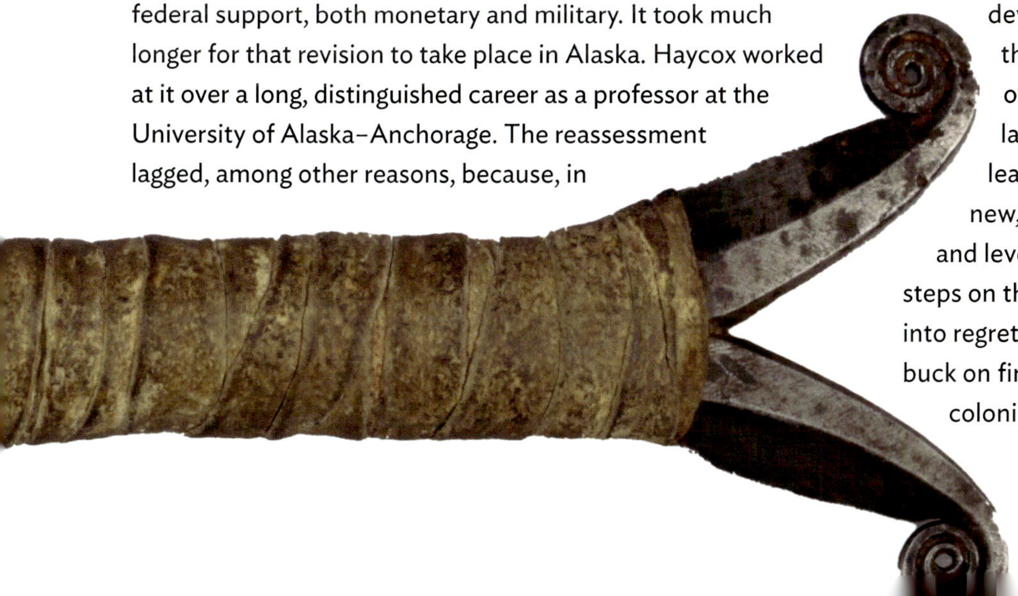

Badge from Alaska Territorial Police, established in 1953 with 36 officers.

III-O-103

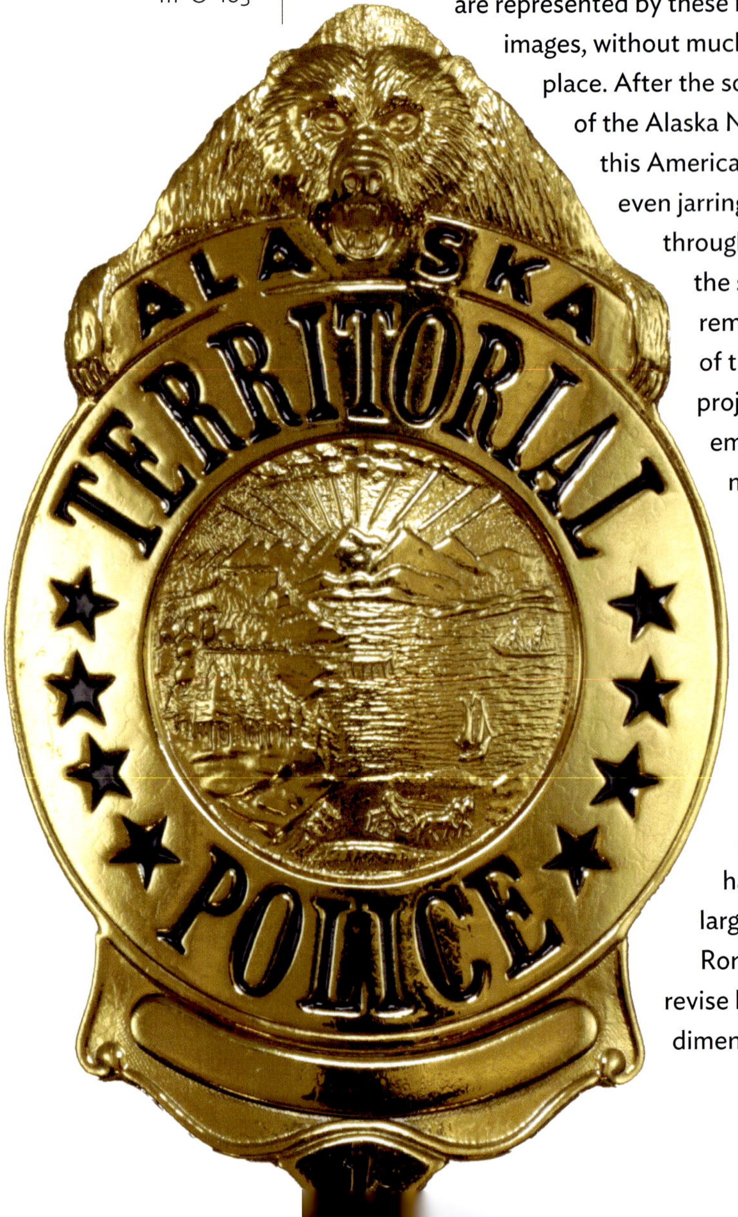

The exhibit barely mentions the passage of these laws. We're still living the story, and you won't find much written explanation of what has happened in the last fifty years. Instead, the message comes in the presentation. The extractive industries are represented by these monolithic objects and images, without much humanity or sense of place. After the soothingly unified design of the Alaska Native part of the exhibit, this American area feels jumbled and even jarring, with multiple pathways through disconnected sections—the story line is complex and remains unsettled. Many of the objects themselves project a different kind of emanation, not as handmade, artistic belongings that still retain a sense of their owners, but as mass-produced products, used up and left behind. (And another important story is missing, too, in the extraordinary ethnic and racial diversity that has come about in Alaska's larger cities since the 1990s.) Ron Inouye himself helped revise history, adding the dimension of prejudice against Japanese and Unangan people to the righteous story of the defense of Alaska during World War II. But he warned that some Alaska museums might be going to extremes, trading one absolute for another, as they turn away from the pioneer myth and colonial story. "History was being expunged and all of a sudden it was indigenous history that was being emphasized and that colonialist idea, it's off to the side," he said. "It's always extremes, . . . looking backwards in the mirror for a hypothetical place that never really existed."

That was true of the old pioneer myth, too. It was a cartoon. Even today it remains the dominant popular image of Alaska, starring bearded tough guys in flannel shirts, with their manly tales of survival and wilderness conquest. The real stories are much more interesting.

Academically, Haycox led the movement to dispose of the pioneer myth, but he didn't want to dispose of the pioneers. "When I got to Alaska in 1970, it was just absolutely clear to me that the self-reliance and the romanticization of the Alaskan past, that history of Alaska, was simply inadequate," Haycox said. "Not to say illegitimate. I mean, there were people who went into the wilderness and led heroic lives. And paved the way for others."

As a co-curator, Haycox helped develop the only chronological part of the exhibit, the timeline in the American section, which is illustrated by charming and surprising objects that speak of adventures and first encounters, and of communities so remote they seem part of another world—the stuff of the romantic version of Alaska, but without the suggestion of triumphal progress. People are in these cases. One can imagine the unpredictable days of the brave young William Healey Dall, exploring for a telegraph route to Siberia in 1865 and 1866, as he gathered and used the miscellaneous articles he carried, here exhibited. And the power of the revenue cutter *Bear*, which for forty-one years governed Alaska's coast, much of that time under the command of its heroic but volatile captain, "Hell Roaring" Mike Healy, and which is depicted from two cultural perspectives: an oil painting and an ivory model made by a Yup'ik or Iñupiaq carver. Here also, a silver trophy given in 1912 to the "King of the Trail," A. A. "Scotty" Allan, in gold rush Nome, a legendary sled dog racer in the four-hundred-mile All-Alaska Sweepstakes, for which promoters built telegraph lines over the Seward Peninsula so they could track the leaders and set betting odds back at the Board of Trade Saloon on Front Street. And nearby, an opera coat worn by Frances Muncaster, who arrived with her husband in 1897 at Candle, the turnaround point for the Sweepstakes, and likely mushed to Nome to see performances wearing this coat.

Historical myths have a purpose. They tell us about ourselves and who we are. That's why they change, although the facts of history stay the same. Because we change. Historian Ross Coen made this point to me—he is the editor of the journal *Alaska History*, and has written extensively about Elizabeth Peratrovich, Alaska's most famous civil rights leader, and the changing meaning of her most famous speech. Peratrovich spoke dramatically to the Alaska Territorial Legislature in 1945 before it passed its anti-discrimination law. Decades later, she was raised as an icon and her speech—of which no verbatim record was made—was re-created, to be repeatedly quoted, performed in historic reenactments, taught to schoolchildren, and made the basis of Peratrovich's canonization, with a state holiday in her honor, her image on a $1 coin, and even her depiction on Google's home page. Peratrovich was a remarkable woman, but Coen showed how her speech was built into a myth representing Alaska Native pride and striving for equality. And then, it changed again. Peratrovich's work and life had aligned fully with the assimilation model of indigenous equality—she was Westernized and led the Alaska Native Sisterhood, which adopted that perspective for her people's advancement. But, Coen said, some Alaska Natives now see her as a symbol of decolonization—the opposite of assimilation—and a proposal has been made to take down a Kodiak statue of Alexander Baranov, the Russian colonial conqueror of Alaska, and replace it with one of Peratrovich.

Coen's work is highly controversial, examining the reality behind a figure who, for Alaska, is on the level of Dr. Martin Luther King Jr. nationally—and he points out that King's image also evolved after his death—but his point is not to destroy the power of an icon but to understand it and what the changing myth says about society. The purpose of the Peratrovich myth is real and valuable. For that matter, the pioneer myth was valuable for those battling to make Alaska a state, buttressing a clear identity and sense of worth. And the Peratrovich myth continues to grow, as do

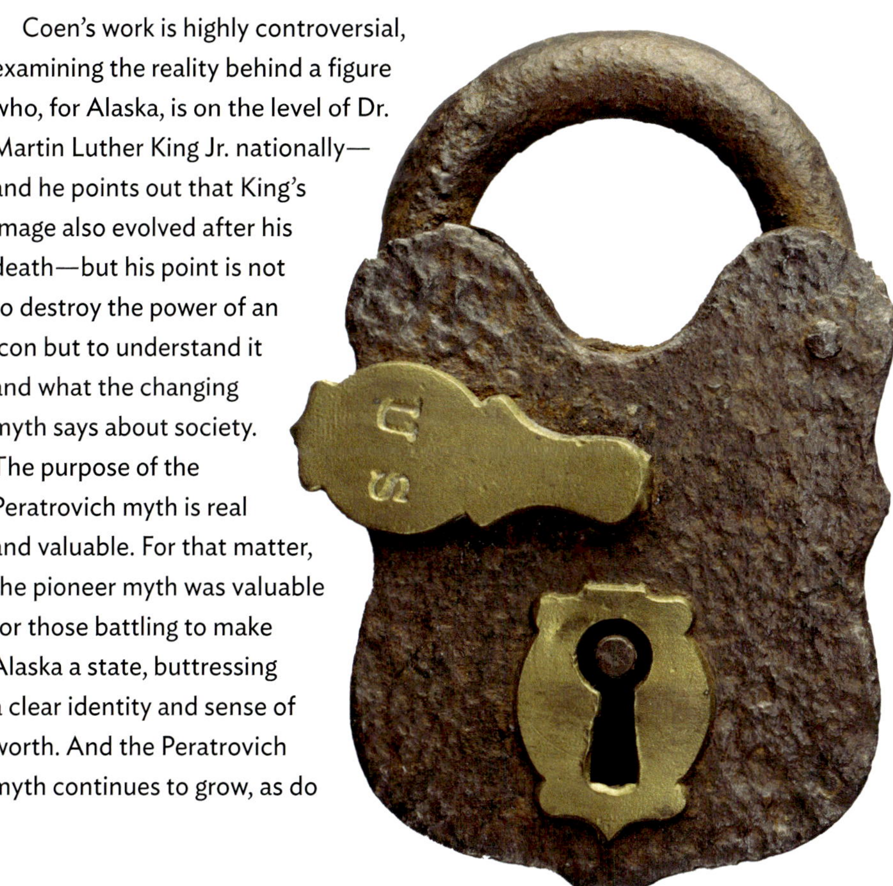

Padlock secured the door of Juneau's first federal jail, circa 1893.

III-O-355

Dugout canoe by John Wallace, Tlingit.
II-B-1893

other tales of Alaska Native resistance, as the indigenous point of view and awareness of past injustices become dominant. But with the death of the pioneer myth, Alaska society as a whole lacks a unifying sense of itself. The exhibit tells us that, in a subtle way, as it moves from topic to topic without connecting them chronologically or thematically. The concept of decolonization suggests rejection of non-Native Alaskan ways, with the unspoken corollary that only indigenous people belong. But that would leave out 80 percent of the Alaska population, for whom the museum also is intended to stand as a touchstone.

The museum staff had many themes in mind when they designed the exhibit. I found an early memo from their planning work. Some of the ideas didn't pan out, as the work progressed and the distinctive, artifact-based style developed, but a few of the big ones clearly did. The document declares, "The exhibition will be composed of many voices." At the top it defines the "Big Idea" as "The landscape of Alaska is inseparable from the experience of being Alaskan." Of course, the place we live always shapes how we live, but Alaska's extremes especially define what it means to be an Alaskan, as we endure its harsh weather, remoteness, dependency on outside support, sparse population, and a land mass so vast it encompasses many regions with various terrains, climates, and biomes—a size and geographic diversity more like a nation than a state. In the exhibit, this idea comes across clearly when you begin looking at the boats. Watercraft are everywhere, often in places where they grab attention and provide landmarks. Alaska has more coastline than all the other states combined—by a lot—and many thousands of miles of great, navigable rivers. Alaskans use boats. Watercraft have allowed people to move around and to live, and they're as different as the conditions in which they were used.

Manning, the curator of exhibitions, uses the boats to explain Alaska to newcomers, who often don't grasp the size and geographic diversity of the state. "The watercraft can help tell that story," she said. "These are the materials that are in this

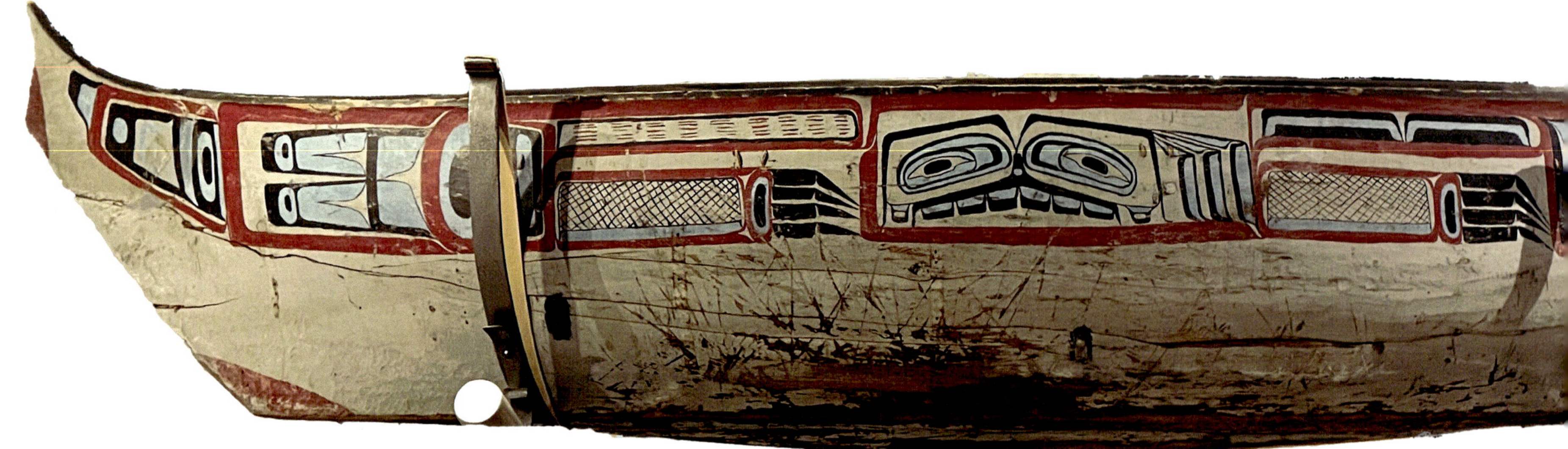

area. So, you have a dugout canoe, that's telling you that there's trees of this size, versus a birch bark canoe, it was lightweight. Then you start looking at the walrus hides around the umiak. The watercraft tell the different geography of Alaska."

The thematic connection through navigation continues with the square-rigged ships of the European explorers and, centered in the twentieth-century part of the exhibit, the double-ended sailing boat that fished salmon in Bristol Bay until 1951. And further on are the tales of shipping access to Alaska and maritime disasters along its coasts, and a huge lighthouse lens that once showed the way, preventing wrecks. Photos and models capture the vast fleet of American ships that fought in the Aleutian Islands in World War II. Even the material on aviation contributes to this story of the struggle of navigating Alaska, of finding its food and resources, and never taming it, but coping with its vastness and surviving. Alaskans have bobbed around on this immensity in every kind of vessel, tiny and vulnerable to its forces, but most of the time finding their way through. It's a metaphor for life in a place much bigger than we are, which we cannot control. The double-ender, elevated above the room and glowing in the light, seems to stand for that sense of vulnerability and perseverance.

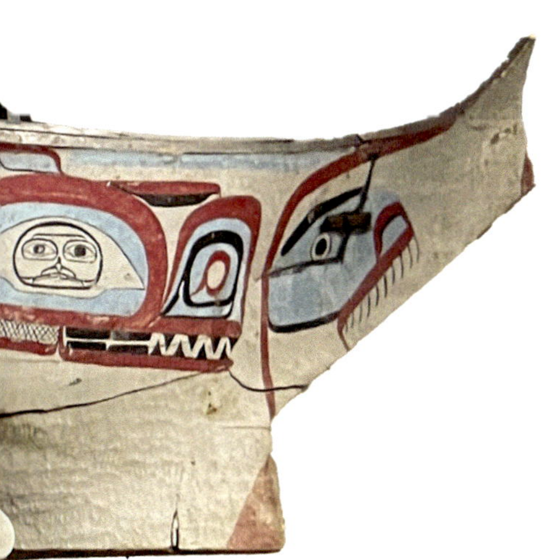

These many boats were individual solutions to the great Alaska challenge. In Banghart's conception of the museum, it's the thinking behind those solutions that create the commonality among Alaska's peoples, and connect the beginning of the exhibit to the end. "The cultures here across the board are the most adaptive and creative to make things function. You're always in preparation of what it is you need to accomplish," he said. "We could connect an ivory-headed toggle harpoon and the pipeline. That connectivity is the ingenuity of the human species doing something with the materials at hand to solve a problem. It's adaptability. It's that creative process."

The landscape itself isn't here. The Alaska Gallery has no windows and few maps or pictures to capture the size or grandeur of Alaska. Instead, we see things made by people, almost all of them in some way responding to that landscape. They are like tracks that Alaskans left behind. Seeing these objects as the paths of people, we can imagine what they were up against. The upward-progressing pioneer myth may be defunct, but these parallel paths of survival hold the power of another truth.

Ivory drum handle.

II-A-3241

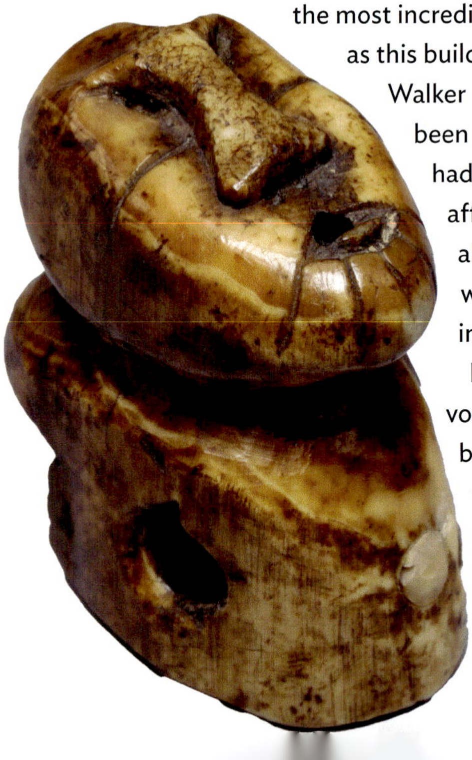

6.

The Kashevaroff building and the museum exhibit opened on June 6, 2016, on time and under budget. That morning, staff members who had worked so long met joyfully for coffee in a messy work room backstage before calmly but hurriedly adding the final labels and details to the display cases. The gallery remained cluttered with tools. A manlift rolled across plywood that had been put down to protect the carpet.

By lunch time, an urgent cleanup began. Soon, dignitaries assembled under the awning outside the front door and a crowd gathered, standing, to hear their speeches. Aak'w Kwaán elder Rosa Miller said, "We welcome you to our ancestral land." Lieutenant Governor Mallott, also Tlingit, said, "We can celebrate, both collectively, symbolically, and really, when we say Alaska can build the most beautiful edifices, we can build the most incredible future, and we can do it together as this building is so emblematic of." Governor Bill Walker noted the good luck that the project had been funded when it was, now that the oil bust had begun and the treasury could no longer afford such expenditures. But little was said about the sesquicentennial of the treaty with Russia, which had been the original impetus for finishing by this date.

Instead, Walker spoke of the present, his voice rich with emotion, his words shaped by an infectious smile. "I cannot describe the feeling one gets going through this building. You feel so much pride to be an Alaskan."

Children from Harborview Elementary School's Tlingit Culture, Language, and Literacy Program, dressed in regalia of bright red and black felt, sang and danced for the gathering. Then, since the building was for future generations, they had the honor of cutting the ribbon.

People poured into the atrium and into the exhibit. Henrikson admitted he held his breath waiting for the first visitors to find errors—I felt the same. But the reaction was overwhelmingly positive.

That night, Banghart called together staff and consultants—all the workers—for a noisy dinner at a casual restaurant, and a party followed at Asper-Smith's house, high up Juneau's steep streets and public stairs.

Alaska and its cultures have continued to change in the years since that day. The English names of some Alaska Native peoples remained matters of lively debate in 2016, between older people who still liked words such as Eskimo or Aleut—names given by outsiders—and younger generations who preferred to return to names their people gave themselves. Now those debates are quieter and their end is in sight. The public perception of extractive industries has also evolved, as oil seems increasingly of the past, but the economic future remains undefined. The controversy about the museum's "Genocide" label erupted well after the museum opened, with the changing perspectives about the nature of colonialism and the suppression of Alaska Native cultures. Coen, the historian, uses newspaper columns from that debate to teach his students about how we interpret the past. Historian Haycox was among those who thought the word *genocide* was incorrect, but over time his view and curator Henrikson's have come closer.

Haycox said the meaning of history changes and its truths can diverge. We need simplifying myths, and he gave credit to Henrikson for the weight he placed on the testimony of elders and storytellers in defining the past. "It's absolutely disrespectful and prejudicial to ignore the oral tradition, even when the oral tradition is ostensibly completely at odds with what might strike a reasonable person as reality. Because the myth is there for a reason. It tells you something about the way that people think of themselves and the way they think of their past." In the museum, he said, that complexity requires visitors to be sophisticated about what they see. "You have to allow the existence of things simultaneously that may be somewhat contradictory."

Objects have their objective truth—in their physicality and provenance—as Henrikson acknowledged, even with his willingness to allow visitors different ways of seeing them. But Hayes, the Tlingit elder who wrote *Blonde Indian*, wondered if indigenous items belong in the museum at all, even though she admires the space. "I think it's beautiful," she said. "I know that it's done with massive respect and truthfulness and authenticity. One of the thought exercises that I like to try to explore is to imagine what something would be like had it not been for colonization." Presumably, the belongings would be part of everyday life, she said. "What would it look like? And I wonder if there would be museums, and if there were, I wonder what they would look like? The artifacts have spirits and they long for home, just as I do."

After finishing the museum project, Banghart went back to work for himself. He still plays in country and western bands, and also has worked in musical theater, creating and performing scores for shows. He values the objects in the museum for their current use, like Hayes, but not only for their original purposes. He was the curator who, early on, preferred to both keep them in the cases and periodically give them back to tribes so they could perform ceremonies—that life that Hayes says these objects long for. But he doesn't restrict his conception of that life only to those objects made by indigenous people. All of the items matter most, he believes, for what they say to people living in the present, as we encounter them. "When I give tours to friends or acquaintances or if I bring somebody in, I always want to point that out. I say, 'Be thinking about the people, the human mind, the human experience that gave voice through these objects. Think about that. Don't look at the object. Go back behind the object. Think of the human being there.' It gives you a totally different perspective. Because you have to drop your preconceived ideology of what they were. They were not what you thought. They were people like yourself."

This may be the deepest message of the museum, the reason why objects must live here—even if they do long for home—and also the reason why the museum had to be made by Alaskans themselves, in their collaborative, loosely organized way. In this setting, everyone is together, all our myths collide, and the tangle of our stories cannot be hidden or ignored. The proximity of these dissimilar things testifies that different truths can live together. As can we. We must share an Alaska that means something different in each of our cultures, and to each of us as individuals. To do so honestly is to see

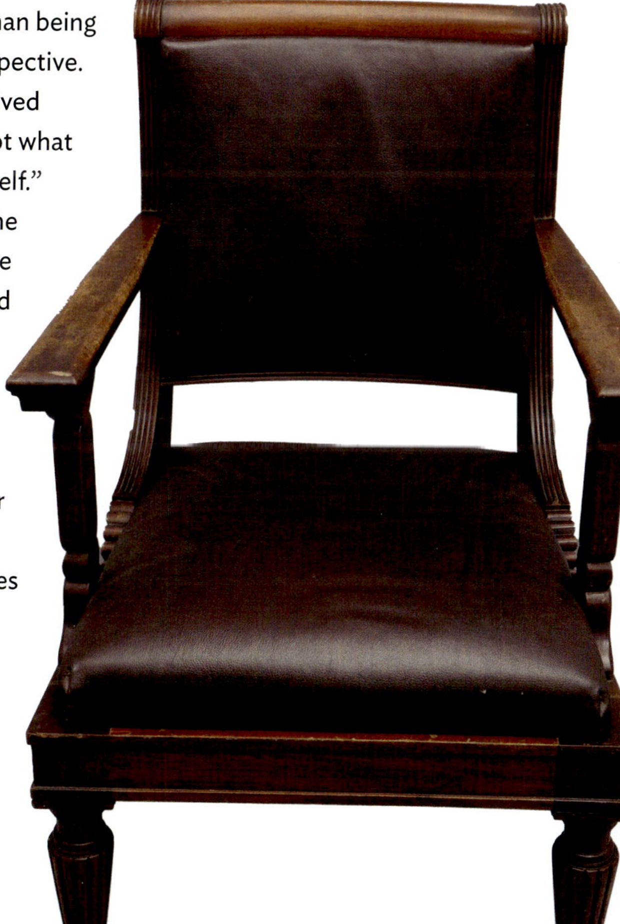

Chair used by former territorial governor Gruening after his election as Alaska's first United States Senator, 1959-69.

2008-37-1

Badge belonging to Henry Lawless of Seattle, recovered from shipwreck of the *Princess Sophia*.

72-99-4

we are not divided among good and bad people, and that even contradictory beliefs can be valid.

The museum can serve as our working model, like a smaller version of our state. The objects can stand in for each of us and our beliefs. We can, then, learn here about being Alaskan, not just as individuals or members of our own cultures, but as part of a whole. What that commonality consists of isn't easy to explain. It's true, as the museum's creators declared, that the landscape defines the nature of being an Alaskan. But isn't there more to it than that? If our state is more than a collection of cultures rattling unconsolidated in a vast space, we should be able to see those patterns here, in the things people left behind.

The answer may lie in simple acceptance and appreciation. Today, as before, the future is uncertain. The Alaska population is shifting and the mainsprings of the economy are in flux. Newly assertive cultural voices speak for their own—as tribes, political perspectives, industries, geographies—and often these groups don't hear one another. The unity of the past has been discarded as flawed, but we still need to connect to a new, better meaning of being Alaskan. I think we can, even if that identity is only emerging. And I think we can witness that emergence here, in the museum's unspoken message of reconciliation. The Alaska identity remains unsettled, but in the museum we can participate in the process of connection, as we adapt and learn respect for other cultures, other people, and the land. This process may yet take a long time, but the materials are here, with the opportunity to absorb and integrate this essential understanding of who we are. That knowledge is on exhibit, if one has the time and openness to see.

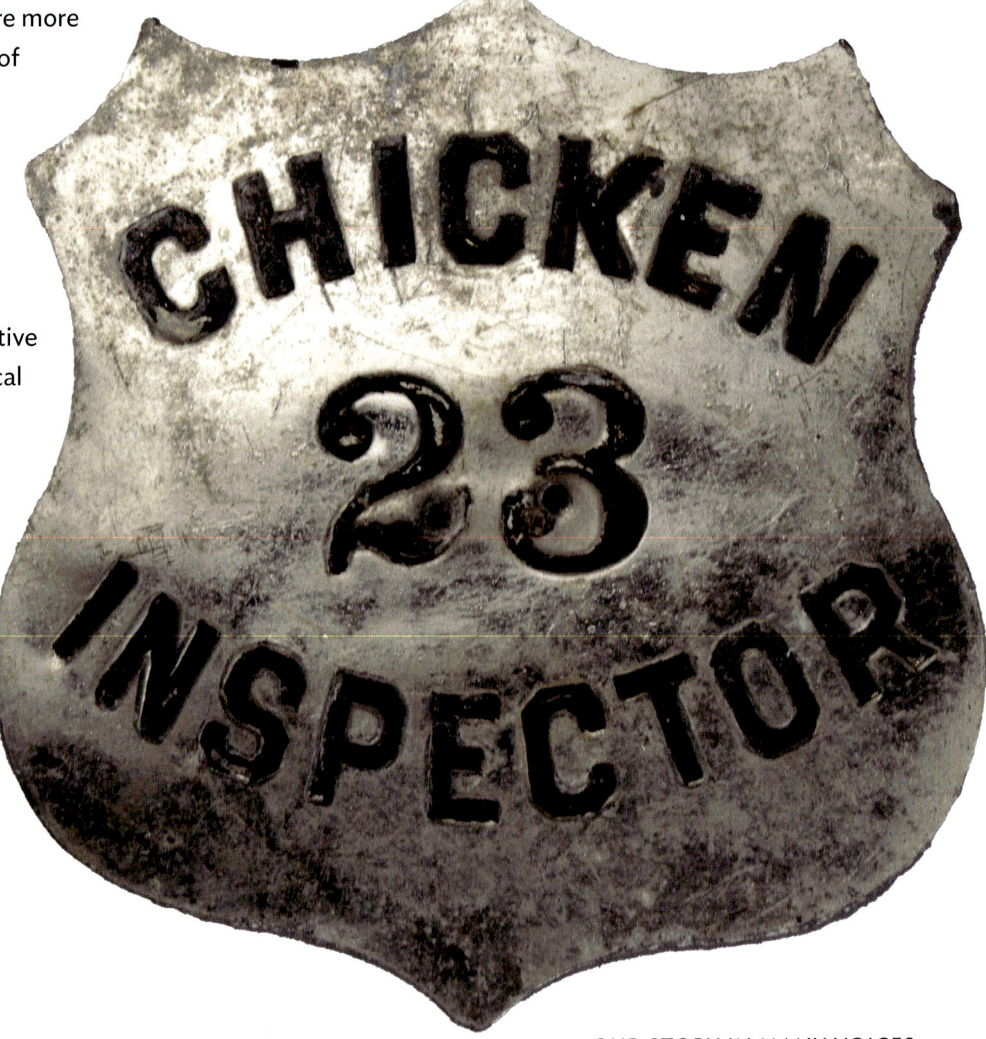

ACKNOWLEDGMENTS

Many people and organizations contributed money and effort for us to make this book, and to allow us to create it independently of the museum itself from the perspective of the observer and critic. This was a unique project.

The Alaska Historical Society sponsored the book, providing the able assistance of Executive Director Joan Antonson. The Atwood Foundation made the first financial contribution. Without the advice and encouragement of its executive director, Ira Perman, this project probably would not have happened. Other critical financial contributions came from the Block Foundation, the Rasmuson Foundation, and the Friends of the State Library, Archives and Museum—the last of which also was instrumental in bringing about the current building itself.

Important early supporters of the book concept included Dalee Sambo of the Inuit Circumpolar Council, Jim LaBelle, a retired leader of Chugach Alaska Corp., and Katrina Woolford, owner of the Store at the Father Andrew P. Kashevaroff Building. University of Alaska Distinguished Professor Emeritus Steve Haycox helped us early gain traction, granted a long interview, and provided much other assistance. We are also grateful to Nate Bauer, former associate director and acquisitions editor for the University of Alaska Press, for capably ushering the book into existence, and to the helpful and highly professional staff of the University Press of Colorado, especially Production Manager Daniel Pratt, who made many important contributions to the maps and layout.

The current and past staff of the library, archives, and museum were extremely generous with their time and knowledge, particularly the curator of collections, Steve Henrikson, whose deep familiarity with the collection is itself an Alaskan treasure. We also gratefully acknowledge Bob Banghart, Brian Wallace, Freya Anderson, Jackie Manning, and Addison Field. Others who gave generously of their time include Aaron Leggett, Bob Sam, Brian Meissner, Ernestine Hayes, Gary Gillette, Judy Bittner, Nadia Jackinsky-Sethi, Tricia Brown, Ron Inouye, and Ross Coen.

After the manuscript reached draft form, several reviewers substantially improved it with their comments (although any remaining errors are our responsibility alone). Two anonymous peer reviewers showed great sensitivity and erudition in their comments. Tom Kizzia read the manuscript and provided many helpful thoughts, as did Henrikson, acknowledged above.

Finally, Charles acknowledges his wife, Sarah Rowland, whose support is unflagging and whose joyful enthusiasm is energizing.

Sarah acknowledges her incredible family, who tell her that she can do anything she wants to do. She is also grateful to the Alaska museum community, a generous and purposeful group of people, and especially to Bob Banghart, who showed her how to have a career meeting people and helping them tell their stories.

SOURCES AND FURTHER READING

This section provides sources for the information found in the book, organized in the order they appear in the text and under the same section headings. I have also added some good general sources that readers can consult on these topics to learn more.

Our best sources are found in the Alaska State Museum itself. The museum labels were compiled from the research and knowledge of dozens of cultural and historical experts and contain a vast store of information, much of which I have relied upon.

I also interviewed a variety of people, some at great length, and kept notes of important moments and speeches. Recordings of interviews, machine transcriptions, and some of the notes are held in the Alaska State Library at the Father Andrew P. Kashevaroff Building (Citation: Alaska State Library, *Our Story in Many Voices* Interviews, 2016–2024, Charles Wohlforth, MS308.) The identities of individuals and their professional titles are cited in the text. Here is a list of the interviews and dates, in alphabetical order, for those who wish to use this material in the future:

Freya Anderson, notes only, March 21, 2023
Sarah Asper-Smith, notes only, September 13, 2022; recorded September 19, 2022
Bob Banghart, recorded October 12, 2022; notes only, December 30, 2022
Judy Bittner, recorded January 30, 2023
Tricia Brown, recorded December 27, 2022
Ross Coen, recorded December 28, 2022
Gary Gillette, recorded February 1, 2023
Stephen Haycox, recorded October 15, 2022
Ernestine Hayes, recorded, December 14, 2022
Steve Henrikson, notes only, June 6, 2016; recorded (in two parts) October 14, 2022
Ronald Inouye, recorded September 22, 2022
Nadia Jackinsky-Sethi, recorded October 7, 2022
Aaron Leggett, recorded October 11, 2022
Byron Mallott, notes only, April 2, 2017
Jackie Manning, recorded October 13, 2022
Brian Meissner, recorded December 23, 2022
Bob Sam, notes only, January 4, 2023
Bill Walker, notes only, June 6, 2016
Brian Wallace, recorded January 2, 2023

The Setting

1.

It's easy to find natural history books about Alaska, but I don't know of a single authoritative book that covers the entire state. For those interested in accessible material on Alaska's nature and peoples, Alaska Geographic (www.akgeo.org/), the nonprofit publishing arm of Alaska's parks and public lands agencies, issues and sells excellent books on each region and many topics.

My own knowledge is based on a lifetime of traveling and reading as a journalist and science writer in Alaska. Sources and firsthand impressions are found in my books *The Whale and the Supercomputer: On the Northern Front of Climate Change* (New York: North Point, 2004), which is about climate change in the Arctic and Interior Alaska, as well as the people and ecosystems there; and *The Fate of Nature: Rediscovering Our Ability to Rescue the Earth* (New York: St. Martin's, 2010), which is about the history and natural and human ecology of the Gulf of Alaska region, particularly Prince William Sound.

To understand Alaska's forests, I relied upon Leslie A. Viereck and Elbert L. Little Jr.'s *Alaska Trees and Shrubs* (Fairbanks: University of Alaska Press, 1972). The fascinating linkages in the Gulf of Alaska ecosystem are explained in Phillip R. Mundy, ed., *The Gulf of Alaska: Biology and Oceanography* (Fairbanks: Alaska Sea Grant College Program, University of Alaska, 2005).

Climate change in the Arctic is a critically important and ever-advancing topic. To find serious science and scholarship, the Arctic Council is an excellent source. This international organization of each of the Earth's Arctic nations distributes accessible updates and observations through its website arctic-council.org/explore/topics/climate/.

2.

The preeminent economic research organization in Alaska is the Institute of Social and Economic Research at the University of Alaska–Anchorage (iseralaska.org), which also produces work for the public on how Alaska's economy works. It published online the best economic history of the state I am aware of: Terrence Cole, "Blinded by Riches: The Permanent Funding Problem and the Prudhoe Bay Effect," January 2004, which, despite its name, is a book-length treatment of Alaska's economy beginning in 1867. The handiest ready source of data on the Alaska economy is the Section of Research and Analysis in the Alaska Department of Labor and Workforce Development (live.laborstats.alaska.gov), which publishes *Alaska Economic Trends*, a monthly online magazine of current economic analysis. I've learned a lot from the experts at both these organizations and relied on them in personal communications.

The history of Alaska's forest products industry is covered in Kathleen Morse, "Southeast Timber Task Force Report," October 1997, prepared for Governor Tony Knowles by the Southeast Regional Timber Industry Task Force, excerpted at www.commerce.alaska.gov/web/dcra/ForestProducts/HistoricalOverview.aspx. Readers who want general information about Alaska Native cultures presented by indigenous people can find material from the Alaska Native Heritage Center in Anchorage (www.alaskanative.net).

3.

See the sources above for information about the Sitka spruce. Freya Anderson, head of Information Services and Historical Collections at the Alaska State Library and Archives, provided information about their services. Background on Evon Zerbetz's stained glass work, *We Are Written in the Layers of the Earth*, comes from a brochure of the same name by the artist, which is distributed by the library.

The Story in the Exhibits

1. Native Alaska

For a recent geographic contribution to the debate on early human migration to North America, see Summer K. Praetorius et al., "Ice and Ocean Constraints on Early Human Migrations into

North America along the Pacific Coast," *PNAS* 120, no. 7 (2023), doi.org/10.1073/pnas.2208738120. Regarding the Kachemak tradition, see Frederica de Laguna, *The Archaeology of Cook Inlet, Alaska* (Philadelphia: University of Pennsylvania Press, 1934).

My main sources in discussing the objects in this part of the exhibit are the labels and background material provided by the co-curators who informed the labels, my interviews with museum staff noted above, and my own observations and experiences in the regions where these things were made.

I explored the story of the Iñupiaq umiak boat in my book *The Whale and the Supercomputer: On the Northern Front of Climate Change* (New York: North Point, 2004), including the transfer of technology between Native and Yankee whalers. Besides my own experience, key sources include Charles Brower, *Fifty Years Below Zero: A Lifetime of Adventure in the Far North* (1942; repr., Fairbanks: University of Alaska Press, 1994), and John R. Bockstoce, *Whales, Ice, and Men: The History of Whaling in the Arctic* (Seattle: University of Washington Press, 1986).

The danger of drowning and exposure in the Alaska outdoors is documented by a database of wilderness deaths kept at akfatal.net; water is overwhelmingly the most common cause of death in the wilderness. An article by Austin Rohl, MD et al., "Photokeratitis," which validates the usefulness of Inuit snow goggles, was published online by the American Academy of Ophthalmology at eyewiki.aao.org/Photokeratitis, and was updated November 9, 2023. Details about the Sanightaaq parka were provided by Ellen Carrlee, the museum conservator.

The discussion of Native spirituality and masks draws on many conversations. My most detailed treatment of the subject, with references to sources, is in my book *The Whale and the Supercomputer*, 249–55. The 2017 story of the young harpooner criticized on the internet is covered by Julia O'Malley, "The Teenage Whaler's Tale," *High Country News*, July 17, 2017.

On James Cook's family, see J. C. Beaglehole, *The Life of Captain James Cook* (Stanford, CA: Stanford University Press, 1974). Regarding the tradition of Athabascan music and song, I relied in part on Siri G. Tuttle and Håkan Lundström, "Transmission of Song-Making in Interior Athabascan Tradition, Alaska," in *Traditional Musics in the Modern World: Transmission, Evolution, and Challenges*, ed. Bo-Wah Leung (New York: Springer, 2018), 89–109.

2. Conquest and Resistance

The text on Russian America upon which I have relied the most is the classic Lydia T. Black, *Russians in Alaska, 1732–1867* (Fairbanks: University of Alaska Press, 2004). The description of Cook's possession ceremony is found in the journal of Lieutenant King in *The Journals of Captain James Cook on His Voyages of Discovery: The Voyage of the* Resolution *and* Discovery, *1776–1780*, ed. J. C. Beaglehole (1967; repr., Woodbridge, UK: Boydell, 1999), 1421–22. See pp. 346–48 and 1417 in that volume for a description of the first encounter with the Chugach people. My understanding of the Chugach people's concept of ownership before contact comes from two books: Frederica de Laguna, *Chugach Prehistory: The Archaeology of Prince William Sound, Alaska* (Seattle: University of Washington Press, 1956); and Kaj Birket-Smith, *The Chugach Eskimo* (Copenhagen: Nationalmuseets Publikationsfond, 1953). The latter volume also informs the sentence about lay readers becoming de facto chiefs, as did an interview with anthropologist Nancy Yaw Davis.

The relative size and importance of Sitka is noted by various historians, including Barbara Sweetland Smith, who indicated in personal communication that in 1819, Sitka's population was 759, while in 1842 San Francisco still had only 196 people and in the 1840s Oregon City had 500. The maximum size of the Russian population was established by Svetlana G. Fedorova, *The Russian Population in America and California*, trans. and ed. Richard A. Pierce and Alton S. Donnelly (Kingston, Ontario: Limestone, 1972). Many other facts about Russian America repeated here come from the museum labels and underlying research by the co-curators.

The information about the American flag on display is from the interviews with Steve Henrikson. The bad conduct of the early American garrison is described in Hubert Howe Bancroft, *History of Alaska, 1730–1885* (1886; repr., New York: Antiquarian, 1959), 606–19. This period and the starvation of indigenous people due to loss of resources are well covered in Don Mitchell, *Sold American: The Story of Alaska Natives and Their Land, 1867–1959: The Army to Statehood* (Hanover, NH: University Press of New England, 1997). I found the quote about the Angoon incident in Peter Segall, "Remembering and Rebuilding: Angoon Residents Commemorate 139 Years since Bombardment," *Juneau Empire*, October 27, 2021.

Ernest Gruening, *The State of Alaska*, rev. ed. (New York: Random House, 1968) is an excellent source on early resource waste. The impact of commercial whaling on Arctic indigenous people is discussed in Don Charles Foote, "American Whalemen in Northwestern Arctic Alaska," *Arctic Anthropology* 2, no. 2 (1964): 16–20. The horrifying fact about prospectors feeding their dogs on the dead bodies of indigenous people is from Allan Alexander Allan, *Gold, Men and Dogs* (New York: G. P. Putnam's Sons, 1931).

Hudson Stuck's work is covered in David M. Dean, *Breaking Trail: Hudson Stuck of Texas and Alaska* (Athens: Ohio University Press, 1988). Sheldon Jackson's role is amply covered in the exhibit labels, as well as in James L. Cox, *The Impact of Christian Missions on Indigenous Cultures: The "Real People" and the Unreal Gospels* (Lewiston, NY: Edwin Mellen, 1991). For Jackson's own perspective, see Sheldon Jackson, *Alaska, and Missions on the North Pacific Coast* (New York: Dodd, Mead, 1880).

Facts and documents about Native citizenship are in the exhibit and available online from the University of Alaska–Fairbanks through materials for a course on federal Indian law at uaf.edu/tribal/academics/112. My column about Molly Hootch was published under the headline "Molly Hootch Never Intended to Sue. But She Is Glad Her Case Changed Alaska," *Anchorage Daily News*, October 28, 2016. My article on Lela Oman is "Lela Oman and the Epic of Qayak," *Anchorage Daily News*, April 20, 1997.

The story of equal rights and World War II in Alaska is covered in Muktuk Marston, *Men of the Tundra: Alaska Eskimos at War* (New York: October House, 1969); and Ernest Gruening, *Many Battles: The Autobiography of Ernest Gruening* (New York: Liveright, 1973). Ross Coen has written extensively about the passage of the anti-discrimination law, as well as its symbolism and impact, in "Elizabeth Peratrovich Day: Constructing a History of Alaska Native Civil Rights," *Pacific Northwest Quarterly* 112, no. 3 (Summer 2021); and, regarding impact, in Ross Coen, "How Alaska's Equal Rights Law Was First Put to the Test," *Anchorage Daily News*, December 2, 2017.

For a comprehensive history of the Alaska Native Land Claims Settlement Act up to its passage, see Donald Craig Mitchell, *Take My Land, Take My Life: The Story of Congress's Historic Settlement of Alaska Native Land Claims, 1960–1971* (Fairbanks: University of Alaska Press, 2001). You can find a helpful brief history of corporate versus tribal status for Alaska Native organizations online at Gregory Ablavsky, "Are Alaska Native Corporations Indian Tribes? A Multimillion-Dollar Question," *scotusblog.com*, April 21, 2021. I wrote about the business difficulties and successes of Native corporations and 1990s anti-Native prejudice in *From the Shores of Ship Creek: Stories of Anchorage's First 100 Years* (Anchorage: Todd Communications, 2014). The state legislation is covered in Joaqlin Estus, "State of Alaska Recognizes Tribes with Historic Bill," *Indian Country Today*, July 30, 2020.

3. American Colony

Information on the rapid change in Alaska's population is explained in Eric Sandberg, "Movers and Population Turnover: Data by State Show Alaska Represents the Extremes," *Alaska Economic Trends* (September 2022).

A good overview of the gold rush years, and census information from the time, can be found in Claus-M. Naske and Herman E. Slotnick, *Alaska: A History of the 49th State*, 2nd ed. (Norman: University of Oklahoma Press, 1987). The National Park Service also has a readable introduction at www.nps.gov/klgo/learn/goldrush.htm. For a clear and concise explanation of the gold standard and how the Klondike discovery (and one in South Africa) changed world economics and American politics, see Thomas Klitgaard and James Narron, "Crisis Chronicles: Gold, Deflation, and the Panic of 1893," *Liberty Street Economics*, Federal Reserve Bank of New York, May 13, 2016, libertystreeteconomics.newyorkfed.org/2016/05/crisis-chronicles-gold-deflation-and-the-panic-of-1893.

Wickersham's life is chronicled in Evangeline Atwood, *Frontier Politics: Alaska's James Wickersham* (Portland, OR: Binford & Mort, 1979). See Terrence Cole, "Blinded by Riches: The Permanent Funding Problem and the Prudhoe Bay Effect," Institute of Social and Economic Research at the University of Alaska–Anchorage, January 2004, iseralaska.org, for more on the impact of World War II and the Cold War, and other economic events in the timeline. On the statehood movement, Alaska Constitutional Convention, Bill Egan, and so on, see Vic Fischer with Charles Wohlforth, *To Russia with Love: An Alaskan's Journey* (Fairbanks: University of Alaska Press, 2012). I was an eyewitness to the *Exxon Valdez* spill as a newspaper reporter; a summary of impacts is provided by the National Oceanic and Atmospheric Administration at darrp.noaa.gov/oil-spills/exxon-valdez.

For timber history, see Kathleen Morse, "Southeast Timber Task Force Report," October 1997, prepared for Governor Tony Knowles by the Southeast Regional Timber Industry Task Force, excerpted at www.commerce.alaska.gov/web/dcra/ForestProducts/HistoricalOverview.aspx. For a book specifically about Juneau's mines, see Earl Redman, *The Juneau Gold Belt: A History of the Mines and Miners* (Juneau: Gastineau Channel Historical Society, 2011). The National Park Service interprets the history of the Kennecott mines at nps.gov/wrst. For a clear explanation of placer mining and its history in Alaska, see Warren Yeend, Peter H. Stauffer, and James W. Hendley II, "Rivers of Gold, Placer Mining in Alaska," published in 1998 by the U.S. Geological Survey at pubs.usgs.gov/fs/1998/0058/report.pdf. For an interesting and broad-ranging history of the oil industry in Alaska, see Jack Roderick, *Crude Dreams: A Personal History of Oil and Politics in Alaska* (Fairbanks: Epicenter, 1997).

Regarding population turnover, see Sandberg, "Movers and Population Turnover." The figure on veterans comes from Chris

Gilligan, "Who Are America's Veterans?" *US News and World Report*, November 11, 2022. On Anchorage integration, see Steve Haycox, "At 100, Anchorage Is More Than Ever a City of Immigrants," *Anchorage Daily News*, September 17, 2015.

The classic book on the Alaska fishing industry in the federal period is Richard A. Cooley, *Politics and Conservation: The Decline of the Alaska Salmon* (New York: Harper & Row, 1963). For the post-statehood period, see Bob King, *Sustaining Alaska's Fisheries: Fifty Years of Statehood* (Juneau: Alaska Department of Fish and Game, 2009).

The story of John Muir's Alaska travels is captured in Kim Heacox, *John Muir and the Ice That Started a Fire* (Guilford, CT: Lyons, 2014). The history of tourism in Skagway is covered in Frank Norris, *Legacy of the Gold Rush: An Administrative History of Klondike Gold Rush National Historical Park* (Anchorage: National Park Service, 1996), which can be found online. Pictures and links to more stories about the wrecks of the *Princess Sophia* and the *Islander* are at an online exhibit from the Alaska State Library at library.alaska.gov. Learn more about the *Norge* from a detailed article posted by the Fram Museum in Oslo at frammuseum.no.

For a powerful account of the war in the Aleutians, see Brian Garfield, *The Thousand-Mile War: World War II in Alaska and the Aleutians* (1969; repr., Fairbanks: University of Alaska Press, 1998). John Cloe, who assisted with the labels in the museum as a co-curator, also wrote extensively about the war in Alaska, including in his book, John Cloe with Michael F. Monaghan, *Top Cover for America: The Air Force in Alaska, 1920–1983* (Anchorage: Air Force Association, 1984).

Terrence Cole's quote is from "Blinded by Riches," 4.

Voicing Alaska's Story

1.

The scientific debate on human migration to North America is discussed in Summer K. Praetorius et al., "Ice and Ocean Constraints on Early Human Migrations into North America along the Pacific Coast," *PNAS* 120, no. 7 (2023), doi.org/10.1073/pnas.2208738120. Ernestine Saanklalaxt' Hayes makes her case in our text for an alternative story. Her book *Blonde Indian: An Alaska Native Memoir* (Tucson: University of Arizona Press, 2006) in part describes her childhood memories in the area where the museum now stands.

An invaluable report on the 1967 museum building gives an authoritative account of how that land was created and includes an aerial photograph from before the fill was placed: Summer Rickman and Emily S. A. Lochart, "Determination of Eligibility for the Alaska State Centennial Museum (Alaska State Museum), Juneau AHRS Site Number: JUN-1124," State of Alaska, Office of History and Archaeology—Short Report 2010–04. The Office of History and Archaeology, located in Anchorage, holds the report.

My 2017 interview with Lieutenant Governor Byron Mallott is referenced above. Henrikson's remarks about Native veterans and the decision to use the word *genocide* in the museum are found in Charles Wohlforth, "Native Memory: Rewriting Alaska History with the Word 'Genocide,'" *Anchorage Daily News*, July 26, 2018. The newspaper debate that followed included columns by Terrence Cole, "We Shouldn't Remove the Shades of Gray from Alaska's History," *Anchorage Daily News*, August 24, 2018; Tony Kaliss, "Genocide: What's in a Word?" *Anchorage Daily*

News, September 7, 2018; and Steve Haycox, "The Dangers of Presentism when Confronting the Past," *Anchorage Daily News*, September 13, 2018.

Henrikson is a remarkable scholar and person. He is profiled and his clan membership explained in this radio piece: Wesley Early, Alaska Public Media, and Kavitha George, "49 Voices: Steve Henrikson of Juneau," *KMXT Kodiak*, October 5, 2018, alaskapublic.org/2018/10/05/49-voices-steve-henrikson-of-juneau. In 2016, Henrikson was cited for Distinguished Service to the Humanities by the governor of Alaska.

2.

Dates in the history of the museum are established in an unpublished document provided and written by Steve Henrikson, "DRAFT TIMELINE; Alaska State Museum/Alaska State Library Historical Collection (formerly Alaska Historical Library and Museum)," December 1996. He also provided many more facts in our interviews. Some of Governor Brady's early story in Alaska, including the letter that I quote, is found in Sheldon Jackson's *Alaska, and Missions on the North Pacific Coast* (New York: Dodd, Mead, 1880). Regarding the last potlatch of 1904, I relied on an email exchange with Henrikson on December 30, 2022, and on an article: Robert W. Preucel and Mary F. Williams, "The Centennial Potlatch," *Expedition Magazine* 47, no. 2 (2005).

I covered the eugenics movement and Alaska Natives in my book *The Fate of Nature: Rediscovering Our Ability to Rescue the Earth* (New York: St. Martin's, 2010); the portion on the 1904 fair in St. Louis, including the quote by W. J. McGee of the fair's anthropology department about displaying living humans, is from Robert W. Rydell, *All the World's a Fair: Visions of Empire at American International Expositions, 1876–1916* (Chicago: University of Chicago Press, 1984).

I relied on Douglas Cole, *Captured Heritage: The Scramble for Northwest Coast Artifacts* (Norman: University of Oklahoma Press, 1995) to learn about museum collectors in the region. The detail about the collector from the Berlin Museum in 1883 comes from Janet Klein, *A History of Kachemak Bay: The Country, the Communities* (Homer, AK: Homer Society of Natural History, 1981). Henrikson was my main source on the strengths and weaknesses of the museum's collection.

Information about Father Andrew P. Kashevaroff, including the quote from the Milwaukee visitor, comes from a short biography written by Henrikson, dated 2020, which is unpublished.

Sources on the bombardment of Angoon are contained in the earlier section "The Story in the Exhibits: 1. Native Alaska."

Benson's biography and disputed ethnicity comes from Michael Livingston et al., "Benny Benson's Hidden Unangax̂ Heritage," report published by the Aleutian Pribilof Islands Association, March 2022, hdl.handle.net/11122/12729. Benson's remark on the moon landing is found in Ann Cameron Siegal, "Flag Contest Helped Tough-Luck Teen Become One of Alaska's Favorite Sons," *Washington Post*, October 17, 2017.

The statehood story and oil-era story are covered above.

3.

My main source on the 1967 centennial, including Don Wright's involvement, is the book described in this section, Tricia Brown, ed., *The View from the Future—2017: Fifty Years After the Alaska Purchase Centennial* (Juneau: Department of Education and Early Development, Division of Libraries, Archives and Museums, 2015). Regarding the statue controversy, see Jacob Resneck,

"Seward Statue Unveiled in Front of Alaska Capitol," *KTOO*, July 3, 2017; and Associated Press, "Petition Seeks Removal of Juneau Statue Honoring Alaska-Purchase Driver William H. Seward," *Anchorage Daily News*, June 23, 2020. When the statue was erected, a group of historians debated its significance, preserved in "What Raising a Statue of William Seward Means to Alaskans 150 Years Later," in special double issue: "The Sesquicentennial of the Alaska Purchase," *Pacific Northwest Quarterly* 108, nos. 2/3 (Spring/Summer 2017): 57–62, https://www.jstor.org/stable/44791020.

The history of the 1967 building and the planning for its demolition are drawn from Rickman and Lochart, "Determination of Eligibility for the Alaska State Centennial Museum," and from interviews with Judy Bittner, the State Historic Preservation Officer and the chief of the Office of History and Archaeology, as well as Bob Banghart, Brian Meissner, and Steve Gillette. Nathan Jackson designed the new flicker feather motif.

The information about the museum's policies on sharing objects with tribes came from interviews with Banghart and Henrikson, and regarding the Kiks.ádi frog hat, Steve Henrikson, "A Link with the People: The Alaska State Museum." *Museums International* (UNESCO Paris) 182, 46, no. 2 (1994): 6–10. Details on the 2004 potlatch in Sitka come from Preucel and Williams, "The Centennial Potlatch," and the December 30, 2022, email exchange with Henrikson.

Newspaper coverage informs the discussion of 1990s prejudice against Alaska Natives, at the time known as "the urban-rural divide." An informative article from the period is Tom Kizzia, "Urban-Rural Divide Widens in Juneau," *Anchorage Daily News*, May 3, 1998.

4.

Asper-Smith saved Aaron Elmore's 2013 email. Background on Paul Gardinier comes from his obituary published in the *Juneau Empire*, June 15, 2022. Background on Jackie Manning is from "Introducing Exhibits Specialist, Jackie Manning," *Alaska State Museums Bulletin*, no. 35 (Winter 2010). The story of the museum's development is based largely on interviews with each member of the staff. I was also fortunate to have discussed the project several times with Senator Johnny Ellis before his death.

See Hayes, *Blonde Indian*; and Rickman and Lochart, "Determination of Eligibility for the Alaska State Centennial Museum." I also learned about the site and the process of demolition and the move from interviews with Meissner, Hayes, Gillette, Banghart, Henrikson, Manning, and Asper-Smith. Some details and dates also come from these works: Russell Stigall, "Alaska Breaks Ground on Museum Archive Project," *Juneau Empire* via Associated Press, January 21, 2013; Matt Miller, "Packing Up 32,000 Pieces of Alaska History," *KTOO*, September 27, 2013; Casey Kelly, "Putting the 'State' in Alaska State Museum," *KTOO*, December 1, 2013; Matt Miller, "Slideshow: Alaska State Museum Demolition," *KTOO*, August 2, 2014.

Ben Didrickson's quote is from Asper-Smith's notes from the meetings with cultural leaders. Chief Peter John was ninety-six years old when I interviewed him in Minto: Charles Wohlforth, "Chief Peter John," *Alaska Magazine*, September 1997.

5.

The installation of the large objects in the exhibit was described to me by staff. Haycox's history of Alaska, originally published in 2002, is Stephen W. Haycox, *Alaska: An American Colony*, 2nd ed. (Seattle: University of Alaska Press, 2020).

The Anchorage Museum discarded the pioneer narrative in 2017. Two takes on that event are: Charles Wohlforth, "At the Expanding Anchorage Museum, a Homegrown Leader Seeks to Remake Alaska's Identity," *Anchorage Daily News*, April 24, 2017; and Steve Haycox, "Museum Gallery Treats History with Disdain," *Anchorage Daily News*, September 21, 2017.

The U.S. Coast Guard maintains a history of the revenue cutter *Bear* online at www.history.uscg.mil/. See also Allan's autobiography, Allan Alexander Allan, *Gold, Men and Dogs* (New York: G. P. Putnam's Sons, 1931). I interviewed Coen, and some of his work on Peratrovich is cited above under "The Story in the Exhibits: 2. Conquest and Resistance."

The early draft memo about planning the exhibit, with the file name "SLAM Exhibition Goals and Objectives," is unsigned and undated. Metadata indicates it came to me from Asper-Smith in March 2015.

6.

The museum's opening ceremony was captured in Matt Miller, "Hundred-Year 'Treasure' of Alaska History and Culture Opens in Juneau," *KTOO*, June 7, 2016. The four newspaper columns involved in the "genocide" debate, which Coen used as a teaching tool, are cited above under section 1 of this chapter.

ALASKA STATE MUSEUM COLLECTIONS ON EXHIBIT

WITH SELECT PHOTOGRAPHS

The use of the word "Eskimo" in this list reflects the museum's collection records, which were compiled when that term was common.

Across the Cultures

89-44-1 Tlingit carved and painted wooden eagle mask by Wayne Price

89-44-2 Tlingit carved and painted wooden shark mask by Wayne Price

91-31-27 Necklace of dentalia shells and glass beads

92-26-1 Coiled lidded willow basket decorated with baleen and carved ivory seal

94-34-1 Carved wooden mask of human face

95-9-1 Eskimo skin scraper of brass and ivory

95-35-1 Even-culture beaded leather hood

96-50-1 Beaded red felt dance hat lined with yellow bandana by Florence Marks Sheakley

96-54-1 Tlingit carved bentwood bowl with inset shells

97-8-1 Tsimshian twined cedar bark basket with knobbed lid and contrasting grass design

97-35-15 Nephrite jade adze blade

97-36-1 Adze comprised of a worked jade head lashed with rawhide to a bone handle

98-7-214 Story pipe made of walrus ivory with carvings of sleds and reindeer, seals and walrus

98-7-378 Athabascan basket of birch bark and spruce root

98-26-1 Tlingit carved wooden mask and earrings by Nathan Jackson, Emma Marks

98-30-1 Beaded wool cloth bag

98-30-3-A Haida metal harpoon point

98-30-3-B Haida wooden sheath for harpoon point

98-32-2 Painted twined spruce root basket by Selina Peratrovich, Nathan Jackson

98-45-14 Tiny woven baleen basket with knob of carved ivory in form of walrus head

98-45-15 Woven baleen basket with knob of carved ivory in form of walrus head

2000-1-2 Carved and painted wooden image titled Whaler by Ron Senungetuk

2000-14-1 Carved cedar folding triptych sculpture by John Hoover

2001-10-11 Tlingit beaded neckpiece made of dark blue wool cloth, depicting eagle

2002-16-20 Yup'ik lidded basket of coiled grass with dyed designs

2003-1-13 Whetstone carved of jade

2003-15-5 Tsimshian plaited cedar bark basket

2005-35-1 Sculpture of walrus head created from found objects, titled Ooger-uk Inua #3 by Larry Beck

2006-18-1 Tlingit spruce-root basket with false embroidery

2006-19-1 Beaded woven robe titled Tsirku River Robe by Lani Hotch

2008-10-1 Gut hat with red trim

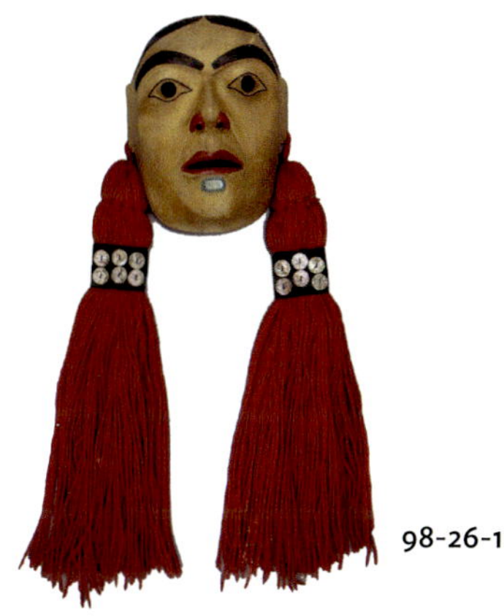

98-26-1

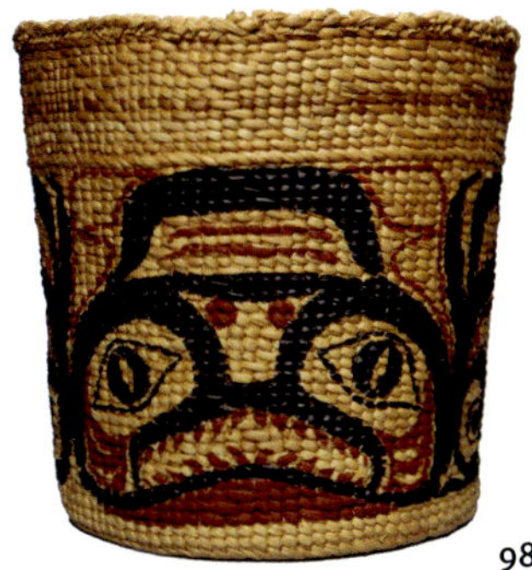

98-32-2

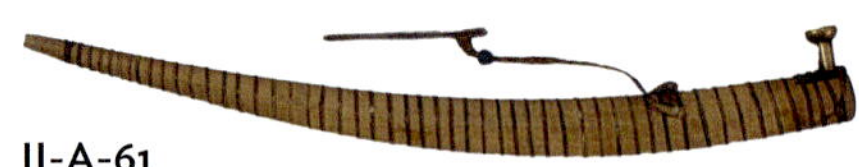
II-A-61

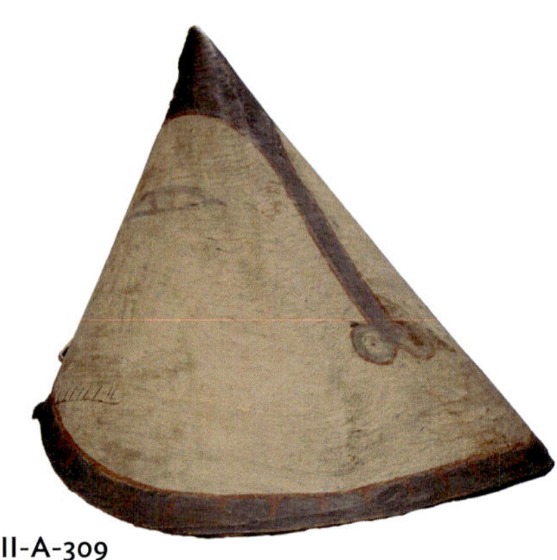
II-A-309

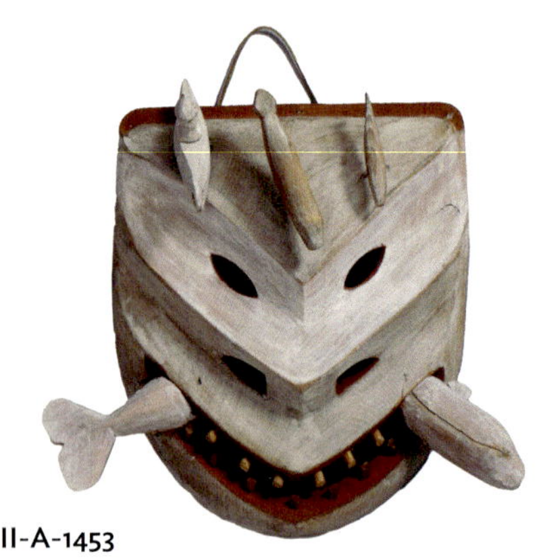
II-A-1453

2010-34-2	Pendant carved from mother of pearl in the shape of a tin.aa with eagle and wolf designs by Mike A. Jackson
2012-6-1	Harpoon line spool formed from sheet of driftwood bent into cylinder stitched with baleen
2013-7-1	Kayak frame with hide lashings and no skin covering present, made in the Norton Sound style
2013-7-2	Kayak frame in King Island style
2014-2-1	Tlingit gold bracelet with killer whale design
2022-8-1	Basketry hat, twined of spruce roots, surmounted with two basketry rings, titled All the Relatives by Delores Churchill, Selina Peratrovich, Holly Churchill, and Donny Varnell
II-A-5	Eskimo drill bow of carved, etched ivory with leather thong attached
II-A-9	Eskimo drill bow of carved ivory with leather thong
II-A-23	Eskimo drill with jade point and ivory handle
II-A-42, 44	Brass smoking pipe
II-A-48	Eskimo smoking pipe of ivory, wood, brass, and rawhide
II-A-50	Eskimo leaden smoking pipe with wooden insets and ivory mouthpiece
II-A-52	Eskimo brass smoking pipe with brass pipe cleaner attached by cord
II-A-55	Smoking pipe of walnut, pewter, and inlaid ivory by Apaata
II-A-61	Eskimo smoking pipe with wooden diamond-shaped stem, brass bowl, and beaded pick attached
II-A-62	Eskimo wood, ivory, and lead smoking pipe with elaborate cleaner attached
II-A-63	Eskimo ivory smoking pipe inlaid with lead and incised designs
II-A-69	Eskimo carved ivory smoking pipe with walrus-shaped bowl.
II-A-143	Eskimo round snuffbox of antler and metal
II-A-309	Eskimo conical painted wooden hunting hat
II-A-310	Inup'iq conical painted wooden hat worn by beluga whale hunters
II-A-311	Eskimo painted wooden hunting visor
II-A-552	Eskimo adze bit of antler and jade with hole for lashing to shaft
II-A-558	Eskimo ulu of antler and jade, broken or unfinished
II-A-559	Eskimo ulu of walrus ivory and jade, with rounded corners
II-A-563	Commercially made ulu of iron and musk ox horn
II-A-564	Eskimo ulu of iron and musk ox horn or bone
II-A-566	Eskimo ulu of iron and ivory with crescent-shaped blade
II-A-618	Eskimo carved and painted wooden paddle
II-A-624	Eskimo ulu of slate and antler
II-A-821	Eskimo jade adze blade
II-A-822	Eskimo jade adze blade
II-A-837	Eskimo jade adze blade
II-A-1428	Yup'ik beaded headdress
II-A-1429	Eskimo beaded headdress with brass and sealskin
II-A-1453	Yup'ik carved and painted wooden mask with minke whale in mouth and figures attached to forehead
II-A-1468	Yup'ik carved and painted wooden mask of human face with glass eyes
II-A-1524	Yup'ik mask of carved and painted wood, with asymmetrical features and feathers attached
II-A-1529	Eskimo carved mask of human-like face with weathered surface
II-A-1581	Eskimo women's bentwood work box
II-A-1582	Eskimo teardrop-shaped bentwood box
II-A-1601	Eskimo triangular painted bentwood dish
II-A-1794	Yup'ik carved and painted wooden spoon with bird design
II-A-1823	Eskimo painted bentwood dipper sewn with vegetable fibers
II-A-1824	Yup'ik round painted bentwood dish kerfed into a rim

II-A-1829	Eskimo painted bentwood rimmed wooden dish with bird decoration
II-A-2239	Eskimo kayak anchor of wood and sealskin
II-A-2266	Oval bentwood dish fastened with nails and pegs
II-A-2381	Eskimo pair of twined grass socks
II-A-2405	Eskimo grass basket of open twined work
II-A-2500	Eskimo flat-bottomed coiled-grass basket with loop-handled lid
II-A-2626	Eskimo painted and carved wooden paddle
II-A-2755	Eskimo adze with blade made from a file and lashed with rawhide
II-A-2779	Ogeanak carved walrus tusk with a walrus man and seven walrus heads
II-A-2881	Eskimo ivory carving of seal with human face
II-A-3048	One pair Yup'ik mukluks, made with oogruk (bearded seal) soles and seal uppers, decorated with various colors of cloth and yarn
II-A-3059	Pair of Siberian slippers of sealskin, cloth, and caribou skin, with multicolored decoration
II-A-3089	Eskimo wooden mouth-pump kayak bailer composed of two halves bound together with cotton string
II-A-3101	Eskimo boat hook of bone, carved like a bird beak
II-A-3251	Eskimo decorated ivory spear rest from kayak
II-A-3366	Eskimo model hunting scene with carved ivory figures
II-A-3438	Eskimo walrus ivory handle for bucket or box, with whale carvings
II-A-3478	Eskimo cylindrical kayak bailer made from two wood pieces bound with cotton string
II-A-3488	Eskimo ivory toggle harpoon head
II-A-3489	Eskimo ivory toggle harpoon head
II-A-3495	Eskimo ivory toggle harpoon head
II-A-3495-B	Eskimo all-metal harpoon head with wooden case.
II-A-3583	Eskimo Wooden paddle with ridge on each side of blade
II-A-3654	Eskimo wooden paddle painted with seals and other mammals
II-A-3663	Eskimo seal float with fur left on, decorated with ivory beads and feathers
II-A-3665 (see p. 106)	Eskimo painted wooden paddle with ridged sides of blade
II-A-3671	Eskimo wooden paddle with hinge down center each side of blade
II-A-3690	Eskimo wooden paddle with rawhide lashing
II-A-3708	Eskimo bird (goose) spear with ivory prongs and sinew wrappings
II-A-3936	Two Eskimo harpoon rests of ivory carved as head and necks of emperor geese with inset eyes of dark wood
II-A-3936-1	Eskimo harpoon rest of ivory carved as head and neck of emperor goose with inset eyes of dark wood
II-A-3936-2	Eskimo harpoon rest of ivory carved as head and neck of emperor goose with inset eyes of dark wood
II-A-3938	Pair of Eskimo unfinished irony harpoon rests carved in shape of beaver teeth
II-A-3952	Eskimo colored-ivory piece of kayak rigging
II-A-3993	Pair of Eskimo walrus tooth harpoon rests incised with black designs
II-A-4156-3	Eskimo seal harpoon dart of wood, ivory, and feathers
II-A-4157-9	Eskimo wooden throwing board with bone or ivory pegs for finger grips, carved-out thumb and finger grooves, and ivory stops
II-A-4166-1	Eskimo seal harpoon dart with oozik socket piece, barbed ivory head, and feathers
II-A-4176	Eskimo coil of rawhide line
II-A-4204	Eskimo braining ball made from skeletal whalebone, for killing seals
II-A-4205	Eskimo harpoon rack of wooden hoop, brace, and legs, edged with ivory and glass bead seal decorations

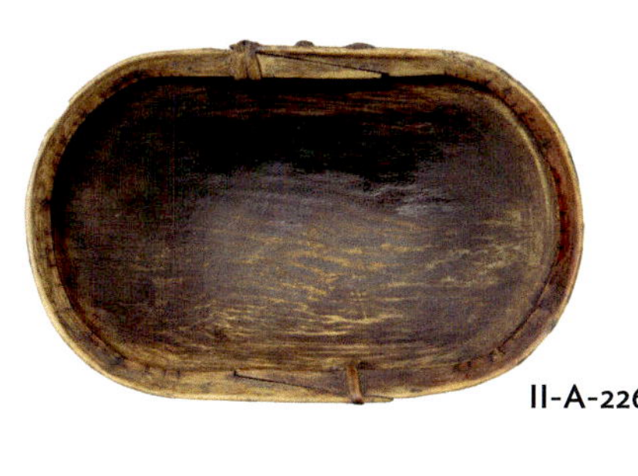
II-A-2266

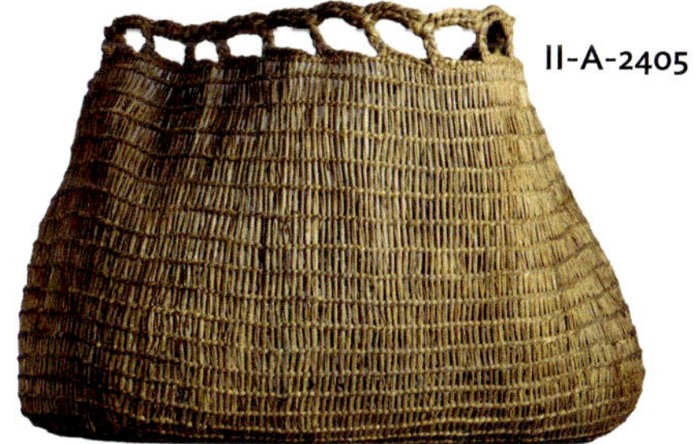
II-A-2405

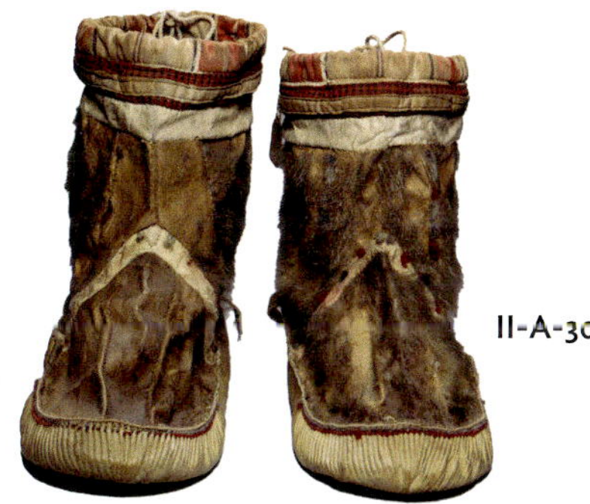
II-A-3048

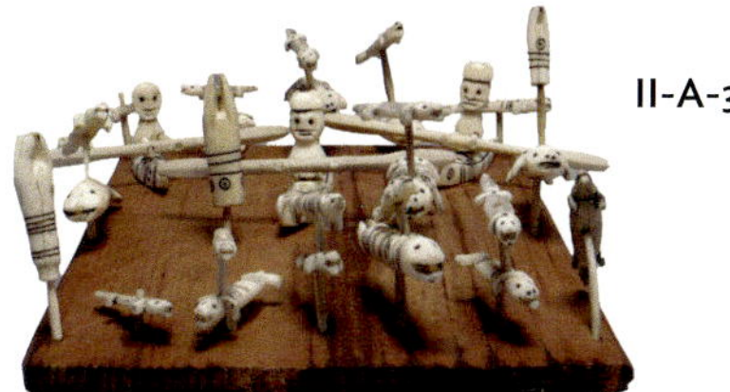
II-A-3366

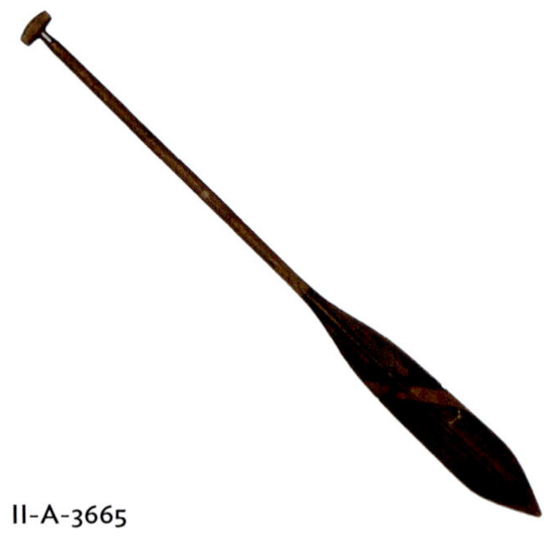
II-A-3665

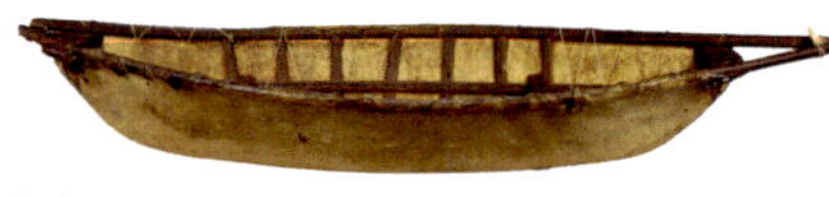
II-A-5104

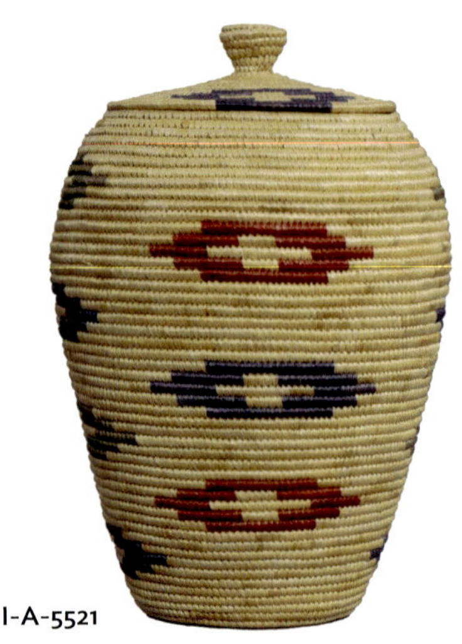
II-A-5521

II-A-4420	Eskimo water bottle carried kayak, made of bladder with ivory mouthpiece, wood stopper, and braided cord
II-A-4575	Eskimo painted boat hook of wood, bone, and rawhide
II-A-4737	Yup'ik basketry rattle coiled in Eskimo style with multicolored dyed gut bands of decoration
II-A-4869	Eskimo round bentwood toolbox spliced with root, hinged with rawhide, with beads and ivory
II-A-4940	Eskimo tanned leather coat of reindeer skin, ornamented with cut and colored tanned hide and fringes
II-A-4941	Eskimo leather apron-type garment tied with leather thongs, with glass beads and fringe
II-A-4969	Three pieces of calfskin parka trim in black and white pattern of diamonds and triangles by Margaret Temple
II-A-4969-A	Piece of calfskin parka trim in black and white pattern of diamonds and triangles by Margaret Temple
II-A-5024	Yup'ik fifteen-foot wooden kayak frame with one hatch, ice breaker, and carved face design and fragment of walrus hide
II-A-5024-A	Eskimo fifteen-foot wooden kayak frame with one hatch
II-A-5024-B	Eskimo wooden kayak seat
II-A-5035	Eskimo coiled-grass oblong-shaped basket and lid with bright multicolored bead and skin appliqué
II-A-5104	Eskimo model umiak with skin over pegged wooden frame
II-A-5407	Carved and painted wooden mask of crow head with mouth containing seal face by Sam Hunter
II-A-5521	Lidded coiled basket with multicolor design by Anna L. Smart
II-A-5678	Yup'ik wooden food dish carved from one piece, with bentwood rim with eight diamonds of white rock inlaid
II-A-5955	Eskimo ivory pipe carved in one piece with bowl, with carvings of dog (wolf?), walrus, and bear and incised scenes of people and animals
II-A-6099	Red ochre-stained bentwood berry bucket with ivory handle by Paul Nagaruk
II-A-6109	Carved wooden mask of asymmetrical, kidney-shaped human-like face by Sylvester Ayek
II-A-6295	Round cardboard box covered with multicolored beadwork on felt and lined with fabric by Lucille Koozaata
II-A-6464	Eskimo old ivory tusk sliced lengthwise and incised with animal, humans, and vegetation
II-A-6467	Eskimo old ivory "tally stick" or story stick incised with humans, animals, and objects
II-A-6570	Eskimo jade and ivory ulu
II-A-6593	Eskimo bentwood box with baleen and rawhide
II-A-6678	Eskimo coiled lidded grass basket
II-A-7103	Eskimo jade ulu blade with elongated semi-lunar shape, very symmetrical
II-A-7121	Baleen basket with ivory disks and carved polar bear head handle by Joe Sikvayugak
II-A-7124	Eskimo large nephrite adze blade, very polished except for top edge
II-A-7128	Eskimo black stone adze blade
II-A-7288	Eskimo ivory and sinew bola
II-A-7358	Baleen basket with carved ivory walrus head finial by Joshua Sakeagak
II-B-7	Tlingit string of red, white, and blue glass beads
II-B-26	String of spherical blue and white glass beads
II-B-82	Tlingit headdress of fabric cap decorated with beads and dentalia shells
II-B-83	Tlingit octopus bag, or beaded pouch with four equal-length extensions at bottom
II-B-343	Tlingit twined spruce-root basket with grass imbrication and multicolored false embroidery
II-B-396	Spruce-root basket with flared walls and false embroidery in "shaman's hat," "tattoo," and "half the head of the salmonberry" patterns by Princess Klonteek

II-B-420 Tlingit twined cylindrical spruce-root basket decorated with three horizontal bands of false embroidery

II-B-584 Tlingit spruce-root basket plaque decorated with alternating rows of overlaid twining and open weave, and solid-weave center

II-B-664 Hand-wrought spear blade with groove down center on both sides

II-B-701 Northern-style varnished and shellacked model dugout canoe, painted with head with teeth at both ends

II-B-747 Tlingit beaded headdress in Iroquois or Mohawk style with bear fur, surmounted by bird with cloth body

II-B-752 Tlingit carved red cedar board from bentwood box

II-B-793 Branch-hafted adze with file bit, lashed with halibut line

II-B-811 Hat woven of split spruce roots, with painted "formline" design of red and black, depicting straight-beaked bird and four pointed star on crown by Charles Edenshaw, Isabel Edenshaw

II-B-836 Tlingit ceremonial blanket clasp of engraved silver

II-B-930 Tlingit hand-forged copper double-dagger

II-B-982 Tlingit shark-tooth earrings with silver fasteners

II-B-1014 Tlingit carved and painted wooden crest hat with abalone and seal teeth

II-B-1226 Tlingit Yakutat-style painted bentwood box with partition

II-B-1306 Tlingit copper double-dagger

II-B-1380 Tlingit hat of red wool trimmed with ermine, rabbit fur, pearl buttons, and human hair

II-B-1395 Plaited cedar-bark basket with square shape and plaid-like effect

II-B-1404 Seal harpoon head made of metal barb inset into wood and bound with twine

II-B-1506 Tlingit green and yellow felt hat with red accents, decorated with buttons, ribbon, feather duster

II-B-1530 Tsimshian carved wooden puppet with jointed arms and legs and moveable head, with accessories

II-B-1601 Tlingit stocking cap-style hat made of red wool flannel with tassel and beadwork

II-B-1619 Haida cylindrical spruce-root basket with four black bands

II-B-1677 Ceremonial tinneh (tin.aa) of hammered copper

II-B-1695 Spruce-root "boater"-style hat dyed purple with grass false embroidery

II-B-1709 Tlingit carved and painted wooden model house post

II-B-1832 Rattle-top spruce-root basket with brown and orange decoration

II-B-1853 Carved and stained wooden maskette of human in contemporary Tlingit style, with human hair in side ponytail, by Rick Beasley

II-B-1864 Tlingit carved modern wooden totem pole with hair tufts

II-B-1883 Chilkat-style woven tunic of mountain-goat hair and cedar bark by Anna Ehlers

II-B-1893 Cutout canoe carved and painted in northern Northwest Coast Native style by John Wallace

II-B-1924 Ceremonial Chilkat-style shirt of black velvet with beaded floral patterns on orange wool trim

II-B-1969 Tlingit wooden smoking pipe with detachable pipe

II-C-9 Tlingit woman's beaded hair ornament

II-C-32 Athabascan model birch bark canoe with colorful painted decorations

II-C-37 Athabascan knife sheath of leather with porcupine quill trim

II-C-103 Athabascan dentalia necklace of shells and beads strung on sinew with tabs and dividers of smoked moosehide

II-C-152 Athabascan "crooked" knife with wooden handle, steel blade filed almost to a point at the tip

II-C-154 Birch stick used as handle for scraping skins

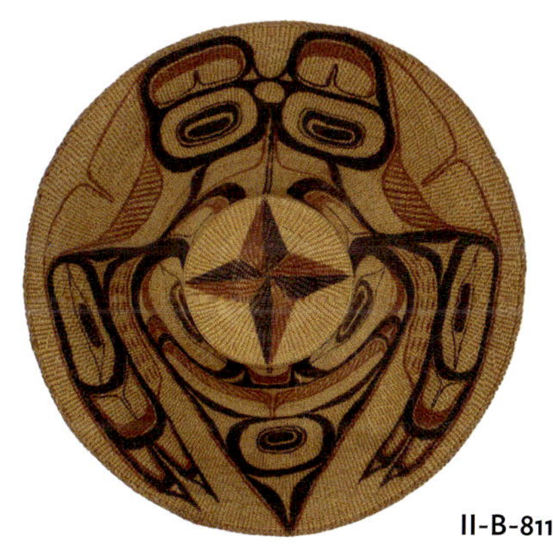

II-B-811

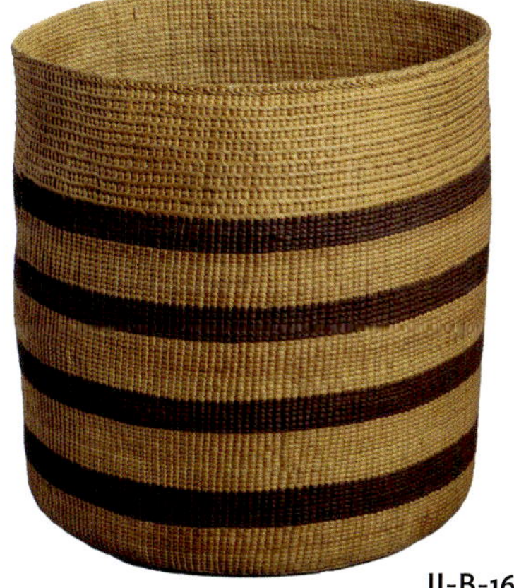

II-B-1619

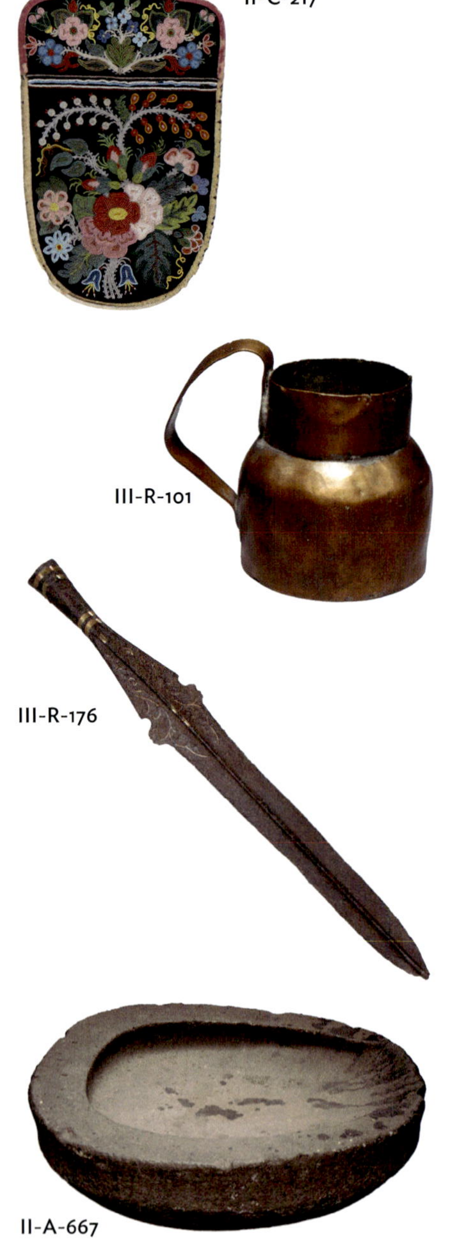
II-C-217
III-R-101
III-R-176
II-A-667

II-C-154-B Birch stick used as handle for scraping skins

II-C-154-C Scraper made from iron trap spring

II-C-199 Athabascan split-willow basket with lid and loop handles

II-C-217 Athabascan beaded wall pocket

II-C-221 Athabascan split-willow basket with loop handles and large flower design

II-C-236 Athabascan large willow-root basket coiled with constricted neck, walrus ivory closure

II-C-242 Athabascan carved and painted black and white wooden mask of woman's face

II-C-294 Athabascan knife of copper with snail-shell shape and leather wrapping

II-C-324 Athabascan beaded fabric panel of "Yakutat Flower" design

II-D-98 Blue and clear trade beads on cotton string

II-F-107 Aleut work basket with overlay design in "bar" diamonds

II-F-124 Aleut covered basket of finely woven grass, with yarn and embroidery floss decoration

II-F-153 Aleut circular lidded woven-grass basket with checkerboard and diamond embroidery

II-F-165 Aleut three-hatch model kayak with stretched hide, bristles, and yarn, and human figures

III-O-121 Knife and handle are all one single piece of iron, with curved blade

III-R-64 Copper spike

III-R-101 Handmade copper mug stamped in Cyrillic letters "PAK"

III-R-111 Wrought-iron spike

III-R-175 Russian round copper snuffbox with inside coated with tin

III-R-176 Koryak spear or lance head decorated with floral designs of overlaid copper and bronze

III-R-232 Small Russian bronze bell with Russian writing engraved around base

IV-B-55 Jade nugget, irregular in shape, from Kobuk River

IV-B-130 Four copper nuggets

IV-B-130-A Copper nugget

IV-B-130-B Copper nugget

IV-B-130-C Copper nugget

IV-B-365 Calcite (green phosphorescence), iron-rich mud

V-A-844 Wall-mounted carved and painted wood with Northwest Coast designs by Jim Schoppert

ED.97-5 Kameleika or gut parka

LC.261-1 Eskimo sealskin pants

LC.435-1 Iqyax or biadarka of wood, skin, and sinew

LC.435-2 Double-bladed igyax, kayak, or biadarka paddle

SJ-II-X-683 Eskimo sled of wood, hide, and bone

Alutiiq / Sugpiaq

93-24-1 Oak bentwood hunting hat decorated with paint, beads, ivory, imitation sea lion whiskers by Jacob Simeonoff

96-32-1 Painted wooden seal decoy helmet by Jacob Simeonoff

2001-10-6 Ivory model of Alutiiq bidarka with two figures hunting sea otter

2001-10-10 Long and thin harpoon blade of ground slate with small grooves to contain poison

2001-10-13 Wooden bow

2004-29-1 Wooden sculpture titled Rites of Passage, in the form of a traditional wooden kayak paddle, painted and decorated with beads and feathers by Jerry Laktonen

2005-4-1 Three-dimensional painted paper harbor seal head by Alvin Amason

2014-9-1 Wooden oil bowl carved in fish shape and repaired with spruce root

2014-9-2 Wooden oil bowl carved in fish shape

2014-21-1 Alutiiq mask of carved and painted white spruce wood, titled Raven Who Married the Chief's Daughter by Perry Eaton

II-A-239 Egg-shaped stone lamp with rounded base

II-A-667 Sugpiaq large stone lamp

II-A-1559 Aleut carved mask of grotesque human-like face with weathered surface and exaggeratedly high forehead

II-A-1560	Aleut mask of carved wood with grotesque human-like face
II-A-1564	Alutiiq carved mask of grotesque human-like face with weathered surface and exaggeratedly high forehead, mouth and chin missing
II-A-1637	Eskimo quiver of red cedar wood
II-A-1644	Eskimo throwing stick of carved wood
II-A-1665	Eskimo stone maul
II-A-1668	Eskimo stone adze
II-A-1674	Alutiiq double-edged stone pick
II-A-1678	Alutiiq elliptical stone oil lamp
II-A-1680	Alutiiq elliptical stone oil lamp
II-A-1739	Eskimo grooved stone sinker
II-A-1744	Eskimo notched stone sinker
II-A-1748	Eskimo slate ulu blade
II-A-1754	Eskimo wedge of shaped bone
II-A-1758	Eskimo wedge of shaped bone
II-A-2015	Eskimo harpoon head with brass blade and extra copper blade, in wooden case
II-A-2023	Eskimo antler dart point with triangular hole
II-A-2554	Eskimo harpoon-style arrow with copper point
II-A-2606	Small Eskimo stone lamp
II-A-2607	Alutiiq stone lamp with groove for wick
II-A-2793	Eskimo oval wooden oil dish in the shape of a merganser, decorated with inlaid white beads
II-A-3093	Eskimo triangular whetstone
II-A-3723	Eskimo copper spearhead
II-A-3920	Model two-hole, cleft bow baidarka (kayak) made of unpainted wood
II-A-4136	Eskimo light brown carved wooden ladle
II-A-4944	Eskimo woman's parka of squirrel furs, ornamentally trimmed with lynx, rabbit, reindeer, fox, and wolverine, and red worsted fabric, without hood
II-A-6852	Pacific Eskimo spruce-root basket, Pacific Eskimo style, with grass false embroidery
II-A-6857	Alutiiq flared cylindrical spruce-root basket with false embroidery of yellow grass
II-F-22	Alutiiq stone lamp
II-F-310	Aleut whaling lance blade of slate incised with Russian letters
II-F-313	Aleut ulu blade of slate; semi-lunar with curve very symmetrical
II-F-317	Aleut slate knife blade with drilled hole
II-F-318	Aleut stone arrowhead or point, chipped from dark stone, leaf-shaped
II-F-321	Aleut slate arrowhead, "Christmas tree" shape
UA/UC-407	Ground squirrel (taxidermy)

Athabascan

91-3-1	Embroidered Tanana sled bag
91-3-2	Beaded Athabascan moccasins
93-1-2	Athabascan carved sheep-horn spoon
95-37-1	Percussion-lock trade gun, smooth bore,
96-51-9	Carved and stained wooden spoon
96-51-12 (see p. 110)	Small elbow adze with metal blade
96-51-14	Athabascan carved and stained wooden mallet
96-51-15	Ingalik carved and stained wedge for splitting wood
96-51-16	Ingalik carved and stained wedge for splitting wood
2000-36-1	Violin and bow
2001-10-3	Sheep horn spoon with carved handle and engraved bowl
2005-15-1	Rattle fashioned from silver sheet metal by Glen C. Simpson
2006-5-1	Painted wooden mask with metal, feather, human hair, etc. by Kathleen Carlo Kendall
2007-15-1	Male Athabascan hunter doll of smoked moose hide with beads
2007-15-2	Female Athabascan doll of smoked moose hide with beads and fur
2008-7-1	Beaded moose-hide Athabascan baby belt or baby carrier by Delores Sloan
2009-10-1	Athabascan girl's beaded dress of caribou skin
2014-11-1	Athabascan carved canoe paddle
I-B-11	Gray jay (taxidermy)

II-A-2606

II-A-2607

II-F-22

II-F-310

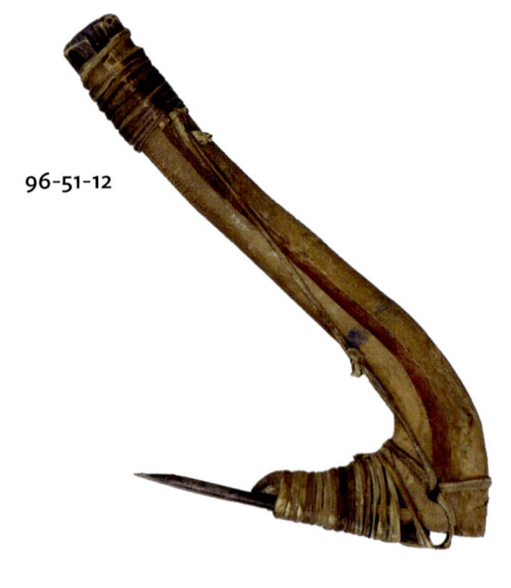

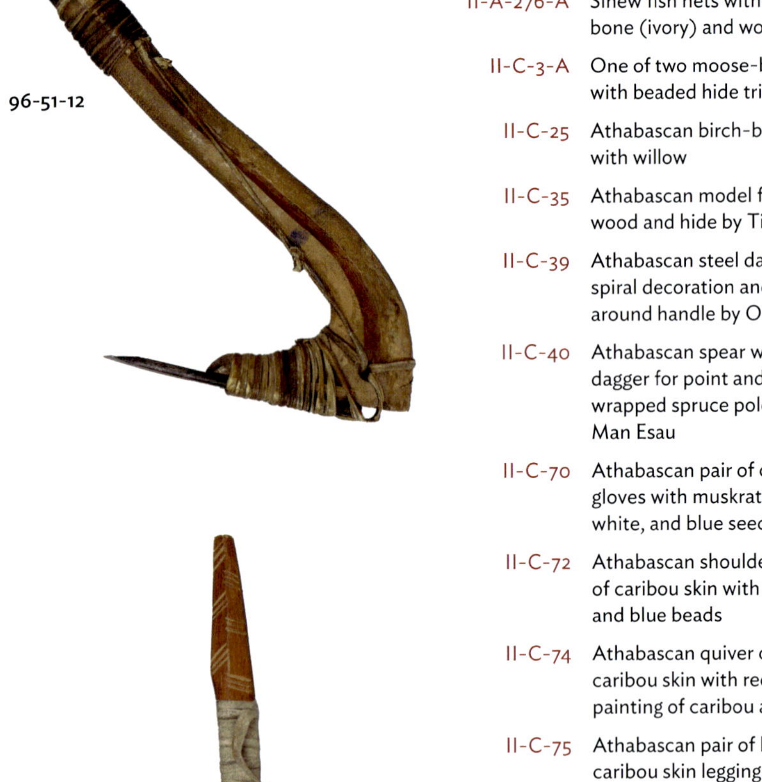

96-51-12

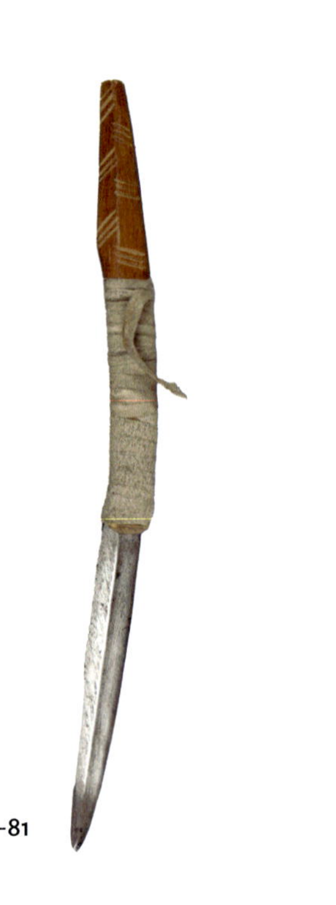

II-C-81

II-A-276-A Sinew fish nets with handles of bone (ivory) and wood

II-C-3-A One of two moose-bone awls with beaded hide trim

II-C-25 Athabascan birch-bark basket with willow

II-C-35 Athabascan model freight sled of wood and hide by Titus

II-C-39 Athabascan steel dagger with spiral decoration and buckskin around handle by Old Man Esau

II-C-40 Athabascan spear with Tena dagger for point and rawhide-wrapped spruce pole by Old Man Esau

II-C-70 Athabascan pair of caribou gloves with muskrat trim and red, white, and blue seed beads

II-C-72 Athabascan shoulder-strap bag of caribou skin with red, white, and blue beads

II-C-74 Athabascan quiver of beaded caribou skin with red ochre painting of caribou and hunter

II-C-75 Athabascan pair of beaded caribou skin leggings with moccasins

II-C-76 Athabascan knee-length dress of caribou skin beaded and fringed

II-C-77 Athabascan pair of beaded and fringed caribou skin mittens connected with beaded cord

II-C-78 Athabascan hood of beaded and fringed caribou skin

II-C-79 Athabascan beaded and fringed caribou skin bag with red ochre interior and beaver tooth and wooden pulls

II-C-80 Athabascan beaded and fringed caribou skin tunic shirt

II-C-81 Athabascan curved knife made of file with wood handle dyed red and rawhide lashing

II-C-84 Athabascan dagger of beveled copper with traditional handle with snail design, wrapped with caribou hide

II-C-89 Athabascan wooden fish spear with caribou antler prongs and steel barbs

II-C-90 Athabascan leather jacket with fur and quill decoration

II-C-91 Athabascan pair of beaded soft leather boots

II-C-100 Athabascan quiver made of caribou leather and decorated with beadwork, paint, and yarn and trade-bead tassels

II-C-118 Carved wooden rattle with six rattle pieces and one fishhook attached to a pole by Joe Joseph

II-C-123 Athabascan skin scraper with wooden handle and blade made from metal saw

II-C-125 Athabascan chisel with steel blade and wood and rawhide handle

II-C-126 Kutchin fish spear with long wooden handle and Y-shaped antler spear ends and bone barbs attached with sinew lashings

II-C-134 Fishhook with bone and wire by Nick Dennis

II-C-136-B Athabascan stone object possibly used as a skin scraper

II-C-140 Athabascan moose-bone skin scraper

II-C-141 Athabascan carved wooden bowl

II-C-142 Athabascan fishhook made from beaver leg bone

II-C-143 Drilled bone fishhook with wire and line by Philip Esal

II-C-147 Athabascan willow-root basket containing basket materials

II-C-147-A Athabascan partly done coiled willow-root basket, polychrome dyed

II-C-147-B Athabascan orange dyed split root

II-C-147-C Athabascan natural split root

II-C-147-D Athabascan red dyed split root

II-C-150 Berry masher carved of one piece of wood (branch and trunk) by Miska Alexia

II-C-153 Athabascan bundle of caribou babiche

II-C-161 Beaver hat with base of machine-stitched navy-blue wool by Malisa Gregory

II-C-165 Set of three birch-bark baskets by Belle Deacon

II-C-165-A One of set of three birch-bark baskets by Belle Deacon

II-C-165-B One of set of three birch-bark baskets by Belle Deacon

II-C-165-C One of set of three birch-bark baskets by Belle Deacon

II-C-166 Athabascan circular peg calendar of carved wood

II-C-176 Athabascan shellacked wooden model of fish or otter trap on a board base with rails or slats held together with string or split root

II-C-177 Otter mask of carved and painted wood with grouse and raven feathers by Billy Williams

II-C-179 Athabascan-style bow with bone string guard, twisted sinew or hide string

II-C-183 Athabascan child's caribou-fawn skin parka, unlined, with fur-trimmed hood decorated with split ears and fur-covered antlers

II-C-186 Athabascan rabbit snare made of two strands of sinew

II-C-192 Athabascan birch-bark baby carrier by Dorothy Titus

II-C-195 Athabascan wooden netting needle

II-C-197 Athabascan birch-bark canoe

II-C-203 Athabascan pair of moose-hide mittens with yarn harness, beadwork, and pom-poms

II-C-208 Athabascan basket of coiled willow, with red and green "V" design

II-C-210 Athabascan scraper of moose bone, with leather thong and terry cloth wrapping

II-C-232 Athabascan rawhide mesh beaver trap

II-C-235 Athabascan dagger of copper with traditional handle with snail design, wrapped with hide

II-C-244-3 Athabascan hunting arrow with metal point

II-C-244-4 Athabascan hunting arrow with metal point

II-C-245-3 Athabascan set of five arrows with bone points and fletching of barred feathers by Steven Northway

II-C-256 Athabascan beaded coin purse shaped like infant's slipper with zipper closing and suede sole

II-C-257 Athabascan glasses case, of smoke-tanned leather with beaded flowers by Pat Metleum

II-C-272 Athabascan drum of scraped skin stretched taut over bentwood frame, painted with dots and lines, laced with rawhide by Stephen Northway

II-C-297 Athabascan beaded and fringed moose-hide gun case

II-C-298 Athabascan beaded moose-hide knife sheath

II-C-312 Athabascan dentalia shell necklace with cross-piece leather dividers and jet-black tube beads

II-C-313 Kutchin beaded moose-hide bag with yarn handle and tasseled fringe

II-C-314 Athabascan beading in intricate floral design on black velvet backed with tan cotton fabric

II-C-316-F Athabascan counting cord of gut, feathers, hair, and hide

II-C-326 Athabascan beaded fabric panel of "Yakutat Flower" design

II-D-21 Athabascan beaded wall pocket

II-D-112 Athabascan drawstring bag or pouch consisting of two beaded discs joined with fabric at sides, with yarn drawstring and tassels

LC.98-1 Kutchin Athabascan snowshoes by Agnes Deaphon, Mrs. Deacon Deaphon

UA/UC-464 Red-backed vole (taxidermy)

Atrium (Eagle Tree)

I-B-51 Townsend's warbler (taxidermy)

I-B-53 White-winged crossbill (taxidermy)

I-B-54 Red-breasted sapsucker (taxidermy)

I-B-77 Bald eagle egg (cleaned)

I-B-238 Red squirrel (taxidermy)

I-B-439 Bald eagle (taxidermy)

I-B-485 Bald eagle (taxidermy)

I-B-493 Bald eagle (taxidermy)

UA/UC-465 Red squirrel (taxidermy)

UA/UC-483 Bald eagle with wings spread as if just landed (taxidermy)

UA/UC-484 Immature bald eagle (taxidermy)

UA/UC-485 Bald eagle chick (taxidermy)

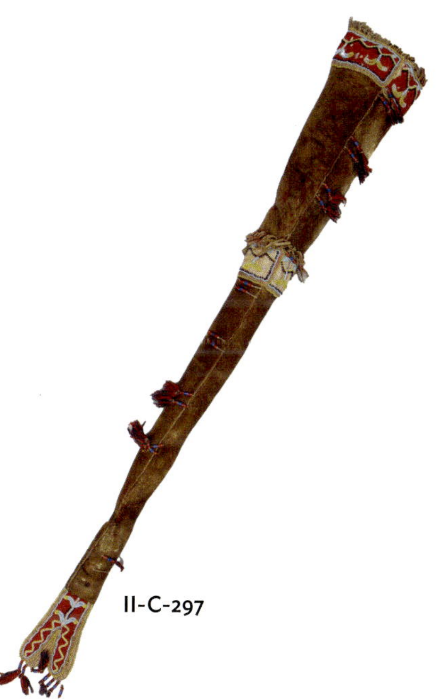
II-C-297

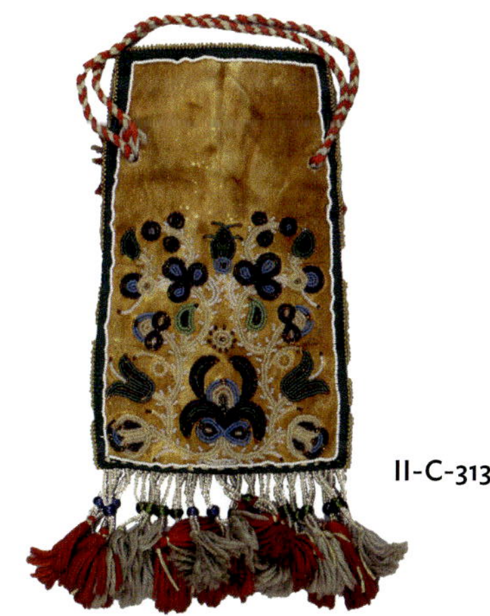
II-C-313

Earth Sciences

92-30-1 Mineral sample of epidote with quartz

92-30-2 Mineral sample of epidote with quartz

97-18-1 Two samples of epidote and quartz

97-18-2 Sample of garnet and almandite

97-18-16 Pelecypod fossil

97-18-19 Sample of orbicular diorite

97-18-21 Leaf fossils

2012-22-1 Large ore sample with a variety of minerals

2012-24-1 Small dark gray rocks in plastic bubble on wooden pedestal with small Alaskan flag that went to the moon with the Apollo 11 mission

II-A-16 Eskimo mouth drill of carved wood and stone

II-A-180 Eskimo tom cod rod with line, sinker, and hook

II-A-180-B Eskimo gray stone sinker for tom cod fishing line

II-A-180-C Eskimo lure with hook for tom cod fishing line

II-A-209 Eskimo fishhook and reddish stone lure with sinker

II-A-225 Eskimo ivory and pyrite plummet

II-A-231 Eskimo fishing sinker and lure

II-A-384 Eskimo drill cup of stone set into wood

II-A-521 Eskimo skin scraper with slate blade lashed to wooden handle with thong

II-A-524 Eskimo skin scraper with black flint blade set in mammoth ivory handle

II-A-551 Eskimo adze bit of antler and jade with notches for extension

II-A-560 Eskimo ulu of jade, mammoth ivory, wood, and sinew

II-A-623 Eskimo ulu of ivory, baleen, and wood

II-A-653 Eskimo knife with slate blade and wooden handle drilled with holes

II-A-655 Eskimo knife with slate blade and pistol-grip-style antler or bone handle

II-A-751 Eskimo lancet with pinched lanceolate-shaped flint blade and straight handle carved from antler

II-A-752 Eskimo lancet with pinched lanceolate-shaped flint blade and straight handle carved from antler

II-A-966 Eskimo jade lancet with antler handle

II-A-973 Eskimo mitlik of jade and antler

II-A-2061 Eskimo tan-colored flint projectile point

II-A-2062 Eskimo tan-colored flint projectile point

II-A-2063 Eskimo tan-colored flint projectile point

II-A-2064 Eskimo tan-colored flint projectile point

II-A-3397 Eskimo ivory toggle harpoon head

II-A-3503 Eskimo ivory toggle harpoon head with blade

II-A-3504 Eskimo ivory toggle harpoon head with blade

II-A-3509 Eskimo ivory toggle harpoon head with jade blade

II-A-3509-A Eskimo ivory toggle harpoon head with blade

II-A-3509-B Eskimo ivory toggle harpoon head with blade

II-A-3542 Eskimo antler toggle harpoon head with flint blade

II-A-3637 Two Eskimo flint projectile points

II-A-3637-A Eskimo flint projectile point

II-A-3637-B Eskimo flint projectile point

II-A-3638 Four Eskimo flint projectile points

II-A-3638-A Eskimo flint projectile point

II-A-3638-B Eskimo flint projectile point

II-A-3638-C Eskimo flint projectile point

II-A-3849 Three Eskimo toggle harpoon heads of ivory with stone blades

II-A-3849-1 Eskimo toggle harpoon head of ivory with stone blade

II-A-3849-2 Eskimo toggle harpoon head of ivory with stone blade

II-A-3849-3 Eskimo toggle harpoon head of ivory with stone blade

II-A-3851-2 Eskimo toggle harpoon head of antler with slate blade

II-A-3851-5 Eskimo toggle harpoon head of antler with slate blade

II-A-3857-3 Eskimo whale harpoon head of bone

II-A-5243 Eskimo spear point of chipped stone and inserted into end of antler shaft, bound with baleen

II-A-5260 Eskimo greenish-black stone braining ball with leather thong

II-A-6623 Eskimo dark brown bone ulu

II-B-224 Stone hat-top hammer

II-B-245 Stone war club of granite, oval-shaped and grooved

II-B-749 Stone artifact in shape of bird head and neck

III-O-888 Wood plaque with moon rock in plexiglass and small Alaska flag

IV-A-6 Light-brown and waterworn limestone piece

IV-A-8 Trachyte porphyry containing phenocrysts feldspar

IV-A-22 Light tan-color pumice stone

IV-A-25 Forty-three small stones of various colors from Aleutian Islands beach, including jasper, agate, and quartz

IV-A-26 Twenty-eight volcanic rocks from Aleutian Islands

IV-A-30 Natural stone resembling pestle or "mano," worn smooth by wave action

IV-A-40 Graphitic schist with metasomatic quartz and coarse grains of pyrite, from Ship Creek

IV-A-41 Greywacke, sandstone

IV-A-50 Actinolite in sericite schist

IV-A-57 Marble

IV-A-59 Flat heart-shaped amulet of concretion, found at Valdez Glacier

IV-A-63 Vial of volcanic ash with cork

IV-A-64 Graphitic schist containing pyrrhotite, galena, and sphalerite

IV-A-67	Muscovite schist
IV-A-99	Two shiny black pieces of coal
IV-A-133	Round ball of polished breccia consisting of sharp fragments embedded in fine-grained matrix
IV-B-2	Red and green waterworn jasper from Moonstone Bay
IV-B-4	Red and green jasper with small amount of brown, from Moonstone Bay
IV-B-22	Calcite from Halleck Harbor
IV-B-66	Quartz crystals from Treadwell Mine
IV-B-110-A	Large mineral sample of native copper
IV-B-120	Pieces of mica
IV-B-120-A	Piece of mica
IV-B-126	Jasper, miniature geode vug, chalcedony
IV-B-156	Kyanite
IV-B-173	Obsidian
IV-B-182	Two agate specimens from Moonstone Bay
IV-B-182-A	Agate from Attu Island
IV-B-182-B	Agate from Attu Island
IV-B-186	Pyrite cubes from Taku Harbor
IV-B-188	Quartz, sulfide-bearing vein
IV-B-201	Vein quartz in schist, weathered ankerite
IV-B-227	Calcite (bornite, "peacock ore")
IV-B-246	Almandite garnet in hornblende gneiss
IV-B-262	Two quartz crystals
IV-B-262-A	Quartz crystal
IV-B-272	Pyrite crystals, quartz
IV-B-279-A	Large white and gray rock with gold flecks, free gold in quartz, from Hirst Chichagof Mine
IV-B-286	Gold, galena, sphalerite in quartz
IV-B-295	Pyroxenite
IV-B-315	Garnet sand in glass bottle with cork
IV-B-325	Tremolite asbestos
IV-B-380	Collection of agates from Attu Island
IV-B-404	Palygorskite from Lemesurier Island
IV-C-32	Rock-bearing marine fossil
IV-C-50	Petrified (fossilized) wood, at one time encrusted with barnacles
IV-D-16	Stone artifact, brownish gray in color
UA/UC-206	Four long glass tubes filled with white sediment, stopped with corks at both ends

Foreign Voyagers

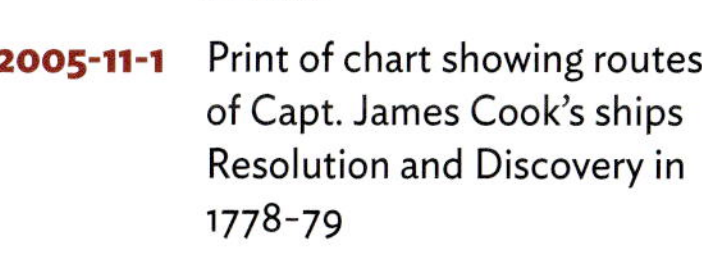

90-14-1	1772 map of Alaska
92-20-1	Engraving depicting Tlingit fishing camp
92-23-1	Russian silver medal depicting Catherine the Great and a ship
93-2-1	Model of Russian ship Slava Rossii by Timothy M. Sczawinski
94-16-2	Sounding lead and rope with depth markings
97-24-1	1773 map of coasts of Siberia and Alaska
2005-11-1	Print of chart showing routes of Capt. James Cook's ships Resolution and Discovery in 1778–79
2010-13-1	White plaster bust of Vitus Bering
2015-30-1 (see p. 114)	Watercolor painting of two Spanish vessels sailing before a forest shoreline and snow-covered mountain range by Mark R. Myers
2015-30-2	Watercolor painting of two large sailing vessels and four canoes by Mark R. Myers
I-B-4	Steller's Jay (taxidermy)
II-B-8	Tlingit string of faceted blue glass beads
II-B-11	Tlingit string of faceted blue glass beads
II-B-27	Tlingit string of spherical red glass beads
II-B-833	Tlingit upper section of deteriorated wooden totem pole featuring likeness of President Abraham Lincoln
II-B-1187	Haida bracelet of grooved wrought iron

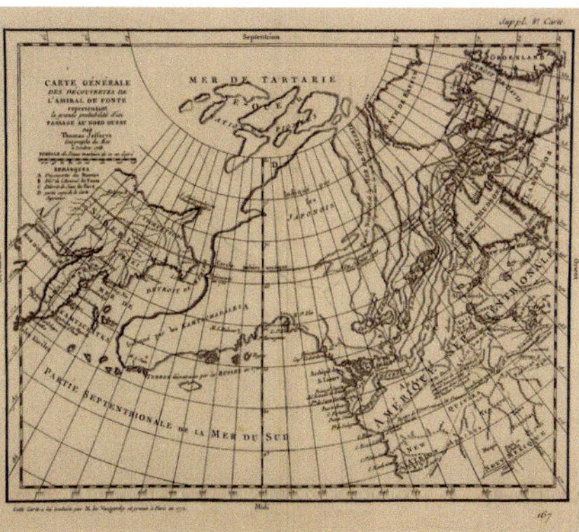

90-14-1

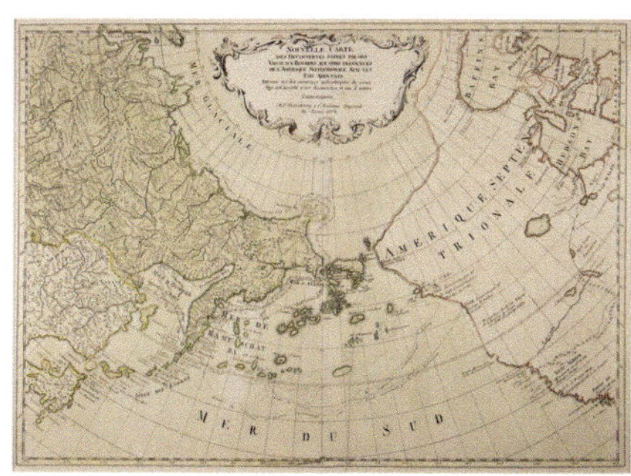

97-24-1

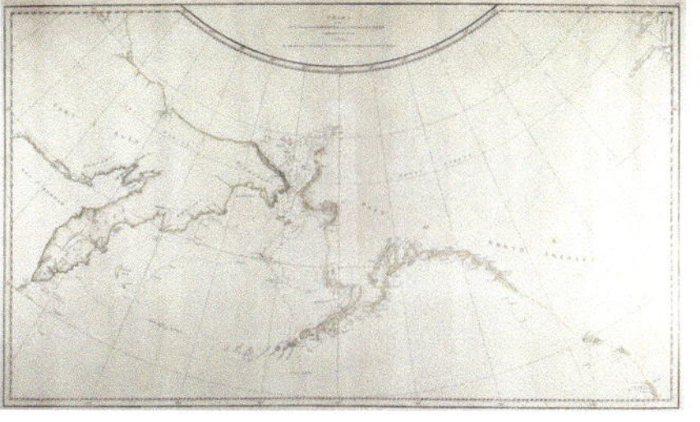

2005-11-1

II-B-1560 Metal halibut hook

II-B-1787 Argillite panel pipe with several carved figures

II-B-1889 Haida carved argillite pipe with realistic portrait of "Westerner" with muttonchop sideburns and beard

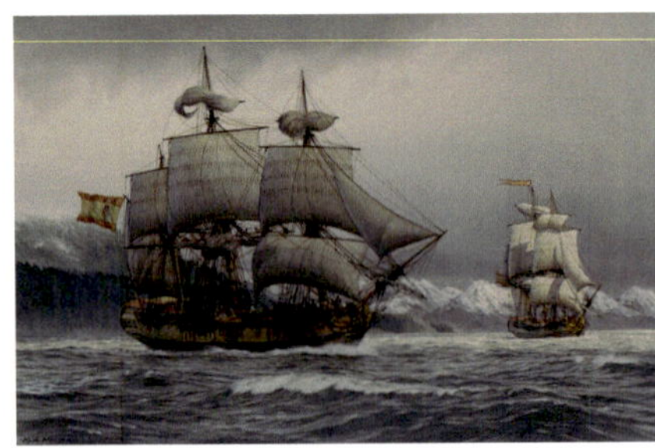

2015-30-1

III-O-14 Round bronze Chinese coin with square center hole, characters on one side and human figures on the other

III-O-1066 Engraving depicting a polar bear

III-R-120 Russian copper kettle

III-R-122 Copper kettle

III-R-123 Iron pot

III-R-213 Two copper spikes from the ship Politkofsky

III-R-213-B Copper spikes from the ship Politkofsky, unbroken

III-R-251-B Nail from St. Michael's Russian Orthodox Cathedral in Sitka, burned in 1966

III-R-251-F Nail from St. Michael's Russian Orthodox Cathedral in Sitka, burned in 1966

III-R-349 Bronze medal, octagonal (oblong with corners cut), featuring images in relief and lettering in Russian Cyrillic

III-R-357 Bronze commemorative medal with man's head on one side, reverse has map and sailing vessel

V-A-144 Print showing incident at sea of the La Perouse Expedition in Lituya Bay, on July 13, 1786

V-A-259 Lithograph of a drawing showing interior of Tlingit house with family gathered around central hearth by Aleksandr F. Postels

V-A-835 Ink and watercolor showing rocks, islands and water with hills, mostly sky by William Ellis

LC.253 Cast-metal reproduction of a Russian possession plaque

Lobby

52-26-1 Dried specimen of either horsefish or sea poacher fish

90-30-2 Gold-dust-filled barnacle removed from ship hull

92-27-1 Plastic vial containing mammoth hair sample

98-7-232 Section of whale jawbone

98-7-333 Mammoth tooth

2003-42-2 Taxidermy mount of a great horned owl on a piece of driftwood by Jerry Howard

2014-4-1 Taxidermy live mount of a female fisher on base resembling stone with stick and moss

2014-4-2 Taxidermy live mount of male hooded merganser duck on driftwood base

2014-4-3 Taxidermy live mount of male green winged teal on driftwood base

2014-4-4 Taxidermy live mount of female green winged teal on driftwood base

2014-4-5 Taxidermy live mount of pygmy owl on wood base

2014-4-10 Nest of twigs, sticks, fur, string, and various other items loosely woven together, containing crow eggs

2014-4-12 Sitka blacktail deer cranium with antlers

2014-4-13 Beaver skull

2014-4-14 Fisher skull

2014-4-15 River otter skull

2014-4-16 Black bear skull

2014-4-17 Wolf skull

2014-4-18 Moose skull

2014-5-1 Taxidermy live mount of female brown bear

I-A-8 Yellow wolf moss (lichen) attached to branch

I-B-2 Rufous hummingbird (taxidermy)

I-B-3 Western flycatcher (taxidermy)

I-B-5 Chestnut-backed chickadee (taxidermy)

I-B-10 Boreal chickadee (taxidermy)

I-B-15 Bonaparte's gull (taxidermy)

I-B-16-A Arctic tern (taxidermy)

I-B-16-B Arctic tern (taxidermy)

I-B-18 Full baleen strip, tapering to point

I-B-22 Sandhill crane (taxidermy)

I-B-23 Trumpeter swan (taxidermy)

I-B-24 Dall sheep (taxidermy)

I-B-36 Blown arctic murre egg

I-B-37 Blown arctic murre egg

I-B-46 Varied thrush (taxidermy)

I-B-48 Common raven (taxidermy)

I-B-49 Osprey (taxidermy)

I-B-50 Rufous hummingbird (taxidermy)

I-B-57 Red-breasted sapsucker (taxidermy)

I-B-58 Northern shrike (taxidermy)

I-B-62 Sharp-shinned hawk (taxidermy)

I-B-65 Red-necked grebe (taxidermy)

I-B-67 Spruce grouse (taxidermy)

I-B-69 Kingfisher (taxidermy)

I-B-70 Oystercatcher (taxidermy)

I-B-72	American robin (taxidermy)
I-B-78	Common eider (taxidermy)
I-B-80	King eider (taxidermy)
I-B-82	Spectacled eider (taxidermy)
I-B-84	Steller's eider (taxidermy)
I-B-106	Fox sparrow (taxidermy)
I-B-142	Glaucous-winged gull (taxidermy)
I-B-143	Pelagic cormorant (taxidermy)
I-B-144	Pigeon guillemot (taxidermy)
I-B-146	Golden crowned kinglet (taxidermy)
I-B-147	Yellow warbler (taxidermy)
I-B-148	Townsend's warbler (taxidermy)
I-B-149	Pine siskin (taxidermy)
I-B-166	Lock from mane of muskox
I-B-167	Two orca teeth
I-B-168	Sea lion tooth
I-B-172	Pair of bulla tympani (ear bones of whale)
I-B-172-A	Ear drums of whale
I-B-172-B	Ear drums of whale
I-B-175	Pair of whale ear bones
I-B-175-A	Ear drum of whale
I-B-175-B	Ear drum of whale
I-B-177-B	Fur seal teeth
I-B-180	Marbled murrelet (taxidermy)
I-B-184	Extra-large whale ear drum
I-B-188	Stomach stone of caribou
I-B-213	Vertebral plate from whale carcass
I-B-222	Rough-skinned newt preserved in vial of alcohol
I-B-226-B	Walrus tusk, corrugated at top end, with convex side with long, longitudinal cracks
I-B-236	*Arctomelon stearnsii* seashell
I-B-243	Sperm whale tooth
I-B-258	Canada goose (taxidermy)
I-B-263	Snow goose (taxidermy)
I-B-264	Bald eagle (taxidermy)
I-B-265	Golden eagle (taxidermy)
I-B-287	Snowy owl (taxidermy)
I-B-292	Common murre (taxidermy)
I-B-293	Surf scoter (taxidermy)
I-B-295	Red-throated loon (taxidermy)
I-B-298	Rhinoceros auklet (taxidermy)
I-B-301	Common loon (taxidermy)
I-B-307	Arctic loon (taxidermy)
I-B-310	American dipper (taxidermy)
I-B-315	Ancient murrelet (taxidermy)
I-B-332	Greater yellow legs (taxidermy)
I-B-336	Mallard drake (taxidermy)
I-B-367	Pair of geoduck shells
I-B-380	Shell of small species of abalone
I-B-393	Murex seashell
I-B-405-1	Sand dollar
I-B-407	Sunray starfish
I-B-409	Starfish
I-B-410	Leather star starfish
I-B-412	Basket starfish
I-B-417	Blood starfish
I-B-422	Giant barnacle
I-B-429	Egg cases of whelk or Oregon triton
I-B-442	Ruffed grouse (taxidermy)
I-B-444	Harlequin duck (taxidermy)
I-B-445	Bohemian waxwing (taxidermy)
I-B-448	Pair of eardrums, possibly of a seal
I-B-448-A	Eardrum, possibly of a seal
I-B-448-B	Eardrum, possibly of a seal
I-B-450	Great blue heron (taxidermy)
I-B-451	Hooded merganser (taxidermy)
I-B-454	Northwestern crow (taxidermy)
I-B-458	Bufflehead bird (taxidermy)
I-B-460	Common snipe (taxidermy)
I-B-466	Willow ptarmigan (taxidermy)
I-B-471	Goshawk (taxidermy)
I-B-473	Northern flicker (taxidermy)
I-B-476	Polar bear (taxidermy)
I-B-477	Wolf (taxidermy)
I-B-484	Brown bear skull
I-B-492	Os penis of a pinniped (probably walrus)
I-B-504	Glacier bear (taxidermy)
I-B-505	Black wolf taxidermy mount walking with hare in mouth
II-B-1	Specimen of *Echinodontium tinctorium* (Indian paint fungus)
II-B-1740	Haida pair of matched house posts with totemic figures repainted
IV-B-125	Quartz crystal
IV-B-199	Calcite on large pyrite cubes (pink fluorescent)
IV-B-376	Quartz crystal
IV-C-6	Pleistocene horse molar (Equus), lower
IV-C-9	Pleistocene bison tooth, upper tooth
IV-C-33	Rock-bearing marine fossil
IV-C-41	Rock-bearing marine fossils
IV-C-74	Fossil tooth with two roots
ED.90-2	Taxidermy wolverine
LC.431-1	Black bear with separate mount (taxidermy)
UA/UC-96	Hardened white shell formation
UA/UC-181	Mammoth tibia bone
UA/UC-404	Willow ptarmigan (taxidermy)
UA/UC-408	Small rodent (vole) mounted (taxidermy)
UA/UC-440	First cervical vertebrae (atlas) of a large mammal, possibly whale

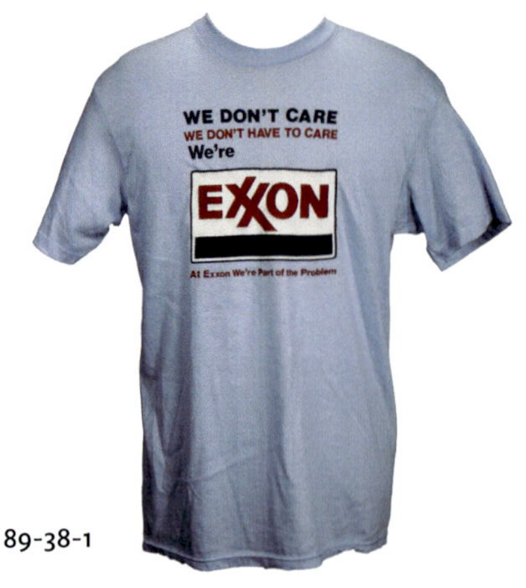

89-38-1

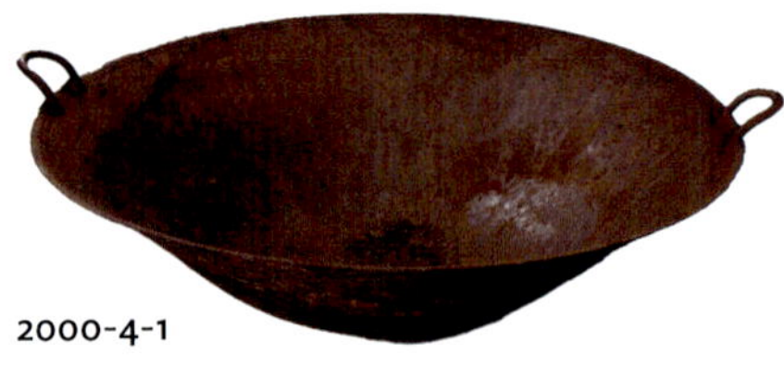
2000-4-1

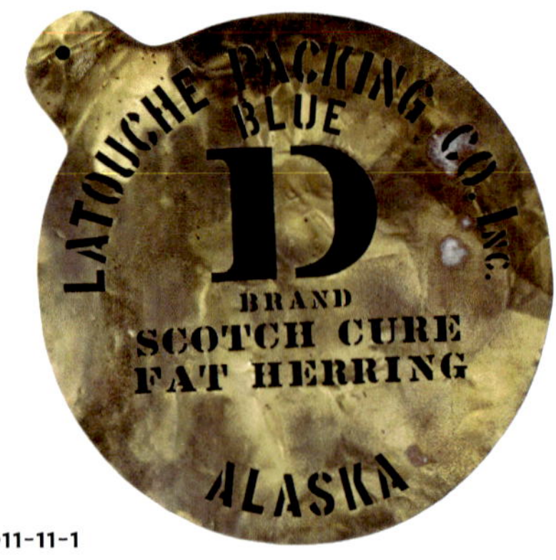

2011-11-1

Maritime

89-38-1 T-shirt satirizing Exxon Valdez oil spill

90-27-1 Postcard satirizing Exxon after the Valdez oil spill by Vern Culp

91-13-1 Wooden rudder from fishing boat

91-45-2 Cape Karluk red salmon can

92-28-18 Fishing float of blue blown glass and rope netting

92-28-20 Fishing float of amber blown glass

94-21-3 Wooden downrigger with cotton line

95-1-3 Downrigger consisting of wooden reel with rope and metal weight and clip

95-1-4 Wood and metal gaff hook

95-2-1 Wooden herring rake

95-4-1 Varnished wooden crate for shipping canned salmon

95-5-1 Printed salmon can

95-22-1 Plaited halibut line with hooks

96-4-1 Tin salmon can with printed paper label

96-60-2 Tin salmon can with red paper label

97-34-1 Wooden fishing sailboat with all gear

98-40-1 Box of six wooden salmon fishing plugs or lures

99-10-1 Wooden canned salmon crate with ink-stamped illustrations

2000-4-1 Large cooking wok

2000-8-1 Scale for weighing salmon cans

2000-9-1 Tin salmon can with printed paper label

2000-29-1 One-pound salmon can with printed paper label

2000-39-1 Wigwam Brand tin salmon can with printed paper label

2001-7-2 Wooden canned salmon crate with label printed on side in black ink

2001-7-4 One-pound salmon can with paper label

2001-18-1 End panel from a wooden salmon can crate imprinted with black ink

2002-13-1 Metal salmon can with red paper label

2002-20-12 Booklet titled How to Serve, How to Buy Canned Salmon

2003-6-1 Salmon can with full-color printed paper label

2003-45-12 Booklet of salmon recipes

2005-9-34 Clock with cylindrical brass housing and leather carrying case

2005-9-36 Stencil kit with wooden rack containing brass number and letter stencils

2005-9-38 Wooden printing block with image of a salmon

2005-9-39 Wooden printing block with image of a salmon

2005-9-40 Wooden printing block with image of a salmon

2005-9-60 Paper stencil

2005-9-76 Paper stencil

2005-20-1 Wooden printed shipping crate for canned salmon

2005-34-1 Metal one-pound salmon can with paper label

2008-6-1 Unsealed and unlabeled gold-colored metal salmon can

2009-3-11 Ceramic plate with Naknek Packing Co. written in script letters at top and salmon pictured at bottom

2010-22-1 Alaska red sockeye salmon can with printed label

2011-3-18 LORAN (long range navigation) C Plotter, Furuno Model LP 1000, circa 1984, in white case with screen and knobs, back-up memory cards, and instruction manual

2011-6-1 Can of pink salmon with color printed label

2011-11-1 Round barrel stencil that reads "Latouche Packing Co., Inc. Blue Brand Scotch Cure Fat Herring, Alaska"

2011-11-2 Rectangular brass box stencil used to mark shipping boxes

2011-20-4 Tin salmon can with printed paper label

2015-1-7 Hinged bronze mold with two iron handles used for forming fishing sinkers

2015-1-8 Hinged bronze sinker mold with two iron handles

2015-1-9 Hinged bronze sinker mold with two iron handles

2015-1-11 Curved trolling weight with an iron ring on one end and brass barrel swivel at the other end for weight attachments

2015-1-12 Curved trolling weight with copper loops at each end for iron rings to attach weight

2015-1-13 9-gauge wire for sinker mold attachments

III-O-13 Round Chinese coin with square center hole, characters on both sides

III-O-290 Ship's deadeye with circular block of ironbark held by iron band to iron plate, with three holes for lanyard

III-O-682-30 Wooden plane, also known as a leveling or sun plane, arc-shaped

III-O-1077 Jar of crude oil from Prince William Sound oil spill of the Exxon Valdez, April 1989

Mining

77-46-2 Canvas pouch containing travel tickets and hardware ads

77-46-3 Canadian Pacific Railway envelope containing travel documents

77-46-6 Handwritten receipt on back of business card of transportation company

77-46-7 Journal containing pressed plants

77-46-10 Handwritten envelope and incomplete preliminary application cards for gold rush camp

92-41-2 Iron socket wrench

92-57-1 Bronze sculpture The Hiker by Louis Potter

92-58-1 Assay balance

93-1-1 Moose-hide jacket

93-1-1-B Fabric yoke decorated with beads (from moose-hide jacket)

93-3-37 Alaska Miners Memorandum Book

93-3-81 Leather gold poke bag

93-12-2 Fragment of wooden pack saddle

93-12-3 Leather yoke

95-3-1 Wood and rope snowshoes

96-28-1 Thanksgiving menu in pencil on cloth

96-30-1 (see p. 118) Brass handheld pocket sextant

97-18-8 Ore sample

97-18-12 Two samples of rhodonite

97-18-26 Sample of crude oil in small bottle

97-22-1 Metal crampon

97-22-2 Wooden crampon

97-22-4 Shot glass of transparent molded glass

97-22-5 Clear glass liniment bottle

99-8-1 Portable alcohol stove made of silver-colored metal

2000-4-17 Printed cardboard box for individual gold brick

2000-27-1 Framed oil painting of prospector with horses near Mt. McKinley by Eustace Ziegler

2002-19-1 Cube-shaped metal canister with screw-top lid and printed paper label

2003-2-1 Deputy U.S. Marshal badge

2003-5-1 Wooden crate for gold bullion, with silver stencils

2003-38-1 Wooden dog sled

2004-1-2 Rolled navigational chart of the Yukon River

2005-9-35 Can of minced sea clams

2007-11-1 Small brass sieve

2007-11-8 Metal and glass mining lamp with sparking mechanism

2007-11-16 Ore sample in canvas bag with paper labels

2007-11-17 Divided clear plastic box containing asbestos ore and milled products

2007-11-18 Enameled iron coffee pot

2007-11-68 Hand-held Geiger counter made of grey metal

2007-11-69 U.S. Bureau of Mines brown safety helmet

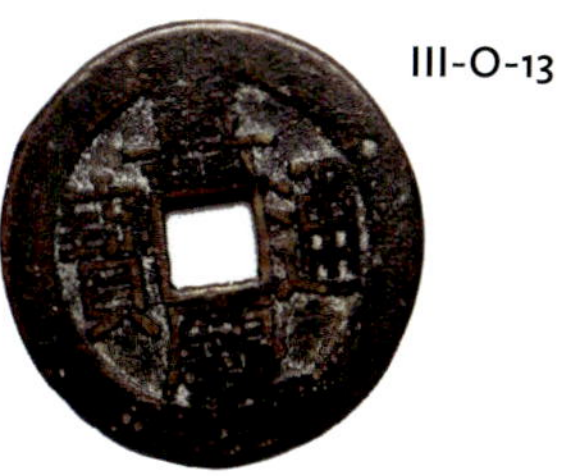

III-O-13

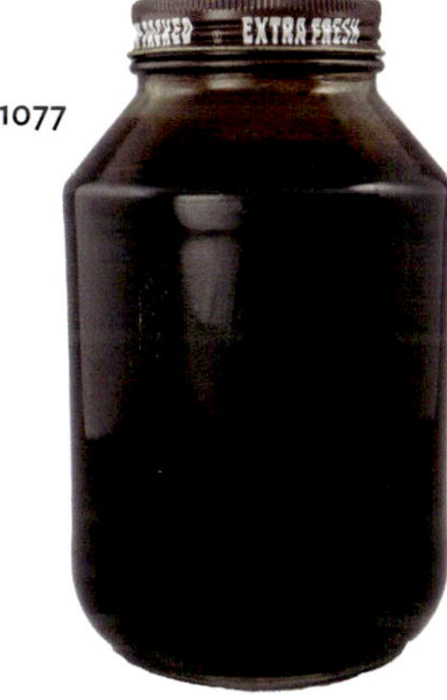

III-O-1077

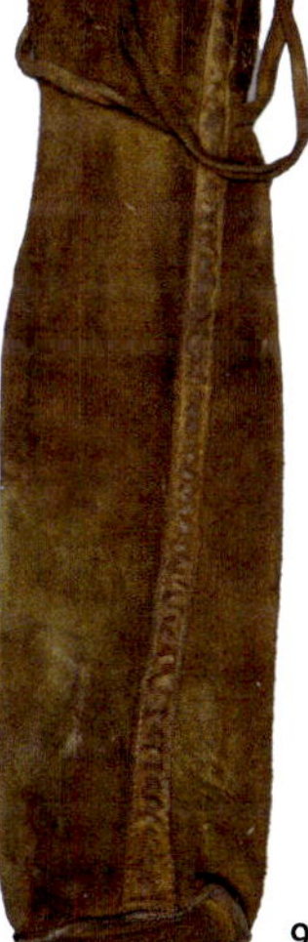

93-3-81

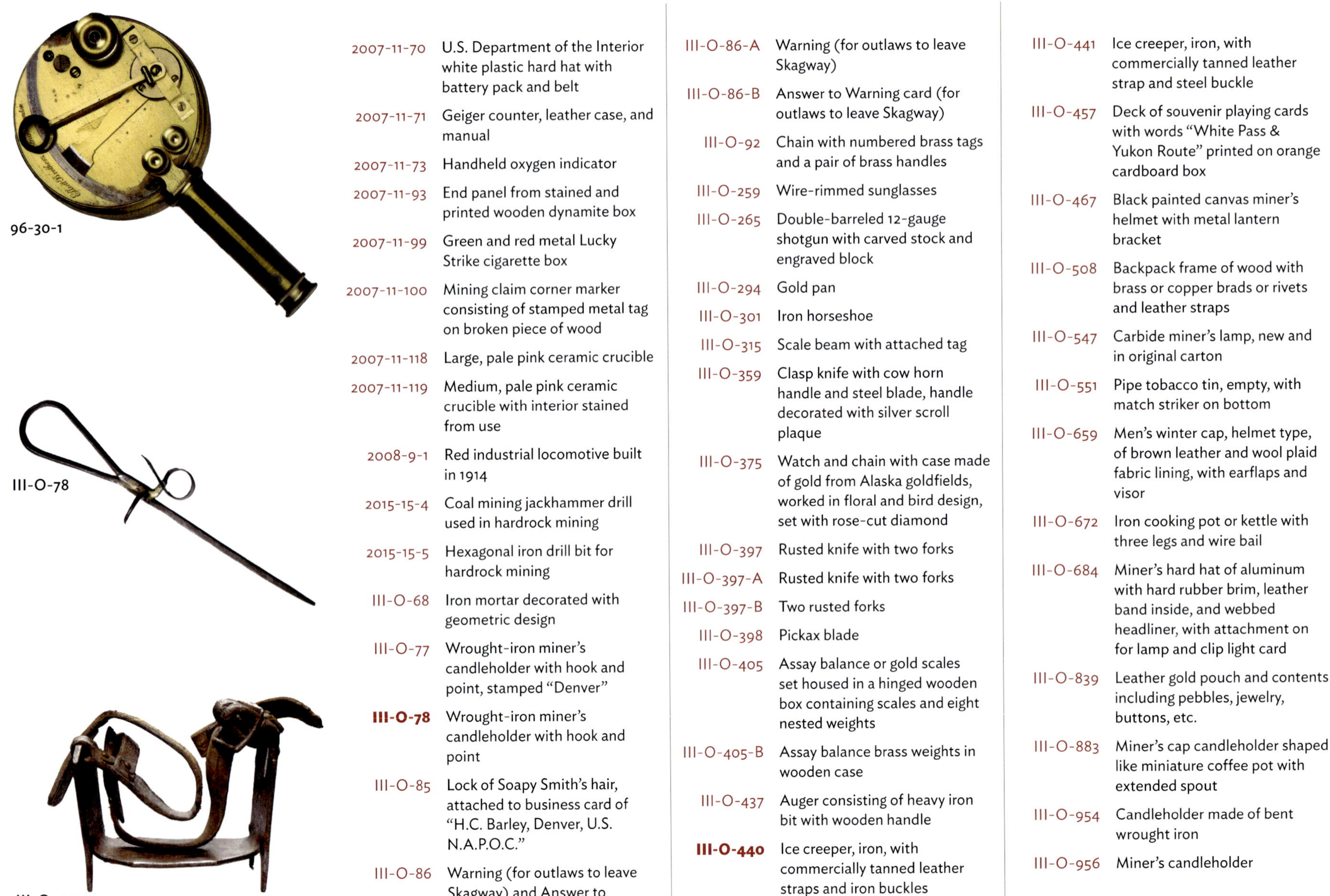

96-30-1

III-O-78

III-O-440

2007-11-70 U.S. Department of the Interior white plastic hard hat with battery pack and belt

2007-11-71 Geiger counter, leather case, and manual

2007-11-73 Handheld oxygen indicator

2007-11-93 End panel from stained and printed wooden dynamite box

2007-11-99 Green and red metal Lucky Strike cigarette box

2007-11-100 Mining claim corner marker consisting of stamped metal tag on broken piece of wood

2007-11-118 Large, pale pink ceramic crucible

2007-11-119 Medium, pale pink ceramic crucible with interior stained from use

2008-9-1 Red industrial locomotive built in 1914

2015-15-4 Coal mining jackhammer drill used in hardrock mining

2015-15-5 Hexagonal iron drill bit for hardrock mining

III-O-68 Iron mortar decorated with geometric design

III-O-77 Wrought-iron miner's candleholder with hook and point, stamped "Denver"

III-O-78 Wrought-iron miner's candleholder with hook and point

III-O-85 Lock of Soapy Smith's hair, attached to business card of "H.C. Barley, Denver, U.S. N.A.P.O.C."

III-O-86 Warning (for outlaws to leave Skagway) and Answer to Warning card

III-O-86-A Warning (for outlaws to leave Skagway)

III-O-86-B Answer to Warning card (for outlaws to leave Skagway)

III-O-92 Chain with numbered brass tags and a pair of brass handles

III-O-259 Wire-rimmed sunglasses

III-O-265 Double-barreled 12-gauge shotgun with carved stock and engraved block

III-O-294 Gold pan

III-O-301 Iron horseshoe

III-O-315 Scale beam with attached tag

III-O-359 Clasp knife with cow horn handle and steel blade, handle decorated with silver scroll plaque

III-O-375 Watch and chain with case made of gold from Alaska goldfields, worked in floral and bird design, set with rose-cut diamond

III-O-397 Rusted knife with two forks

III-O-397-A Rusted knife with two forks

III-O-397-B Two rusted forks

III-O-398 Pickax blade

III-O-405 Assay balance or gold scales set housed in a hinged wooden box containing scales and eight nested weights

III-O-405-B Assay balance brass weights in wooden case

III-O-437 Auger consisting of heavy iron bit with wooden handle

III-O-440 Ice creeper, iron, with commercially tanned leather straps and iron buckles

III-O-441 Ice creeper, iron, with commercially tanned leather strap and steel buckle

III-O-457 Deck of souvenir playing cards with words "White Pass & Yukon Route" printed on orange cardboard box

III-O-467 Black painted canvas miner's helmet with metal lantern bracket

III-O-508 Backpack frame of wood with brass or copper brads or rivets and leather straps

III-O-547 Carbide miner's lamp, new and in original carton

III-O-551 Pipe tobacco tin, empty, with match striker on bottom

III-O-659 Men's winter cap, helmet type, of brown leather and wool plaid fabric lining, with earflaps and visor

III-O-672 Iron cooking pot or kettle with three legs and wire bail

III-O-684 Miner's hard hat of aluminum with hard rubber brim, leather band inside, and webbed headliner, with attachment on for lamp and clip light card

III-O-839 Leather gold pouch and contents including pebbles, jewelry, buttons, etc.

III-O-883 Miner's cap candleholder shaped like miniature coffee pot with extended spout

III-O-954 Candleholder made of bent wrought iron

III-O-956 Miner's candleholder

III-O-967	Medicine chest consisting of gold-lettered black tin box with hinged lid and wire handle, containing medications and first aid equipment
III-O-1011	Brochure containing timetables, fares, descriptions, photos, etc.
IV-A-23	Seven types of radioactive rocks from Southeast Alaska
IV-A-23-1	Radioactive rock from Moira Sound
IV-A-23-2	Radioactive rock (fluorite) from Mt. Bokan
IV-A-23-3	Radioactive rock from Gardner Bay
IV-A-23-4	Radioactive rock from Mt. Bokan (commercial ore from discovery lode)
IV-A-23-5	Radioactive rock from Mt. Bokan
IV-A-23-6	Radioactive rock from Salmon Bay (jasper)
IV-A-23-7	Radioactive rock from Dall Bay (schist)
IV-A-33	Five diamond-drill core sections
IV-A-33-1	Quartz core sample
IV-A-33-4	Mica schist core sample
IV-A-35	Drill core of quartz diorite with hornblende and biotite
IV-A-46	Diamond drill core, altered diorite composed of plagioclase feldspar
IV-A-53	Altered monzonite
IV-A-72	Two specimens of light tokeen marble
IV-A-72-A	Large piece of light tokeen marble, used in State House Building
IV-A-125	Coal
IV-B-21	White quartz containing iron sulfide (pyrites), from Funter Bay
IV-B-23	Red jasper from Gambier Bay
IV-B-45	Cream-color palygorskite (mountain leather) from Lemesurier Island
IV-B-54	Jade nugget, roughly pear shaped, flat on one side, from Kobuk River
IV-B-59	Copper ore from Copper River
IV-B-68	Uranium ore
IV-B-75	Quartz and gold
IV-B-83	Galena, tetrahedrite, and azurite, from Keno Hill, Canada
IV-B-85	Galena, sphalerite, quartz, pyrrhotite, and gold, from Chisana
IV-B-100	Glass tube containing small garnets from Yakataga sand
IV-B-102	Four pieces of chalcopyrite from Bonanza Mine, Copper River
IV-B-102-A	Chalcopyrite from Bonanza Mine, Copper River
IV-B-102-B	Chalcopyrite from Bonanza Mine, Copper River
IV-B-102-C	Chalcopyrite from Bonanza Mine, Copper River
IV-B-102-D	Chalcopyrite from Bonanza Mine, Copper River
IV-B-107	Malachite and azurite from Kougarok Valley
IV-B-155	Garnets in biotite schist
IV-B-160	Native bismuth from Charley Creek
IV-B-162	Cinnabar in quartz, from Kuskokwim
IV-B-162-A	Cinnabar in quartz, from Kuskokwim
IV-B-162-B	Cinnabar in quartz, from Kuskokwim
IV-B-166	Orpiment with realgar & cinnabar from Red Devil Mine
IV-B-175	Galena in quartz vein, small amounts of chalcopyrite
IV-B-177	Asbestos
IV-B-178	Gypsum from Chichagof Island
IV-B-194	Drill core sample from Alaska Juneau Gold Mine
IV-B-209	Chrysolite on asbestos
IV-B-221	Five pieces of copper
IV-B-224	Five samples of malachite from Whitehorse Copper Mine
IV-B-232	Stibnite ore, antimony sulfide in quartz, from Van Klein Mine
IV-B-251	Vial of platinum nuggets
IV-B-263	Cassiterite (placer tin) in a vial
IV-B-276	Chalcopyrite and pyrrhotite
IV-B-278	Two specimens of pyrite
IV-B-278-A	Pyrite
IV-B-278-B	Pyrite
IV-B-283	Gold crystals in a quartz lined vug within a siliceous rock containing dispersed small pyrite crystals
IV-B-300	Cinnabar
IV-B-301	Galena from Unuk River
IV-B-307	Galena in quartz vein
IV-B-321	Galena from Fisher Claim, Keno Hill Mine

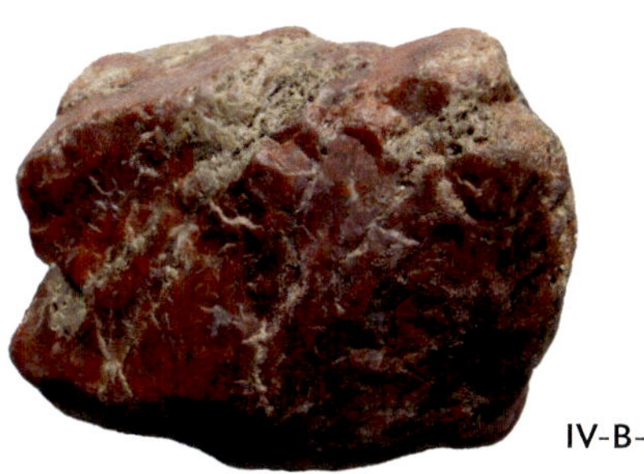
IV-B-23

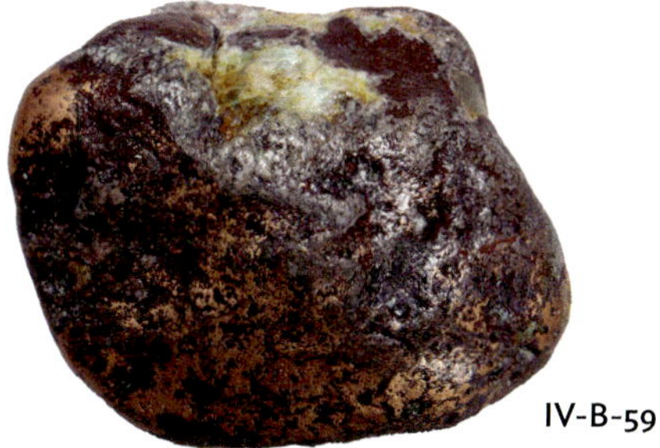
IV-B-59

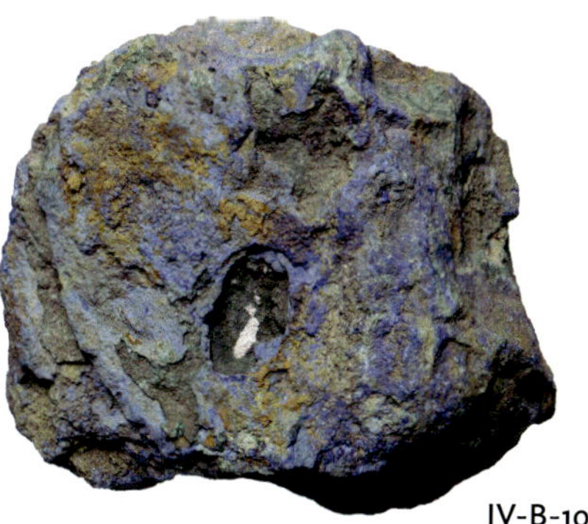
IV-B-107

IV-B-326 Tremolite, actinolite

IV-B-340-A Sphalerite, pyrite, bornite, scheelite (fluorescent), chalcopyrite

IV-B-340-B Sphalerite, pyrite, bornite, scheelite (fluorescent), chalcopyrite

IV-B-379 Abundant galena imbedded in manganiferous ankerite

IV-B-383 Placer tin, cassiterite, from Cape York

IV-B-391 Several pieces of placer tin, cassiterite, from Hot Springs district

IV-B-391-A Placer tin, cassiterite, from Hot Springs district

IV-B-391-B Placer tin, cassiterite, from Hot Springs district

IV-B-396 Vial of scheelite ore, fluorescent

IV-D-6 Bar of smelted pig iron

V-A-462 Watercolor showing man with pack train of six horses crossing mountain pass by Edward J. FitzGerald

UA/UC-308 Metal drill bit

UA/UC-325 Horse skeleton

Modern Alaska

90-12-1 Army-style U.S. park ranger felt hat with leather band

90-16-1 Wrangell civil defense police badge

91-23-1 Russian child's hat of felt and fur

91-30-1 Attu grass basket with lid by Mrs. Michael Lokanin

92-21-40 Soviet-era Russian-made outboard boat engine

92-21-44 Snowmobile

93-3-53 Blue cotton bonnet

93-3-54 White and blue cotton bonnet

93-19-1 Cone-shaped milk carton

94-4-3 Camera and accessories

94-10-1 Glass milk bottle

95-6-1 Metal safety helmet with decal

96-51-10 Wood, rope, and metal yoke for carrying water buckets

97-6-1 White rubber "bunny boots" with metal valve for inflation and deflation

97-17-1 Mixed-media portrait drawing of President Dwight D. Eisenhower

97-20-1 Anchorage Stealers jersey

98-19-1 Record album of Alaska-themed choral music

98-36-3 Alaska Brand root beer can

98-43-1 Survey altimeter in round painted green metal case, with green woven cotton strap

99-11-1 Pair of mukluks

99-11-2 Army Air Corps cloth hood with fur lining

99-15-1 Clear glass milk bottle with printed text in red ink

99-15-4 Cardboard ice cream container

2000-4-15 Ice skates

2000-4-39 Portable typewriter with case and instruction manual

2000-4-42 Red metal lantern

2000-4-43 Toaster

2000-22-12 Alaska Brand plastic water bottle with paper label

2000-28-1 Phonograph record album in a cardboard jacket titled *Sounds of Alaska*

2003-4-2 WWII portable air raid siren

2003-13-1 Alaska veterans of WWI white and brown cap with gold trim

2003-13-2 Plastic bottle with red cap and printed paper label for smoked salmon bits

2003-21-4 Round blue campaign button printed "Fran Ulmer/Ernie Hall" in white letters

2003-46-1 Men's one-piece wool bathing suit, red with white stripes

2005-17-1 Wool U.S. Army uniform jacket c. 1942

2005-17-2 WWII military hat with leather band and brass insignia

2005-17-3 WWII military bronze pin with propeller and wings

2005-17-4 WWII oval military bronze plate with aviator wings in relief

2005-17-6 Military dog tags

2005-17-7 Purple heart medal in presentation box

2008-28-8 Brown felt Alaska State Trooper hat with chin strap

2008-36-1 Black leather and wool Japanese naval officer's bill cap from WWII

2008-38-7 White molded foam hat from political campaign

2009-13-1 Navy blue campaign button McCain-Palin '08

2009-13-2 White campaign button with multicolored lettering that reads "Alaska / Where Men are Men and the Women . . . run for Vice President!"

2009-13-3 Campaign button showing Sarah Palin as Rosie the Riveter

2009-13-4 Campaign button with Palin photo and pink accents that reads "THE HOTTEST VP / ALASKA GOVERNOR SARAH PALIN / From the COOLEST STATE"

2010-7-1 WWII military white felt bunny or Little Abner boots

2010-19-1 Red Alaska-themed print cotton party dress and replica petticoat dress crinoline

2010-21-35 One-quart vanilla ice cream container showing Mat Maid Eskimo girl logo

2011-21-6 Small poster with detailed instructions on what to do in a blackout or air raid

2012-2-8 Japanese propaganda poster depicting Japanese soldier killing two American soldiers in chaotic battle scene

2012-17-71 White and blue round political pin supporting Bill Hudson for State House

2012-17-72 Blue and white round political pin supporting Arliss Sturgulewski for governor

2012-17-73 Rectangular blue pin supporting Arliss Sturgulewski and Jim Campbell campaign

2012-17-74 Round yellow and black political pin supporting Aaron Isaacs

2013-10-1 Radio in wooden cabinet with telescoping antenna

2013-12-2 Japanese WWII wooden ammunition box

2013-14-1 Red, white, and blue oval pin-back button from Mike Gravel campaign

2013-14-2 Round, red and white campaign button supporting Red Swanson for Senate

2013-14-3 Round, red and white pin-back button from the state Senate campaign of Bill Ray

2013-14-4 Red, white, and blue round pin-backed button with the image of bee, reading "DON'T BE STUNG / 'VOTE FOR STANG'"

2013-14-5 Round pin-back button with horizontal red, white, and blue stripes, reads "KeepKeith"

2013-14-6 Round pin-back button in red, white, and blue, reading "People / Pollock / Progress"

2013-14-12 Blue and yellow round pin-back button from a campaign of Governor William Egan

2013-14-15 Green, black, and white round pin-back button from a campaign of Nick Begich for Congress

2013-14-17 Yellow, blue, and white oval pin-back button from the campaign of Laurence "Larry" Carr

2013-14-19 Blue and yellow round pin-back button from the campaign of Egan and Boucher

2013-14-20 Red, white, and blue round pin-back button reading "I'm for Mike"

2013-68-1 Service medal from the Alaska Territorial Guard, with ribbon-covered pin and presentation box

2015-14-1 Tabletop metal grain grinder with wood handle

I-B-27 Caribou (taxidermy)

I-B-278 Short-tailed shearwater (taxidermy)

II-A-4970 Fur hat made of wolverine head, calfskin, muskrat, beaver trim, and wolverine tails attached with red yarn by Emma Atsitmok

II-A-6704 Grass basketry hat with brim and red and black designs by Hazel Lake

II-A-6844 Fur seal hat, helmet-shaped, with earflaps by Loulare Wassille

II-C-106 Athabascan child's hat made of black velvet and trimmed with marten and cotton cloth

II-F-128 Aleut covered thimble basket in plain twined weaving with silk floss overlay design by Jennie Golley

II-F-135 Aleut twined basket of wild rye grass in plain twined weaving with overlay flower and zigzag design by Mary Snigaroff

III-M-47 Women's two-piece bathing suit made of sealskin

III-O-2 U.S. Navy binoculars with case

III-O-218 Pen with clear plastic handle, printed, and black plastic grip, Esterbrook point 2668

III-O-392 Women's oval with fringe of horsehair lace

III-O-845 Pre-WWI knitting machine

III-O-946 Graniteware coffeepot with hinged lid with knob on top

III-O-971 Miner's lunch pail with lid with wire and wood handle

III-O-980 Set of collar, muff, and hat of white ermine fur

III-O-980-A White ermine collar

III-O-980-B White ermine muff

III-O-980-C White ermine hat

III-O-1002 Two oval metal campaign buttons with safety-pin fasteners on reverse

III-O-1002-A Oval white metal campaign button says "Cowper / FOR GOVERNOR" in red and black

III-O-1002-B Oval white metal campaign button says "Cowper / FOR GOVERNOR / VOTE November 4" in red and black

III-O-1047 Six-pack of Chinook Alaskan Amber beer

Octopus Room

92-1-1 Mixed-media art on paper titled "Rain on the Parade" by Ray Troll

92-18-1 Oil on canvas painting of waterfall by David Mollett

97-26-1 Drawing in colored pencil on paper titled Cannery Dance V by Carolyn Reed

97-35-7 Eskimo human figurine of carved bark

98-7-124 Model ship (Mosquito Fleet) on wheels of walrus ivory

98-7-197 Model of steam whaling ship of walrus ivory, bone (foremast), and twisted reindeer sinew by Happy Jack (Angokwazhuk)

2000-1-1 Pair of carved and painted wooden images titled Bering Strait Visions by Ron Senungetuk

2004-26-1 Collages of images of underwater plants and animals by Roxanne Turner

2006-24-1 Aleut model kayak and doll by Mikhail Snegirev, Mary Ellen Frank

2009-22-1 Doll of elderly woman making a basket by Rosalie Paniyak

II-A-3086 Eskimo wooden-headed doll dressed in gut parka

II-A-3087 Eskimo doll with composition head, dressed in Eskimo woman's clothing, including squirrel-hide parka

II-A-4292 Model sailboat of baleen by Tony Pushruk

II-A-5527 Baleen model boat, umiak type with mast, two sails, and rudder by George Imergan

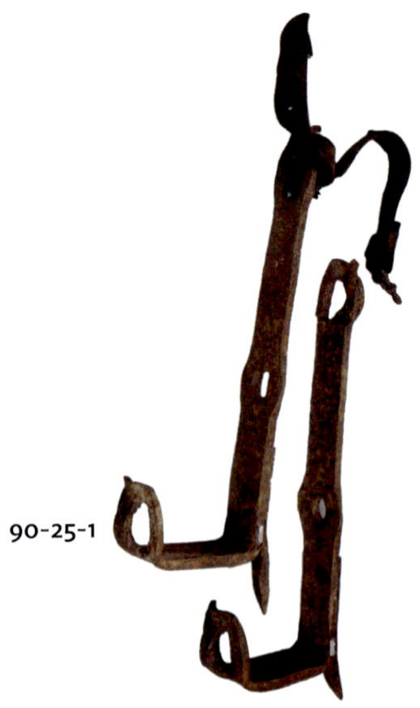
90-25-1

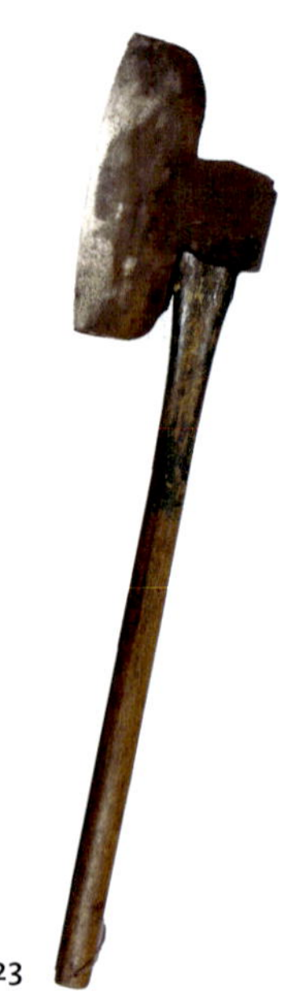
2000-4-23

II-A-6116	Eskimo doll in ceremonial gut parka, with embroidered face of bleached skin
II-A-6262	Carved and incised mastodon ivory model sailboat by Carl Iyakitan
II-A-6263	Carved and painted mastodon ivory model sailboat by Arnold Iyakitan
II-A-6264	Carved and painted mastodon ivory model sailboat with dark sails by Arnold Iyakitan
II-A-6322	Eskimo model umiak made of skin, with wooden paddles
II-A-7317	Doll of female figure in gut parka holding bundle of wood, with head of carved and painted wood with wolverine tail hair by Dolly Spencer
II-B-1352	Model Haida canoe with two paddles, mast and seat, stained and painted with bird heads
II-B-1532-A	Male doll dressed in multicolored beaded white felt
II-B-1542	Twined spruce-root doll with removable hat and basket by Annie Lawrence
II-B-1948	Stuffed doll of leather, cloth, beads, fur, feather and embroidery
II-B-1970	Doll with headdress and white felt blanket with beadwork by Nancy Jackson
II-C-27	Athabascan birch-bark doll basket carrier with doll
II-C-218	Athabascan model birch-bark canoe with red, black, and white trimmed gunwales, with paddle
II-C-282-1	Athabascan doll of male figure of painted white suede leather and fur, with beaded moose-hide clothing by Doris Charles
II-C-282-2	Athabascan doll of female figure of painted white suede leather and fur, with beaded moose-hide clothing by Doris Charles
V-A-117	Ink and charcoal drawing depicting village and various activities by George Ahgupuk
V-A-361	Painting shows gray house on pilings by Rie Munoz
V-A-869	Woodblock relief print depicting large red and black raven over ochre-colored curled seal, with blue background and vertical black tree branch shapes, on white Japanese paper by Dale DeArmond

Oil and Timber

90-25-1	Iron tree climbing spikes
91-18-5	Old-growth forest conservation political bumper sticker
96-27-1	Grumpy the Bear bumper sticker about clear-cutting
98-3-1	U-shaped bike lock and key from protest
2000-4-23	U.S. Forest Service broadax
2000-15-1	Cross-section of power cable
2004-1-1	Cross section of a Sitka spruce tree trunk
2005-8-1	Humble Oil and Refining Company red hooded goose-down parka
2009-17-1	U.S. Coast Guard bright orange floatation coat
2011-21-14	Square coaster with Alaskan flag promoting wood pulp manufacturer
2015-12-1	Orange plastic housing for metal copper coil mounted on spring
2015-12-2	Steel drill bit with threaded top and cutting head with three spinning wheels
2015-12-3	Steel drill bit
2015-12-4	Yellow plastic cone-like shape at one end of device with electrical cord protruding from other end
2015-15-6	Hard hat of bare metal with spots and spills and leather strap
2015-15-8	Circular saw blade
2015-23-1	Dark green parka with fur ruff
2015-23-2	Snow pants
2015-23-3	Green hard hat inner fittings with elastic lace

III-O-74 Souvenir pulp sample in the form of a rectangular card, printed with advertising text

III-O-848 Springboard, made of one piece of wood, reinforced with iron plate

III-O-849 Two-person crosscut saw

III-O-532 Plastic desk paperweight with vial of crude oil inside

III-O-930 Wooden ox yoke

III-O-950 Specimen bottle filled with crude oil and labeled, with black plastic cap

III-O-1078 Used oil pompon of long thin strips of different-colored paper material

LC.437-1 Two-person chainsaw with yellow power head and stinger

UA/UC-300 Ax of iron and wood

Orientation

95-13-7 Twined spruce root doll by Annie Lawrence

95-34-1 Lithographed icon of St. Nicholas with gold-toned embossed metal

2004-8-4 Doll with wooden face and cloth-covered body, dressed in fur boots and parka of duck feathers, fur, and hide

2005-12-1 Wooden Athabascan woman doll in fabric Euroamerican dress, picking berries by Mary Ellen Frank

II-A-1481 Yup'ik carved and painted wooden mask with red, white, and black geometric designs

II-A-1599 Eskimo wooden box carved in shape of human head with removable face as lid, decorated with beads

II-A-4903 Eskimo ivory carving of human figure

II-A-5028 Eskimo fossilized ivory carving of stylized human head and torso

II-A-5435 Eskimo ivory carving of dance scene depicting four seated drummers and one standing, moveable dancer

II-A-5554 Ivory carving of blanket toss scene on base section of ivory tusk, with several figures by Frank Illanna

II-A-5634 Carved ivory dance scene on baleen base with seated drummer and male dancer with raven mask by Mike Pullock

II-A-6325 Miniature King Island mask of carved and painted wood by Tony Pushruk

II-A-6326 Miniature King Island mask of carved and stained wood by Mary Pushruk

II-A-6837 Eskimo carved wooden doll head and torso with bead eyes

II-A-7318 Doll of male seal hunter wearing gut parka and backpack by Dolly Spencer

III-O-803 Square, ornate metal frame contains painting on porcelain of dark-haired young woman

III-R-146 Icon of silver-colored metal with repousse, depicting Christ

V-A-602 Carved and painted wooden mask with horsehair by Jim Schoppert

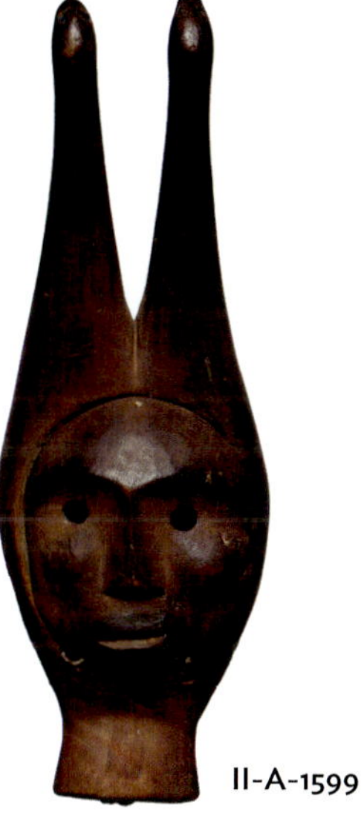

II-A-1599

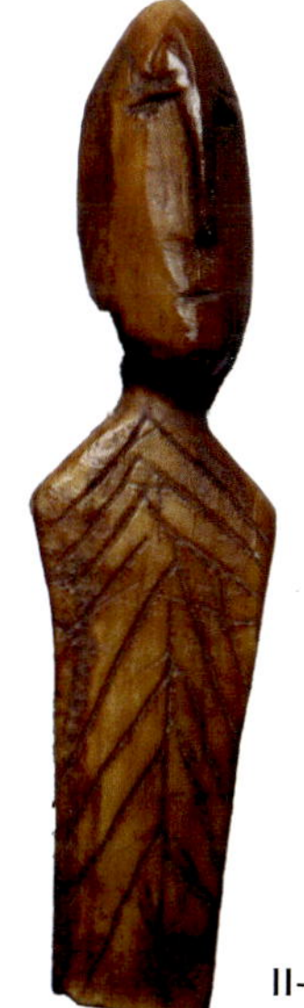

II-A-4903

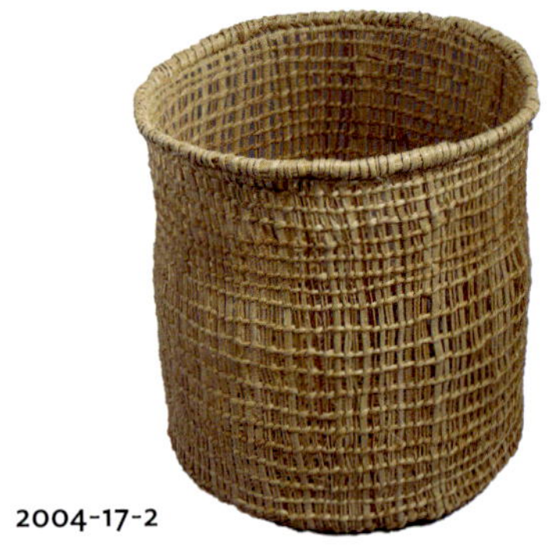
2004-17-2

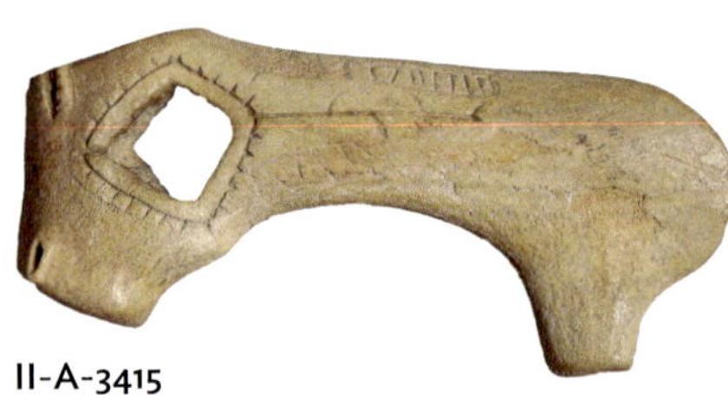
II-A-3415

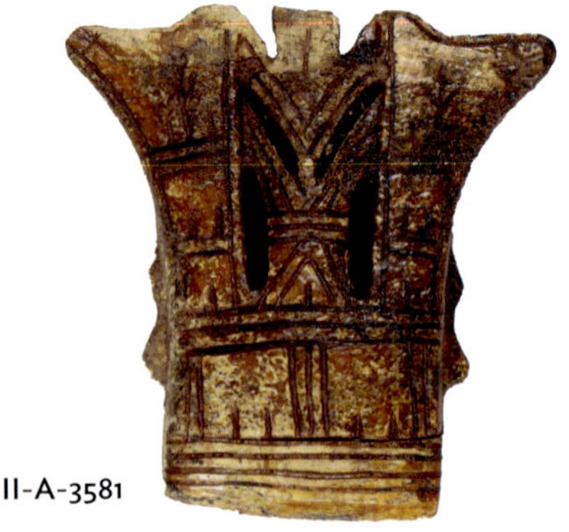
II-A-3581

Origins

94-31-1	Fragment of conical twined basket
95-12-1	Fragments of hemlock twined basket
98-7-331	Mammoth tooth
98-7-334	Walrus skull
2004-17-2	Replica of Thorne River Basket (94-31-1), made of twined spruce roots with openwork between rows by Delores Churchill
2006-31-2	Tlingit carved wooden bow
I-B-209	Lower jaw of mammoth, with grinders
II-A-909	Eskimo wrist guard made of incised and carved mammoth ivory
II-A-922	Eskimo wrist guard made of incised mammoth ivory carved in bear shape
II-A-928	Eskimo wrist guard made of incised and carved mammoth ivory, with slits and center hole
II-A-1007	Eskimo drum handle made from antler
II-A-1316	Eskimo ivory mouthpiece for harpoon float
II-A-1776	Sugpiaq stone lamp carved with animals and human head and shoulders
II-A-1958	Eskimo walrus-ivory ulu handle in form of fish
II-A-1998	Eskimo flint flaker haft of mammoth ivory with no blade
II-A-2248-A	Eskimo walrus ivory bird carving drilled with holes
II-A-2249	Eskimo carved and incised ivory ulu handle
II-A-2254-A	Eskimo ivory carving of fox
II-A-2255	Eskimo ivory carving of bear, incised and drilled
II-A-2628	Eskimo ivory artifact
II-A-2629	Eskimo ivory artifact
II-A-2642	Eskimo toggle with bird design, all links carved from one piece
II-A-2788	Eskimo ivory carving of caribou head
II-A-2958	Part of Eskimo sinew spinner, made from circular flat stone with wood rod
II-A-3184	Eskimo ivory carving of eight walrus heads on a bar
II-A-3187	Eskimo carved and drilled walrus ivory toggle in the shape of a whale
II-A-3191	Eskimo carved and drilled ivory carving of whale
II-A-3223-B	Eskimo carved and drilled ivory carving of water bird
II-A-3228-B	Eskimo carved and drilled ivory carving of sea bird
II-A-3229	Eskimo carved and drilled ivory carving of sea bird
II-A-3230	Eskimo carved and drilled ivory carving of sea bird with young on back
II-A-3241	Eskimo carved ivory face for a drum handle
II-A-3242	Two Eskimo carved ivory faces
II-A-3242-A	Eskimo carved ivory face
II-A-3242-B	Eskimo carved ivory face
II-A-3243	Two Eskimo carved ivory faces cut off drum handles
II-A-3243-A	Eskimo carved ivory smiling face cut off drum handle
II-A-3243-B	Eskimo carved ivory sad face cut off drum handle
II-A-3258-A	Eskimo ivory carving in dumbbell shape with faces at each end
II-A-3261-B	Eskimo ivory carving of female figure
II-A-3292-C	Eskimo carved and drilled ivory carving of bird
II-A-3294-C	Eskimo ivory carving of whale with yellow-brown color, no features, small notch in center of tail
II-A-3299	Eskimo ivory carving of composite animal blending human, seal, and walrus
II-A-3327	Eskimo carved ivory link chain with wood pendant with two human faces
II-A-3376	Eskimo toggle harpoon head of ivory or bone
II-A-3378	Eskimo ivory toggle harpoon head
II-A-3381	Eskimo ivory toggle harpoon head
II-A-3388	Eskimo ivory toggle harpoon head
II-A-3392	Eskimo ivory toggle harpoon head
II-A-3395	Eskimo ivory toggle harpoon head
II-A-3399	Eskimo ivory toggle harpoon head

II-A-3408 Eskimo ivory engraved bag handle

II-A-3415 (see p. 124) Eskimo bone arrow straightener

II-A-3420 Eskimo carved antler quiver stiffener in the shape of a caribou head with a pointed opposite end and bead eyes

II-A-3421 Eskimo carved antler quiver stiffener in the shape of a caribou head with a pointed opposite end, engraved with hunting scene

II-A-3451 Eskimo engraved piece of brown ivory

II-A-3569 Eskimo ivory toggle harpoon head

II-A-3579 Eskimo carved ivory object, part of a sinew twister

II-A-3581 (see p. 124) Eskimo carved and incised ivory ornament

II-A-3593 Eskimo ivory toggle harpoon head

II-A-3594 Eskimo ivory toggle harpoon head

II-A-3599 Eskimo ivory ovoid sinew spinner, convex on both sides, engraved

II-A-3757 Eskimo winged object of polished and engraved walrus ivory

II-A-3970 Eskimo ivory toggle harpoon head

II-A-4508 Eskimo carved wrist guard

II-A-4661 Eskimo whale talisman carved of old ivory

II-A-4841 Carved ivory story or snow knife

II-A-5030 Eskimo carved dark brown ivory artifact with slot such as could hold blade

II-A-5038 Eskimo carved and incised dark brown ivory female figure with head and parts of legs missing

II-A-5105 Small Okvik walrus ivory figure of a woman with carved face and Okvik style of incised decoration

II-A-5106 Okvik walrus ivory figure of a woman with carved face and Okvik style of incised decoration

II-A-5107 Eskimo ulu handle of carved and incised walrus ivory, with serrated curved edge and bird's head and neck

II-A-5108 (see p. 126) Eskimo walrus ivory harpoon socket piece with incised line decoration

II-A-5117 Eskimo carved ivory object with oval shape, one side convex and incised

II-A-5124 Eskimo dark brown carved and incised walrus ivory object with hollowed-out center and base

II-A-5133 Eskimo brown ivory or bone artifact, oblong with carving of human head

II-A-6493 Eskimo carved ivory harpoon head

II-A-6596 Eskimo carved and incised sinew twister

II-A-6916 Eskimo ivory knife handle with incised design of double parallel line, with groove for blade

II-A-6956 (see p. 126) Eskimo ivory object in flat wing shape with two oval lobes, each with slanted tear-drop slit outlined with incised grooves

II-A-6965 Eskimo dark brown ivory dish with whale's tail handle

II-A-6966 Eskimo small dark-brown ivory spoon with whale's tail handle

II-A-7007 Eskimo ivory doll of very small female standing on base

II-A-7010-A Eskimo small ivory carving of water bird

II-A-7010-D Eskimo ivory carving

II-A-7052 Eskimo drilled and incised carved ivory toggle harpoon head with ground slate blade

II-A-7170 Eskimo needle case of brown ivory, human figure style

II-A-7171 Eskimo tiny doll of brown ivory, facial features slightly carved

II-B-845 Tlingit heraldic painted wooden screen depicting thunderbird carved in three pieces attached to panels

II-B-1884-B Tlingit relief-carved and painted panel from red cedar bentwood box with bear design

IV-C-59 Mastodon tooth

UA/UC-297 Mammoth tusk

UA/UC-442 Two large mammoth tusks

UA/UC-461 Petroglyph in the form of an abstract face

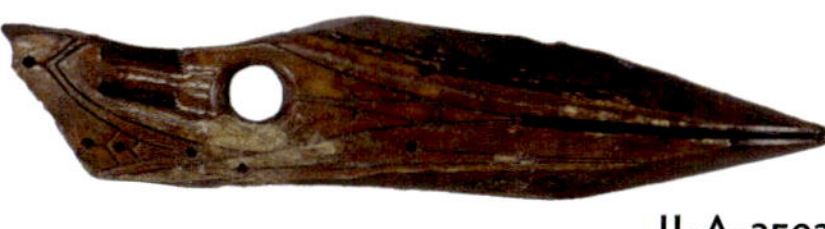

II-A-3593

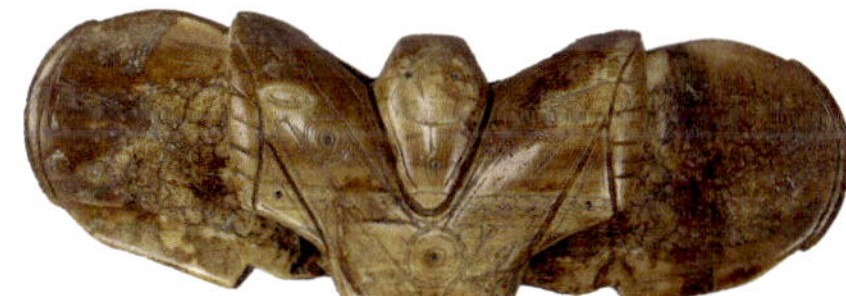

II-A-3757

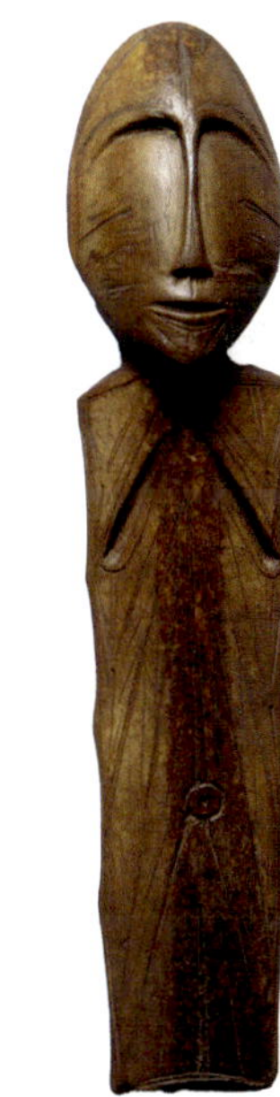

II-A-5105

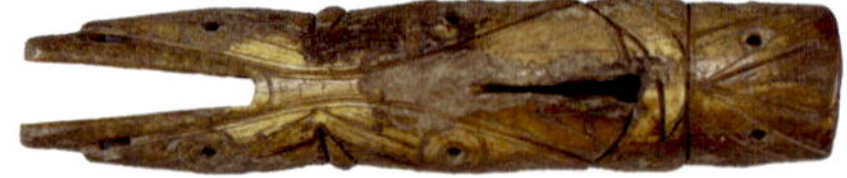

II-A-5108

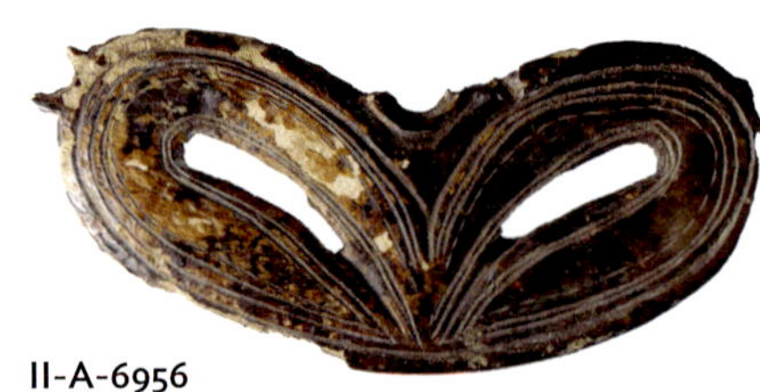

II-A-6956

Political History

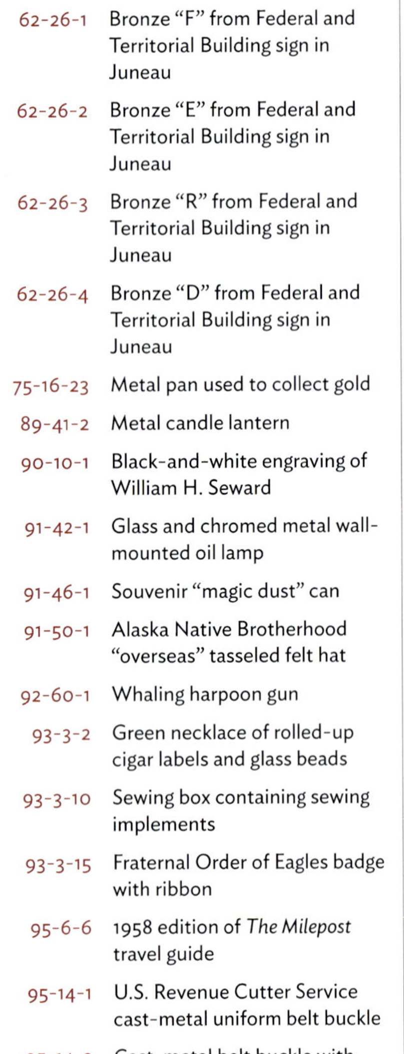

62-26-1 Bronze "F" from Federal and Territorial Building sign in Juneau

62-26-2 Bronze "E" from Federal and Territorial Building sign in Juneau

62-26-3 Bronze "R" from Federal and Territorial Building sign in Juneau

62-26-4 Bronze "D" from Federal and Territorial Building sign in Juneau

75-16-23 Metal pan used to collect gold

89-41-2 Metal candle lantern

90-10-1 Black-and-white engraving of William H. Seward

91-42-1 Glass and chromed metal wall-mounted oil lamp

91-46-1 Souvenir "magic dust" can

91-50-1 Alaska Native Brotherhood "overseas" tasseled felt hat

92-60-1 Whaling harpoon gun

93-3-2 Green necklace of rolled-up cigar labels and glass beads

93-3-10 Sewing box containing sewing implements

93-3-15 Fraternal Order of Eagles badge with ribbon

95-6-6 1958 edition of *The Milepost* travel guide

95-14-1 U.S. Revenue Cutter Service cast-metal uniform belt buckle

95-14-2 Cast-metal belt buckle with eagle

95-18-1 Leather-bound bible

96-30-2 Brass inclinometer with bubble level, engraved scales

96-30-3 Glass chronograph scale with wooden case by George Davidson

96-60-1 Tin salmon can with paper label

97-1-1 Naval officer's bicorn hat of fur felt with ribbon and braid trim

97-23-1 Circular baleen and pine ditty box with lid

2000-4-3 Iron bear trap with chain

2000-4-16 Gray lidded enamel-ware coffee pot

2000-4-40 Miner's candle holder made from one piece of iron

2000-26-3 Color lithograph of a painting of a flock of jaegers by L. A. Fuertes

2000-31-1 Framed oil painting on canvas depicting pioneer outside cabin by Sydney Laurence

2001-24-2 Business card printed in black ink on heavy ivory paper

2001-30-1 "Alaska's Flag" song sheet music

2002-1-10 Blank identification card from the Department of Civil Defense

2002-22-2 Cardboard sign advertising Iditarod Kennel Club's St. Patrick's Day Dog Race in Iditarod, Alaska

2003-1-1 Sewn bag of gut and sinew decorated with colored wool

2003-1-4 Tlingit carved wooden comb handle

2003-1-6 Miniature version of a Tlingit shaman mask, carved and painted wood

2003-1-10 Ivory bow drill handle engraved with hunting scenes

2003-1-16 Labret carved from large flat oval black stone disk

2003-1-42 Russian fine-toothed comb of bone

2003-1-44 Black velvet rectangular shoulder boards or epaulets with fabric ties and shell-shaped metal ornaments

2003-12-1 Pressure cooker

2003-13-21 Red, white, and blue banner reading "Serving Our Country"

2003-22-1 Small painted wood model of the Mile 0 Alaska Highway sign

2003-33-10 Postcard printed in blue ink on blue paper with six small Alaska flags attached

2005-41-1 Painting of seal rookery by Henry W. Elliott

2006-6-4 Watercolor, ink, and gouache on paper depiction of raft run aground on river sandbar by Lt. Charles A. Gloster

2007-11-21 Metal sample-splitter frame and pans, for separating minerals

2008-17-2-A Small round gold-frame reading glasses

2008-17-3 Sleek walking stick with a carved bone handle

2008-17-4 Mahogany lap desk inlaid with brass and copper wire and mother of pearl

2008-37-1 Carved wooden chair with padded leather back and seat, made c. 1959

2009-19-20 Fifteen-page brochure of FAQs about obtaining public land in Alaska, for WWII veterans

2010-9-1 Pen and pencil drawing of seals, a whale, and birds, with attached handwritten note by author by Henry W. Elliott

2011-20-2 Bobble-head souvenir of William H. Seward from minor-league baseball game

2013-2-1 Bronze mountain howitzer, Model 1835, from the wreck of the sailing bark Torrent

2013-65-1 Diphtheria poster showing a black and white photo of three women in nurses' uniforms and one man wearing a suit

2014-16-1 Lithograph made from original hand drawing showing whaling industry in the Bering Sea by Benjamin Russell

II-A-4105 Eskimo ivory piece engraved with dog sleds (old style), hunting scenes, and cannery with queued workers

II-A-5134 Ivory replica of Coast Guard Cutter Bear

II-A-7353 Eskimo ivory cribbage board made from a walrus tusk with carved ivory sledding figures and scrimshawed map

II-B-1314 Tlingit spruce-root basket with orange decoration

II-F-126 Aleut basketry-covered bottle of wild rye with embroidery floss decoration by Mary Snigaroff

II-F-166 Aleut model three-hatch baidarka with hunter figures and paddles

III-M-23 Round Masonite plaque with inscription about 1963 inauguration of Governor Egan and Secretary Wade

III-O-5 Eight Matanuska bingles (tokens) issued in 1935 by the Alaska Rural Rehabilitation Corporation

III-O-5-A Brass $5 bingle (token)

III-O-5-B Brass $10 bingle (token)

III-O-5-C Aluminum $1 bingle (token)

III-O-5-D Aluminum fifty-cent bingle (token)

III-O-5-E Aluminum twenty-five-cent bingle (token)

III-O-5-F Aluminum ten-cent bingle (token)

III-O-5-G Aluminum five-cent bingle (token)

III-O-5-H Aluminum one-cent bingle (token)

III-O-8-G Trade token marked "S. Applegate, Umnak" and "Good for 20 cents in Exchange"

III-O-16 Three-part heating device for baijiu, a liquor often served warm

III-O-21 Pair of screw-type handcuffs and key

III-O-26 Two-string Chinese musical instrument (jing hu), a smaller form of the erhu, with wood and snakeskin body, silk strings, and bow of bamboo and horsehair

III-O-31 Pair of wooden shoes, left has leather heel with copper nails

III-O-42 Wooden U.S. boundary marker shaped as square in cross section with pyramidal point

III-O-43 Cast iron U.S. boundary marker, painted and repainted

III-O-60 Embossed glass bottle with siphon cap

III-O-81 Handmade Alaska flag with gold appliqué on blue silk by Benny Benson

III-O-93 Ruan (Chinese stringed instrument) made of wood, size known as *zhong ruan* (middle ruan)

III-O-102 Hunting knife with curved single-edge steel seven-inch blade, copper guard, and deer-antler handle riveted with copper rivets

III-O-103 Gold Territory of Alaska police badge with inscription in blue

III-O-119 Curved cribbage board made of elephant ivory set in wooden frame

III-O-140 Violin with bow and papier mâché case

III-O-141 Banjo

III-O-150 Wooden washboard

III-O-184 WWII Japanese magazine with thirty rounds ammunition

III-O-193 Copper box with inscribed lid, full of dirt from the birthplace of William H. Seward, Florida, NY

III-O-198 Ice axe

III-O-216 Gold nugget-encrusted watch and chain

III-O-219 Calf stanchion, handmade of a branch bent into a "U" shape

III-O-220 Wooden scoop with metal rake for gathering blueberries

III-O-236 Whale harpoon with cone-shaped tang

III-O-243-B WWII Japanese hand grenade

III-O-244-A WWII U.S. mortar (60mm M1 and M2 shell)

III-O-246 WWII Japanese aircraft combat ammunition

III-O-246-A WWII Japanese aircraft combat ammunition, red-colored projectile

III-O-246-B WWII Japanese aircraft combat ammunition, yellow-colored projectile

III-O-247 Two WWII Japanese 50 mm caliber shells

III-O-247-A WWII Japanese 50 mm caliber shell

III-O-295 Prospector's iron mortar and pestle

III-O-297 Ten bronze letters of various widths with recessed backs and holes for mounting

III-O-311 Hand-lettered parchment display copy of Alaska Constitution, bound in blue Morocco

III-O-312 Smith Premier No.4 typewriter mounted on oak base with metal carrying case

III-O-314 Gavel of carved and incised mammoth ivory head, walrus ivory handle

III-O-324 U.S. Navy black ribbon hatband, lettered in gold

III-O-347 Rifle, Winchester Model 1876, lever action, .45-60 caliber with octagonal barrel

III-O-352	H. W. Chapman whale gun
III-O-354	Howard pocket watch, white gold, with enamel Alaska flag
III-O-355	Iron padlock with brass fittings
III-O-368	Cane with gold knob-style head embossed with flourished and floral designs, smooth top, and black shaft
III-O-406	Silver teaspoon with flag on handle
III-O-410	Original design for the Alaska territorial flag, painted with blue paint on construction paper by Benny Benson
III-O-414	Rusted metal ice creeper or crampon with leather piece
III-O-420	Painted horse or mule jawbone used as a musical instrument
III-O-435	Territory of Alaska Highway Patrol badge of silver-plated brass
III-O-446	White wool opera cloak, heavily trimmed with embroidery, crochet, lace and cording, lined with chiffon
III-O-465	Early motion-picture camera with accessories
III-O-491	Black top hat of black beaver and felt, with grosgrain ribbon edging brim
III-O-495	Handsewn American flag with thirty-six stars
III-O-500	William Henry Seward's black broadcloth cape
III-O-505	Gold nugget pocket watch and chain with fob
III-O-506	Gold nugget, pounded flat, in pendant set with a diamond and gold link chain
III-O-601	Toy metal wind-up car with white wheels
III-O-616	Radio in wood veneer case with glass-covered round dial with broadcast band and four knobs
III-O-669	Gold nugget
III-O-671	Gold nugget with small ring attached
III-O-856	Sailor's white jumper with navy-blue wool cuffs and square collar, red braid around left sleeve eye
III-O-931	Sterling silver engraved dog sledding trophy cup
III-O-968	Child's wooden sled with metal straps on runners
III-O-972	Man's winter hat of brown plaid wool lined with red wool flannel, hood style, with fur-lined ear flaps and neck band and black twill ties with black yarn pompons
III-O-1023	Solid brass Bomb Lance Shoulder Whaling Gun and Bomb Lance projectile
III-O-1023-A	Solid brass Bomb Lance Shoulder Whaling Gun
III-O-1023-B	Bomb Lance projectile for whaling
III-O-1049	Formal evening gown of red taffeta
III-R-95	Iron shrapnel cannonball or case shot with Bormann time fuse
III-R-196	Copper cup, tinned
III-R-197	Copper cup, tinned
III-R-286	Russian musket, cal. 69, with imperial double-headed eagle marked on brass butt plate
III-R-328	Russian infantry officer's sword with curved blade, scabbard of dark brown leather with brass fittings
III-R-341	Small white porcelain teapot with purple line and scroll design
IV-A-34	Test tube filled with colored volcanic ash from Valley of Ten Thousand Smokes, Katmai National Monument, Alaska Peninsula
IV-B-346-1	Copper nugget, roughly person shaped, crystal formations on flat side
V-A-70	Watercolor painting depicting a skin-covered boat with a crew of Alaska Natives by Henry W. Elliott
V-A-71	Watercolor painting of seal drive by Henry W. Elliott
V-A-738	Hand-colored lithograph on paper of sailing ships by Benjamin Russell
V-C-26	Framed photograph of Governor John G. Brady
LC.447-1	Hardcover book, *Travels in Alaska* by John Muir
SJ-I-A-582	Formerly sealed letter of agreement, 1881 peace treaty
SJ-V-A-46	Late 1800s Ketchum Patent Percussion Hand Grenade with egg shape and fins
SJ-V-A-63	Russian round, dry biscuit
SJ-V-A-160	Russian survey marker
SJ-V-C-14	American whale gun of brass and wood, mounted on wood block
SJ-V-D-8	Oil painting of the USS *Pinta* by G. E. Fowler

Resilience

90-4-1	Leather-bound bible
92-9-1	Silver print aerial photo of corralled reindeer herd
92-14-5	Silver spoon engraved with Tlingit bird design by Rudolph Walton
92-24-1	Hide pennant publicizing Eskimo-run trading company by Point Hope Trading and Reindeer Company
94-1-1	Sewing machine
94-2-1	Russian cocked or tricornered hat
94-39-1	Russian silk paisley caftan trimmed with silver and gold braid trim and pearls
98-1-1	Explosive shell casing made of steel
99-20-1	Wooden reindeer collar carved from wood pieces lashed with leather
2000-12-1	Two-piece silk dress by Lily Yaquan
2000-34-15	Pair of salt and pepper shakers carved from curved cylinders of walrus ivory with scrimshaw image of hunter dragging seal by Howard Weyahok (Howard Rock)
2001-10-1	Commercial drawknife used as a "blubbering knife" or scraper for seal hides
2001-10-4	Small Russian brass box embossed with crucifix, containing metal vials, scissors, brush, and sponge
2001-10-9 (see p. 129)	Elaborate Russian cast-metal censer for Orthodox services

2001-10-12 Russian brass lampada or suspended oil lamp

2002-16-1 Boxed set of six steak knives with scrimshawed ivory handles by Howard Weyahok (Howard Rock)

2002-16-4 Pin of walrus ivory with engraved scene of reindeer sled by Howard Weyahok (Howard Rock)

2002-18-1 Alaska Native Sisterhood appliquéd velvet sash

2003-31-1 Pencil drawing on caribou skin of corrals and two cabins in winter by Milo Minock

2006-4-1 Pair of bas-relief heads of hand-cut, unprinted paper bound like a book, titled What Have We Become? by Nicholas Galanin

2007-17-2 Reversible silk marshal ribbon

2010-11-1 Fur seal hat, hatbox, and lid

2010-12-1 U.S. military shell, Civil War period, identified as ten-pound Parrott shell, 2.9 inches caliber

2011-12-2 Carved ivory Madonna figurine by L. Okpealuk

2012-3-1 Yellow and red Alaska Native Brotherhood felt overseas-style hat with an ANB insignia and pin

2012-3-2 Alaska Native Brotherhood sash made from moose hide with red accents

2013-52-1 Tlingit war helmet of wood, abalone, and human hair by Tommy Joseph

2013-52-2 Carved yew wood collar with leather, sinew, and opercula by Tommy Joseph

2013-52-3 Torso armor of wooden slats, sinew, and leather by Tommy Joseph

2013-52-4 Two-piece leather armor by Tommy Joseph

2013-52-5 Deer-hide leather leggings with feet by Tommy Joseph

2014-14-3 Metal forceps with curled pointed jaws wide handles curled on one end

2014-14-7 Metal syringe

2014-14-9 Syringe kit with three vials, two needles, one syringe, and one case

2014-14-14 Dental picture with hexagon-shaped handle and narrow point

2014-14-15 Dental picture with hexagonal handle

2014-14-17 Dental mirror

2014-17-1 Small steel historic engraved handcuffs with formline design, titled Indian Children's Bracelets by Nicholas Galanin

2014-19-1 Tlingit-style wooden dagger with sheath by Tommy Joseph

2015-3-1 Double-ended carvel-planked round-bottomed hull with steam-bent ribs and frames by John Davis Sr., Roderick Davis, Davis and Son

2016-4-1 Blue and white Alaska Native Sisterhood felt hat with an ANS insignia by Adeline DeCastro

2016-9-1 Two large rusty metal daggers sculptures titled Double-Headed Language Dagger #2 (Gunalcheesh) by Da-ka-xeen Mehner

I-B-440 Seal (taxidermy)

II-A-3362 Russian calendar made from painted and incised walrus tusk

II-A-3474 Eskimo carved serrated bone nose bit for reindeer

II-A-3475 Eskimo carved serrated bone nose bit for reindeer with rawhide loops

II-A-4864 Detailed ivory model of MS North Star

II-A-6592 Doll of Howard Rock (Weyahok) wearing parka and mukluks by Dolly Spencer

II-B-690 Slat armor of hardwood (crabapple and yew) and bear sinew

II-B-813 Carved alder wood oil dish in the shape of a sea lion, inlaid with abalone, bone, and beads by Rudolph Walton

II-B-848 Tlingit-style spoon of Dall sheep and mountain goat horn, with engraved silver details by Rudolph Walton

II-B-954 Tlingit small spruce-root hat with five basketry rings and detailed black and red painting

II-B-986 Pocket watch with an engraved silver case

II-B-987 Silver watch case (no works) engraved with Northwest Coast-style designs

II-B-989 Tlingit silver bracelet engraved with killer whale formline design

II-B-1110-1 Carved and painted interior house post with clan crest by Rudolph Walton

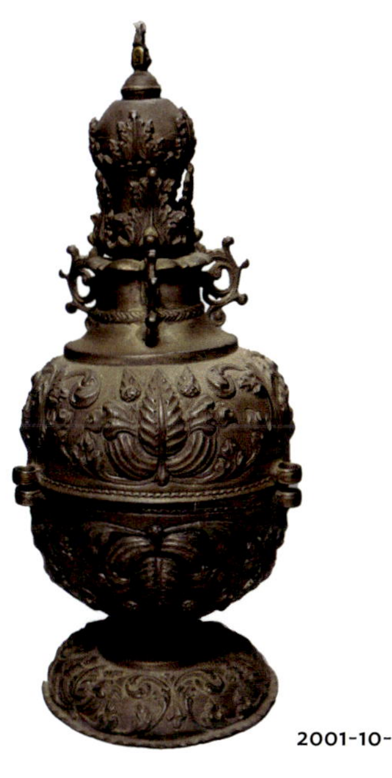

2001-10-9

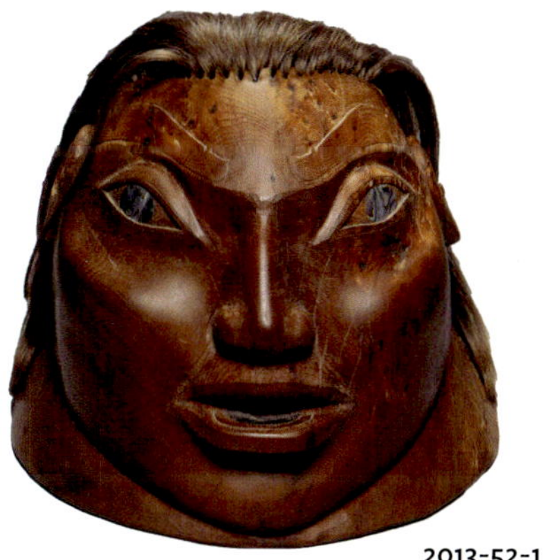

2013-52-1

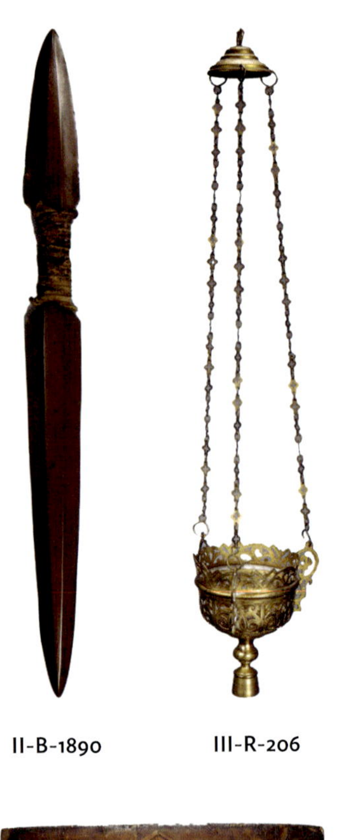

II-B-1890 III-R-206

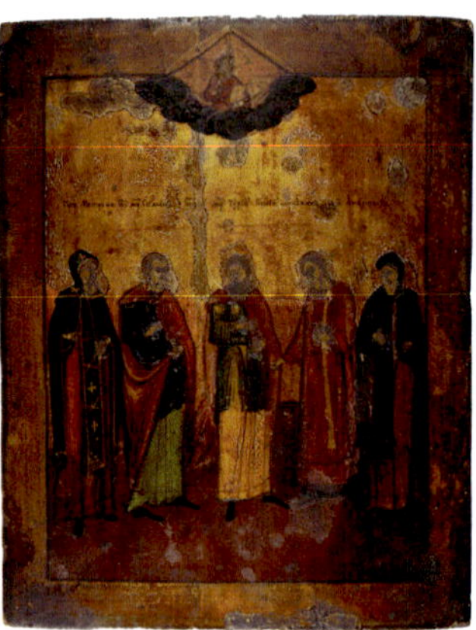

III-R-168

II-B-1110-2	Carved and painted interior house post with clan crest by Rudolph Walton
II-B-1433	Tlingit oversized carved and painted wooden globular rattle painted with humanoid face, with attached human hair
II-B-1799	Tlingit bear crest hat of carved wood with abalone, copper, and sea-lion whiskers
II-B-1890	Tlingit double-dagger of copper with leather
II-B-1896	Haida wooden bow carved with formline designs
II-C-149	Athabascan wooden peg calendar with brass hinges and clasp, iron nails, and screws
III-O-23	Screw-type shackle or handcuff with a 13.5-inch length of chain
III-O-35	Japanese branding iron for seal skins, with wooden handle
III-O-114	Peg calendar of drilled wood with cord for hanging
III-O-117	Saami (Lap) carved wooden doll with jointed arms and legs, wearing hat
III-O-416	U.S. Marine Corps navy blue uniform with brass buttons and gold braid
III-O-416-A	Jacket from U.S. Marine Corps navy blue uniform with brass buttons and gold braid
III-O-416-C	Trousers from U.S. Marine Corps navy blue uniform with yellow grosgrain ribbon stripe
III-O-530	British Sea Service percussion cap pistol
III-O-600	Silver-colored metal police badge in shape of seven-point star with words "Police Officer" in black
III-R-8	Handmade round copper snuffbox
III-R-32	Wick trimmer, scissor-like metal implement
III-R-125	Russian icon of wood and glass
III-R-129	Velvet-covered Russian bible
III-R-131	Silver-plated cross pendant with embossed crucifix
III-R-135	Oval ceramic medallion representing St. Xenia
III-R-141	Square ceramic medallion with picture of St. Matena
III-R-142	Square paper icon of St. Nina, patron of Georgia, with metal back with cardboard and metal frame
III-R-144	Icon oil painting on silver metal with silver halo
III-R-148	Icon of silver-colored metal with repoussé, oil-painted depiction of Mary and Child
III-R-151	Painted icon representing Christ, St. Nicholas, and Mary
III-R-157	Russian brass seal with wooden handle to make impressions on wax seals
III-R-159	Russian brass hand blessing cross with raised figures
III-R-163	Lampada with red glass bowl set in bronze cup with three elaborate lugs for chains for hanging
III-R-166	Icon painted with egg tempera on wood panel showing figure of bishop
III-R-167	Icon painted with oil paint on wooden panel, with silver repoussé, showing Holy Mother and four other figures
III-R-168	Icon in egg tempera on wood panel, showing five saints with Christ above
III-R-169	Old icon of Russian-made tapestry, representing King David
III-R-171	Brass schoolhouse bell with iron handle
III-R-202	Icon showing Christ
III-R-203	Icon of Holy Mother and Christ Child
III-R-204	Small icon of Christ
III-R-205	Wooden peg calendar in disk shape with drilled holes for keeping track of dates and metal loop for hanging
III-R-206	Lampada with red glass bowl set in bronze cup with three elaborate lugs for chains for hanging
III-R-208	Hand-lettered Divine Liturgy of the Russian Orthodox Church, text in Church Slavonic
III-R-210	Silver-covered icon of Christ, done in oil paint on wood
III-R-211	Ceramic medallion icon with picture of saint
III-R-212	Ceramic medallion icon with picture of two saints
III-R-228	Certificate from Russian-American Company to Tlingit chief
III-R-233	Nine small cannonballs, possibly canister shot

III-R-233-1 Small cannonballs, possibly canister shot

III-R-233-2 Small cannonballs, possibly canister shot

III-R-233-3 Small cannonballs, possibly canister shot

III-R-233-4 Small cannonballs, possibly canister shot

III-R-233-5 Small cannonballs, possibly canister shot

III-R-233-6 Small cannonballs, possibly canister shot

III-R-233-7 Small cannonballs, possibly canister shot

III-R-233-8 Small cannonballs, possibly canister shot

III-R-233-9 Small cannonballs, possibly canister shot

III-R-238 Russian iron ladle with small bowl of the type used in metalworking to melt small amounts of lead

III-R-242 Russian wrought-iron chopping tool

III-R-243 Metal table fork with wooden handle

III-R-258 Bronze bell with Russian inscription

III-R-264 Small hardcover book titled The School and Family, Russo-American Primer

III-R-299 Russian icon, painted on wood, with picture of Christ with silver perforated halo

III-R-350 Silver medal with Imperial double-eagle and monogram of Alexander I on one side, Russian inscription on other side. Loop at top for cord or chain

V-A-170 Painting depicting an Eskimo taking a gun away from a white man by Kivetoruk Moses

V-A-547 Drawing showing winter scene and man riding on runner of reindeer sled by Kivetoruk Moses

LC.99-1 Feast dish carved from one piece of wood, in the form of a beaver, decorated with formline design and opercula

LC.378-1 Metal round snuffbox with bird design and chain by Rudolph Walton

LC.438-1 Small child's tunic is made bright red wool with grey cuffs and neckband, front is beaded with two-headed eagle and floral designs

LC-443 Set of Russian Orthodox vestments: phelonion, epimanikia, epitrachelion, zone, nabredennik

LC.443-1 Blue phelonion or cape, vestment for Russian Orthodox clergy

LC.443-2 Epimanikia, or cuffs that lace onto wrists, vestment for Russian Orthodox clergy

LC.443-3 Epitrachelion, or long garment that hangs down front from neck, vestment for Russian Orthodox clergy

LC.443-4 Zone, or ribbon belt with ties, vestment for Russian Orthodox clergy

LC.443-5 Fabric rectangle with appliquéd cross, vestment for Russian Orthodox clergy

LC.478-1 Booklet titled Tlingit / Short Stories with formline design by Robert Davis

LC.478-2 Booklet titled SAM / ALUTIIQ with log cabin-built store on cover

LC.478-3 Booklet titled K'qizaghetnu Ht'ana with people in canoe on cover

LC.478-4 Booklet titled AAHAHAANAAQ with cover showing person sitting on grass

LC.478-5 Booklet titled ALQUTAXˆ UKUXˆTALTXIN? (AKUTAN / Eastern Aleut) with cover showing people near winter cabin

SJ-I-A-522 Sealed letter of agreement, 1899 truce

SJ-I-A-832 Pair of child's high-top shoes of cloth and leather, with serrated top edges

SJ-II-N-97 Yup'ik reindeer skin boots with decorative stitchery and leather inserts

SJ-V-C-2 American bomb fragment with triangular metal point, sharp tip, and hole in opposite end

SJ-V-C-6 Leather surgical case containing numerous tools

SJ-V-C-23 Small child's dress with notation, on printed muslin with tiny parasols

UA/UC-31 Tlingit wooden sign with gilded letters: "Kow-ee Auk Chief 1884"

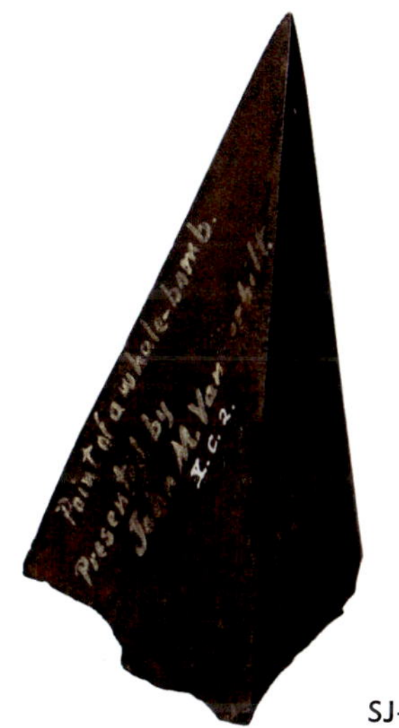

SJ-V-C-2

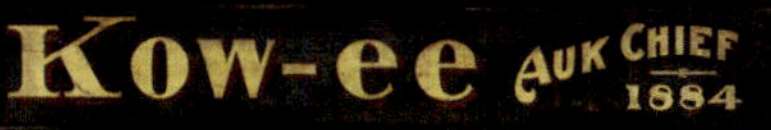

UA/UC-31

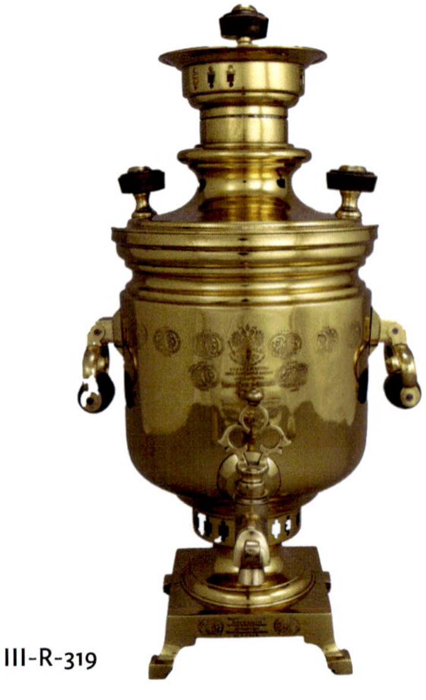
III-R-319

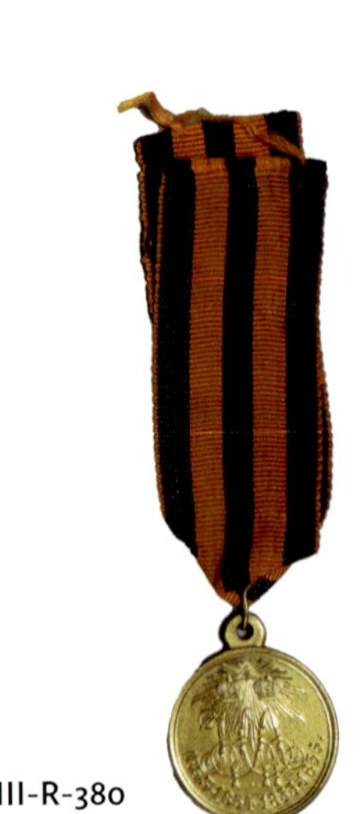
III-R-380

Russian Alaska

79-17-2	Color engraving of Baie D'Awatcha, Siberia
90-6-1	Russian steamship cannon
93-7-1	Russian dagger or kindjal
94-18-1	Russian iron scale inlaid with brass
98-11-1	Lacquer box of word or papier-mâché with painted scene of man and woman
98-15-1	Russian ruble note
2000-5-1	Tea strainer of gold-washed silver
2001-10-8	Russian stamped tray of silver-plated copper with brass handles and feet
2007-12-1	Oil painting of Russian Orthodox church in Sitka by Lesley Jackson
2008-11-12	Wood and brass fragment of hub from ship's wheel from shipwreck of Kad'yak
2008-11-83	Large bronze rudder pintle recovered from the Kad'yak shipwreck
2008-11-91	Large bronze gudgeon and pin recovered from the Kad'yak shipwreck
2012-14-1	Watercolor painting of Sitka by Aleksandr F. Postels
2015-7-1	Marble bust of William H. Seward with green marble base with brass plaque by Chauncey B. Ives
I-B-501	Sea otter (taxidermy)
II-A-1639	Eskimo arrow with harpoon-style copper point and ivory and wood shaft
II-B-851	Tlingit stone pipe bowl carved in form of sleeping sea otter
II-F-171	Aleut model baidarka (kayak) of skin stretched over wood frame, with two model figures dressed in gut parkas
III-O-517	Iron key
III-O-518	Brass escutcheon with keyhole
III-R-43	Corroded metal horseshoe
III-R-46	Large stoneware cup with handle and matching saucer, with white background with Wedgwood-style blue and white relief decorations
III-R-53	Paper knife made from copper spike
III-R-57	Russian brass mortar and pestle
III-R-58	Incised copper spike
III-R-59-A	Wooden peg
III-R-67	Hammer of iron and wood
III-R-68	Whale-bone hammer with wooden handle
III-R-69	Metal weights
III-R-70	Tea brick branded with "M"
III-R-72	Pair of brass hinges mounted on mahogany block
III-R-73	Ornate brass door handle with iron pin
III-R-74	Brass key
III-R-75	Wrought-iron pike
III-R-76	Russian wrought-iron scissors
III-R-77	Iron scraper
III-R-80	Iron latch hook
III-R-81	Metal hasp
III-R-82	Iron padlock and key that screws in
III-R-83	Abacus of metal and wood with glass beads
III-R-85	Russian mangle with corrugations and carved geometric design
III-R-86	Wood roller
III-R-96	Wrought-iron founder's rammer or bar shot with double end
III-R-97	Wrought-iron bar shot, with double end
III-R-98	Wrought-iron founder's rammer with double end
III-R-102	Wrought-iron pitchfork
III-R-103	Metal boot jack
III-R-105	Wrought-iron square
III-R-106	Wrought-iron spike
III-R-108	Russian copper hinge
III-R-115	Wrought-iron ax head
III-R-116	Wrought-iron ax
III-R-150	Russian double-headed eagle plaque of cast bronze
III-R-186	Copper kettle, tinned, with iron handle
III-R-195	Cast-iron pot
III-R-198	China cup and saucer
III-R-201	Brass plate from grave, with Russian inscription
III-R-215	Brick of fired clay
III-R-219	Complete brass samovar, tinned, with wood handle grips
III-R-221-A	Hinge from last standing Russian blockhouse at Sitka
III-R-221-B	Hinge from last standing Russian blockhouse at Sitka
III-R-221-C	Hinge from last standing Russian blockhouse at Sitka

III-R-223 Copper caulking iron

III-R-285 Russian small cannon

III-R-319 (see p. 132) Russian brass samovar set with wooden handles

III-R-319-A Russian brass samovar

III-R-319-B Russian brass samovar tray

III-R-319-C Russian brass samovar drip cup

III-R-319-D Russian brass samovar teapot

III-R-319-E Russian brass samovar lid

III-R-319-F Russian brass samovar stack

III-R-345 Small Russian travel samovar

III-R-346 Two Russian tea glasses each consisting of a brass holder and crystal glass

III-R-346-1 Russian tea glass consisting of a brass holder and crystal glass

III-R-346-2 Russian tea glass consisting of a brass holder and crystal glass

III-R-347 Russian medal of copper alloy with bust of Catherine on one side, Russian inscription on reverse, and loop at top for cord or chain

III-R-348 Gold alloy medal with bust of man on one side, Russian inscription on reversed side

III-R-380 (see p. 132) Round bronze medallion issued to Crimean War veterans, with orange and black ribbon of Order of St. George

III-R-381 Cross-shaped Order of St. George medallion of white-enameled gold metal

V-A-50-4 Watercolor painting on paper of Sitka circa 1860, one of set of four by Lt. Schreiben

V-A-116 Watercolor painting depicting Unalaska with three-masted vessel anchored offshore by Henry W. Elliott

V-A-142 Copy of Emanuel Leutze's Signing the Alaska Treaty by Lynn Fausett, Helen (Wessells) Henry

V-A-268 Watercolor painting depicting Baranoff's castle in Sitka by Katherine Delaney Abrams

V-A-270 Watercolor painting depicting St. Michael's Cathedral in Sitka by Katherine Delaney Abrams

V-A-272 Watercolor of St. Michael's Cathedral in Sitka by Edward Chamberlain

V-A-489 Drawing shows Aleuts hunting in baidarkas by Henry W. Elliott

V-A-533 Color lithograph by Englemann from Kittlitz's drawing of small boy with string of fish talking to adult with dog and pointing to Russian fort by Baron Kittlitz

LC.447-2 Leatherbound Russian veterinary book

LC.448-1 Carved ivory figurine of bear with elongated neck and cub

LC.448-2 Carved ivory figurine of bear with hole drill

LC.448-3 Carved tortoise shell comb

LC.448-4 Miniature carved wood musket

LC.448-5 Carved ivory chess piece (pawn)

LC.448-6 Glass stopper or piece of stemware repurposed and shaped into labret

LC.448-7 Obsidian projectile point

LC.448-8 Fragment of obsidian projectile point

LC.448-9 Carved ivory bird game piece

LC.448-10 Carved and drilled ivory game piece in the figure of a bird with ears

LC.448-11 Carved and drilled greenish ivory swimming animal figurine

LC.448-12 Brass clothes button with image of phoenix bird, French text

LC.448-13 Brass clothes button with image of phoenix bird

LC.448-14 Brass clothes button with image of phoenix bird, French text

LC.448-15 Brass clothes button with image of phoenix bird

LC.448-16 Brass clothes button with image of phoenix bird

LC.448-17 Wood bottle stopper

LC.448-18 Wood bottle stopper

LC.448-19 Brass spigot with valve

LC.448-20 Copper alloy valve handle with delicate three ring pattern at top

LC.448-21 Copper alloy valve handle

LC.448-22 Shallow copper drinking vessel

LC.448-23 Rolled copper cone ornament

LC.448-24 Rolled copper cone ornament

LC.448-25 Molded copper candleholder

LC.448-26 Russian terra cotta clay pipe bowl with incised or stamped decorations

LC.448-27 Copper alloy circular adornment with eroded lion head figure

LC.448-28 Broken round pipe stem with irregular ridges

LC.448-29 Fragment of enamel triptych panel depicting religious figures

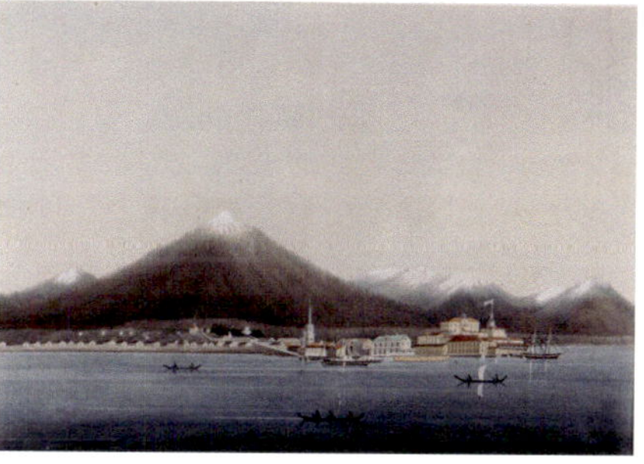

V-A-50-4

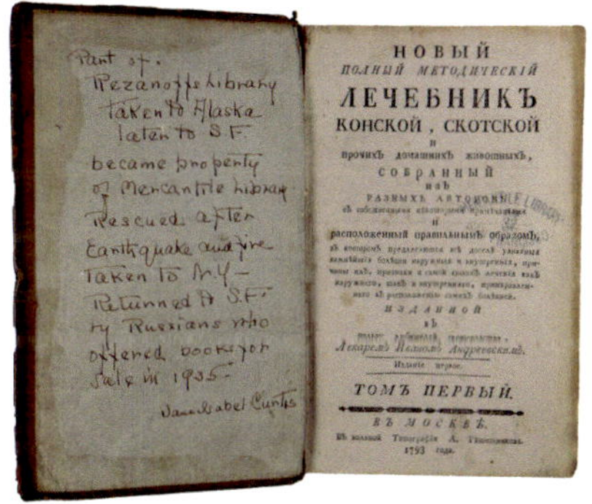

LC.447-2

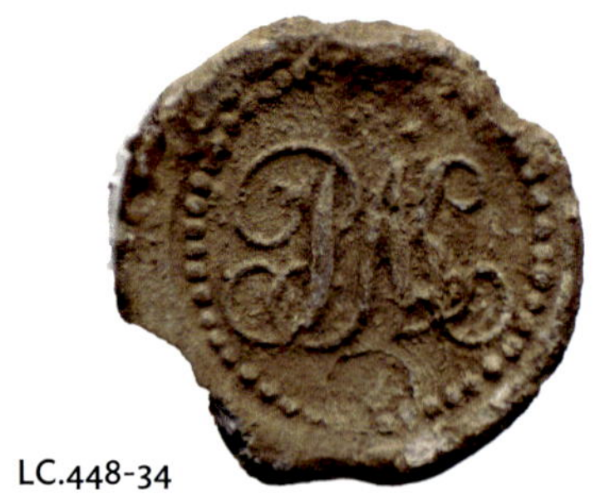
LC.448-34

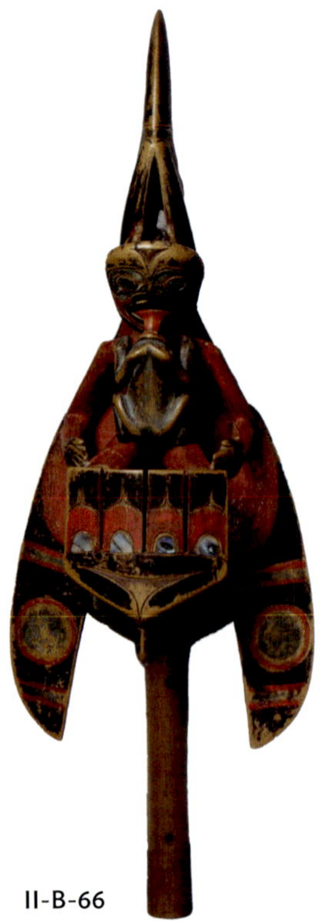
II-B-66

LC.448-30 Triptych panel depicting religious figures

LC.448-31 Lead seal with text "P.A.K. T"

LC.448-32 Lead seal with text "P.A.K. G"

LC.448-33 Lead seal with text "P.A.K."

LC.448-34 Lead seal with text "P K"

SJ-II-N-18 Fox trap made of bone, wood, and sinew

SJ-II-N-19 Fox trap made of small log, with bone supports, and inserts in end of log and deadfall with metal spike

SJ-V-A-27 Russian metal shears

SJ-V-A-28 Russian metal knife

SJ-V-A-45 Russian respirator of grass stuffed into coil of cedar bark, for steam baths

SJ-V-A-66 Russian brass cannon with double-headed eagle symbol

SJ-V-A-90 Russian metal grappling hook

SJ-V-A-164 Russian wrought-iron candlestick

SJ-V-D-11 Native-drawn map of New Archangel in Russian Period

Southeast Alaska

91-49-1 Tlingit carved children's toy canoe

92-25-1 Engraved sheep-horn bowl

92-56-1 Painted wooden clam shell rattle by Jim Schoppert

92-56-2 Painted wooden mussel shell rattle by Jim Schoppert

95-37-2 Halibut hook of wood and spruce root and design of human wrestling octopus

98-22-1 Beginning of Tlingit woven spruce root basket

98-32-3 Ball made of spruce root bark, with crocheted cover of white yarn

98-32-4 Ball made of spruce root bark

2007-18-1 Silver bracelet engraved with formline design of killer whale, with humanoid face as whale's eye by Nicholas Galanin

2009-11-1 Tlingit spruce-root basket for spoons

2009-30-1 Carved and painted raven rattle with abalone inlay and red felt by Archie Cavanaugh Jr.

2010-34-1 Cut and carved mother of pearl eagle pendant by Mike A. Jackson

2012-4-3 Spoon of horn of mountain sheep, with inlaid abalone

2012-9-1 Carved and painted wooden Eagle Man mask decorated with copper and hair by Archie Cavanaugh Jr.

2013-8-1 Carved and painted wooden mask with abalone inlays and opercula shells by Norman Jackson

2013-8-2 Carved and painted wooden bear mask with inlaid abalone eyes and teeth by Norman Jackson

2015-11-1 Carved and painted wooden young raven mask with feathers by David A. Boxley

2015-24-2 Densely patterned robe with several rows of raven's tail tattoos and bands of lightning patterns by Kay Field Parker and Vicki Soboleff

2016-2-1 Remains of a Tlingit "raven's tail" robe

2016-5-1 Tlingit soapberry spoon carved in a light-colored hardwood with formline design

2019-4-1 Worn black stone hammer or maul with carving of bird's head on one end

II-B-60 Haida carved and painted wooden bird rattle

II-B-63 Tlingit carved and painted wooden rattle used for ceremonies in form of raven with reclining humanoid figure on its back holding frog

II-B-66 Tlingit carved and painted wooden rattle used for ceremonies in form of raven with reclining humanoid figure on its back holding frog, with inlaid abalone

II-B-91 Tlingit stone maul with wooden handle

II-B-98 Tlingit stone maul carved of tuff, with a bear's head motif

II-B-100 Stone maul carved in shape of owl's head

II-B-127 Handheld stone wedge with grooves

II-B-130 Stone adze bit of salificied tuff

II-B-135 Green stone adze bit

II-B-136 Green stone adze bit

II-B-140 Stone adze bit of jade

II-B-180 Oval whetstone made of mudstone

II-B-205 Stone tobacco mortar of diorite

II-B-217 Stone sloping-grip hammer decorated with U-shaped grooves

II-B-218 Stone stirrup hammer

II-B-221 Stone T-hammer

II-B-222 Stone stirrup hammer, incomplete

II-B-225 Stone hat-top hammer, finely finished

II-B-232 Small hat-top hammer

II-B-241 Fragment of stone stirrup hammer

II-B-261 Smoothly finished granite stone mortar with flattened base

II-B-294 Bone harpoon point with three barbs and elliptical hole

II-B-364 Broad, shallow woven spruce-root basket

II-B-440 Twined spruce-root basket, undecorated and folded

II-B-514 Tlingit twined split spruce-root basket with "half the head of the salmonberry" and "tying" designs

II-B-672 Dagger with steel blade, flat on one side and convex on opposite side, and wooden handle wrapped in cord

II-B-769 Carved, painted, inlaid yellow cedar chief's staff

II-B-788 Tlingit carved wooden halibut hook with devil fish motif, suckers, and head with horns at bottom

II-B-789 Tlingit carved wooden halibut hook decorated with depiction of bird wearing spruce-root hat, lashed with twine and halibut line

II-B-796 Adze, branch-hafted and lashed with rawhide

II-B-810 Tlingit painted spruce-root hat with six basketry rings and ermine skin

II-B-815 Tlingit Dall sheep horn spoon

II-B-831 Carved, stained, and painted bentwood box with with curved tops on sides

II-B-832 Tlingit doll of child in spruce-root cradle

II-B-857 Tlingit carved yellow-cedar face stamp with octopus design

II-B-861 Chilkat blanket with diving whale and raven designs

II-B-883 Carved sheep-horn spoon with geometric design of lines and half-circles on handle

II-B-889 Tlingit seal oil skimmer with flat perforated bowl

II-B-914-A Small formline patterns for weaving Chilkat robes, in bent birch-bark circular box

II-B-914-B Bent birch-bark circular box

II-B-915 Fifteen balls of mountain goat hair yarn for weaving Chilkat blankets, in various colors of native dye

II-B-923 Tsimshian soapberry spoon carved of swamp maple with handle carved with face of animal with very long ears

II-B-938 Spoon carved of mountain sheep horn with eagle head handle

II-B-940 Northwest Coast-style wooden spoon carved with two heads

II-B-943 Carved wooden spoon with formline painting

II-B-962 Tlingit small carved wooden dish with concave sides and convex ends

II-B-976 Haida carved goat-horn spoon with several human and animal figures carved in the round on the handle

II-B-981 Tlingit pair of shark-tooth earrings with engraved gold bands and silver fasteners

II-B-983 Tlingit silver earrings shaped like shark teeth, with engraved gold bands

II-B-990 Tlingit grooved silver nose ring

II-B-1010 Replica carved and painted crest hat in form of eagle, with human hair plume by Kailian-ish, Augustus Bean

II-B-1040 Enormous carved wooden spoon with mud shark carving nailed to handle

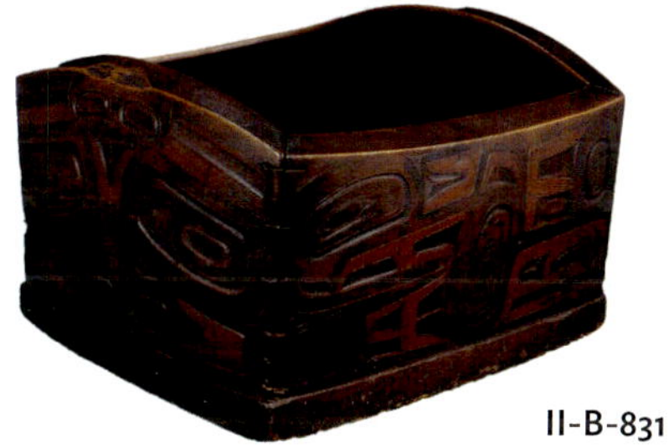

II-B-831

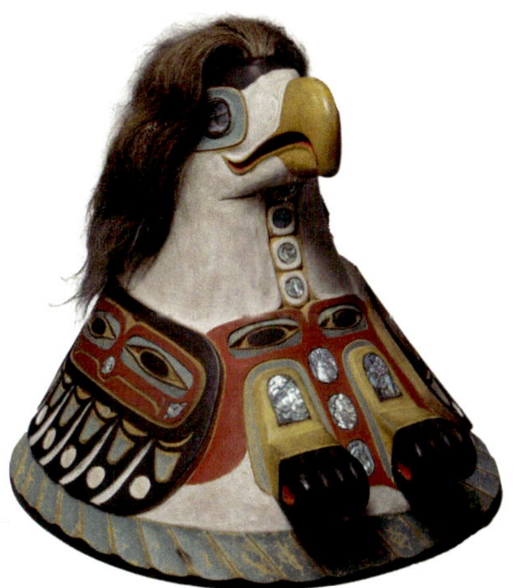

II-B-1010

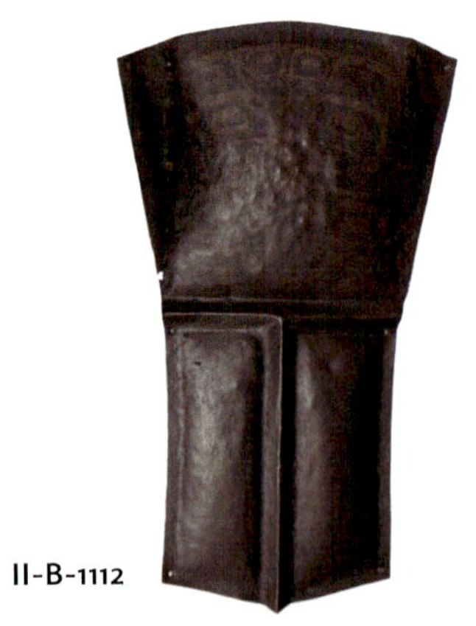

II-B-1112

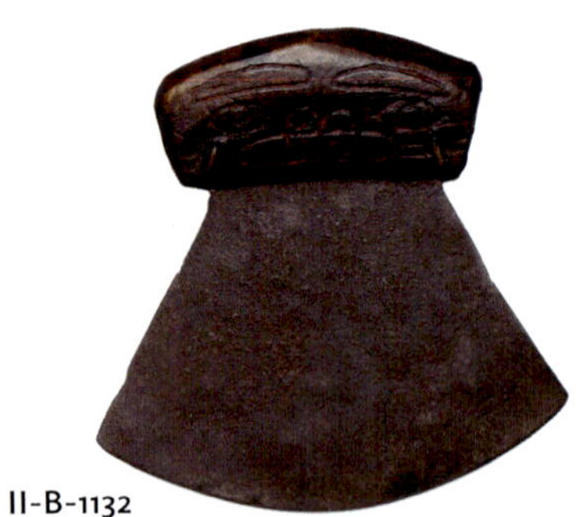

II-B-1132

II-B-1257

II-B-1044 Wooden food tray carved from single piece of wood, with inset opercula

II-B-1046 Tlingit carved wooden sea lion figure with bird-quill whiskers from a crest hat

II-B-1063 Tlingit pipe with brass top, abalone inlay, and long cherrywood stem

II-B-1073 Carved wooden fish club

II-B-1074 Crabapple wood club for killing salmon or halibut carved in shape of wolf head

II-B-1078 Carved alder-wood snuff mortar

II-B-1089 Small "crooked knife" with straight pointed iron blade and wooden handle wrapped with thong

II-B-1090-A Knife with iron blade and wooden handle wrapped with cotton cord

II-B-1092-A Crooked knife with iron blade and worked bone handle wrapped in leather

II-B-1093 Two "crooked knives"

II-B-1093-B "Crooked knife" with curved handle carved with eagle head and wrapped with cotton cord

II-B-1097 Pipe bowl carved from wood with two seated figures

II-B-1098 Fire-making set consisting of wooden hearth and wooden drill

II-B-1098-A Wooden hearth from fire-making set

II-B-1099 Tlingit wooden cylindrical container with stopper

II-B-1105 Leather ammunition pouch with bone nozzle

II-B-1112 Tlingit tinneh (tin.aa) of copper with painted design

II-B-1123 Carved wooden dance baton in the shape of a Winchester rifle with head of Kooshdahkah

II-B-1131 Hand-hewn and painted red cedar Chilkat pattern board

II-B-1132 Ulu of iron, copper, and carved wood

II-B-1170 Iron harpoon point

II-B-1171 Iron harpoon point

II-B-1174 Haida labret

II-B-1223 Painted bentwood storage box with inlaid opercula

II-B-1234 Halibut float carved of wood in shape of bird

II-B-1257 Large rectangular carved and painted bentwood box with slab lid by Captain Carpenter

II-B-1328 Set of gambling counters in case with bone and leather closure

II-B-1329 Two Tlingit gambling game pieces of carved wood

II-B-1330 Two Tlingit wooden labrets, each set both sides with abalone

II-B-1361 Bone harpoon head of skeletal whalebone, used for sea otter, with point missing

II-B-1372 Carved horn spoon of yellow and brown color

II-B-1398 Barbed bone harpoon point

II-B-1403 Seal harpoon head made of steel barb set into piece of horn and wrapped with twine

II-B-1405 Seal harpoon (metal) with sinew cord and wooden sheath

II-B-1423 Bear snare of seven strands of moose hide wound with split spruce root

II-B-1427 Tlingit pair of carved wooden brushes used for tattooing

II-B-1427-A Tlingit carved wooden brush used for tattooing, with eagle head

II-B-1427-B Tlingit carved wooden brush used for tattooing, only half of handle carved

II-B-1549 (see p. 137) Strand of amber and blue trade beads

II-B-1559 (see p. 137) Tlingit coat of white ermine furs with multicolored trim and decorations

II-B-1597 Tlingit carved and painted wood raven crest hat

II-B-1598-B Bundle of spruce root

II-B-1598-C Bundle of spruce-root weft

II-B-1598-G Bear tooth

II-B-1629 Tlingit carved iron dance-cane head or hair ornament with totemic design

II-B-1640 Northwest Coast snowshoes made of wood, rawhide, cord, and rope

II-B-1643 Carved and painted wooden eagle rattle with face on the belly by Leo Jacobs

II-B-1719 Tlingit wool and cotton beaded ceremonial pouch with four extensions

II-B-1776 Copper ulu with rolled handle

II-B-1777 Copper ulu with leather-covered handle

II-B-1789 Silver bracelet engraved with designs of dogfish or shark and eagle

II-B-1802 Tlingit ceremonial headdress with abalone fin and human hair

II-B-1820 Tlingit spruce-root basket with red and black "checkerboard" and "winding around" patterns

II-B-1840 Carved and painted wooden crest hat depicted frog crest of Kiks.adi clan of Sitka, with abalone and ermine

II-B-1845 Haida grease dish of dark wood with raven's-head design

II-B-1846 Carved and painted wooden eagle headdress with beak that opens by Nathan Jackson

II-B-1858 Wooden canoe-shaped grease dish

II-B-1862 Large carved and painted wooden mask of human face with frog in mouth by Wayne Price

II-B-1870 Bone trap stake with carved wolf head

II-B-1881 Tlingit sewn wool felt robe decorated with buttons

III-O-63 Powder horn made of cow horn flattened to one inch thick

III-O-349 Flintlock musket with flint, brass dragon insignia, Barnett-London, 1876

LC.430-1 Large bentwood box carved and painted with "formline" design, with lid inlaid with opercula by David A. Boxley, Zach Boxley

Tourism

90-29-1 Bar of soap with printed wrapper

91-31-26 Silver spoon engraved with totem pole design

92-14-8 Tlingit engraved silver teaspoon

92-49-1 Silver-plated teapot from steamship

93-3-31 Nome commemorative spoon with gold-panning design and box

96-48-1 Carved and stained yellow cedar porpoise-shaped inlaid dish by Silversmith Jim

97-15-2 Silver cigarette box inlaid with lapis lazuli and turquoise by William Spratling

98-7-1 thru 59 Carved ivory billiken figures with features incised in black

98-7-60 Carved ivory billiken figure with features incised in black by Happy Jack (Angokwazhuk)

98-7-61 thru 65 Carved ivory billiken figures with features incised in black

98-7-208 Cribbage board carved from walrus tusks and decorated with sculptures of seals and a whale by Happy Jack (Angokwazhuk)

98-7-213 Cribbage board carved from walrus tusk with freely turning wheels and carvings of seal, fish, and a man driving a sled with two dogs by Happy Jack (Angokwazhuk)

98-9-1 Hammered copper bowl with lid, decorated with deer antlers by Albert Berry

2002-23-1 Suitcase with stickers

2002-25-6 Eskimo doll dressed in fur clothing

2002-25-8 Eskimo dolls (mother and baby) dressed in fur clothing

2008-31-1 Salad or dessert plate used with Pacific Coast Steamship Co. logo

2009-3-4 Red and black souvenir felt hat with "Greetings from Alaska" printed on one side and picture of musher with dogs and sled on the other

2009-8-7 Souvenir bone china waste bowl with SS Princess Louise pictured

2009-8-12 Souvenir bone china cup and saucer with Tonsina Road House pictured

2009-8-14 Metal-framed desk calendar bearing Alaska Territory seal

2009-8-15 Souvenir porcelain dessert plate with picture of town of Sitka

2009-8-21 Souvenir bone china cup and saucer with picture of sled dog

2011-25-1 Pickle fork and salt spoon from silver serving set with totem pole design

II-A-2789 Walrus tusk carved as thirty-one intertwined animals in the Nunivak Island style

II-A-2971 Circular baleen basket and cover with ivory knob carved as mountain sheep's head probably by Lloyd Pikok

II-B-825 Haida Argillite flute (recorder) inlaid with skeletal whalebone and abalone, with carving of fish with shaman lying on his back, and raven design on flute body by George Gunya

II-B-950 Tlingit dagger modeled after traditional fighting daggers, with copper blade and horn handle carved with humanoid head with abalone and fur

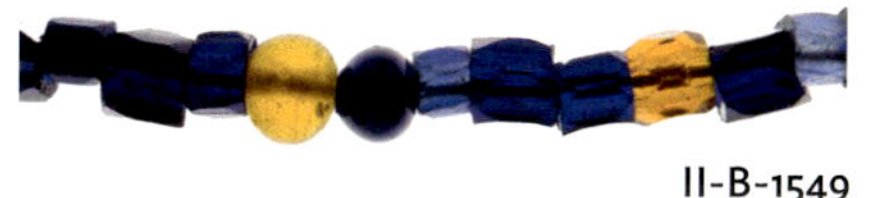

II-B-1549

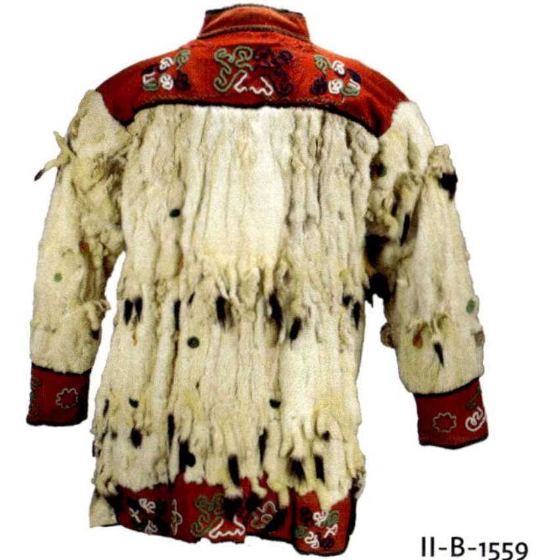

II-B-1559

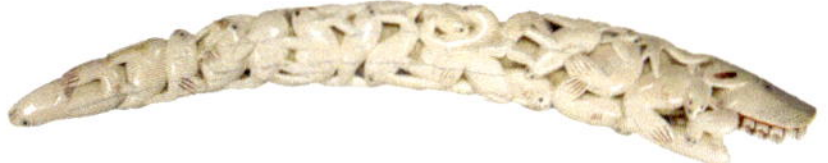

II-A-2789

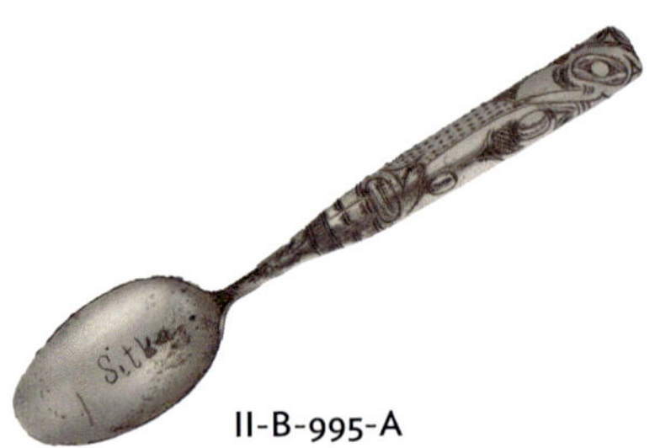

II-B-995-A

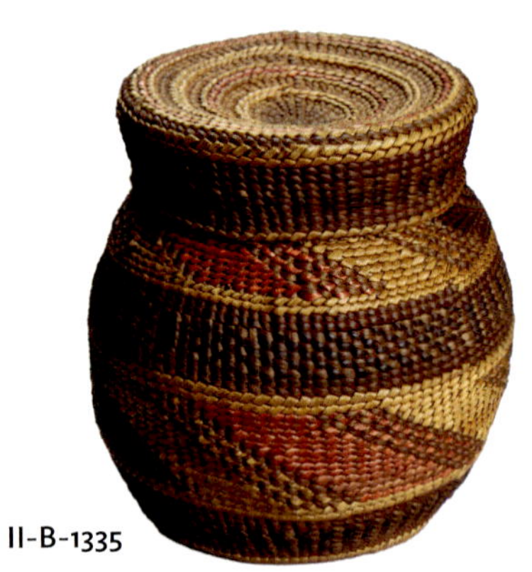

II-B-1335

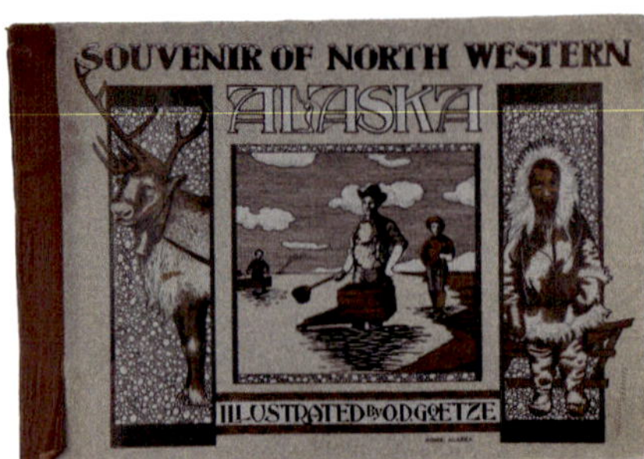

III-M-12

II-B-953 Model totem pole by James Watson

II-B-995-A Silver spoon with front of handle engraved with profile of raven by Silversmith Jake

II-B-1030 Argillite model totem pole

II-B-1304 Model of Haida house carved from argillite by Charles Edenshaw

II-B-1335 Twined spruce-root basket with cover, unusual shape, several false embroidery patterns

II-B-1964 Model totem pole carved of yellow cedar, with thunderbird figure at top with large wings by Lincoln Wallace

III-M-12 Book, paperback album-type, containing photographs circa 1900

III-O-831 Kodak automatic folding camera and case

III-O-910 Folding Brownie camera and cardboard box

III-O-973 Sterling-silver souvenir demitasse spoon, with miner panning gold on bowl, and mining equipment with walrus on handle

III-O-974 Sterling-silver souvenir teaspoon with husky dog on bowl, and totem pole handle

III-O-975 Sterling-silver souvenir demitasse spoon, with gold prospecter handle

III-O-976 Sterling-silver souvenir teaspoon with ships on ocean scene in bowl, and gold nuggets depicted on handle

V-A-732 Carved wooden mask showing walrus face stained red ochre, with fork and spoon for tusks by Jim Schoppert

Transportation

90-1-2 Athabascan bear-hide gloves

90-30-4 Glass vial containing panned gold sample

92-21-33 (see pp. 139) Seat from dirigible Norge

92-21-37 Wooden propeller from first commercial flight in Alaska

92-21-73 (see pp. 139) Aviation fuel can

92-37-3 Tourist map for Alaska Highway

92-37-4 Alaska Airlines deck of playing cards

92-47-1 Piece of fabric from the dirigible Norge

93-9-4 Dish from the wreck of the Princess Sophia

93-9-5 Cabin door lock from the wreck of the Princess Sophia

96-30-5 Set of metal proportional dividers in leather case with printed paper instructions

96-63-1 Small bar of soap in wrapper promoting Alaska marine tourism

2000-18-1 Aviation map board game lithographed on metal

2000-19-18 Circular button pin promoting the MV Wickersham

2000-22-3 Metal button with paper face and printed lettering used as ID badge

2001-1-1 Commercially made cleaver

2003-43-14 White metal ruler with Pacific Northern Airlines logo

2007-22-1 Small white plastic Alaska Coastal Airlines bag given out to passengers

2008-11-1 Oval porcelain bowl with Alaska Steamship Co. logo

2008-11-2 Oval porcelain plate with Alaska Steamship Co. logo

2008-11-3 Oval porcelain plate with Alaska Steamship Co. logo

2008-11-4 Round porcelain plate with Alaska Steamship Co. logo

2008-11-8 Brass binoculars from SS Aleutian

2008-11-9 Porcelain juicer cover from SS Aleutian

2008-11-16 Porcelain teacup with Alaska Steamship Co. logo

2008-11-17 Porcelain demitasse teacup with Alaska Steamship Co. logo

2008-11-18 Porcelain saucer with Alaska Steamship Co. logo

2008-11-20 Glass salad dressing carafe and stopper

2008-11-21 Copper bell, clapper, and hook from wheelhouse SS Aleutian

2008-11-23 Bronze port light (porthole) from the SS Aleutian

2008-31-2 Drinking glass with Alaska Pacific Steamship Co. logo

2009-19-3 Bakelite hard hat with heavy fabric liner

2011-3-1 Large brass and glass masthead light

2011-3-3 Small blue-green snuff bottle

2011-3-4 Brown glass mange medicine bottle

2011-3-6 Brass and glass porthole recovered from the Princess Sophia

2011-3-8 Small brass oil-burning table lamp with clear glass chimney

2011-3-10 Mechanical telegraph to communicate between captain and engine room on the Princess Kathleen

2011-5-4 Brass surveying transit with small crate

2011-24-1 Red wool Filson jacket worn by Shell Simmons, cofound of Alaska Airlines

2012-11-1 Acrylic painting of Norge airship in stormy sky over water by Dan DeRoux

2013-12-1 Round clock and winding key from the skipper's room on the SS Alaska

2013-13-3 Red Alaska Airlines carry-on bag

2013-35-1 Steering wheel from the SS Jefferson

2013-35-3 Pilot's peaked black cap with flag of Alaska Steamship Company

2015-4-1 Ceramic chamber pot with Canadian Pacific Railway logo

2015-6-1 Small glass jar with groves for screw top, swirls on sides, star on bottom

2015-6-2 Clear glass bottle with cork

2015-6-3 Tan-colored cloth work jacket

2015-6-6 Brass and copper block letter "A"

2015-6-7 Brass and copper block letter "L"

2015-6-8 Brass and copper block letter "L"

2015-6-9 Brass and copper block letter "S"

2015-6-11 Brass and copper block letter "N"

2015-6-12 Brass and copper block letter "D"

2015-6-13 Brass and copper fragment of letter from sign

2015-6-14 Brass and copper block letter "R"

2015-6-15 Stamped lead anti-friction bar

2015-6-16 Large wooden maul heading

2015-6-17 Wooden plane with coffin body style and compassed bed

2015-6-18 Wooden saw handle with two metal screws

2015-6-19 Wooden tool handle with rounded end and metal ring attached

2015-6-20 Leather sailmaker's palm

2015-6-21 Rusted stamped metal luggage tag with small leather strap attached

2015-6-23 Wooden brush with coiling around brush end

2015-6-24 Wooden tool handle

2015-6-25 Wooden paintbrush handle

2015-6-26 Black razor handle with gold-colored metal pins and no blade attached

2015-6-27 Wooden brush

2015-6-28 Wooden brush

2015-6-29 Rubber hot water bottle

2015-6-30 Leather gold poke with large gash on side and top sealed with wax

2015-6-32 Tuxedo jacket

2015-6-33 Yellow silk wall covering with ribbon-like pattern

2015-6-35 Black rubber galoshes or overshoes to fit a women's narrow shoe with a moderate (one-inch) heel

II-A-3318 Eskimo carved ivory model of Amundsen's airship Norge

III-O-47 Leather key tag attached by wire to bent copper key

III-O-57 China carafe with monogram CPN

III-O-58 End of heaving line tied in a monkey-fist knot

III-O-59 Leather and metal collar for large dog

III-O-66 Brass speaking trumpet

III-O-87 Metal steam gauge

III-O-254 Ring buoy from Princess Sophia

III-O-288 Radio receiver in black wooden case

III-O-384 Parts of dirigible Norge

III-O-384-A Section of framework of Amundsen's airship Norge

III-O-384-B Aluminum gasoline valve from Amundsen's airship Norge

III-O-384-C Links of aluminum chain from Amundsen's airship Norge

III-O-497-1 Fresnel lighthouse lens of concentric annular sections of glass prisms

III-O-497-2 Pieces of the Cape Spencer Lighthouse clockwork

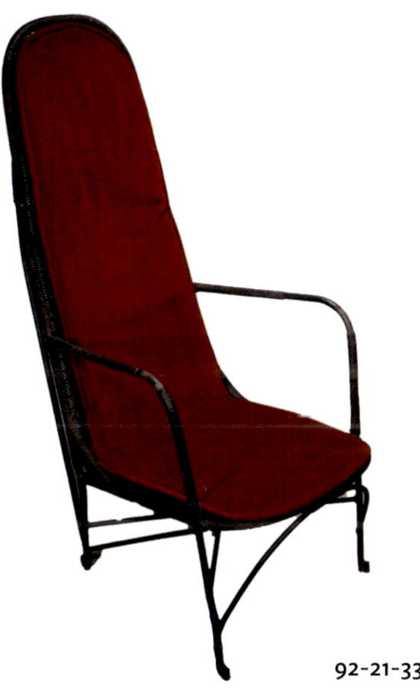

92-21-33

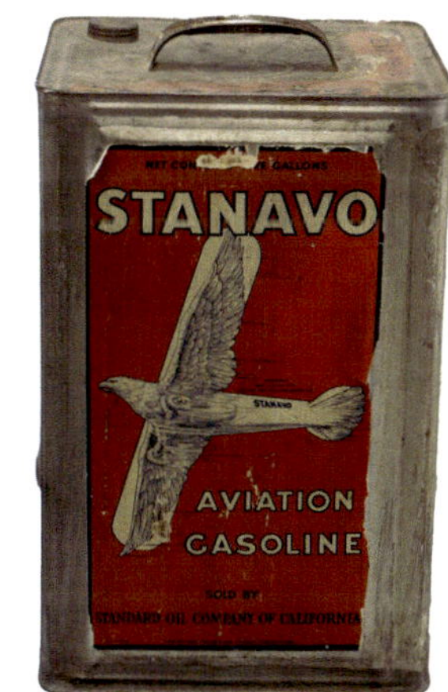

92-21-73

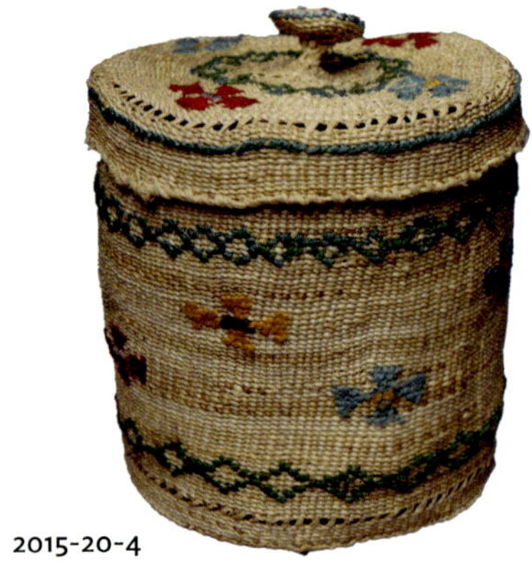
2015-20-4

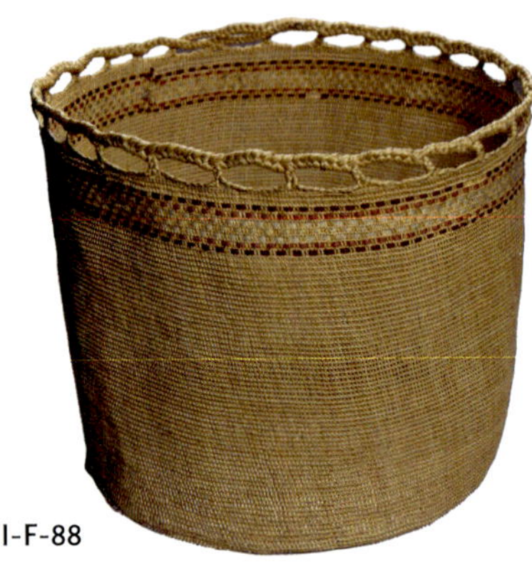
II-F-88

- III-O-513 Brown leather pouch and lock inscribed "First official flight, Alaska, via air mail, Juneau, Whitehorse, Fairbanks, May 18, 1938"
- III-O-525 Octagonal box with star design, made of driftwood from the wreckage of the Princess Sophia
- III-O-829 Distinguished flying cross medal with blue, white, and red grosgrain ribbon
- III-O-857 Ship officer's hat, white with black band and visor
- III-O-891 Dish for individual butter pat, of white china with "CPN co" insignia
- III-O-892 Three pieces of engraved silverplate tableware, two spoons and a fork
- III-O-892-1 Engraved silverplate soup spoon
- III-O-892-2 Engraved silverplate soup spoon
- III-O-892-3 Engraved silverplate dinner fork
- III-O-983 Painted wooden model ferry with full rigging by Gene Davis
- III-O-1034 Dietz kerosene lantern
- III-O-1034-A Dietz kerosene lantern

Unangax̂ (Aleut)

- 90-7-1 Aleut basket
- 90-7-2 Aleut basket
- 97-35-10 Aleut basketry-covered bottle
- 98-24-1 Lidded grass basket with colorful embroidered designs by Jennie Krukoff
- 2000-2-1 Twined grass basket with knobbed lid and multicolored false embroidery
- 2010-33-1 Round beaded grass basket woven in traditional Aleut style, with silk false embroidery by Arlene Skinner
- 2010-33-2 Freeform beaded grass basket woven in the traditional Aleut style by Arlene Skinner
- 2011-13-1 Aleut carved wood fishing club
- 2011-13-2 Wooden throwing board decorated with ivory
- 2012-12-1 Traditional Unangan bentwood visor with painted designs and ivory, whisker, feather, and bead adornments by Gertrude Svarny
- 2013-53-1 Aleut-style headdress made with red and black glass beads and bone hair pipes by Jolene Petticrew
- 2015-9-1 Tiny beaded basketry-covered bottle by Sharon Kay
- 2015-10-1 Parka made from tufted puffin skins and sealskin trim with decorative woven ribbon at cuffs and hem
- **2015-20-4** Aleut lidded grass basket with embroidery floss
- 2015-27-1 Wine bottle covered with twined raffia and twined cap with knob by Agnes Thompson
- II-F-11 Aleut piece of ivory with decorated area on one edge of engraved circle and dot
- II-F-16 Unangax double comb of carved antler
- II-F-17 Aleut oval stone lamp of black stone
- II-F-18 Aleut spear head of carved and notched bone
- II-F-29 Aleut small egg-shaped stone lamp
- II-F-57 Aleut carved ivory spoon
- II-F-71 Aleut wooden bowl repaired with baleen strips
- II-F-72 Aleut pair of model or child's mukluks of hair seal
- II-F-74 Aleut ivory carving of man with tusked face
- II-F-79 Aleut pump drill with wooden shaft and pump, iron point, and string and wire lashing
- II-F-81 Aleut finely woven lidded basket with multicolored embroidery
- II-F-84 Aleut twined basket of wild rye in open-work twining with geometrical design of multicolored wool yarn
- II-F-85 Aleut twined basket of wild rye in open divided-warp twining with overlay pattern in pink, blue, and green wool yarn
- **II-F-88** Aleut twined basket of wild rye in open divided-warp twining with multicolored wool yarn embroidery at top

II-F-94 Aleut twined basket of wild rye in divided-warp twined weave with overlaid pattern in blue, red, and black yarn

II-F-110 Aleut work basket

II-F-118 Aleut twined basket of wild rye with plain and divided-warp weaves and yarn decoration

II-F-120 Aleut partially finished basket of wild rye alternating open and plain twined weaving, with silk floss decoration

II-F-123 Aleut covered basket of open-work twining with embroidery floss decoration by Sophie D. Pletnikoff

II-F-125 Aleut basket with lid, finely woven grass with wool embroidery

II-F-127 Aleut twined basket of wild rye in divided-warp and open-twined weaving, with overlay decoration

II-F-134 Aleut twined basket and top, of plain and crossed-warp weaving with silk floss overlay decoration

II-F-136 Aleut twined covered basket of wild rye grass in plain and crossed-warp weaving, decorated with overlaid butterfly design

II-F-137 Aleut twined basket of wild rye in plain twining and crossed-warp weave, with silk thread decoration

II-F-139 Aleut basket with lid, with multicolored decoration

II-F-139-A Aleut small, very thin, woven grass basket with lid and embroidered details

II-F-139-B Aleut finely woven grass basket lid with swirl pattern embroidered on knobs

II-F-140 Aleut cigar case with inner sleeve, embroidered with some open weave

II-F-141 Aleut telescoping card case of plain twined weaving of wild rye with multicolored bands

II-F-142 Aleut telescoping card case of plain twined weaving of wild rye with multicolored bands

II-F-143 Aleut grass wallet imbricated with many-colored quill, closure of loop and china button

II-F-144 Aleut flat, oval-shaped woven grass basket with concentric rings decoration

II-F-147 Aleut grass basket woven around a bottle, with triangle and flower false embroidery

II-F-148 Aleut wallet of woven grass, lined with yellow-green silk and embroidered

II-F-150 Aleut glass bottle with flaring spout above constricted neck and wooden top, covered with areas of plain twined weaving with overlay design

II-F-151 Aleut basket of wild rye in alternating weaves, with flared scalloped rim and handle bound with twisted grass, roses pattern in silk floss overlay

II-F-152 Aleut rye-grass basketry-covered bottle and cap

II-F-154 Aleut circular lidded woven-grass basket with colored fibers woven in and multicolored geometric designs

II-F-155 Aleut woven basket with silk floss decoration, in course of construction on wooden form

II-F-168 Aleut model two-hatch baidarka with figures, of wood and gut

II-F-175 Aleut cylindrical shaped wooden basket-making form with square shaped handle off center on one end

II-F-177 Aleut eighteen ivory labrets ranging in size

II-F-177-B Aleut plug-shaped carved ivory labret

II-F-177-C Aleut carved ivory labret

II-F-177-E Aleut carved ivory labret

II-F-177-K Aleut carved ivory labret

II-F-177-R Aleut carved ivory labret

II-F-192 Aleut fish basket of finely woven grass with three bands of differently colored fiber

II-F-195-A Aleut small spear with ivory point, feathers, and crisscross lashing along entire shaft

II-F-270 Aleut three barbed bone harpoon heads

II-F-270-A Aleut barbed bone harpoon head

II-F-270-B Aleut barbed bone harpoon head

II-F-270-C Aleut barbed bone harpoon head

II-F-271 Aleut slate ulu blade with drilled hole

II-F-276 Aleut carved barbed and notched ivory fishhook

II-F-279 Aleut small lidded woven-grass basket with open-weave and thread decoration by Anfesia Shapsnikoff

II-F-280 Aleut lidded woven-grass basket with open-weave and thread decoration

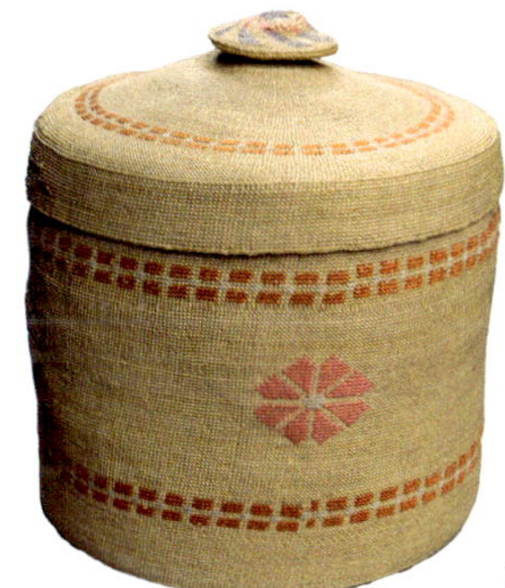

II-F-139

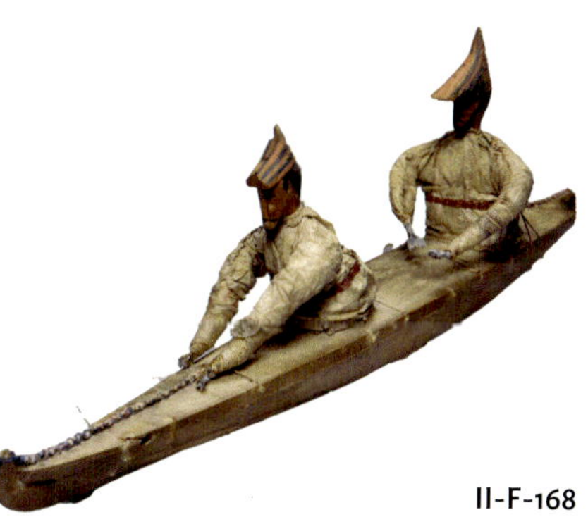

II-F-168

II-F-285	Aleut basket of twined beach grass in "May basket" shape with roses and "Greek key" embroidery
II-F-289	Aleut belt woven of finely twined beach grass, backed with navy blue silk and embroidered with roses, leaves, and zigzags
II-F-292	Aleut ivory labret with blue glass bead inset
II-F-293	Aleut stone labret
II-F-296	Aleut berry basket with top of scalloped open work with braid, with yarn embroidery
II-F-298	Aleut woven grass lidded basket and top with decoration of open weave and embroidery
II-F-299	Aleut woven grass lidded basket and top with embroidery decoration by Maggie Prokopiuff
II-F-301	Aleut Unalaska-style woven grass basket and lid, with multicolored diamond-shaped embroidery
II-F-302	Aleut small woven basket with lid, embroidered with kayak figures by Tatiana Zoachney
II-F-303	Aleut small woven beach-rye basket with lid, with purple floral embroidery by Eunice Neseth
II-F-305	Aleut glass inkwell and lid covered with woven grass in Attu-type pattern with tiny geometric designs
II-F-308	Aleut grass twined basket and lid with multicolored overlay fleur-de-lis design
II-F-311	Aleut whaling lance blade of slate (with point broken off) incised with Russian letters
II-F-330	Aleut basketry-covered bottle with long, narrow neck and bulbous lower section, with cork
II-F-333	Aleut woven grass "fish basket" with braided grass cord around top edge and handle across top
II-F-334	Aleut woven grass basket with lid and flower and leaf embroidery design by Mary Snigaroff
II-F-335	Aleut basketry-covered inkwell with stopper, decorated with multicolored false embroidery
II-F-339	Aleut woven grass basket with lid, decorated with open weave and embroidered with ovals
II-F-340	Aleut carved and incised ornament in shape of seal

World War II

93-10-1	Boxed deck of flashcards to study international signals
94-3-1	Model of USS *Alaska* by Keith Thomson
94-13-5	Army-issue "K-Bar" knife
95-36-1	Watercolor on paper titled What a Dump Warren Beach
96-23-4	Watercolor on paper titled Beautiful Storage Area by Warren Beach
96-23-5	Watercolor on paper titled Big Gun Ammo Storage, Sitka by Warren Beach
96-43-1	Air Force sextant housed in wooden case
96-45-1	Glass Coca-Cola bottle with metal cap and contents intact
96-59-1	Painted wooden barracks box with metal hardware
98-31-1	Japanese sake bottle
98-31-2	Japanese geta sandals
98-31-3	Japanese wooden paddle-shaped rice spoon
98-44-4	Olive green military hat with red accents
2000-4-26	Khaki waterproof fabric rain parka or anorak
2000-22-2	White sugar ration in cellophane wrapper
2000-28-2	Color postcard showing soldier in parka on beach in Hawai'i
2002-1-1	U.S. Navy blue wool face mask for cold weather protection
2002-2-1	WWII model 1917 A1 metal helmet with leather liner
2003-4-1	Wood and rawhide snowshoes with leather straps and metal buckles
2003-13-17	U.S. Army Ski Team goggles with case
2003-13-18	Red circular embroidered patch with black hourglass design
2003-13-24	Round blue embroidered patch with white polar bear head and gold star
2003-13-28	Round blue embroidered patch with red-centered white star below two gold wings
2003-24-1	Japanese officer's sword and scabbard c. 1934
2003-24-2	Japanese Nambu Model 14 pistol with custom jade grips
2003-24-3	Japanese Imperial Army helmet
2003-33-1	Blue twill cloth patch with embroidered gold stars of Alaska's flag and letters "ATG" in white
2004-15-1	Canteen cover made of fur-lined khaki canvas
2004-15-2	WWII Japanese cold-weather coat
2007-23-1	Japanese khaki canvas overcoat
2007-23-2	Japanese khaki wool hat with fur trim and yellow felt star
2004-69-1	U.S. Army parka shell
2004-70-1	WWII U.S. Coast Guard uniform jumper with a sail collar
2004-70-2	WWII U.S. Coast Guard uniform drop-front bell-bottom trousers
2004-70-6	U.S. Coast Guard white sailor's cap
2006-30-1	WWII brass identification plate with Japanese writing

2008-29-1	Fold-over leather bag marked "Army Air Force," decorated with the hand-painted logos of the Alaska Defense Command and Aleutian Islands
2008-36-2	Pair of wooden Japanese Army skis from WWII
2008-41-1	Olive green rain hat
2009-4-1	Blank paper identification tag worn by prisoners of war
2009-4-6	Two metal dog tags attached to a metal chain
2009-4-16	U.S. Army dull gold medallion attached to ribbon with red, white, blue, navy blue, and black vertical stripes
2009-4-17	U.S. Army round medallion with helmeted woman with shield and raised sword surrounded by oak log and leaves, with yellow ribbon with red, white, and blue stripes
2009-4-18	U.S. Army WWII victory medal showing woman with broken sword, with red ribbon with rainbow stripes
2009-4-19	U.S. Army medal for Asiatic Pacific campaign, showing servicemen on a shore, with yellow ribbon with red, white, and blue stripes
2009-4-20	U.S. Army good conduct medal showing an eagle on a book, with red ribbon with white stripes
2009-4-25	Blue shield-shaped 11th Air Force, U.S. Army embroidered patch with diagonal gold wing and red-centered star
2009-4-30	WWII fuzzy tan fabric patch with a seal balancing the D of "ADC" on its nose
2009-4-31	U.S. Army 44th Infantry Division patch showing back-to-back blue 4s on a yellow background
2009-4-34	U.S. Army Kiska Task Force round embroidered patch with blue background and silver border and black-handled knife at center
2009-19-1	Two-piece aluminum mess kit used by U.S. Army in Alaska during WWII
2009-19-9	Shield-shaped patch with royal blue background, red and white star with gold wings, and seven smaller gold stars
2009-19-10	Blue and white embroidered patch of the U.S. 10th Mountain Division, showing two crossed red swords
2009-19-11	Embroidered patch of WWII Alaska Support Signal Command, showing zig-zag, compass rose, and signal flag
2009-19-22	Red, white, and blue embroidered patch with green border, for Northwest Service Command
2010-22-3	Pair of metal crampons with canvas strips
2010-22-4	Army green canvas bag with a tattered cardboard liner
2010-22-5	Hand-painted plywood sign of 344th Fighter Squadron logo of a bird with cigar, bowler hat and shoes, and slingshot behind its back
2010-22-6	Padded leather hat to protect the head when boxing
2010-22-43	Full-length army-green wool coat with brass buttons with eagles
2010-22-49	Large army-green duffel bag
2010-29-1	Bayonet with a wooden handle that attaches to a rifle
2012-2-13	Green parka with brown fur ruff and stenciled black letters on back
2012-21-1	Brown leather Alaska Air Corps cap with shearling and fabric lining
2013-61-1	WWII pair of heavy leather pants lined with shearling
2015-22-1	Jacket of U.S. Navy Engineers uniform, with ribbon bars
2016-10-1	U.S. Army air knee-high suede boots fully lined with sheepskin
III-O-100	Knife evidently forged from a piece of shrapnel with shrapnel unchanged at handle part of knife
III-O-155	WWII Japanese aluminum mess kit with metal handle
III-O-161	White porcelain bowl with blue five-pointed star inside
III-O-163	WWII Japanese megaphone
III-O-164	WWII Japanese brass bugle
III-O-165	WWII Japanese gas mask with cloth carrying bag
III-O-167	WWII Japanese metal canteen with cork held by leather strap, with carrying harness
III-O-174	WWII Japanese khaki wool military cap
III-O-175	WWII Japanese khaki-colored wool uniform jacket, lined with canvas
III-O-178	WWII Japanese entrenching shovel with knobbed wooden handle
III-O-182	WWII Japanese mortar shell, painted black with yellow and red stripes, inscribed copper band
III-O-183	WWII Japanese field sighting level for mortar, with leather case
III-O-189	WWII Japanese package of medical supplies wrapped in printed paper
III-O-189-A	WWII Japanese tan paper wrapping, white with blue and red
III-O-189-B	WWII Japanese tan paper wrapping, white with blue and red
III-O-191	WWII Japanese 37 mm anti-tank gun on wheels
III-O-206	Khaki-colored can of corned beef hash
III-O-207	Khaki-colored can of meat and rice
III-O-240	WWII Japanese rifle, Model 99 (Long), 7.7 mm rifle, bolt action, with carrying strap
III-O-243-A	WWII U.S. Army "pineapple" hand grenade
III-O-364	WWII Japanese cast-iron charcoal heating stove, painted light green
III-O-1042	Doormat from the U.S.S Juneau
V-A-507	Drawing of group of Russian men in uniform by Henry Varnum Poor
V-A-962	Ink wash and crayon drawing on Strathmore paper, depicting head and shoulder view of two soldiers in khaki green military uniforms by Henry Varnum Poor

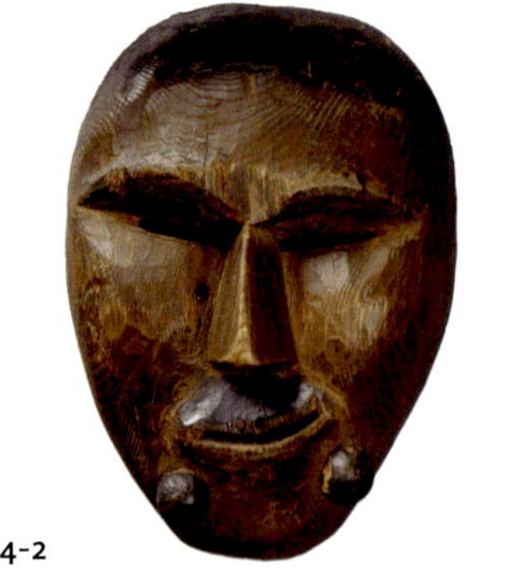

94-34-2

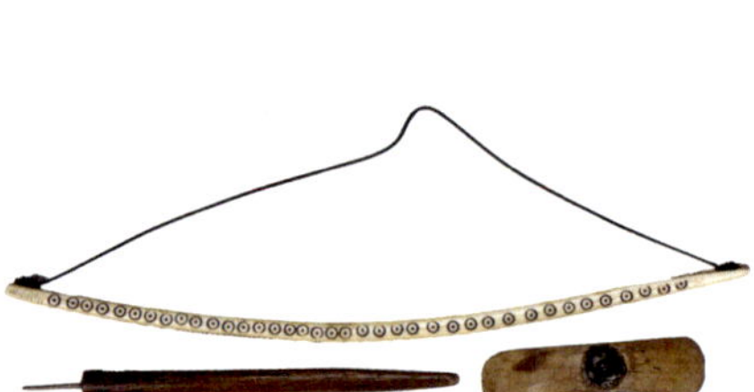

98-7-241

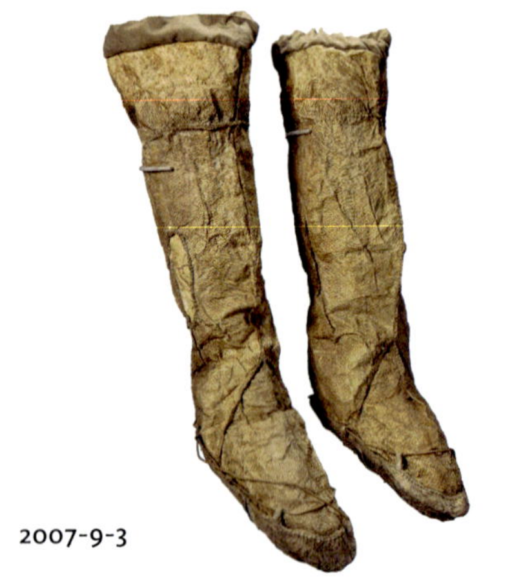

2007-9-3

Yup'ik / Saint Lawrence Island Yupik / Iñupiat

92-2-44 Eskimo decorated ivory fastener

94-34-2 Carved and painted wooden mask of human face

96-16-3 Eskimo whale amulet of carved jet

96-51-11 Carved and stained Eskimo wooden dish

98-7-240 Ulu with engraved ivory handle and metal blade

98-7-241 Eskimo bow drill

98-45-3 Eskimo ulu with metal blade and ivory handle

2000-35-1 Wooden seal net float with ivory pendants

2003-36-1 Shallow oval miniature wooden bowl with handle and painted fish

2003-36-2 Painted miniature wooden ladle with painted fish

2005-19-1 Yup'ik open-weave basket with braided rim and drawstring by Nan Kiokun

2007-9-3 Salmon-skin mukluks

2008-30-2 (see p. 145) Ink drawing on bleached reindeer hide showing dancers, drummers, and observers by Milo Minock

2014-3-1 Loon headdress shaped like a head band, with beak at front

2015-5-1 Iñupiat model umiak from wood and animal skin and sinew

2015-5-2 Iñupiat miniature boat bailer

2015-5-3 Iñupiat miniature seal float

2015-5-4 Iñupiat miniature seal float

2015-5-5 Iñupiat miniature seal float and harpoon

2015-5-6 Iñupiat miniature harpoon

2015-5-7 Iñupiat miniature harpoon

2015-5-8 Iñupiat miniature boarding knife

2015-5-9 Iñupiat miniature whaling spade

2015-5-10 Iñupiat miniature blubber fork

2015-5-11 Iñupiat miniature harpoon point

2015-5-12 Iñupiat miniature likely boat bailer

2015-5-13 Iñupiat miniature likely boat bailer

II-A-120 Eskimo saucer-shaped pottery oil lamp

II-A-153 Eskimo carved and painted square wooden paint box with leather pull attached to lid

II-A-206 Eskimo tom cod rod with line and sinker

II-A-244 Eskimo ivory fishhook lashed with thong

II-A-277 Two Eskimo stone weights for fish nets, lashed with baleen

II-A-277-A One of two Eskimo stone weights for fish nets, lashed with baleen

II-A-279 Eskimo baleen dip net with iron weight beneath

II-A-291 Eskimo carved bone fin-toggle in the shape of a whale head, decorated with beads

II-A-293 Eskimo carved wooden effigy in the shape of a whale

II-A-296 Eskimo carved graphite whale

II-A-297 Eskimo carved wooden whale

II-A-299 (see p. 145) Eskimo carved wooden animal head, decorated with beads

II-A-300 Eskimo carved wooden seal, decorated with quills and beads

II-A-301 Eskimo carved wooden projectile point case in the shape of a whale, decorated with beads

II-A-312 (see p. 145) Eskimo painted wooden hunting visor

II-A-314 Eskimo painted wooden hunting visor

II-A-316 Eskimo painted wooden snow goggles with visor

II-A-318 Eskimo painted wooden snow goggles with visor, for hunting

II-A-320 Eskimo painted wooden snow goggles with visor

II-A-322 Eskimo wooden snow goggles

II-A-323 (see p. 145) Eskimo wooden trough-shaped snow goggles

II-A-324 Eskimo wooden snow goggles

II-A-326 Eskimo wooden spectacle-type snow goggles

II-A-328 Eskimo bone spectacle-type snow goggles

II-A-336 Eskimo pair of ivory ice creepers with iron points and leather thongs

II-A-351 (see p. 146) Eskimo wooden-handled ice scratcher for seal hunting, with three claws lashed to one end with commercial string

II-A-358 Eskimo set of wooden wound plugs and seal drag

II-A-362 Eskimo set of ivory seal indicators

II-A-372-B Eskimo wood harpoon drag painted with whales, walrus, and human figure

II-A-373 Eskimo wooden seat with whale carving and ivory decorations

II-A-377 (see p. 146) Eskimo carved wooden umiak seat with whale design

II-A-429 Eskimo mesh gauge of ivory with wooden handle

II-A-432 Eskimo bone mesh gauge

II-A-441 Eskimo baleen mesh gauge

II-A-448 Eskimo ivory mesh gauge with wooden piece

II-A-451 Eskimo wooden net shuttle

II-A-469 Eskimo wooden net shuttle

II-A-493 Eskimo wooden reel or shuttle with vegetable fiber string

II-A-509 Eskimo skin scraper with green-gray stone blade lashed to handle

II-A-526 Eskimo skin scraper with brown slate-like blade lashed on with vegetable fiber binding

II-A-569 Eskimo ulu of iron and ivory

II-A-581 Eskimo ulu of iron and bone

II-A-585 Eskimo ulu of slate and bone

II-A-798 Eskimo adze made of jade, antler, and leather

II-A-818 Eskimo adze made of stone, ivory, and leather

II-A-848 Eskimo adze made of jade, antler, and sinew

II-A-923 Eskimo wrist guard made of incised and carved mammoth ivory

II-A-924 Eskimo wrist guard made of incised and carved mammoth ivory, with slits

II-A-926 Eskimo ivory thumb guard with inlaid bead

II-A-930 Eskimo wrist guard made of incised and carved mammoth ivory, with slits

II-A-958 Eskimo iron saw with ivory handle

II-A-995 Eskimo mitlik of iron and antler

II-A-1056 Eskimo needle case made from carved and incised wing bone

II-A-1067 Eskimo needle case made from carved and incised antler

II-A-1095 Eskimo needle case made from carved and incised ivory, with dangling pieces shaped like heart and pair of horns

II-A-1102 Eskimo needle case made from ivory carved in human shape, with attached creaser and burnisher

II-A-1109 Eskimo thimble or thumb guard made from oogruk (bearded seal), bias tape, and porcupine quill

II-A-1117 Eskimo ivory comb with wooden handle

II-A-1166 Eskimo ivory housewife fastener

II-A-1167 Eskimo ivory housewife fastener

II-A-1168 Eskimo ivory housewife fastener

II-A-1170 Eskimo ivory housewife fastener

II-A-1198 Eskimo iron bodkin with carved ivory handle

II-A-1224 Eskimo carved ivory boot creaser

II-A-1233 Eskimo carved and incised ivory bodkin

II-A-1400 Eskimo dance fan of sealskin, feathers, and beads

II-A-1409 Eskimo earrings of ivory, bone, beads, and copper

II-A-1410 Eskimo earrings of ivory, hide, brass, and beads

II-A-1414 Aleut pendant beaded earrings with string of beads connected between

II-A-1451 Yup'ik kidney-shaped mask of carved and painted wood, with asymmetrical features

II-A-1452 Yup'ik oval-shaped mask of carved wood with one side flattened and small seal figures attached

II-A-1454 Yup'ik carved and painted wooden mask shaped like paddle with handle upwards and a seal face

II-A-1457 Mask of body of loon with fish in mouth by Edward Kiokun

II-A-1485 Eskimo carved and painted wooden mask of red, white, and black, with fangs

II-A-1504 Eskimo carved and painted wooden mask of human-like face

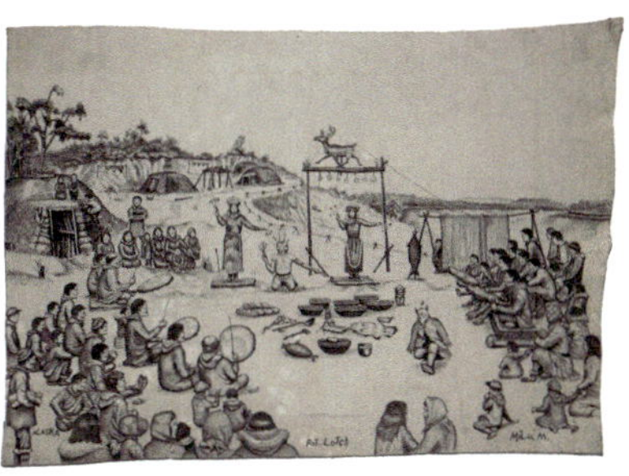

2008-30-2

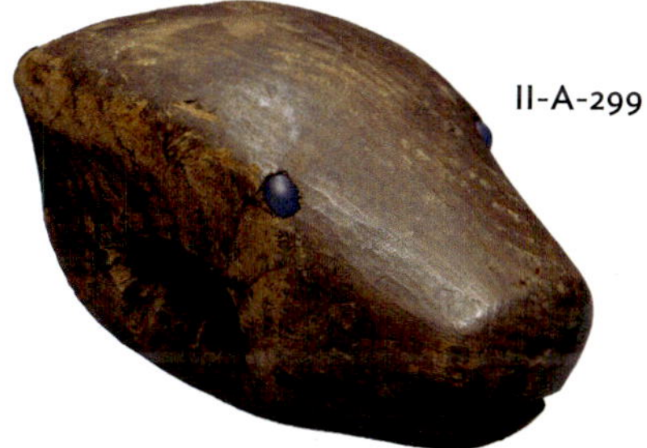

II-A-299

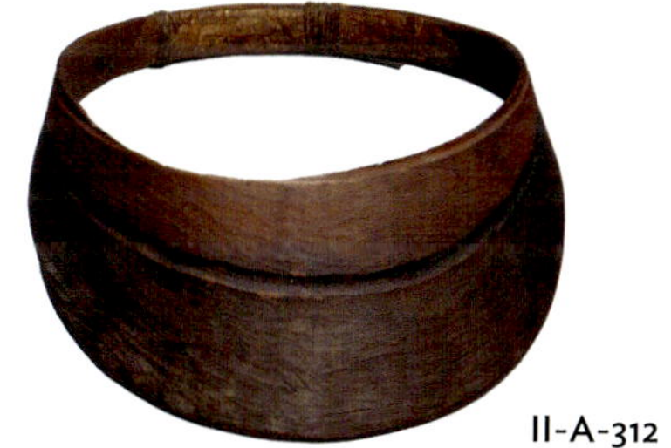

II-A-312

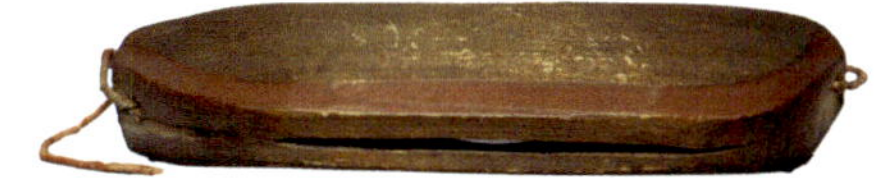

II-A-323

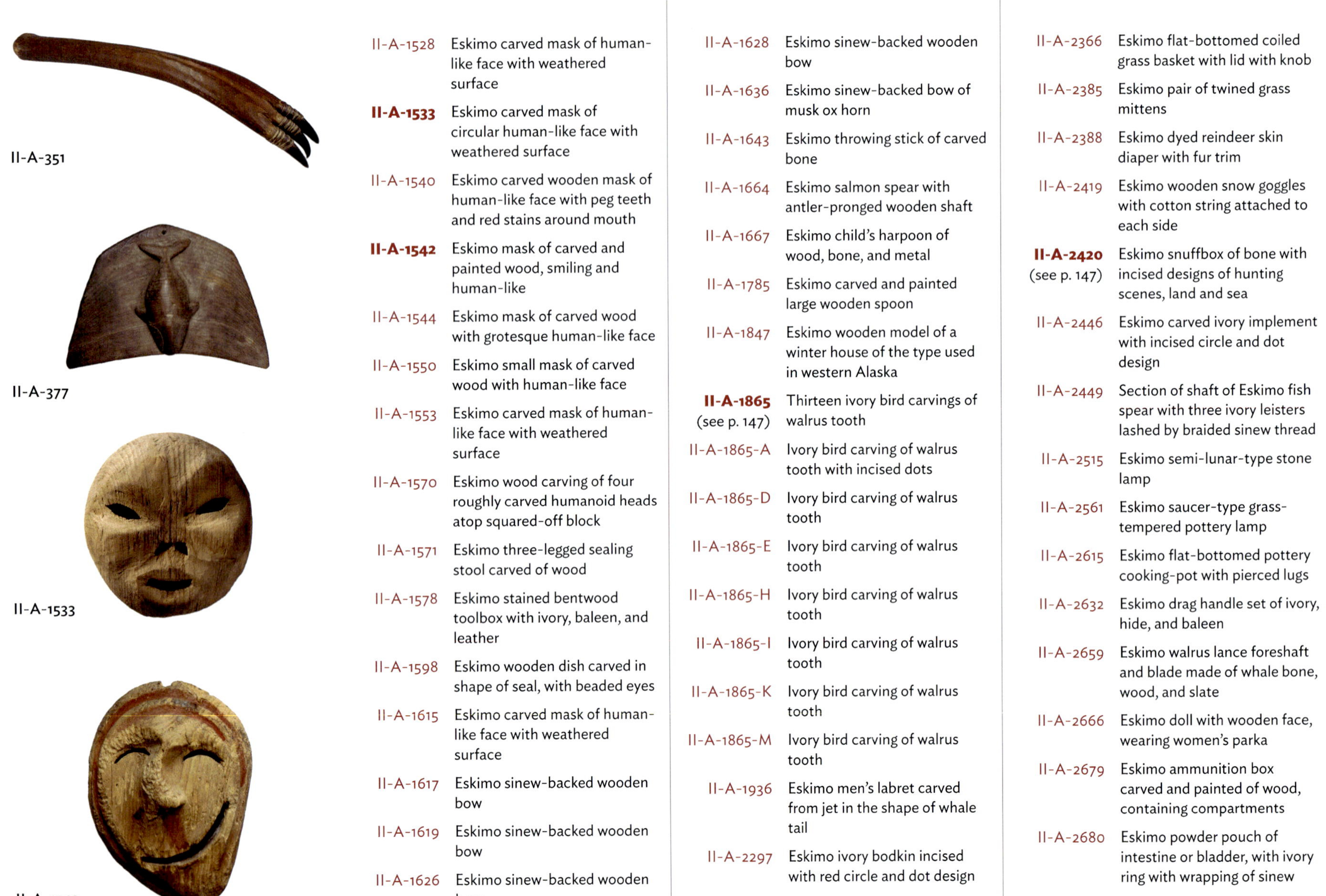

II-A-351

II-A-377

II-A-1533

II-A-1542

II-A-1528 Eskimo carved mask of human-like face with weathered surface

II-A-1533 Eskimo carved mask of circular human-like face with weathered surface

II-A-1540 Eskimo carved wooden mask of human-like face with peg teeth and red stains around mouth

II-A-1542 Eskimo mask of carved and painted wood, smiling and human-like

II-A-1544 Eskimo mask of carved wood with grotesque human-like face

II-A-1550 Eskimo small mask of carved wood with human-like face

II-A-1553 Eskimo carved mask of human-like face with weathered surface

II-A-1570 Eskimo wood carving of four roughly carved humanoid heads atop squared-off block

II-A-1571 Eskimo three-legged sealing stool carved of wood

II-A-1578 Eskimo stained bentwood toolbox with ivory, baleen, and leather

II-A-1598 Eskimo wooden dish carved in shape of seal, with beaded eyes

II-A-1615 Eskimo carved mask of human-like face with weathered surface

II-A-1617 Eskimo sinew-backed wooden bow

II-A-1619 Eskimo sinew-backed wooden bow

II-A-1626 Eskimo sinew-backed wooden bow

II-A-1628 Eskimo sinew-backed wooden bow

II-A-1636 Eskimo sinew-backed bow of musk ox horn

II-A-1643 Eskimo throwing stick of carved bone

II-A-1664 Eskimo salmon spear with antler-pronged wooden shaft

II-A-1667 Eskimo child's harpoon of wood, bone, and metal

II-A-1785 Eskimo carved and painted large wooden spoon

II-A-1847 Eskimo wooden model of a winter house of the type used in western Alaska

II-A-1865 (see p. 147) Thirteen ivory bird carvings of walrus tooth

II-A-1865-A Ivory bird carving of walrus tooth with incised dots

II-A-1865-D Ivory bird carving of walrus tooth

II-A-1865-E Ivory bird carving of walrus tooth

II-A-1865-H Ivory bird carving of walrus tooth

II-A-1865-I Ivory bird carving of walrus tooth

II-A-1865-K Ivory bird carving of walrus tooth

II-A-1865-M Ivory bird carving of walrus tooth

II-A-1936 Eskimo men's labret carved from jet in the shape of whale tail

II-A-2297 Eskimo ivory bodkin incised with red circle and dot design

II-A-2366 Eskimo flat-bottomed coiled grass basket with lid with knob

II-A-2385 Eskimo pair of twined grass mittens

II-A-2388 Eskimo dyed reindeer skin diaper with fur trim

II-A-2419 Eskimo wooden snow goggles with cotton string attached to each side

II-A-2420 (see p. 147) Eskimo snuffbox of bone with incised designs of hunting scenes, land and sea

II-A-2446 Eskimo carved ivory implement with incised circle and dot design

II-A-2449 Section of shaft of Eskimo fish spear with three ivory leisters lashed by braided sinew thread

II-A-2515 Eskimo semi-lunar-type stone lamp

II-A-2561 Eskimo saucer-type grass-tempered pottery lamp

II-A-2615 Eskimo flat-bottomed pottery cooking-pot with pierced lugs

II-A-2632 Eskimo drag handle set of ivory, hide, and baleen

II-A-2659 Eskimo walrus lance foreshaft and blade made of whale bone, wood, and slate

II-A-2666 Eskimo doll with wooden face, wearing women's parka

II-A-2679 Eskimo ammunition box carved and painted of wood, containing compartments

II-A-2680 Eskimo powder pouch of intestine or bladder, with ivory ring with wrapping of sinew

II-A-2682 Eskimo ammunition box carved from one piece of wood curved to shape of powder horn, containing compartments

II-A-2685 Eskimo set of ivory bird bolas, also incorporating feathers, sinew, and quills

II-A-2693 Eskimo basketry model fish trap with separate gate

II-A-2695 Eskimo wooden bullet mold hinged with nailed-on piece of leather

II-A-2702 Eskimo carved wooden model umiak with holes, pegged with figures

II-A-2703 Eskimo carved wooden model kayak with holes, pegged with figures

II-A-2794 Eskimo human-like face carved of burl wood with inset ivory eyes

II-A-2858 Eskimo model Kazhgie with ivory dancing figures in wooden box

II-A-3024 Eskimo headband of white sealskin lined with cotton, decorated with polka-dot cotton cloth, yarn stitching, reindeer fur, and muskrat

II-A-3027 Eskimo football of sealskin, walrus gullet, and seal bristles

II-A-3028 Eskimo sealskin cap with visor and lined with seal fur, decorated with contrasting geometric parquetry of eider duck

II-A-3049 One pair Eskimo child's knee boots with oogruk (bearded seal) soles and seal fur uppers, with red and white accents

II-A-3056 One pair Eskimo child's mukluks of dried salmon skin, decorated with various colors of cloth and yarn

II-A-3062 Pair of Eskimo dance mitts of sealskin with all fur removed, covered with sewn-on puffin beaks

II-A-3070 Eskimo ceremonial object made of fox pup skin turned inside out and painted red-brown, with carved and painted wooden human face

II-A-3078 Eskimo wooden doll with muskrat-fur parka

II-A-3294 Three Eskimo ivory carvings of whales

II-A-3294-A Eskimo ivory carving of whale with shovel-shaped tail

II-A-3294-B Eskimo ivory carving of whale with dark brown color and "right whale"–style mouth

II-A-3434 Eskimo jade labret

II-A-3440 Eskimo ivory arrow shaft straightener carved in shape of caribou fawn with folded legs

II-A-3470 Eskimo ridged, wooden masher

II-A-3473 Eskimo wooden-handled boot hook with ivory tine

II-A-3645 Eskimo adze with wooden handle, walrus tusk blade, and hide lashings

II-A-3647 Eskimo child's parka of swan's-down with brown fur trim

II-A-3648 Eskimo seal float made from whole sealskin, with carved ivory and wood float plugs

II-A-3649 Eskimo bird dart with wooden shaft and ivory points

II-A-3658 Eskimo ice scoop of wood, caribou horn, and baleen mesh

II-A-3661 Eskimo snow shovel of wood and bone

II-A-3667 Eskimo spear with wooden handle and glass point

II-A-3681 Eskimo painted and decorated wooden box drum

II-A-3682 Eskimo drum of walrus bladder on wooden frame

II-A-3707 Eskimo bird spear with ivory prongs and sinew and cotton cord wrappings

II-A-3726-1 Eskimo slate blade

II-A-3727 Pair of Eskimo wood and rawhide snowshoes

II-A-3745 Eskimo carved wooden blubber pounder in shape of swimming sea bird

II-A-3747 Eskimo triangular unpainted box lid with inset beads

II-A-3750 One Eskimo seal-shaped quid or snuffbox with brass and copper strips riveted on and inlaid bead eyes (lid missing)

II-A-3860 Two Eskimo whale toggle harpoon heads of bone with slate blades

II-A-3860-1 Eskimo whalt toggle harpoon head of bone with slate blade

II-A-3954 Two Eskimo fish spear heads with ivory tridents mounted in wood

II-A-3954-1 Eskimo fish spear head with serrated ivory tridents lashed to wood with baleen and string

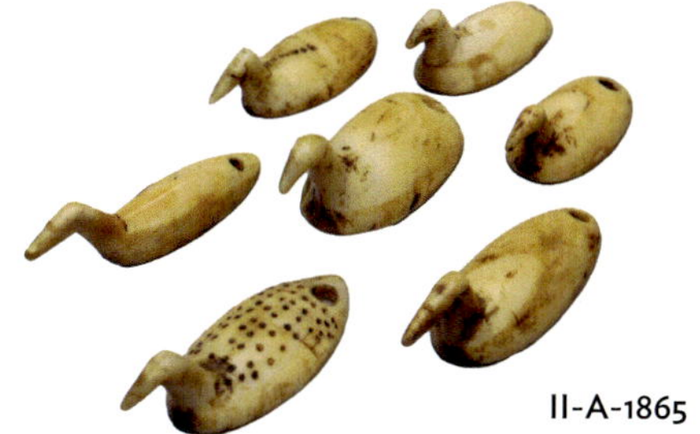

II-A-1865

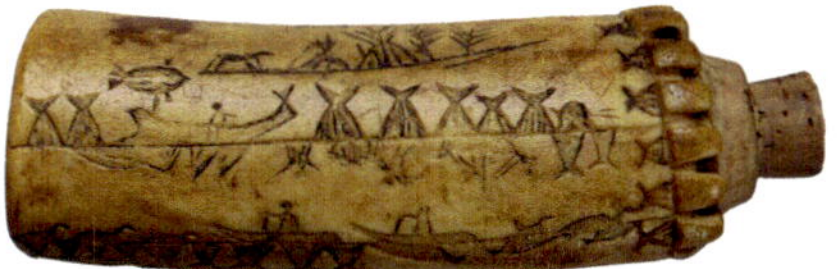

II-A-2420

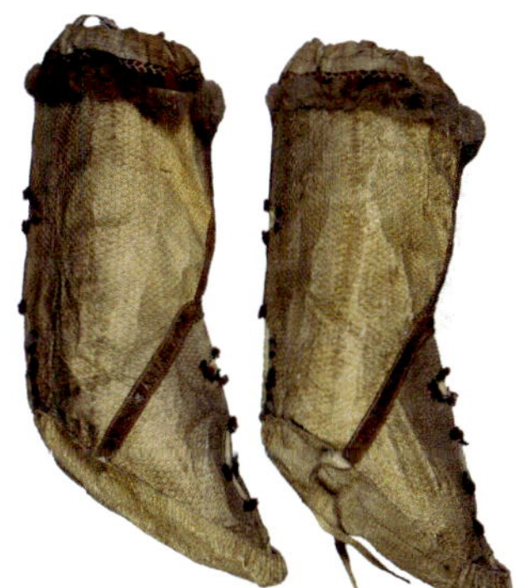

II-A-3056

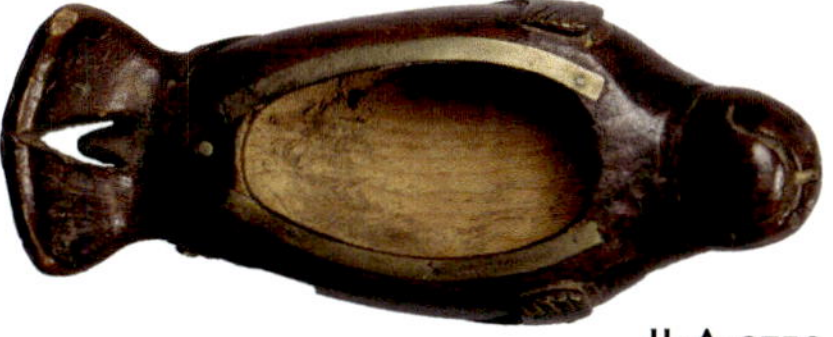

II-A-3750

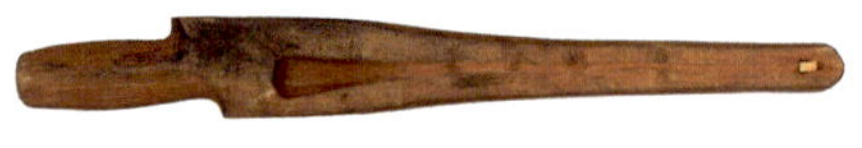
II-A-4168

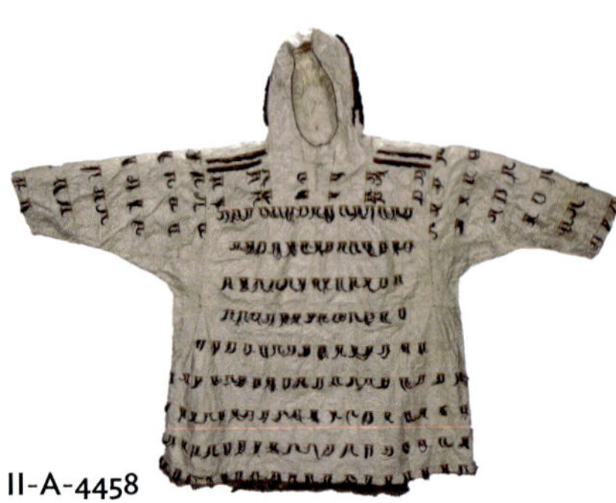
II-A-4458

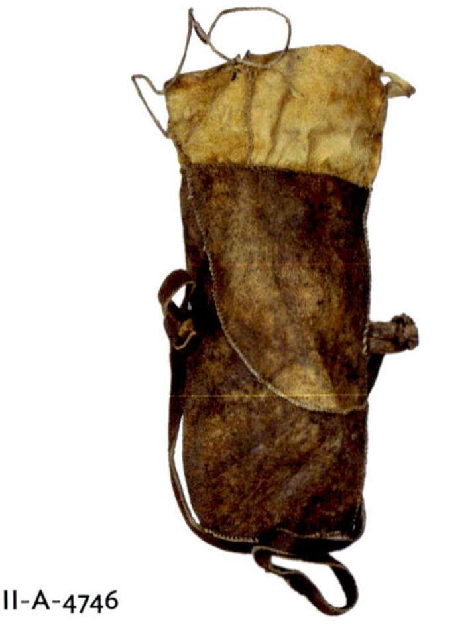
II-A-4746

II-A-3954-2	Eskimo fish spear head with serrated ivory tridents lashed to wood with baleen and string
II-A-4096	Eskimo seal fur and skin bag with envelope-type flap with carved ivory buttonhole closure and red embroidery
II-A-4155	Eskimo toy food tray carved of ivory
II-A-4157-6	Eskimo wooden throwing board with bone or ivory pegs for finger grips, carved-out thumb and finger grooves, and ivory stops
II-A-4160	Eskimo harpoon dart with throwing stick
II-A-4160-A	Dart shaft of wood with flared feathers and ivory socket and head
II-A-4160-B	Throwing board with wood peg finger brace (one missing), carved-out thumb groove, and ivory stops
II-A-4167	Eskimo staff or stout pole for use with snowshoes, with iron spike and ring of antler lashed with rawhide
II-A-4168	Eskimo wooden throwing board with red stain and ivory stop
II-A-4169	Eskimo wooden throwing board with finger hole
II-A-4171	Eskimo wooden throwing board with finger hole and ivory peg at grip, decorated with glass beads and metal button
II-A-4181	Eskimo walrus harpoon with ivory probe and foreshaft, oosik socket piece, and seal head decoration
II-A-4207	Eskimo meat sled with wooden sides and deck with ivory runners
II-A-4208	Eskimo hinged wooden box in form of walrus head, decorated with flat carved ivory bear head and two bird heads, with seal teeth used for tusks, and tacks for eyes
II-A-4225	Pair of Eskimo identical dance fans or finger wands made from circular basketry, fur, and feathers
II-A-4318	Eskimo woman's squirrel parka with hood, elaborately trimmed with tassels of fur strips and red yarn
II-A-4413	Eskimo ivory labret with large blue bead in center
II-A-4458	Siberian Yupik gut parka (kamlaika)
II-A-4483	Eskimo bone net gauge
II-A-4542	Eskimo throwing board
II-A-4560	Eskimo carved wooden throwing board
II-A-4561	Eskimo carved wooden throwing board
II-A-4562	Eskimo carved wooden throwing board
II-A-4564	Eskimo carved wooden throwing board
II-A-4582	Eskimo arrow with wood shaft capped with ivory and bone detachable point secured with line, with arrows
II-A-4591	Eskimo carved wooden throwing board with ownership mark
II-A-4595	Eskimo carved bone net hook
II-A-4634	Miniature wooden raven mask painted black by Tony Pushruk
II-A-4636	Eskimo scraper and handle made of flint
II-A-4655	Eskimo slate ulu with elaborately carved fossil ivory handle
II-A-4692	Eskimo mattock with wooden handle and whalebone blade held together by leather thong
II-A-4723	Eskimo of carved and incised ivory
II-A-4745	Eskimo dance headdress of machine-sewn cotton and canvas with snowy owl feathers, sealskin, and baleen by Otto Okpealuk
II-A-4746	Eskimo child's berry picking bucket made of seal skin, sewn with sinew and reinforced with grass, with strap handle made of commercial leather by Wilsa Allockeok
II-A-4765	Eskimo ceremonial object used in whaling, consisting of whale charms made from leather, with fur tufts
II-A-4808 (see p. 149)	Siberian Yupik bird skin parka by Mrs. Apata
II-A-4816	Eskimo man's reindeer-skin parka with white trim
II-A-4836	Pair of child's mukluks of sealskin and fur trim with commercially tanned leather soles of black and green felt top with twisted pink and brown yarn drawstring by Mary Snyder

II-A-4840 Carved ivory story or snow knife by Elsie Billie

II-A-4845 Eskimo ceremonial dance mask or headdress of whitewashed carved wood and feathers, with fish and harpooned human-faced seal or beluga whale figure

II-A-4935 Eskimo umiak with driftwood frame lashed with rawhide and wire

II-A-4948 Eskimo fur stowing bag for furs, clothing, etc., made of sealskin and ornamented with beads, fur, and fringe

II-A-4950 Iñupiat waterproof suit made of single piece of sealskin

II-A-4985 Eskimo fossilized ivory carving of miniature kayak with human

II-A-5011 Eskimo carved ivory bodkin with ivory chain (one link) and a wolf's head design

II-A-5013 Eskimo carved wooden pear-shaped snow goggles with triangular blue glass eyepieces and cotton string

II-A-5018 Eskimo dark-brown leather belt with two rows of reindeer teeth, still set in the gums, and beads

II-A-5149 Eskimo wooden sled model with human figure

II-A-5150-B Eskimo carved wooden snow goggles

II-A-5153 Eskimo carved and incised ivory seal-shaped "toggle" attached to rawhide line

II-A-5237 Eskimo wooden carving of human head and torso with removable snow goggles attached by sinew

II-A-5285-A Eskimo wooden, pegged, and stained throwing board

II-A-5285-E Eskimo fish spear of barbed ivory with string

II-A-5286 Carved, darkly stained wooden seal mask by Peter J. Seeganna

II-A-5299 Eskimo small mallet or hammer made of dark brown bone and baleen

II-A-5302 Eskimo small adze with wooden handle and stone blade, lashed with sinew

II-A-5350 Bering Sea Eskimo model kashim (aka qasgi or men's house) of ivory frame and skin covering, containing several figures engaged in music and dance

II-A-5398 Carved and painted wooden mask of seagull body with fish in mouth, decorated with human faces by Sam Hunter

II-A-5406 Carved and painted wooden mask in form of seal with fish in mouth, with human face on back and carved kayak attached near tail by Andy Gump

II-A-5410 Carved and painted wooden mask of wolf head with animal in mouth by Sam Hunter

II-A-5413 Carved and crayoned wooden mask of blue whale body, with human face on back and smaller whale in mouth

II-A-5417 Pair of man's finger rings, or dance fans, made of bentwood circles bound with split root, decorated with feathers

II-A-5604 Carved wooden mask with open round holes for mouth and eyes containing dangling ivory and baleen ornaments by Sylvester Ayek

II-A-5605 (see p. 150) Carved wooden mask with ivory labret by Earl Mayac

II-A-5673 Tom cod fishing outfit with wood, ivory, and baleen rod and various implements by Jacob Ahkinga

II-A-5774 Small ball of bleached seal skin and oogruk (bearded seal) with diamond appliqué trim and stuffed with caribou hair by Clara Tiulana

II-A-5782 Carved and painted wolf mask with ivory teeth by Frank Ellanna

II-A-5981 Eskimo carved ivory labret

II-A-6327 Miniature King Island mask of carved and stained wood by Mary Pushruk

II-A-6510 Eskimo carved ivory housewife fastener

II-A-6512 Eskimo carved ivory housewife fastener

II-A-6513 Eskimo carved ivory housewife fastener

II-A-6516 Eskimo carved ivory housewife fastener

II-A-6517 Eskimo carved ivory housewife fastener

II-A-6523 Eskimo carved ivory housewife fastener

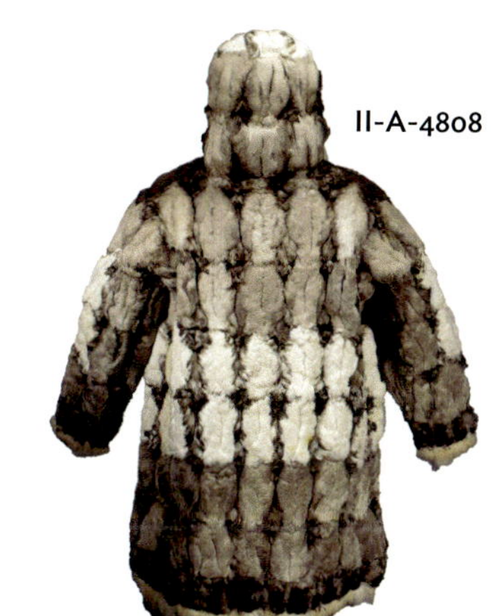
II-A-4808

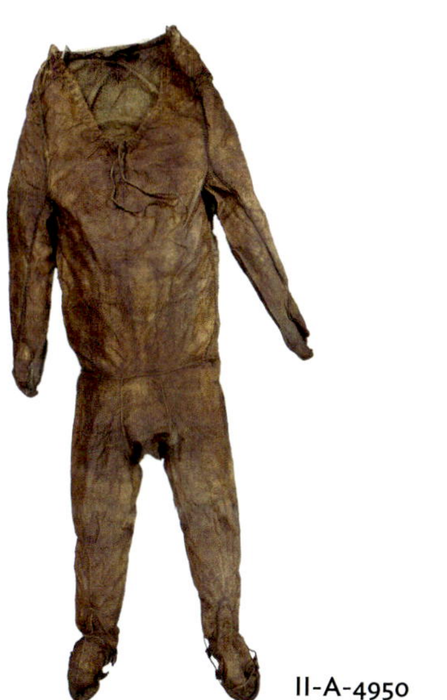
II-A-4950

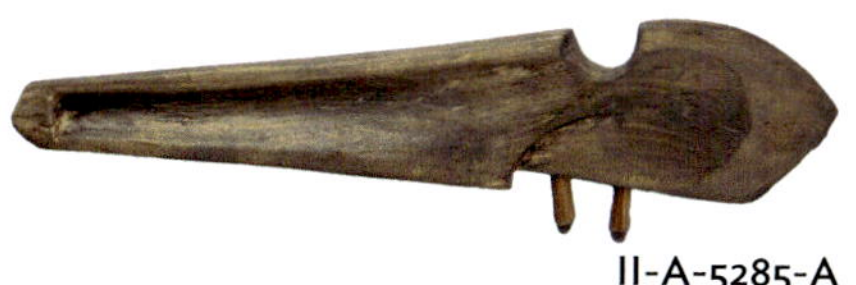
II-A-5285-A

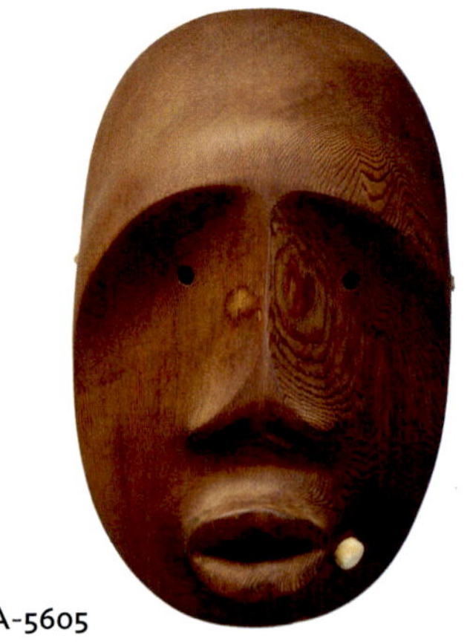

II-A-5605

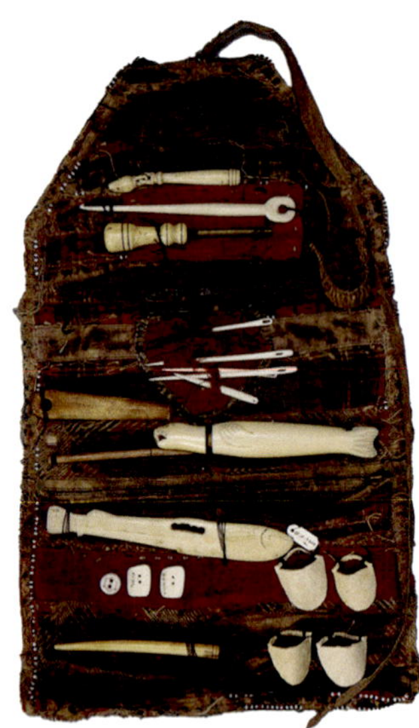

II-A-7300

II-A-6551	Eskimo white and black stone labret
II-A-6582	Eskimo grappling hook of wood, iron, and rawhide
II-A-6618	Eskimo fish lure with fish-shaped carved ivory shank and metal hook made from nail
II-A-6710	Eskimo small skin drum with wooden frame and handle carved as bird holding fish
II-A-6718	Ivory carving of Donald Duck with scrimshaw features by Jonathon Johnson
II-A-6749	Eskimo ulu of ivory and metal
II-A-6758	Eskimo awl of metal and ivory
II-A-6768	Eskimo net gauge of ivory, wood, and rawhide
II-A-6822	Eskimo tom cod outfit with reel-type wooden rod with ivory tips and baleen line
II-A-6831	Eskimo pottery paddle made of whale bone with concentric circles design
II-A-6845	Seal mittens, short style, with band of fur seal trim around tops by Annie Evans
II-A-6853	Iñupiat bentwood bucket with ivory ornaments (seals, whales, etc.)
II-A-6881	Eskimo ball made of dried fish skin with seams reinforced by tanned leather
II-A-7092	Eskimo jigging rod made from flat piece of wood cut to form an angle, with fish-shaped lure and hook of ivory and auklet bills
II-A-7099	Eskimo ulu with ivory handle and slate blade
II-A-7117	Eskimo mottled ivory scraper with stone blade and handle curved for easy holding with flat section on one side for thumb rest
II-A-7205	Eskimo white ivory needle, very thin with small eye
II-A-7271	Eskimo ivory housewife fastener
II-A-7300	Eskimo sewing kit
II-A-7300-A	Eskimo fabric sewing kit exterior with pockets for storing sewing needles, thimbles, awls, etc.
II-A-7300-C	Sewing thimble made of skin
II-A-7300-D	Sewing thimble made of skin
II-A-7300-E	Sewing thimble made of skin
II-A-7300-F	Sewing thimble made of skin
II-A-7300-G	Ivory handle carved in a fish shape, for sewing tools
II-A-7300-H	Ivory and wood needle case carved into a seal shape
II-A-7300-I	Sewing pin or point made of antler
II-A-7300-J	Ivory awl handle and iron sewing pin
II-A-7300-L	Ivory sewing needle tied with monofilament
II-A-7300-M	Ivory sewing needle tied with monofilament
II-A-7300-N	Ivory sewing needle tied with monofilament
II-A-7300-O	Ivory sewing needle tied with monofilament
II-A-7300-P	Ivory sewing needle tied with monofilament
II-A-7300-Q	White ivory button attached to needle with monofilament
II-A-7300-R	White ivory button attached to needle with monofilament
II-A-7300-S	White ivory button attached to needle with monofilament
II-A-7300-T	Ivory sewing needle case carved in shape of animal
II-A-7300-U	Ivory handle with copper alloy tube, for sewing tools
II-A-7300-V	Ivory crochet hook
II-A-7300-W	Ivory awl with seal-like face on handle
II-A-7300-X	Two leather sewing thimbles
II-A-7377	Yup'ik carved and pigmented wood "welcome stick" or ayaruq decorated with feathers, grass, and cord
LC.444-1	Photographic print of man sharpening whale tools by Joel Bennett

INDEX

Page numbers followed by f indicate illustrations

ABOUT THE AUTHOR AND DESIGNER

Charles Wohlforth, who was an Alaska resident for more than fifty years, is author of a dozen books and numerous articles covering science and the environment, politics and history, medicine, and as-told-to biography. He has won many awards. His book *The Whale and the Supercomputer: On the Northern Front of Climate Change* won the *LA Times* Book Prize. He served two terms on the Anchorage Assembly and was a newspaper columnist and radio host. He also edited the labels for the Alaska State Museum. He graduated magna cum laude from Princeton University in 1986, has four adult children, and currently lives in New Jersey. Learn more at www.wohlforth.com.

Sarah Asper-Smith, a lifelong Juneau resident, has worked independently and collaboratively as a curator, exhibit designer, and graphic designer in museums in all parts of Alaska. In 2011, she earned a master's degree from the University of Fine Arts in Philadelphia, studying Museum Exhibition Planning and Design to fulfill a need for Alaskans to tell Alaskan stories in museums. Her work has included co-curatorial exhibit development of the permanent exhibits at the Alaska State Museum. She gets home from the museum via a series of public staircases rising through Juneau's mountainside neighborhoods.